ENHANCING SELF ESTEEM

Second Edition

Diane Frey, Ph.D.
Professor of Counseling
Wright State University
Dayton, Ohio

C. Jesse Carlock, Ph.D.
Psychologist in Private Practice
Dayton, Ohio

A Companion Book
to
Practical Techniques for Enhancing Self Esteem

ACCELERATED DEVELOPMENT
A member of the Taylor & Francis Group

ENHANCING SELF ESTEEM
Second Edition

10

Printed in the United States of America

Technical Development: Tanya Dalton
Delores Kellogg
Marguerite Mader
Sheila Sheward

Cover Illustration: David Loop

Library of Congress Cataloging-in-Publication Data

Frey, Diane.
Enhancing self esteem / Diane Frey, C. Jesse Carlock. -- 2nd ed.
p. cm.
Includes bibliographies and index.
ISBN 1-55959-004-1
1. Self-respect. 2. Self-respect--Problems, exercises, etc.
I. Carlock, C. Jesse. II. Title.
BF697.5.S46F73 1989
158'.1--dc20 89-84336
CIP

LCN: 89-84336

For additional information and ordering, please contact:

ACCELERATED DEVELOPMENT
A member of the Taylor & Francis Group
1900 Frost Road, Suite 101
Bristol, PA 19007

1-800-821-8312

*This book is dedicated
to
my mother,
Helen Frey,
who continually gives me
the greatest gift of all—
the activation of the
potential for positive
self esteem.*

D.F.

*To my father,
Bill Carlock,
who inspired my belief
that I can
make my dreams come true . . .*

*To my mother,
Marge Carlock,
who gives me hope by showing
through her life that blooming
can happen at any age . . .*

and,

*To my loving mentor,
Virginia Satir,
Who generously gave of herself.*

C.J.C.

FOREWORD

(First Edition)

Isn't it peculiar that we all know that low self esteem in an individual is a prime factor in defeating oneself. All the manuals on success point indirectly to low self-worth through pointing out that self-confidence is the key to success. Few show the steps that can be taken to achieve this. The underpinnings of low self-confidence are low self esteem. One does not value oneself, but instead sees oneself in negative contrast to someone else. People are constantly prodded to have self-confidence—confidence in self, which means to value self. Hardly any of these proddings show how one can take that long journey from low self-worth to self-confidence. Coming to self-confidence, high self-worth, is a long journey, but not necessarily in time. It is more in awareness and knowledge. What does one have to experience to become aware of, to learn about, to accomplish this? Remember the journey is long because it is an about-face attitude in relation to yourself. Yesterday you felt like nothing and today you unconditionally feel that the world is a better place because you are here. You know you are worthwhile; you know you have meaning; you know you have something to offer and are worthy to receive. How can that big leap occur? It does little good to know you have no confidence except to make you feel worse. What makes it possible to take the risk, develop hope, martial the energy to change, *and* have the skills to change? The world is completely new to the person with confidence as contrasted to the person of low self-worth.

Someone with low self-worth has developed a style of life to which he/she has become habituated. It is like a familiar dress. It isn't so pretty or comfortable, but it is there. You can count on it. When someone pays you a compliment and you feel worthless about yourself you have conditioned yourself to apologize: You feel tight. When you have high self-worth and someone pays you a compliment, you genuinely thank them and recognize inwardly that you mutually share good taste. Your juices flow and you are happy. What a change! Before you wondered if you deserved it, were they buttering you up, etc., etc.? Your insides were swirling with guilt and anxiety.

What kind of life is it when you don't feel guilty or anxious anymore? You have to get used to a whole new set of feelings about yourself as well as new communication with others.

When I have asked myself the question, "Why do so many people feel undeserving?" I come up with the observation that they are brought up that way. We usually get very little training in valuing ourselves. "Be nice to others" usually means at the expense of yourself. "Don't think well of yourself because it is selfish."

Many of us have been conditioned to fear our egos. An ego is the window of the self. Egos are bad, we are told. Get egos out of the way. Be a doormat. Actually an ego can guide you to self-defeating or self-enhancing behavior and feelings. It depends on what kind of experience one has and what kind of messages one gets early in life. A nurtured, harmonious ego can only give joy to its owner and to others. One doesn't have to take from others when one has it him/herself.

Learning to value oneself, having high self esteem, having self confidence can happen to anyone despite past learnings. We all have internal wisdom, we have left and right brains. We have hearts. If we can accept that we have the capacity to place people on the moon, we can accept that we can elevate our feeling of value toward ourselves. Anyone associated with space travel knows that it takes much knowledge, skill, awareness, and judgment to make a successful moon trip. We can apply the same approach to ourselves. We can acquire knowledge to learn how the human being functions; we can acquire the skill to be effective human beings.

Virginia M. Satir
October, 1983

PREFACE

"Everything has its beauty but not everyone sees it" (Confucious). This book is intended to help people see beauty in other people and beauty in themselves.

Self esteem, the degree to which one values self, is the fertilizer which nourishes one's talents, resources, and abilities. The more positive and pervasive the self esteem the richer the soil within which one can grow.

The purpose of this book is to help others in planting seed, fertilizing, and developing the soil of positive self esteem. It has been well established that positive self esteem is a better predictor of achievement than are achievement tests themselves. It is also widely accepted among those in helping professions that poor self esteem is the root cause of many other behavioral and emotional problems such as teenage pregnancies, eating disorders, depression, child abuse, juvenile delinquency, and anxiety, to name just a few. While many helpers intervene only with the symptoms of such problems, many other helpers are realizing more frequently that it is more effective to help others with the more basic problem of low self esteem.

This book is distinctive from other books on self esteem in numerous ways. Many books on self esteem focus either on theory or practice. This book takes theory of self esteem and translates it for the reader into practice. In this way it stands alone among all other books on self esteem. Activities and techniques suggested have been field tested by us over the past eleven years. We have used these techniques in a variety of settings, both academic and clinical, and with a great variety of individuals including children, adolescents, young adults, adults, and senior citizens. The diversity of people within each of these age ranges has been quite extensive—gifted children, mentally retarded children, battered women, displaced home-makers, and men in midlife crises, to name a few. All of these experiences have been valuable in developing techniques and activities which are very effective in enhancing self esteem.

Another unique characteristic of this book is its **system-atic** approach to enhancing self esteem. Many other inter-ventions in the literature suggest a somewhat haphazard method of helping. In this book are suggested a specific sequence and phase-wise progression of enhancing self esteem, thus enabling helpers to be more effective. The four phases of intervention are a result of extensive literature review and practice by these authors.

In addition, theory and practice of this book incorporate cognitive, emotive, and behavioral aspects of individuals. Other books on self esteem often focus on only one of these aspects. Readers will readily see the importance of all three of these dimensions being interwoven throughout the book.

This book is appropriate for anyone who is interested in helping others enhance their self esteem. Readers also can learn ways to enhance their own self esteem. Counselors, teachers, social workers, parents, psychologists, ministers, employers all can benefit by theory and methods presented.

We believe that the greatest gift anyone can give another is the activation of potential for positive self esteem. We give this gift to you; we hope you pass it on to others.

CONTENTS

LIST OF ACTIVITIES

LIST OF FIGURES

LIST OF TABLES

CHAPTER 1

TERMINOLOGY AND THEORIES OF SELF ESTEEM

Historically, ever since ancient Greece, individuals have been admonished to "Know thyself." Interest in the self, self-concept, and self esteem has continued throughout history. Shakespeare said, "To thine ownself be true, and it must follow as the night the day, thou canst not then be false to any man." Biblical verse indicates "Love thy neighbor as thyself," implying the necessity to have positive regard for oneself is in order to love one's neighbor (Scofield, 1917).

In the book *The Psychology of Self Esteem*, Branden (1971) stated,

> There is no value-judgment more important to man—no factor more decisive in his psychological development and motivation—than the estimate he passes on himself.

> This estimate is ordinarily experienced by him, not in the form of a conscious, verbalized judgment, but in the form of a feeling, a feeling that can be hard to isolate and identify because he experiences it constantly; it is part of every other feeling, it is involved in his every emotional response. (p. 109)

To understand individuals psychologically, one must understand their degree of self esteem, the process of its development, and those standards by which esteem is judged.

Combs (1971) stated that "The self is the star of every performance, the central figure in every act" (p. 39). Individuals see the world through the filter of self; therefore, view of self colors and influences all of how one thinks, feels, and acts. Self-concept is the frame of reference for all perception. Thus, the fact that the study of self has been pursued for centuries suggests the significance of understanding oneself and others. Many counseling and psychotherapy theories posit that self esteem problems are underlying causes of various kinds of psychopathology. Even preventative mental health efforts and effective education have central themes of understanding self-concept and enhancing self esteem. Although various psychological theories view self somewhat differently, common agreement exists as to its importance.

SELF-THEORY AND DEFINITION

Around the turn of the century considerable interest in self-theory was evident. In 1890 William James defined self as the sum of all a person can call his/her own: physical self, psychological traits, feelings, family, significant others, possessions, avocation, and vocation. Cooley (1902) introduced the concept of a "looking-glass self." He believed that by seeing ourselves in a looking glass we are more aware of how others perceive us, and we are affected by these perceptions. Between 1902 and 1940 interest in the self waned and interest in behaviorism increased.

Hall and Lindzey (1957) distinguished between two different meanings of self in modern psychology. *Self was defined as the person's attitudes, feelings, and evaluations of oneself. The second meaning of self was defined as a process of thinking, remembering, and perceiving.*

Secord and Backman (1964) *defined self as the individual's attitudes toward self.* Self-concept development was described as a result of social learning, primarily role and identification learning.

Wylie (1961) indicated that a proliferation of self-theories, such as Freud's emphasis on ego development, the neo-Freudian's priority on self, and the evolution of humanistic psychology and its interest in phenomenology, aided in the increased importance self-theory received in professional literature.

Hall and Lindzey (1970, 1978) mentioned over 20 different ideas about self and Hinsie and Campbell (1970) devoted 10 pages in their psychiatric dictionary to the definition of ego and related concepts. Recently, an increasingly large body of research has been devoted to the study of these theories and concepts. In Table 1.1 is a brief summary of theorists and their definitions of self.

In this historical review of literature, the terms "self," "self-concept," "self esteem," and "self-acceptance" are often used interchangeably, however, distinctions can be made.

SELF-THEORY AND THE JOHARI WINDOW

The Johari Window (Luft, 1969) accurately described the self as being composed of aspects known and not known to the self as well as aspects that are known or unknown by others. The uneven nature of self-concept development also can be understood from this model (Figure 1.1).

	Known to Self	Not Known to Self
Known to Others	**I. Open**	**III. Blind**
Not Known to Others	**II. Private**	**IV. Unknown**

Figure 1.1. Johari window.

Note. From *Of Human Interaction* (p. 13) by J. Luft, 1969, Palo Alto, CA: National Press. Copyright 1969 by National Press. Adapted by permission.

Area I, the Open area, represents aspects of self that are known to the individual and others. Included are three basic elements of human behavior: thoughts, feelings, and behaviors. This area affords much growth potential because if an

TABLE 1.1
Theorists and Definitions of Self

Theorist	Definition Of Self
Alfred Adler	Environment and heredity are basic elements of personality. Life scripts of the individual determine how self is created.
Raymond Cattell	Self organizes personality traits, determines consistency among them, and adds structure.
Erik Erikson	Concepts of self are organized into roles which help one relate to environment.
Prescott Lecky	Self is the unifying force of personality. Individuals reject that which does not fit their value structure and accept that which does. Self is consistent with these values.
Abraham Maslow	Each person has a desire to maximize his/her potential. In reaching potential, individuals become self-actualized.
Carl Rogers	Self is seen as being composed of real self, ideal self, and perceived self. The more congruent these are, the more adjusted the individual is.
Donald Snygg and Arthur Combs	The phenomenal field the individual has greatly determines self. The self develops and maintains itself in a manner consistent with individual values, perceptions, and experiences.
Harry Stack Sullivan	Self is similar to defense mechanisms. It guards against anxiety by selectively perceiving interactions from the environment. Self, thus, is a system.

individual has an awareness of self he/she can channel energy to nurture, maintain, or change that part of him/herself. The person also can benefit from feedback from significant others because this area is known to them.

Statements such as the following could represent Area I:

"When you told me I was late, I felt guilty and decided to meet you on time at our next appointment." (This statement includes an awareness of feedback from others and an awareness of feelings, thoughts, and behaviors.)

"I am glad you told me you like my new shirt. I like it so much that I bought another one like it but in a different color." (Again, there is a reflection of awareness of feelings, thoughts, behaviors, and feedback.)

"Thank you for supporting my idea about where to have the party. I felt satisfied with the place also." (This statement shows an awareness of thoughts, feedback, and feelings.)

If a person feels threatened, Area I will not increase because an individual is less likely to disclose to others in the presence of perceived threat. Use of force to help a person disclose something to others is not desirable because it leads to defensiveness and resentment.

Area II represents thoughts, feelings, or behaviors known to self but hidden from others, and is, therefore, called the Private area. Such statements as "I hope he doesn't find out I was drinking," or "She will never know I have on torn underwear," are representative of Area II. This area allows for change, however, inasmuch as an awareness is present on the part of the individual. Area II becomes smaller as trust and acceptance are developed in interpersonal relationships.

Area III is the Blind area, represented by those behaviors, thoughts, and feelings not known to the individual but known to others. For example, someone might know that you have a spot on your sleeve and you do not know it. This area also is open to change, if the individual is open to feedback from others. Such statements as the following could represent this area: "You think I am attractive," "You see me as confident," "My friends think I am kind." Accuracy of self-perception is related to accuracy of perception of significant others. Feedback from others is critical.

Area IV, the Unknown area, represents one's thoughts, feelings, and behaviors not known by anyone. These aspects of oneself could have been known at one time, but have since been repressed to the point that they are forgotten or perhaps one's life experiences have not allowed for knowledge of self in a particular area yet. For example, one might not know how he/she would react in a terrible automobile accident because that has not occurred. Others would have no idea of the possible reaction either. Possibly these thoughts, feelings, and behavior are latent and unknown. They may be under the surface of oneself and unknown until an event surfaces them, such as when a relatively benign person commits murder. Such hostility may have been brewing for years unknown to self and others. Area IV is not likely to change significantly in typical human relationships. Circumstances which may cause change are the unleashing of repressed thoughts, feelings, or behaviors; a dramatic life event; and/or the process of aging and developing more fully as a person.

All four areas in the Johari Window are typically of different size. As healthy human interaction occurs, Area I increases, thus causing changes in the other quadrants also. The Johari Window represents the whole self. Areas I, II, and sometimes parts of Area III represent the self-concept—those thoughts, feelings, values, and attitudes one claims as representative of who the person is. Areas I, II, and some parts of III include self for self, self for others, and ideal self. The self-concept includes physical self, psychological self, and spiritual self in relation to the environment. Self-concept has both structure and function. All behavior can be related to self-concept as one's behavior is related to one's perceptual set and one's perceptual set is influenced by self-concept. Self-acceptance refers to the degree to which one is comfortable with the self-concept.

DEFINITIONS OF SELF ESTEEM

Self esteem is an evaluative term. It refers to negative, positive, neutral, and/or ambiguous judgments that one places on the self-concept. Self esteem is an evaluation of the emotional, intellectual and behavioral aspects of self-concept. Self esteem is not self-love, but the evaluation one places on self-concept.

People with high self esteem themselves, consider themselves worthy, and view themselves as equal with others. They do not pretend to be perfect, they recognize their limitations, and they expect to grow and improve.

Those low in self esteem generally experience self-rejection, self-dissatisfaction, self-contempt, and self-disparagement. The manner in which such low self esteem is manifested is discussed more fully in Chapter 5. Figures 1.2 and 1.3 are illustrative of high and low self esteem. An activity entitled "I'm Not Perfect But . . . Parts of Me are Excellent" further elaborates the idea of positive self esteem.

Self esteem has two interrelated components: the feeling that one is competent to live and the feeling that one is worthy of living. Being competent includes the confidence one has in his/her mind, feelings, and behavior as these relate to the reality of one's existence. Feeling worthy means affirming oneself and feeling self-respect.

Ideal Self

Overlaying all three areas related to self-concept of the Johari Window is the concept of ideal self. Ideal self refers to the way one would like to be. Aspirations and goals for the ideal self are exhibited in statements such as the following: "I want to become a painter." "I would like to improve my typing skills." "I want to become more self-assertive." Healthy goals are desirable, achievable, believable, conceivable, and measurable. In addition, they need to be flexible. Within a healthy person much compatibility exists among and between Areas I, II, III, and ideal self. If much discrepancy occurs in these areas, then anxiety is

(Continued on page 10)

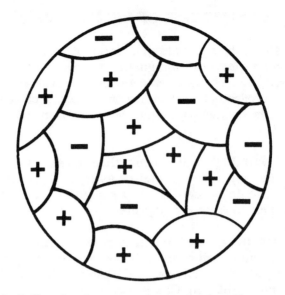

Figure 1.2. Self and sub-personalities—high self esteem.

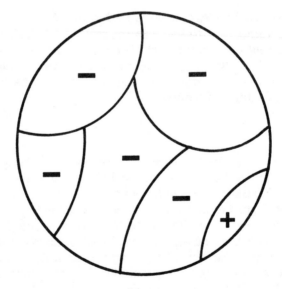

Figure 1.3. Self and sub-personalities—low self esteem.

ACTIVITY 1.1 I'M NOT PERFECT BUT . . . PARTS OF ME ARE EXCELLENT

Introduction

The purpose of this activity is to illustrate that persons with high self esteem consider themselves worthy, but do not feel that they are perfect. They realize areas in which they can grow and improve.

Participants

Individual or group.

Procedure

Make a list of 3 to 6 for each of the following:

- something you're embarrassed about;
- some of your failures;
- some of your weaknesses;
- some things you don't like about yourself.

In a small group or by yourself:

- Process some of what you wrote (nondefensively and preserving your self esteem).
- How did you feel writing each?
- How did you feel talking about your items and hearing other peoples?
- What did you discover?

Now each person, one at a time, go through your list and say, "I may not _____ (describe imperfection), but PARTS OF ME ARE EXCELLENT."

- Describe your feelings.
- What relationship does this have to self esteem?

Variation

Place each imperfection on one 3x5 index card. Shuffle and distribute cards. Each person then reads the cards as if they were his/her own and explains the imperfection and the problems it causes, why he/she hates to let go of it, but what he/she hopes to do to correct it.

Outcomes

What did you learn from this experience?

───────

created. Healthy people deal directly with this anxiety, and as a result, the anxiety is brief in duration. On the other hand, nonadaptive individuals react to anxiety by hiding, masking, distorting, or denying and as a result anxiety persists. Area I decreases in size and the person begins to lose grasp of the self. Much energy is needed to hide or disguise this loss, and consequently, interpersonal functioning is handicapped.

Rogers (1951, 1961) developed a representation of the fully functioning person which is generally referred to as "self-theory:"

1. The individual has an interest tendency toward actualizing self.

2. The individual has the capacity and tendency to symbolize experiences accurately. (A corollary statement is that he/she has the capacity and tendency to keep self-concept congruent with experience).

3. The individual has a need for positive regard.

4. The individual has a need for positive self-regard.

5. Tendencies 1 and 2 are most fully realized when needs 3 and 4 are met. More specifically, tendencies 1 and 2 tend to be more fully realized when:

   a. The individual experiences unconditional positive regard from significant others.

b. The pervasiveness of the unconditional positive regard is made evident through relationships marked by an exchange of empathic understanding between and among individuals.

6. If the conditions under 5 are met to a maximum degree, the individual will be a fully functioning person.

Fantasy Self

In addition to the concepts of ideal self, real self, and self as seen by others (presenting self), several other concepts of self have been postulated. These include the fantasy self—the person one would like to be if unencumbered by reality (i.e., "If I were not female, I could be President of the United States," "If I were taller, I could be promoted faster"), ego ideal—the person one feels he/she should be (i.e., "I should be more patient, more tolerant"), or future self or possible self—the person one may become (i.e., "I am going to be 50 pounds thinner"). The greater the congruence between the real self, what one is, and the ideal self, how one would like to be, the better self esteem and psychological adjustment one experiences.

Congruency is to be viewed as a goal toward which one strives. More frequently than not, varying degrees of discrepancy occur between ideal self and real self. To believe that one must attain this congruence in order to be happy only sets one in a vicious cycle which leads to lowered self esteem. Activity 1.2 at the end of the chapter helps participants to become aware of different types of self.

Unstable Self

The concept of the unstable self is particularly related to the discussion of self esteem. When individuals have a stable self-concept, they value and accept themselves and feel secure about self. Such people can answer confidently and positively the question, "Who am I?" The person with an unstable self is unable to consolidate the various selves into a stable aggregate because he/she cannot deal effectively with the negative elements perceived in self. Individuals with unstable self-concepts generally have low self esteem, but are capable of viewing themselves in a flattering way. This, however, is just one extreme of their ambivalence. When such individuals view themselves positively, it is very positive; when they view themselves negatively, it is very negative. This casting about for an acceptable self causes the self-concept to remain very fluid and unstable.

Unstable Self and Deficient Self Esteem

Deficient self esteem and the unstable self can be considered correlates of each other. A determination cannot be made as to what the exact cause and effect relationship is. Apparently a circular-causal relationship exists between the two. Individuals lacking in self esteem are likely to be very influenced by their environment. If the environment is perceived as favorable, self esteem rises. If the environment is perceived as unfavorable, their self esteem is lowered. For example, if one receives feedback that he/she is a poor dancer he/she may feel terrible about self. If the next partner feels he/she is a good dancer, he/she may feel terrific about self. Adequacy seems to hinge upon the environment. On the other hand, individuals with high self esteem are less influenced by the environment. They feel that they can master the environment and, thus, their self esteem is relatively stable. For example, a person of high self esteem might respond to varying feedback about his/her dancing ability by telling self that a large sample for appropriate feedback is needed or maybe lessons are necessary. This alone does not cause one to believe that he/she is a terrible person. No radical restructuring needs to occur as a result of the changing environment. In this case, self esteem is not situationally specific, easily modified by external conditions. Conditions which influence low self esteem and unstable self are discussed in much greater detail in Chapter 3, The Social System and Self Esteem, and Chapter 4, Internal Dynamics of Self.

Self-Estimate

The term "self-estimate" refers to how people rate themselves with regard to a particular characteristic. One might have generally low self esteem, but admit to one positive quality, usually one that is not valued by the individual. For example, individuals might generally regard themselves negatively but admit that they are considerate. On the other hand, one might have generally high self esteem but admit to being a terrible letter writer. The self-estimate thus refers to the evaluation of those thoughts, feelings, and behaviors one has that are all a part of the self-concept. In Figure 1.4 are illustrated low self esteem, unstable self, and self-estimates.

IMPORTANCE OF SELF ESTEEM

This survey and review of self terminology reveals the importance of self-theory. In recent decades leading psychologists and helping professionals substantiated the central role of positive self esteem for the development of a healthy personality:

Carl Rogers: "If I were to search for the central core of difficulty in people as I have come to know them, it is that in the great majority of cases they despise themselves, regarding themselves as worthless and unlovable."

Eric Fromm: "Love of others and love of ourselves are not alternatives. On the contrary, an attitude of love towards themselves will be found in all those who are capable of loving others.

Stanley Coopersmith: "Probably the most important requirement for effective behavior, central to the whole problem is self esteem."

Virginia Satir: "My dream is to make families a place where adults with high esteem can develop. I think we have reached a point where if we don't get busy on dreams of this sort, our end is in sight. We need a world that is as good for human beings as it is for technology."

Bruno Bettelheim: "With some qualifications I suggest that nothing is more characteristic of mental well being than a healthy self respect, a regard for one's body and its functions, and a reasonably optimistic outlook on life."

Abraham Maslow: "No psychological health is possible unless this essential care of the person is fundamentally accepted, loved and respected by others and by himself..."

Numerous studies point toward the relationship between self esteem and academic achievement. Bennis and Nanus (1985) in their book, *Leaders*, discuss the four common characteristics their research found in the nations' leaders. One of these characteristics is high self esteem. In addition another importance of self esteem is related to parenting. Parents high in self-esteem tend to rear children of high self esteem. Parents of low self esteem tend to rear children of low self esteem.

Researchers still seek answers to questions such as "Who am I?," "How can I feel better about myself?" and "How can I maximize my potential?" Keat (1974, p. 47) stated that self-concept is "the single most important variable in an individual's life." This opinion is shared by many others (Durbin, 1982; Satir, 1988; and Frey, 1988).

In a recent Gallup Poll commissioned by Schuller (1982), however 35% of Protestants interviewed believed they had strong self esteem, only 39% of Catholics reflected a feeling of self esteem, and only 40% of those of "other faiths" believed they had strong self esteem. Schuller (1982) stated that the deepest need of individuals is to feel worthwhile.

SUMMARY

Oliver Wendell Holmes stated, "Most of us die with our music still inside us." How this happens to individuals is the topic of the next chapter. The development of individuals with high or low self esteem also will be reviewed in the following chapter. Methods for helping one to enhance self esteem are the major focus of the remainder of this book.

1.

Low Self Esteem

2.

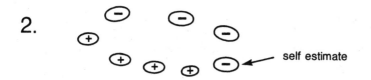 ← self estimate

Unstable Self (Sub-personalities or self estimates not mended together)

3.

i.e. poor dancing skills, therefore, I am generally worthless.

i.e. possibility of poor dancing skills

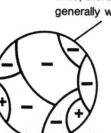 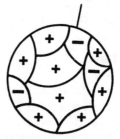

Low Self Esteem with Positive Self Estimates

High Self Esteem with Negative Self Estimates

Figure 1.4. Low self esteem, unstable self, and self estimates.

ACTIVITY 1.2 WHAT IS REAL?

Introduction

This activity focuses on the different facades of self. It is an identity phase activity. (See Chapter 6)

Time Required

Minimal time—30 minutes; time could be unlimited.

Participants

Adults or children in grade 4 or above

Setting

Office or classroom

Materials

None—could use paper and pencil

Procedure

"What is REAL?" asked the Rabbit one day when they [the Skin Horse and Rabbit] were lying side by side near the nursery fender, before Nana came to tidy the room. "Does it mean having things that buzz inside you and a stick-out handle?"

"Real isn't how you are made," said the Skin Horse. "It's a thing that happens to you. When a child loves you for a long, long time, then you become REAL."

"Does it hurt?" asked the Rabbit.

"Sometimes," said the Skin Horse, for he was always truthful. "When you are Real you don't mind being hurt."

"Does it happen all at once, like being wound up," he asked, "or bit by bit?"

"It doesn't happen all at once," said the Skin Horse. "You become. It takes a long time. That's why it doesn't often happen to people who break easily, or have sharp edges, or have to be carefully kept. Generally, by the time you are Real, most of your hair has been loved off, and your eyes drop out, and you get loose in the joints and very shabby. But these things don't matter at all, because once you are Real you can't be ugly, except to people who don't understand." (Williams, 1958, pp. 16-17)

What does being "real" mean to you?

What people have helped you feel "real?"

How have you been hurt when you became more "real" with someone? Are the benefits worth the risk of possible hurt?

How can you be real and still protect yourself from getting hurt too badly?

Why does it take longer for some people to become real than others?

Do you know anyone who is "real?"

How real do you think you are?

Share a time when you felt most real.

Have you ever been "almost close" to someone? Talked with them, and thought to yourself, "Will we ever stop being pleasant, indirect, scared of facing each other?" "Will we ever trust and let our ashamedness show?" "Will we treat each other tenderly?"

Outcomes

The participants begin to develop an awareness of different types of "self"—ideal self, real self, fantasy self, self for others (Open area of Johari Window), self for self (Private area of Johari Window).

REFERENCES

Bennis, W.G., & Nanus, B. (1985). *Leaders: The strategies for taking change.* New York: Harper & Row.

Branden, N. (1971). *The psychology of self esteem.* New York: Bantam Books.

Combs, A. W. (1971). What can man become? In D. Avila, A. Combs, & W. Purkey (Eds.), *The helping relationship sourcebook.* Boston: Allyn and Bacon.

Cooley, C. (1902). *Human nature and social order.* New York: Charles Scribner.

Durbin, D. (1982). Multimodal group sessions to enhance self concept. *Elementary School Guidance and Counseling, 16*(4), 288-296.

Frey, D. (1988). *Intimate relationships, marriage and family* (Instructors' Manual). New York: Macmillan.

Hall, C. S., & Lindzey, G. (1957, 1970, 1978). *Theories of personality,* (1st, 2nd, & 3rd ed.). New York: John Wiley and Sons.

Hinsie, L. E., & Campbell, R. (1970). *Psychiatric dictionary* (4th ed.). New York: John Wiley and Sons.

James, W. (1890). *Principles of psychology.* New York: Holt.

Keat, D. (1974). *Fundamentals of child counseling.* Boston: Houghton Mifflin.

Luft, J. (1969). *Of human interaction.* Palo Alto, CA: National Press.

Rogers, C. (1951). *Client centered therapy.* Boston: Houghton Mifflin.

Rogers, C. (1961). *On becoming a person.* Boston: Houghton Mifflin.

Satir, V. (1988). *The new peoplemaking.* Mountain View, CA: Science and Behavior Books.

Schuller, R. (1982). *Self esteem: The new reformation.* Waco, TX: Word Publishing.

Scofield, D. D. (Ed). (1917). *The Holy Bible.* New York: Oxford University Press.

Secord, P. F., & Backman, C. (1964). Personality theory and the problem of stability and change in individual behavior: An interpersonal approach. *Psychological Review, 63,* 21-32.

Williams, M. (1958). *The velveteen rabbit or how toys become real.* New York: George H. Doran Company.

Wylie, R. C. (1961). *The self concept.* Lincoln, NE: The University of Nebraska Press.

CHAPTER 2

SELF-CONCEPT DEVELOPMENT

Infants are not born with a self-concept. At birth, the infant cannot distinguish between self and environment. Klein (1976) defined the infant's identity as "w-ego" to illustrate how the infant's identity is fused with those around it. Gradually, through interaction with parents, significant others, and peers, children form their self-concept. This early learning is unique because it determines the perceptual screen through which later experiences are filtered (White, 1975). Although people continue to learn throughout their lives, this early learning is very significant.

MODALITIES OF LEARNING SELF-CONCEPT

Direct Experience

The self-concept may be developed from direct experience or perception of the physical world without any social mediation. For example, when a child falls while trying to climb beyond capabilities, he/she soon recognizes physical limitations. Also, when an infant cries, he/she soon learns this brings a certain response from parents. Self-concept is generally first developed in this manner, this process also continues through life and is referred to as the direct-experience modality.

Nonverbal

The self-concept may be socially mediated without language as in cases where nonverbal communication is the main mode of learning. This also is an early learning mode for children because they relate to the world first in a nonverbal fashion. Montagu (1971) reported the significance of early infant learning through touch (a nonverbal medium of communication). He found that babies who are not touched develop a condition called marasmus, which involves a lack of appetite, weight loss, and death. Touching infants stimulates both physical and psychological development.

Children also learn through other modes of nonverbal communication. For example, children learn to read facial expressions as a way of determining if a parent is upset, happy, or angry. Individuals also discern tone of voice as a positive, negative, or neutral indicator. Others' feelings are learned by infants through nonverbal communication and have a major effect on self esteem development (Demos, 1982). Assessing the meaning of spatial distance also is accomplished through the nonverbal learning modality. For example, a child learns that people stand closer to those they like. The nonverbal learning modality also develops throughout life as as way of learning about self.

Verbal

Self-concept also may be socially mediated through language, the verbal modality. If individuals hear others tell them they are worthless often enough, they eventually believe it. Negative feedback, dishonesty, deception, and excessively high expectations are often expressed verbally. Of course, people also can use the verbal modality to express negative ideas to themselves through self-thoughts and self-talk.

The degree, intensity, and duration of each of these modalities is related to factors such as age of the individual, physical condition, and environment. Naturally, infants rely on the direct-experience modality because they have no verbal language. When individuals are in a foreign country they may need to rely on nonverbal communication. For the deaf, the nonverbal modality is most significant. Likewise, for the blind, the verbal modality is dominant.

FACTORS INFLUENCING SELF-CONCEPT DEVELOPMENT

Human Interaction

Human interaction or environment is more likely to influence the development of self-concept than is interaction without human meaning. A grade of C means little until someone adds meaning to it by stating, "That's good improvement," or asks, "Can't you do better?"

Social Learning

Social learning begins at birth. It generally is agreed that the most significant influence on the development of self-concept comes from the major parental figure and/or the person with whom the young child identifies most. This figure is often the mother, but with the increasing divorce rate and more and more single parents, the father also may be the significant adult. This person also could be a grandparent living in the child's home, as in the concept of the nuclear and extended families, or an older sister or brother who is responsible for the younger child. Regardless of who represents this parental figure to the child, no disagreement exists over the fact that parents or parental figures with high self esteem tend to rear children with high self esteem; parents or parental figures with low self esteem tend to rear children with low self esteem (Eskilson, Wiley, Muehlbauer, & Dodder, 1986; Gecas & Schwalbe, 1986; Kawash, Kerr, & Clewes, 1984; Walker & Greene, 1986).

When parental absence exists in a home situation the level of self esteem of children is affected. Miller (1984) found father absence to have more of a negative effect on male children's self esteem than on females'. The information supports the concept that the importance of fathers in child development has been greatly underestimated. According to Amato (1986) the father-child relationship was at least as strongly associated with child self esteem as was the mother-child relationship.

Rosenberg (1965) found that maternal indifference is more likely to produce low self esteem in children than overt dissatisfaction. Apparently, if the mother, as major parental figure, is interested enough to chastise the child, that level of interest produces higher self esteem in the child. A feeling of significance to others is essential in the development of adequate self esteem.

Harlow's (1971) studies of infant monkeys demonstrated that without association and sharing with others, the young monkeys seemed to have no identity or concept of themselves and they became insecure and disturbed.

Spitz (1965) discovered that without stimulating, affectionate, interpersonal contacts, orphaned babies became apathetic, withdrawn, fearful, and often failed to thrive physically or psychologically. Fraiberg (1968) termed this same emotional pattern at later age "disease of nonattachment" and described it as involving people who are incapable of forming psychological bonds with others.

Sullivan (1953) suggested that by the age of six weeks, the infant has the concept of self as either "Good Me in a Good World" or "Bad Me in a Bad World." Erikson (1968) described the first year of life as one where trust or mistrust is established. In the early years, other factors affecting self-concept development are the amount of stimulation and instruction given to the child and the amount of freedom balanced by discipline.

Longitudinal data supporting the importance of early childhood influences on self have all yielded consistent results (Chrzanowski, 1981). Bayley (1951) and the Fels Institute (1962) longitudinal studies both demonstrated the effects of parental behavior in the first six years of a child's life and his/her behavior in later years. In the longitudinal studies by Terman (1921) and Sears (1980), those gifted children who expressed positive feelings about self also expressed positive feelings about self as adults. Bloom (1964) found that half of what can be attributed to the variance in adult aggressiveness in males and dependence in females appears to be present at age four. Gordon (1962) found that the "I" emerges at age three and the child's self-concept becomes a central factor in what type of person he/she will become. These results demonstrate the centrality of the parental role in the development of self-concept.

School and Self-concept. School is the second most important environment in the development of self-concept. Social relationships with peers most often develop through the school environment and these relationships serve as the feedback source for the development of self esteem.

Davidson and Long (1960) found that a positive correlation exists between children's perception of themselves and the school environment. The teacher, like the parents at an earlier age, encourages the child, balances freedom and discipline, and aids the child in becoming more independent. To the child, worthiness often becomes related to academic achievement. When a child does well in school, he/she feels good about self. When the child does not receive adequate positive feedback, the child often internalizes this feedback in the form of low self esteem.

As a result of these findings Covington (1984) suggested that teachers should use a more frequent noncompetitive learning structure whenever possible to enhance self esteem. Examples of such approaches are mastery learning, cooperative learning, and contractual forms of learning. In addition to "how" we learn, equally important is "what" one learns. Students need to be encouraged by teachers to develop the belief that the ability to learn is an ever-improving capacity (Bachman & O'Malley, 1986; Covington, 1984). Teaching students learning-to-learn skills and problem-solving strategies enhances their view of acquired knowledge which provides greater capacity for future learning and enhanced self esteem. Leo Buscaglia said this perhaps more poetically when he said, "Maybe the essence of education is not to stuff you with facts but to help you discover your uniqueness, to teach you how to develop it, and then to show you how to give it away." Students who acquire a positive sense of self in school have a greater chance of succeeding later in life.

Adolescents most often develop a heightened concern about self-concept. One of the major developmental tasks of adolescence is to forge an identity. Self-assessment that occurs at this period leads to such questions as "What am I like?," "What should I become?," "How good am I?," and "How should I judge myself?" Rosenberg (1965) stated three major reasons for heightened concern about self-concept at this age. First, late adolescence is a time of major decision making—decisions need to be made about career, marriage, religion, and family. Second, adolescence is a time of rapid physical change. Height, weight, and sexual characteristics all change suddenly. Secord and Jourard (1953) found that the feelings one holds concerning body closely approximate the feelings one has about self. At a time when body image is quickly changing, self esteem is easily jolted (Offer, 1982). Associated with these changing physical characteristics also are new attitudes about self, others, and life in general. Third, the period of adolescence is a time of status ambiguity. There are no clear expectations for adolescents in society. Sometimes they are treated like children and sometimes they are treated like adults. Consequently, they become confused about their rights and privileges. Evaluation of self is always made with reference to certain criteria; society sets forth standards by which self-evaluation occurs. These standards tend to both change over time and vary across age groups. Answers to the questions "Who am I?" and "Where am I going?" are not easily found during this stage of development.

Although these common experiences of self esteem development exist for both boys and girls, there are some differences in sources of self esteem for boys and girls. Rochlin (1980) stated that most women desire to have a male child. The culture seems to value males more and validate their experiences more readily. Males have more appropriate avenues for dealing with aggression and other emotions. These emotions are often vented through sports, high achievement, positive body image, and the acquisition of power.

Similar behavior on the part of females is not validated by society. Females have generally not been encouraged to participate actively in sports, acquire power, or be achievement oriented. Females also report a greater attitude of body dissatisfaction than do males (Notman, 1982). This can be seen in the epidemic rise of anorexia and bulimia. Notman (1982) also stated that society encourages girls to suppress feelings of oppression and to become passive. Thus, a greater frequency of depression exists in females. Females tend to feel more vulnerable as a result of not being encouraged to think autonomously. They develop fewer internal levels of control and are more sensitive to changes in their environment. They have more unstable selves than males. These sex role differences in the development of self esteem have lead adolescent boys to place more value on school performance as it helps to define their self esteem while adolescent girls place more value on popularity in peer relationships in defining their self esteem (Walker & Greene, 1986). These vicissitudes in self esteem for males and females lead to different sources of low self esteem.

Parenting and Self-concept. Purkey (1970) stated that parent's influence on children's self-concept was equally strong in adolescence as in childhood. Rosenberg (1965) discussed some characteristics of parents and home environment which influence self esteem. He found that children whose fathers were engaged in authoritarian occupations and where physical violence was used as a disciplinary tool, displayed low self esteem. Rosenberg's (1965) research also indicated that Jewish children have higher self esteem than do Protestant or Catholic children.

Divorce and disrupted families have a profound impact on the development of self esteem. Rosenberg's study (1965) found that the effect of a divorce on a child's self esteem is related to three factors: religion of the family, mother's age at the time of the divorce, and whether remarriage occurred. According to Rosenberg, if a child comes from a Catholic or Jewish family, divorce has a clear effect on the child's self esteem; however, little effect can be seen on self esteem in the case of Protestant families. These effects are believed to be related to the religious teaching about divorce. If the mother is young, according to Rosenberg (1965) the child's self esteem will suffer. Divorce at a young age has the effect of lowering the self esteem of the mother and, hence, the child. If remarriage occurs, the child is more negatively affected than if no remarriage takes place. The negative effect of remarriage is particularly strong among older children (prepubescent and adolescent).

Rosenberg (1965) also found that only children have higher self esteem than do others with one or more siblings. Birth order has less important effects on a child's self esteem than the number of siblings. Also, boys whose siblings are mostly sisters show higher self esteem than those surrounded by brothers.

In more recent studies (Long, 1985; Wiehle, 1985; Wyman, Cowen, Hightower, & Pedro-Carroll, 1985) similar results of divorce upon self esteem have been demonstrated. Parental discord appears to lower self esteem of children, develop more negative attitudes by children to parents, develop an external locus of control in children, develop higher anxiety in children, and fewer sources of social support.

Group Membership. To a considerable extent, self esteem depends on the social evaluation of the groups with which one identifies. Low self esteem is frequently associated with membership in underprivileged or outcast groups. Rosenberg (1965) also discovered, however, that self esteem is more a result of one's position within a group rather than the rank of the group compared to other groups. This explains adolescent's strong adherence to the norms of their subculture rather than the general social norm of society. It also would explain the case of boys in a family of mostly girls having higher self esteem. Position within a group becomes very important to self esteem. A student attending a high school for gifted individuals, for example, might have a self-estimate of very average intelligence compared to other students in the school. In reality, of course, this student is probably above average in intelligence compared to all groups of students.

Mack (1987) discussed the issue of dual identity of Blacks in the United States. Although many ethnic and racial groups face such a challenge, the experience for Blacks in America is distinguished by the fact that the qualities attributed to Blacks is in opposition to the qualities rewarded in American society. The difficulty in reconciling diametrically opposed images into one personality poses an extreme challenge for Blacks. Often the result is low self esteem.

In a sense, self esteem can be related to a broader group with which one can/cannot identify. For example, in discussing the Alaskans of the Pribilof Islands, Johnson (1982) indicated that as the United States Government has continued to treat these Alaskans as inferior, self esteem problems have developed. The lifestyle of the Pribilofs is quite different from the "average" United States lifestyle thus making it difficult for the Alaskans to identify with the mainstream of United States culture, thus resulting in poor self esteem. This also is true of the minority groups who have a difficult time identifying with other cultures.

How a nation is viewed compared to other nations can affect self esteem of individuals as self esteem relates to national pride.

Heredity

Heredity and maturation influence self-concept development indirectly. What one has inherited either physically or behaviorally influences others' perceptions of self and others' behavior toward one. An inherited physical handicap, for example, does not cause negative feelings but rather the negative feelings result from the dismay, embarrassment, or disgust others might display toward the handicapped person.

Recent research on brain dominance patterns indicates brain dominance preferences influence verbal and non-verbal communication (Herrmann, 1988). According to Herrmann (1988) four dialects are classified according to brain quadrants: the language of logic and reason, the language of structure and control, the language of feelings and emotions, and the language of intuition and imagination. If you happen to be born with a brain dominance pattern which prefers intuition and imagination and your parents and most of your teachers favor the pattern of logic and reason and structure and control, likely you will feel out of the ordinary in a negative way, and then begin to develop low self esteem.

Sex

The sex with which one is born can effect self esteem. The effect of sex role on self esteem was greater for females than for males in a study reported by Lamke (1982). In the same study it was found that masculine and androgynous individuals had higher levels of self esteem than feminine and undifferentiated individuals.

It seems that girls attribute higher levels of self esteem to boys and conversely, boys, attribute lower levels of self esteem to girls (Robinson-Awana, Kehle, & Jenson, 1986). These sex role differences and how they further effect self esteem are discussed in the later chapter on women and self esteem.

Maturational Rates

Maturational rates also affect others' reactions to self. Often, differential treatment is given to early and late maturers, which results in different self-concepts between these two groups, and consequently results in different behavior of the members of the two groups. Early maturers who are treated as adults often develop favorable self esteem, whereas, late maturers who are treated as children develop more negative attitudes about self. Sometimes, when late maturers finally develop in late adolescence, they continue to live with poor self esteem, functioning under earlier perceptions of self. Havighurst (1972) suggested that failure to master developmental tasks through behavioral, cognitive, and affective maturation results in greater maladjustment, social disapproval, and increased difficulty in mastering more advanced tasks.

Because the self-concept continues to grow in the direction in which it began, early childhood is a critical period in development, although self-concept can be changed to some degree throughout one's life span.

Beliefs, Values, Attitudes, Morals

How easily a person is able to satisfy personal needs helps to determine the level of self-concept. If needs are routinely met, positive self esteem will develop; if needs are not satisfied, frustration, hostility, and anger could result.

Needs are generally categorized as either physical or psychological. Maslow's (1954) hierarchy of needs is represented as follows:

1. Physical needs
2. Safety needs
3. Love needs
4. Esteem needs
5. Self-actualization needs.

Because these needs are in an hierarchical pattern, the higher needs (esteem and self-actualization) can be satisfied only when the lower needs (physical and safety) have been met. Sometimes an individual functioning at a higher need level may not understand or accept his/her lower need level. Persons operating at different levels often do not understand each other. All these interactions affect one's self-concept. For example, if a child has high love and esteem needs and is only given input relative to physical and safety needs by his/her parents, this child will find it difficult to develop self-concept to his/her full potential. If one spouse has high physical needs and the other has a high love need, this could cause self esteem problems in both. If a person lives in an environment where values or morals differ from his/her own, low self esteem could result.

For example, if a woman lived in an environment which highly valued premarital and liberalized sex and she did not value this, she might interpret her morals and values to be wrong and, consequently, come to believe she was inadequate. Or, a person may believe that capital punishment is effective. If many of those around him/her think that this belief is foolish and give him/her that feedback, he/she may begin to think he/she is foolish and inadequate, thereby lowering self esteem. If individuals live in an environment with different values than their own, this incongruency can create self esteem problems. For example, if parents value athletic prowess and the child is very nonathletic, self esteem problems can develop in the child.

Cognitive Dissonance and Perceptual Field

An individual's perceptual field (Figure 2.1, number 5) and ideas which he/she holds about him/herself are related to a concept called cognitive dissonance by Festinger (1957). Festinger posited that when one is presented with a feeling, thought, or behavior which is contrary to his/her belief and value system, it creates dissonance for the individual. This dissonance has associated anxiety. Either the person changes his/her belief system or negates and/or changes the newly presented information. Thus, selective perceptions occur as the individual strives for consistency. (This concept is discussed more in Chapter 3.)

Self In Process

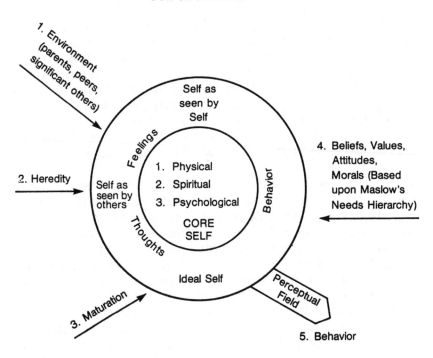

Figure 2.1. Self in process.

Note. From *The Authenic Counselor* (p. 88) by J. J. Pietrofesa, 1971, New York: Houghton Mifflin. Copyright 1971 by Houghton Mifflin. Adapted by permission.

Combs and Snygg (1959) stated that self-concepts seem to vary in two aspects; Some self-perceptions appear to be more central and stable than others, thus resisting change; concepts of self vary in clarity also. Some parts of self are very accurately perceived while others are not. Consequently, perceptual field plays a distinct role in how one envisions self and as a result how one behaves.

As the factors of heredity; maturation; environment; and beliefs, attitudes, values, and needs become more aware to the developing self, the individual engages in a process of evaluating these factors, internalizing them and attributing them to self as seems appropriate. Throughout this process of identity formation, social learning is a central process. The amount of learning about self that is based on feedback from and sharing with others is very significant.

A 400 year-old quote aptly summarizes social impact on the development of self esteem.

If you treat an individual as he is that's all that he will be. Only if you treat him as he ought to be, will he have a chance to become what he ought to be and could.

PSYCHOLOGICAL PATHOGENS

Marion (1981) stated that the way adults interact with a child has a long-lasting effect on the child's self esteem and behavior. The child developing from childhood through adolescence into adulthood may encounter numerous psychological pathogens to self-concept from others. Some of these pathogens can continue throughout one's life. The following is a representation of them: (The first ten pathogens are from Yamamoto, 1972).

1. Lack of Consistency and Limits

Adults often are not consistent in their demands; nor are they consistent in all cases with other adults. Chronic inconsistency is a definite deterrent to positive self esteem. Often, adults do not share similar goals for the children in their care. Discrepancies between different groups of adults also occur in a child's life.

Children need limits and often they will probe until they find a level of consistency. If this level cannot be found, their own behavior becomes increasingly disorganized and they become more anxious, insecure, and angry.

2. Overcoerciveness

Some parents are too controlling with their children. They give them constant attention and supervision. Nearly everything a child does is checked and double checked. The child soon learns that he/she is inadequate.

3. Perfectionism and Criticality

Often goals set for children by adults are ill-defined and constantly accelerated. Pursuit of idealized goals and/or perfection leads to chronic frustration leading to poor self esteem. The child develops a concept of never having done enough, of always having to try harder, do better.

Adults who tend to be perfectionists usually are too critical—expecting too much too soon. Expectations which are too high for the child or which come sooner than the child is capable of responding, lead to lowered self esteem. Thompson and Rudolph (1983) learned that most of children's low self esteem is formed from negative evaluations placed upon them by adults.

These parents find it difficult to offer praise. Small positive accomplishments of the child are overlooked and the focus is too much on deficiencies. Recognition is very important to a developing child. Lack of it serves only to augment a child's low self esteem.

4. Lack of Mastery

When a child does not develop a sense of adequacy because he/she does not understand his/her role in life and the skills involved in it, self-concept is not enhanced. Insufficient structure from adults is often the cause, as is the case when a child does not know what is expected of him/her and, therefore, cannot master it. When a child does not know how to be a contributor or provider in the culture, a sense of mastery is lacking. For example, if parents expect their child to parent them and give them the love and nurturing they missed as children (as is often the case in abusive homes) the child will inevitably feel inadequate because he/she does not specifically understand the role nor have the skills to master it. When a child can master the various skills of life at appropriate times such as walking, talking, reading, he/she receives positive feedback and has self esteem enhanced.

5. Overindulgence

Catering too much to a child's desires often results in lowering the child's opinion of him/herself by creating a dependency and helplessness on the part of the child.

6. Rejection by Significant Adults

Children, through their own unique perceptual sets, experience rejection in many ways that are unseen by adults. Death, divorce, and serious illness of valued adults can often be perceived as rejection by the child. Being ignored is another form of rejection which many children face. Often parents reject a child who most represents aspects of him/herself which he/she does not like. Rejection serves as a very definite deterrent to self-concept development.

7. Identification with Adult Maladjustment

When a child identifies early in life with a maladjusted adult, the influence on the child's self-concept can be dramatic. Adults who misuse drugs or are physically abusive to each other often provide very poor models for children. Children develop some of these behaviors themselves and then dislike themselves because of it.

8. Dishonesty and Deception

Decreased ability to cope with the difficult realities in life, involvement in a web of deception, and increased confusion about reality are the penalties a person pays for excessive dishonesty and deception. Guilt feelings also may be a consequence to the individual.

A double standard exists in our culture making dishonesty and deception a minor offense for adults but major maladaptive behavior for children. This double standard justly infuriates children and also can disillusion them about others and themselves.

9. Family Stress

Communication problems in families are a source of stress which can lead to feelings of low self esteem. When parents seldom actively listen to a child but mostly quarrel with the child and/or give commands, problems develop. Offer (1982) stated that the more parents agree on methods of parenting, the more positive the self esteem of their children.

Sibling rivalry is another source of stress. Children frequently compete with each other for the attention, love, and recognition of parents. Self-concept problems arise when the child experiences failure in the endeavor.

Instability of the family as manifested by a poor marital relationship of the parents and/or often threatened separation or divorce can result in the child feeling insecure, worried, nervous, guilty, and rejected. These factors lead to self-concept problems.

10. Abnormalities and Deviations

Pronounced physical differences in children often lead to self-concept difficulties. Children of exceptionally high intelligence and/or exceptionally handsome appearance often expect that good aspects of life should come to them with little investment on their part. When this does not occur, such children become very confused. On the other hand, children of exceptionally low intelligence and/or homely physical appearance expect little of life and, unfortunately, in reality receive little. Any deviation, whether physical, intellectual, spiritual, or emotional, which aids the child in feeling "odd" or out of place with others, can lead to low self esteem. Such children often become apathetic or listless.

11. Cultural Changes

At a time when societal and cultural values are being challenged and changed, children often have difficulty in adapting. The role of family, school, and religion are currently in a state of flux. Guidelines for behavior consequently are becoming more and more vague. Children, therefore, feel it is more difficult to develop a sense of adequacy when society does not clearly state what is valued. Boredom and a loss of pride in accomplishment develop in children. The psychological problems concommitant with these changes can negatively affect positive self-concept development.

12. Feedback Ratios

Some children hear mostly or solely negative feedback from parents and significant others. If the feedback is in the form of behavior it is commonly known as punishment. Rewards include a smile, a positive statement, a simple thank you, or even a pat on the shoulder. Punishments can include anything that is ego-reducing—a frown, silence, deprivation of privileges, or caustic remarks. Research in the ratio of rewards or positive feedback to punishment and/or negative feedback indicates five rewards for every one punishment is optimal in aiding children to develop to their potential (Stevenson, Keen, & Knights, 1963). When the ratio falls to two rewards for every one punishment, neurotic behavior begins to develop and feelings of inadequacy and inferiority also arise. When the ratio drops to one to one or below, feelings of despair arise.

There are, of course, qualitative differences in rewards and punishment. Certain punishments are more devastating than others and some rewards can set a person on an emotional "high." This rewards/ punishment ratio model can, however, be helpful in viewing the type of information children hear about themselves. If children experience mostly punishment, an obvious correlate is that they will begin to develop low self esteem.

Frequently parents and significant others are un-aware of how negatively they relate to children. They assume the child understands that positive behavior is appreciated and they do not comment about it. At the same time, they are quick to tell a child what is not appreciated. In part, this attitude is culturally induced inasmuch as individuals frequently "take for granted" that which is satisfactory or positive and become very vocal about that which is negative to them. Also, people assign a weighted value to the feedback they receive. If it is received from someone they respect, they accept it. If they do not value the person, they do not accept it. This is related to the concept of competence and positive self esteem. Others might feel a person is very competent, but if the person does not value their feedback, he/she is not going to feel competent. This pattern's destructive effects on self-concept development can be readily seen.

13. False Conceptions

Parents and significant others to the child often confuse the child's identity with his/her behavior. A boy is told he is a "bad boy" when he snacks too soon after dinner. The parent admonishes the child's personhood, rather than focusing on the behavior of snacking.

Instead of being told a behavior is unacceptable, the child is told he is unacceptable, "bad." Identification of self with actions often leads to feelings of inadequacy, remorse, and inferiority.

14. Involuntary Identification

Children are sometimes forced into engaging in behavior which is beyond their capacity by parents whose own low self esteem leads them to live vicariously through their children. Parents want their children to be what they themselves did not become. On the other hand, some parents force their children to become carbon copies of themselves, rather than allowing the child to blossom into whatever he/she is to become, thus negating the child's needs. In either case, feelings of inadequacy and unworthiness are often the result for both parents and children.

15. Materialism

Placing high values on material things rather than on one's self-worth can result in feelings of low self esteem. It's common for people to believe that having a lot of "things" will increase their psychological worth. One's material wealth or affluence cannot bring one feelings of worthiness. Often, guilty and ambivalent feelings result from these circumstances, and such guilt becomes very destructive to self esteem.

16. Repeated Failures

When an individual experiences repeated failures, self-worth can be greatly diminished or destroyed. In response to repeated failures, individuals appear to adapt behavior at one end of a continuum or another. They often drop out of society or become compulsive overachievers in an attempt to overcompensate for their feelings of inadequacy.

17. Procrastination

When accomplishing tasks is repeatedly delayed, a toll is taken on self esteem. Each delay is interpreted as a reflection of lacking discipline and, consequently self esteem is diminished again and again.

18. Lack of Meaning and Direction in Life

Often when people feel no purpose to their life, no direction or goals, they wander aimlessly. They feel that life is meaningless. This dynamic has been referred to frequently as the existential paradox. Feeling no meaning or direction, these individuals lack adequate self esteem.

These pathogens are not mutually exclusive. One can be the recipient of several of these dynamics. These also can be prevalent during one stage of development and not another or throughout life. Pathogens can be manifested by direct experience, nonverbal communication, and/or verbal communication. The intensity, duration, and frequency of these pathogens help to determine how deficient in self esteem the individual might become and how open to positive change the person might be.

SUGGESTED GUIDELINES
FOR ENHANCING DEVELOPMENT

Oaklander (1978) suggested the following guidelines to parents and other adults to remedy some of these pathogens and enhance self esteem:

Listen to, acknowledge, and accept the child's feelings. Treat the child with respect and acceptance. Give specific praise and constructive criticism.

Be honest.

Use "I" messages rather than "you" messages: "I am annoyed because of the volume of your stereo" rather than "You are so noisy." Along with consistency, give the child space to learn how to manage life. Give responsibilities, independence, and the freedom to make choices. Involve the child in opportunities to experiment and pursue interests.

Respect the child's uniqueness.

Be a good model—think well of yourself.

Avoid being judgmental.

Accept the child's judgment.

Respect the child's feelings. Do not contradict as negative feelings emerge.

SUMMARIZATION

In Figure 2.1 is a summarization of factors, structure, and process of self-concept mentioned previously.

Four sources (environment; heredity; maturation; and beliefs, values, attitudes, morals) of input to self-concept involve both nonverbal and verbal communication received by the individual. The inner circle, *core self* represents Areas II (Private) and IV (Unknown) of the Johari Window (Figure 1.2). The outer circle represents Areas I (Open) and III (Blind) of the Johari Window with the exception of the *Ideal Self*, which could be known to self or only private. One's totality, his/her feelings, thoughts, and behaviors, are a part of this outer circle. One's thoughts and feelings are filtered through a *perceptual field* (number 5 in Figure 2.1) resulting in behavior consistent with one's perception of the environment.

Healthy self esteem depends on a synthesis of all these sources in order to develop harmonious regulation of positive self esteem. At varying times in one's life one might rely on one source more than another, but all sources need to be integrated. (For example, a young child relies more on the environment as a source of self esteem than does an adult. An adult might rely more on values and beliefs as a source of self esteem.) This is a common, healthy pattern of moving from a predominantly external locus of control to an internal locus of control with regard to sources of self esteem.

PHASES OF SELF-CONCEPT DEVELOPMENT

Strang (1970) stated that change in self-concept may occur at any time but is particularly common at the beginning of new developmental phases, for example, when going from infancy to childhood, when entering school, at prepubescence, at adolescence, and at early maturity. A pattern of development of self-concept, corresponding to developmental phases of life discussed by Erikson (1968) and Havighurst (1972) might exist.

Hamachek, (1988) postulated the idea of evaluating self-concept and ego development within Erickson's psychosocial framework. Possible behaviors and implicit attitudes associated with positive and negative self esteem at five stages of development have been outlined (Hamachek, 1988). Developmental differences in self-concept and self esteem among kindergarten through twelfth grade students also has been researched by Brinthaupt and Lipka (1985). In addition Clarke and Gesme (1988) have developed affirmations which are specific for each cluster of developmental learnings from birth through adulthood. This is a very helpful method of validating individuals with feedback which is especially specific to their current developmental concern. The end of this chapter includes an activity based on developmental affirmations for enhancing self esteem.

CHARACTERISTICS OF
FULLY FUNCTIONING INDIVIDUALS

(Positive Self Esteem)

If one passes through these phases of self-concept development and develops positive self esteem, he/she can be described as being "self-actualized" or as having a fully functioning self. Maslow (1954) has postulated the characteristics of "self-actualized" persons:

1. They are realistically oriented.

2. They accept themselves, other people, and the natural world for what they are.

3. They have a great deal of spontaneity.

4. They are problem centered rather than self-centered.

5. They have an air of detachment and a need for privacy.

6. They are autonomous and independent.

7. Their appreciation of people and things is fresh rather than stereotyped.

8. Most of them have had profound mystical or spiritual experiences although not necessarily religious in character.

9. They identify with mankind.

10. Their intimate relationships with a few specially loved people tend to be profound and deeply emotional rather than superficial.

11. Their values and attitudes are democratic.

12. They do not confuse means with ends.

13. Their sense of humor is philosophical rather than hostile.

14. They have a great fund of creativeness.

15. They resist conformity to the culture. (p. 327)

Kelly (1962) stated that the fully functioning person thinks well of self; thinks well of others; recognizes the importance of relationships with others; sees self as part of a world in movement, in process of becoming; is optimistic, sees the value of mistakes, develops and holds human values; lives consistently with self-values; and is creative.

In 1962, Maslow described the fully functioning person, the self-actualized individual, as having the following attributes:

1. Acceptance of inner core of self.

2. Expression of inner core of self.

3. Minimal presence of ill health, neurosis, psychic loss, or diminution of basic human personal capacities. This inner core is good, but although biologically based is weak.

4. Selfishness and unselfishness fused into higher super-ordinate unity.

5. Conscious, preconsciousness, unconsciousness integrated.

6. Conative, cognitive, affective, and motor more synergic.

7. Aesthetic perceiving, creating, and peak experiences are central aspects of life and of psychology and educational rather than peripheral. (p. 36)

Combs (1962) described the fully functioning individual as:

1. Seeing him/herself in positive ways,

2. Having a identification with others,

3. Being open to experience and acceptance,

4. Having a rich and available perceptual field.

These characteristics form what can be described as healthy self-concept resulting in positive self esteem. They are the goals toward which many strive throughout their life. Developing healthy self-concept is, thus, a process, not a fixed, rigid idea of self. This process was summarized in Figure 2.1 entitled *Self in Process.* The process is fluid and changing as one develops, interacts with the environment, and assimilates what one has learned and experienced. (Wallace, Cunningham, & Del Monte, 1984).

FUTURE CONSIDERATIONS

Problems and difficulties which can occur in this process of self-concept development are more fully elaborated in the subsequent chapters. Through a thorough understanding of these difficulties, one can more effectively help those of low self esteem. Methods by which counselors, others, and self can intervene in the development of more positive self esteem also are discussed in detail in subsequent chapters.

ACTIVITY 2.1   ROOTS OF SELF-CONCEPT

Introduction

This activity helps one to understand the effect of others, especially parents, on self-concept development.

Time Required

30 to 45 minutes

Participants

Adults or children of age 9 or above

Setting

Office or classroom

Materials

None

Procedure

Who in your family criticized you? What did they criticize about you? All parents use prejudicial and critical remarks.

Considering your mother and father separately, how did each feel about self? Physical self? Social self? Emotional self? Intellectual self? Spiritual self?

How did you win recognition in your family?

How did your family react to your accomplishments? Failures?

What did it mean to be a good boy or girl in your family?

Whose opinions counted in your family? Were your feelings/thoughts listened to? Valued?

Think of your mother and father separately—what did they expect of you? I expect you to . . .

How did your mother and father express the four basic emotions: anger, joy, sadness, fear?

Who in your family encouraged your interests? Skill? How?

What are the mistakes you made that you still feel bad about? What happens to you when you make a mistake? What do you feel?

Did your parents have a life theme such as "drinking themselves to death," "committing suicide," "making it," "succeeding in business," "never quite making it?"

How did your parents manipulate you? With guilt? Fear? Criticalness? Sweetness? False compliments?

How do you copy your parents? (Appearance, values, education, work, how they had fun, listening patterns, attitudes.)

What did you have to do, to be, in order to be accepted and loved by your parents?

Make a list of unspoken Do's and Don'ts from each parent who reared you. (Don't show your feelings; Be smart but not smarter than I; Flirt but don't be sexual; See me as a perfect parent.)

How important was it for you to do well? What was expected of you in school, in social situations, at home? How important were chores, housework, jobs?

Power Structure in the Family

Think back to childhood and consider mother's and father's negative traits and moods:

1. *Faults*
2. *Weaknesses*
3. *Negative feelings about him/herself, partner, and you*
4. *Sins of omission, what he/she did not do for you*
5. *Bad moods*
6. *Negative philosophies*
7. *Fears*
8. *Needs*
9. *Ways of dealing with emotions*
10. *Reaction to criticism*
11. *Bad habits*
12. *Chronic ailments*
13. *Prejudices*
14. *Ways of handling conflict or anger*
15. *Negative reactions*
16. *Negative slogans*
17. *Unfulfilled desires*
18. *Excuses*
19. *Reaction to failure*
20. *Complaints*
21. *What was sacrificed*
22. *Areas of incompetence*
23. *Ways of showing disapproval*
24. *Things that embarrassed him/her*

Look at which traits you adopted, rebelled against, or are totally free from. (It is rare to be free of more than 10 per cent.)

Outcome

Helps one gain a better understanding of ones roots of self-concept.

———

ACTIVITY 2.2 CUTTING LOOSE FROM PARENTS

Introduction

The following activity is intended to help an individual become more aware of the interactional effects of parents on self-concept and self esteem.

Time Required

15 to 30 minutes

Participants

Ages 9 or above

Setting

Office or classroom

Materials

None

Procedure

Close your eyes and sit comfortably. Imagine sitting in a room where you feel very safe. In a moment, one of your parents will walk through the door. Get relaxed, breathe slowly and deeply, as you watch your parent walk through the door and sit with you. Make some kind of contact. Pay attention to how you feel as you do this. Feel good? O.K. If not, try something different if you like.

Just sit with your parent for a while. Really look at your parent—how do you feel as you look? Tell your parent how you feel. Express all the things you've wanted so badly to say. It's time to clear your mind. It's time to finish off any old business. It feels good to clear the slate. Be aware of your feelings as you do this.

Now switch and be your parent and respond. How do you feel about what your child has said? Tell your child how you feel. And tell him/her how you feel about him/her.

Outcome

The person gains insight into the interactional effects of parents upon ones self-concept and self esteem.

ACTIVITY 2.3   ACTIVITY INVENTORY

Introduction

This activity helps an individual to discover the various aspects of self as presented in this chapter. It comes from the **identity phase of intervention.** *(Refer to Chapter 6.)*

Time Required

30 minutes

Participants

Adults and children in grade 3 or above

Setting

Office or classroom

Materials

Paper
Pen or pencils
Code sheet or chalkboard or way to present codes

Procedure

On a sheet of paper place numbers 1 through 20. List at least 20 things you like to do. When you have finished this, take each item and decide which following code(s) apply.

Put an "N" next to things which are self-nurturing.

Put an "A" next to things you enjoy doing alone.

Put an * next to items you do regularly.

Beside each activity place a date when you intend to give yourself that gift.

Put a "B" next to items which are primarily BODY activities.

Put an "S" beside items which are primarily social in nature.

What did you learn from this activity? Did you notice any patterns? What goals might you now set for yourself?

Outcome

Helps individuals to explore various aspects of self.

————————

ACTIVITY 2.4   NAME/SYMBOL INVENTORY

Introduction

*This activity helps a person to become more aware of how symbols affect self esteem. It is from the **identity phase of intervention** presented in Chapter 6.*

Time Required

1 hour or more; each step in the procedure requires approximately 10 minutes.

Participants

Age 8 and older

Setting

Office or classroom

Materials

Books of baby names
Paper
Pen or pencil
Crayons, chalk, or paint

Procedure

Look up your name in available books of names, for example, **4,000 Names for Your Baby.** Record the meaning of your name.

Ask your parents or guardians how your name was selected and for what reason.

Write any names or nicknames which you have used (or have been called) throughout your lifetime. Beside each, record what this word means to you, what images it conjures up, and your feeling reaction to each.

Select some nicknames you might like to have for yourself. Choose names which focus on your strengths.

Get feedback from others regarding the nicknames you selected and ask them to make any additions.

Draw some symbols which represent you and things you're concerned about. Why does this have meaning to you?

What did you learn about yourself from this activity? What were your feelings throughout the activity?

Outcome

Helps one become more aware of how symbols affect self-esteem.

ACTIVITY 2.5   STORY EXCHANGE

Introduction

This is an activity in self-disclosure which can be done individually or in a group. It highlights one's various self-estimates. It is an identity phase activity as presented in Chapter 6.

Time Required

10 minutes—minimal to several days or weeks

Participants

Adults and children

Setting

Classroom or office

Materials

None

Procedure

Exchange short little stories from your life to illustrate different qualities you admire or dislike in yourself. (Examples, not being able to let go of worry, goodheartedness, and so forth).

Outcomes

Such little stories or recollections usually help one to become more aware of the attributes he/she has found throughout life.

———

ACTIVITY 2.6 THE FAMILY

Introduction

This is an excellent activity for children, but can be adapted for adults also. It is an identity phase activity. (See Chapter 6.)

Time Required

Approximately 40 minutes

Participants

Children or adults

Setting

Office or classroom

Materials

Paper
Pen or pencil
Chalkboard or flipchart

Procedure

The dynamics and relationships of the family are constant sources of confusion for children. [The following activity is] designed to help [people] explore and accept their feelings about their families.

Ask the [participants] to describe their feelings about their older and younger sisters and brothers. Recount some of your own experiences to participants first.

Ask the [participants] who have brothers and sisters to write an essay describing their relationship(s) with them . . . only children may write on the topic: "Why I would like to have a brother or sister." It is always an enlightening experience to have [participants] compare the two types of papers.

Have [participants] write about a situation in which members of their families showed kindness and understanding toward one another.

Give [participants] the opportunity to talk or write about what it would be like to be an orphan.

Ask each [person] to write a composition describing how each member of his family, including himself, is unique and different. How do these differences contribute to a stronger family?

Using voting technique ... ask ... the following questions:

1. How many of you like one parent more than the other?

2. How many of you have no father living at home?

3. How many of you have ever wished that one of your family members would go away and stay away?

4. How many of you have ever wished that you were dead?

5. How many of you wish you were the father or mother?

6. How many of you have ever disliked your mother, if only for a moment?

7. How many of you have ever disliked your father, if only for a moment?

8. Did you notice how many other people had the same feelings as you?*

Outcomes

Enables one to better understand the influence of family on self esteem.

---

*Note. From 100 Ways to Enhance Self-concept in the Classroom: A Handbook for Teachers and Parents (pp. 217-218) by J. Canfield and H. C. Wells, 1976, Englewood Cliff, NJ: Prentice-Hall. Copyright 1976 by Prentice-Hall. Reprinted by permission.

ACTIVITY 2.7   ENHANCING SELF ESTEEM DEVELOPMENTALLY

Introduction

This activity helps children and adults to understand the changing development of self esteem as one matures. It focuses on the developmental needs of individuals at different ages and their importance to the development of positive self esteem.

Time Required

10 to 20 minutes

Participants

Adults and children

Setting

Classroom, home, or office

Materials

Affirmation Ovals (Clarke & Gesme, 1988)

Procedure

Think of a child or an adult whose behavior you would like to see changed. Visualize this person, imagine how he/she looks and what the person is doing. Glance at the affirmation ovals used through the age range of this person. Choose one which you want this person to believe. With a partner, share how that person's behavior could be different when he/she has incorporated the affirmations you selected. An example of this might be Clark and Gesmes' affirmation oval for 6 to 12 year-olds: "I love you even when we differ; I love growing with you." If parents feel they want a child to be like them, difficulty may occur when the child reaches this age range. This is a time for exploration of individual interests for the child. To be avoided is the concept of "You must be interested in my interests." The hassling and arguing children do at this age with parents is not to be taken personally. It is part of the developmental task of understanding one's uniqueness. An important aspect to the development of self esteem is to share with the child through verbal and non-verbal methods e.g., "I love you even when we differ." When children experience this they have less of a need to challenge parents and adults.

Another developmental affirmation technique from Clarke and Gesme (1988) is aimed at helping adolescent self esteem: visualize your teenager at earlier developmental ages. Take one stage at a time. Visualize what was happening in his/her life and yours at that time. If you are unaware of developmental stages, use the affirmation ovals for specific time periods as your guide. Take the red affirmation ovals (Birth-6 months) and think about your child during the first six months. (The affirmations for this period of time are "I'm glad you are alive," "You belong here," "What you need is important to me," "I'm glad you are you," "You can grow at your own pace," "You can feel all of your feelings," "I love you and I care for you willingly.") Next review the orange affirmations, and so on through the various stages of your child's development. If there were affirmations at any stage of which you were not aware or you did not give your child, give them now. Give the affirmation verbally, tell your child what was happening at that time. The child may scoff at the idea or act as if he/she does not care. If so, give them feedback anyway. Giving the appropriate age specific feedback to a child is vital to the development of positive self esteem.

Outcome

Encourages one to view self esteem as a development process.

———

REFERENCES

Amato, P. (1986). Father involvement and the self-esteem of children and adolescents. *Australian Journal of Sex, Marriage and Family, 7*, 6-16.

Bachman, J., & O'Malley, P. (1986). Self-concepts, self-esteem, and educational experiences: The frog pond revisited (again). *Journal of Personality and Social Psychology, 50*, 1, 35-46.

Bayley, N. (1951). Development and maturation. In H. Helson (Ed.), *Theoretical foundations of psychology.* New York: Van Nostrand.

Bloom, B. (1964). *Stability and change in human characteristics.* New York: John Wiley and Sons.

Brinthaupt T., & Lipka, R. (1985). Developmental differences in self-concept and self esteem among kindergarten through twelfth grade students. *Child Study Journal, 15*, 3, 207-221.

Canfield, J., & Wells, H.C. (1976). *100 Ways to enhance self-concept in the classroom: A handbook for teachers and parents.* Englewood Cliffs, NY: Prentice-Hall.

Chrzanowski, G. (1981). The genesis and nature of self esteem. *American Journal of Psychotherapy, 35*, 38-46.

Clarke, J., & Gesme, C. (1988). *Affirmation ovals.* Plymouth, MN: Daisey Press.

Covington, M. (1984). The self-worth theory of achievement motivation: Findings and implications. *The Elementary School Journal, 85*, 1, 5-20.

Combs, A.W. (1962). A perceptual view of the adequate personality. In ASCD Yearbook 1962, *Perceiving, behaving, becoming* (pp. 50-64). Washington, DC: Association for Supervision and Curriculum Development.

Combs, A. W., & Snygg, D. (1959). *Individual behavior: A perceptual approach to behavior.* New York: Harper and Brothers.

Davidson, H. H., & Long, G. (1960). Children's perceptions of their teacher's feelings toward them related to self perception, school achievement, and behavior. *Journal of Experimental Education, 29*, 107-118.

Demos, E. V. (1982). Facial expression in young children: A descriptive analysis. In T. Field & A. Fegel (Eds.), *Emotion and early interaction.* Hillsdale, NJ: Erlbaum Associates.

Erikson, E. (1968). *Identity: Youth and crisis.* New York: Norton.

Eskilson, A., Wiley, M., Muehlbauer, G., & Dodder, L. (1986). Parental pressure, self-esteem, and adolescent reported deviance: Bending the twig too far. *Adolescence, 21,* 83, 501-514.

Fels Institute. (1962). Motivational and ability determinants of young children's intellectual achievement behavior. *Child Development, 33,* 3, 643-661.

Festinger, L. (1957). *A theory of cognitive dissonance.* Stanford: Stanford University Press.

Fraiberg, S. (1968). The origin of identity. *Smith College Studies in Social Work, 38,* 2, 79-101.

Gecas, V., & Schwalbe, M. (1986). Parental behavior and adolescent self esteem. *Journal of Marriage and the Family, 48,* 37-46.

Gordon, I. J. (1962). *Human development from birth through adolescence.* New York: Harper and Row.

Hamachek, D. (1988). Evaluating self-concept and ego development within Erickson's psychosocial framework: A formulation. *Journal of Counseling and Development, 66,* 354-360.

Harlow, H. F. (1971). *Learning to love.* New York: Ballantine Books.

Havighurst, R. (1972). *Developmental tasks and education* (3rd ed.). New York: David McKay.

Herrmann, N. (1988). *The creative brain.* Lake Lure, NC: Bain Books.

Johnson, S. (1982). New day for Alaska; Pribilof islanders. *National Geographic, 162,* 186.

Kawash, G., Kerr, E., & Clewes, J. (1984). Self-esteem in children as a function of perceived parental behavior. *The Journal of Psychology, 119,* 3, 235-242.

Kelly, E. C. (1962). The fully functioning self. In ASCD Yearbook, *Perceiving, behaving, and becoming.* Washington DC: Association for Supervision and Curriculum Development.

Klein, G. (1976). *Psychoanalytic theory: An exploration of essentials.* New York: International Universities Press.

Lamke, L.K. (1982). The impact of sex-role orientation on self-esteem in early adolescence. *Child Development, 53,* 1530-1535.

Long, B. (1985). Parental discord vs. family structure: Effects of divorce on the self-esteem of daughters. *Journal of Youth and Adolescences,* 19-27.

Mack, F. (1987). Understanding and enhancing self-concept in black children. *Momentum, 18,* 22-28.

Marion, M. (1981). *Guidance of young children.* St. Louis: C.V. Mosby.

Maslow, A. M. (1962). Some basic propositions of a growth and self-actualizing psychology. In ASCD Yearbook 1962, *Perceiving, behaving, becoming* (pp. 34-39). Washington, DC: Association for Supervision and Curriculum Development.

Maslow, A. M. (1954). *Motivation and personality.* New York: Harper and Row.

Miller, T. (1984). Parental absence and its effect on adolescent self-esteem. *International Journal of Social Psychiatry, 30,* 4, 293-296.

Montagu, A. (1971). *Touching: The human significance of the skin.* New York: Harper and Row.

Notman, M. (1982). *Seminar on self esteem development and sustenance.* Boston: Harvard Medical School.

Oaklander, V. (1978). *Windows to our children.* Moab, UT: Real People Press.

Offer, D. (1982). *Seminar on self esteem development and sustenance.* Boston: Harvard Medical School.

Pietrofesa, J. J. (1971). *The authentic counselor.* Chicago: Rand McNally.

Purkey W. W. (1970). *Self concept and school achievement.* Englewood Cliffs, NJ: Prentice Hall.

Robinson-Awana, P., Kehle, T., & Jenson, W. (1986). But what about smart girls? Adolescent self-esteem and sex role perceptions as a function of academic achievement. *Journal of Educational Psychology, 78,* 3, 179-183.

Rochlin, G. (1980). *The masculine dilemma.* Boston: Little, Brown.

Rosenberg, M. (1965). *Society and the adolescent self image.* NJ: Princeton University Press.

Sears, R. (1980). *Sources of life satisfaction.* Stanford, CA: Stanford University Press.

Secord, P., & Jourard, S. (1953). The appraisal of body-cathexis and the self. *Journal of Counseling Psychology, 17,* 343-47.

Spitz, R. (1965). *The first year of life.* New York: International Press.

Stevenson, H. W., Keen, R., & Knights, R. (1963). Parents and strangers as reinforcing agents for children performance. *Journal of Abnormal and Social Psychology, 67,* 183-186.

Strang, R. (1970). *Helping your child develop his potentialities.* New York: Award Books.

Sullivan, H. S. (1953). *The interpersonal theory of psychiatry.* New York: Norton.

Terman, L. (Ed.). (1921). *Genetic studies of genius.* Stanford, CA: Stanford University Press.

Thompson, C., & Rudolph, L. (1983). *Counseling children.* Monterey, CA: Brooks Cole.

Walker, L., & Greene J. (1986). The social context of adolescent self-esteem. *Journal of Youth and Adolescence, 15,* 4, 315-322.

Wallace, J., Cunningham T., & Del Monte, V. (1984). Change and stability in self esteem between late childhood and early adolescence. *Journal of Early Adolescence, 43,* 253-257.

White, B. (1975). *The first three years of life.* Englewood Cliffs, NJ: Prentice Hall.

Wiehle, V. (1985). Self-esteem, attitude toward parents, and locus of control in children of divorced and non-divorced families. *Journal of Social Service Research, 8,* 1, 17-28.

Wyman, P., Cowen, E., Hightower, D., & Pedro-Carroll, J. (1985). Perceived competence, self esteem, and anxiety in latency-aged children of divorce. *Journal of Clinical Child Psychology, 14,* 1, 20-26.

Yamamoto, K. (1972). *The child and his image.* Boston: Houghton Mifflin.

CHAPTER 3

SOCIAL SYSTEM AND SELF ESTEEM

In Chapter 2 on self-concept development, were addressed both the influence of psychological and the genetic factors on self esteem and the effect of one's position in the social system on self esteem were addressed. Self esteem lies within the person as well as in the person's system of social interactions. This chapter emphasizes the influence of the culture-sub-culture, the family, and other social interactions on self esteem (see Figure 3.1, Influences of social systems on self esteem).

CULTURE-SUBCULTURE

The American culture places a strong emphasis on the accumulation of wealth, power, and prestige with stress on productivity and upward mobility. As the economy and unemployment rates rise and fall and as rapid and drastic transitions occur in career, family forms (remarried families, single parent families, etc.) and geographic locale, individuals experience variability in the level of self esteem. For example, a study by Clausen (1976) revealed that middle class men who were downwardly mobile were prone to psychosomatic ailments, self-defeating behavior, anxiety, and feelings of inadequacy. Even positive transitions (for example, job promotions, mar-riage) are stressful (Holmes & Rahe, 1967). A more thorough analysis of the effects of change on self esteem is discussed in Chapter 8 entitled "Transitions and Self Esteem."

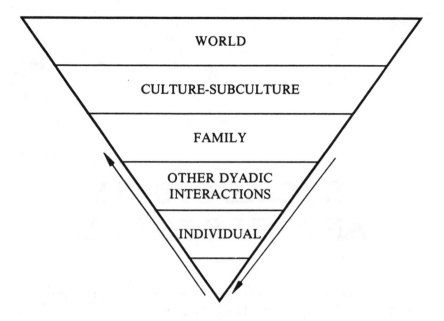

Figure 3.1. Influences of social systems on self esteem.

As can be seen from Figure 3.1, the subculture to which a person belongs also influences self esteem. Whether an individual is a member of the American Medical Association, Gay Liberation, Black Caucus, National Organization of Women, Alcoholics Anonymous, Overeaters Anonymous, or some other organization or institution, that membership influences how one feels about self. If one is a member of the American Medical Association or the Junior League, the association will likely enhance one's esteem. If one is Black, Gay, overweight, or in some other negatively valued subculture, self esteem is likely to suffer since our society does not readily accept and appreciate differences. Joining a minority organization can provide support for the person's self esteem in a nation which demonstrates limited acceptance of individual differences. Such groups provide desperately needed support and affirmation. Breaking societal norms results in explicit disapproval and discrimination which ultimately have the potential of eroding self esteem. Individuals labeled deviant tend to exaggerate their deviance as a defense against, an attack upon, or fulfillment of society's label. Schur (1971) explained that when an individual's behavior is discovered and labeled deviant and his/her life becomes organized with a self-concept of being deviant, one is then set apart and becomes deviant. The positions one holds in the culture, one's social status, deviancy-normalcy, attractiveness-unattractiveness affect one's self esteem.

Our culture also rewards attractive people. Many studies have demonstrated the weight given to physical attractiveness in initial social contracts (Gambrill & Richey, 1985). Negative effects can be controlled, however, with appropriate interpersonal skills.

FAMILY

Self-concept is formed gradually through direct experience and through social mediation. In the area of social mediation, the family is the primary and most powerful teacher. Through family interaction (through words, voice tone, touch, eyes), individuals develop an early picture of themselves. This picture is often incomplete and distorted. In large measure, peoples' relationship to themselves are influenced by the families in which they were reared.

CONTEXT OF BIRTH

From the very beginning people receive messages about self. Think back for a moment about your birth. Describe the context in which you were conceived. That is, where were you conceived? What was the relationship like between your seed mother and seed father at that time? (ex, one-time fling; rape; out of a loving, committed relationship). Were you a first child? Last child? First boy? Replacement for a child who died? Were you welcomed into the world? Were they glad you were the sex you were? What was happening in the world? (historical context).

Then, write a fantasy of your birth. Imagine you are in your mother's womb. Write about that experience. Describe how each member of your family feels about your birth. Imagine the actual birthing experience—what was it like? Describe how you came into this world.

The context of your birth can heavily influence your early beginnings. Your perceptions of this are just as important as the actual facts. Be in touch with both. Were you welcomed into this world? Someone who was born out of wedlock and whose adolescent parents were forced to marry would have a very different beginning than someone born to parents who were more mature, settled in a marriage, or otherwise committed relationship, and ready to have a child. Being born in the midst of an economic depression would be different from being born during a time of prosperity. Being born after several miscarriages influences the expectations one would carry. A birth around the time of significant deaths (for example, parents) bears certain strains. A fourth girl child born before the long awaited birth of a boy might carry yet another set of feelings about herself.

From the beginning, children draw certain conclusions about themselves based on observations and interactions with parental figures. We collect conclusions in our growing up about our own power, others' power, our worth (judged by responses of others which come to us), and our freedom to be separate and connected. These conclusions are based as much on touch and tone of voice as on words. This is especially true of younger children and infants who have not developed their language capacity.

Reflect on the following:

If you are a girl,

how did your mother treat herself?

how did your mother allow others (male/female) to treat her?

how were you treated by same sex parent? Opposite sex parent?

how does your mother treat your father?

how does your father treat your mother?

If you are a boy,

how did your father treat himself?

how did your father allow others (male and female) to treat him?

how were you treated by same sex parent? Opposite sex parent?

how does your father treat your mother?

how does your mother treat your father?

Through the direct/indirect means outlined above, we begin to put a picture together about our worth. Based on your answers to the above questions, what conclusions do you think you drew?

FAMILY ROLE

In looking at the family system as a whole, children often have a tendency to try to relieve the pain, fill in the holes, hide the shame in a malfunctioning family. They do this by adopting a variety of roles in the family: hero, scapegoat, mascot, and lost child (Wegscheider, 1981; Black, 1982)

Each role attempts to pick up functions or express parts which are not being performed or permitted by the chief architects of the family, the parents. Children, being young, dependent, lacking in adult skills and resources, can never adequately make up for or repair the "family machine." This, then, becomes a major root source of not feeling good enough. Children can never adequately compensate for such deficiencies though miraculously, as young as they are, they do help establish the family equilibrium.

What was your role in your family of origin?

Sculpt your family by using small dolls, clay, or friends to play different family members, or make a drawing. Use space, gestures, posture, facial expressions, direction to convey relationship and attitudes. How would your mother be in relation to your father? Now, where would the first born be in relation to them? Second born? Third born? Make it a moving sculpture if you like. How does each feel? What is the posture of each? What is your role in this sculpture? What functions do you serve? What do you need?

You can find clues about your script/role in your given names, nicknames, in how you were labeled as a kid, and in what predictions were made about you.

For example:

"You'll never have any friends."

"You're just like your father: You'll never amount to anything."

"You've got the gift of good luck."

"She's the brains of the family."

"She's our little pet."

"He's the little man of the family."

Part of the motivation for adopting these roles is out of compassion and love; another part is out of survival needs. Each of these roles results in both deficiencies and strengths (see Figure 3.2).

Family Norms/Family Rules
(Carlock & Hagerty, 1988; Curran, 1983; Karpel, 1986; Satir, 1983, 1988; Whitaker & Napier, 1978).

A number of dimensions of family climate can influence the development of self esteem:

1. How positive or negative, critical or encouraging is the family?

(Continued on page 68)

Role	Deficiencies	Strengths
HERO	• builds worth on doing rather than being • emotional self under-developed • seeks approval • doesn't know how to relax and play • lacks spontaneity • trouble admitting when wrong	• possess leadership abilities and sense of responsibility • high achievement • restores pride to family • independent • helpful
MASCOT	• fears (s)he doesn't belong • fragile • insecure • fears breaking down	• knows how to get dependency needs met • fun to be with • reduces tension and anxiety in the family system
SCAPEGOAT	• defiant • acts out • distances others • draws anger and attack	• knows how to get attention • able to express anger and tolerate other people's anger • able to break rules, break confluence with the system
LOST CHILD	• timid, shy • isolated • withdrawn • doesn't get needs met • low energy • afraid to take risks • difficulty making decisions	• excellent observers • avoids becoming target of criticism, abuse • self-sufficient

Figure 3.2. Family roles.

2. How well does the family allow connection and disconnection?

3. Are individual differences acknowledged and appreciated?

4. Is the family flexible enough to allow other people to enter the system now and then?

5. Is the family overprotective/underprotective? Are members given responsibilities, independence, guidance in accordance with their abilities?

6. Are generational boundaries adhered to? That is, are mother and father clearly at the top of the hierarchy? Are parental functions in their hands only? Are alliances between one parent and the children discouraged? Are there clear rules defining the relationship between parents and children?

7. Is there variety and resilience in interpreting events?

8. Does the family stress accountability, commitment, admission and repair of wrongs, and forgiveness without attack of members worth?

9. Are vulnerability, dependency, and neediness permitted without judgment?

10. Is each person separate though a part of the family?

11. Do dialogues occur in relationships and are relationships reliable and constant over time. Are mistakes and differences expected, acknowledged, and accepted?

12. Is there a relatively stable level of emotional contact and accessibility?

13. Does the family support maturation and change of values through life experience? Is learning and growth expected and encouraged?

14. Are family members able to interact with nonfamilial world?

15. Does give and take occur among members?

16. Do members show respect for each other, communicating that each is valued and their feelings and contributions are important?

17. Are humor and playfulness used to reduce shame and reframe highly charged emotional material?

18. Is communication direct, clear, specific, and honest versus indirect, vague, and dishonest?

19. Are members willing and able to protect others in the family?

20. Can people depend on each other?

21. Does hope and belief exist that effort and involvement in the family will pay off?

22. Is scapegoating distributed so that one person is not blamed and dumped on?

23. Are family rules flexible, human, appropriate, and subject to change versus rigid, inhuman, and non-negotiable?

Reflect on your family of origin as well as your current family as you consider the preceding questions. What are the strengths and weaknesses of your family? Set two to three goals to improve the weak areas and appreciate the good parts of your family. Check your views against the views of other family members. Through this sharing you will learn more about others' perspectives and be able to move closer.

SUPPORT NETWORK

The healthy individual has a support network of approximately 55 people upon whom to draw. While the accuracy of that specific number is debatable, the point is that people need many others available to them to support the different aspects of their lives. Support persons are positive resources to draw upon in crisis as well as to simply maintain a healthy way of life. According to Gambrill and Richey (1985) the average number of friends people report is 15; intimate or close friends, six. However, some people are quite happy with just a few friends and infrequent social contacts.

Social relationships provide a sense of belonging and validation for our beliefs, feelings, and self-worth (Gambrill & Richey, 1985). According to Gambrill and Richey (1985) they also can provide assistance in learning new skills and handling problems as well as information to deal with particular situations. On the lighter side, social relationships offer the enjoyment of sharing activities. Since social relationships are reciprocal, they also provide opportunities for us to give to others in these same ways (Gambrill & Richey, 1985). Gilles (1976) outlined the individual circle of support, as shown in Figure 3.3, as family and close friends, limited friendships, and potential friendships and acquaintances.

Assessing Your Network

Individuals can identify their major interpersonal support systems using Figure 3.3 as a base, adding or deleting satellites as appropriate. The following items can be used to help individuals evaluate their satellite network.

1. Place satellites at appropriate distance/closeness from self.

2. List major persons in each satellite.

3. List five adjectives to describe each person in each satellite.

4. Describe how each person is supportive or nonsupportive.

5. As the individual gets an overview of his/her satellite system:

    a. Decide whether or not other satellites are needed. For example, if interest groups are lacking one might wish to join a club or group of some kind.

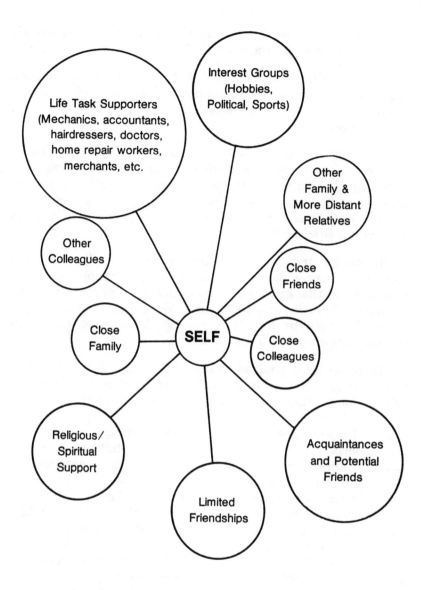

Figure 3.3. Support satellites.

NOTE: Figure is original. Idea initiated from Gestalt Institute of Cleveland (1979).

b. Determine if any satellites are weak in that too few people are included in the satellite.

In completing consideration of the list, the individual will begin to have a sense of how supportive his/her network is and where gaps need to be filled. Adequate support is a safety net for self esteem.

In many locations every day we have opportunities to expand our social contacts: work, clubs and organizations, book stores, grocery stores, buses, trains, airplanes, parties, anywhere you frequently find yourself. Taking advantage of such every day settings to initiate even brief contacts with people can result in a much richer social life.

If you are involved in an interest group such as a chess club or wilderness camping club, such organizations provide a mutual focus that can make conversations easier to initiate and maintain. Consider how well your goals are likely to match the goals of others in the same setting. Make sure that your expectations are realistic for the setting.

Being aware of your own interest areas can help you decide where to go to meet individuals with similar interests and values. Check which of the following you would enjoy:

_____ volunteer work
_____ sports
_____ exhibit/shows
        (antiques, auto-
        mobiles, horses,
        computers, etc.)
_____ cultural events
        (music, drama,
        opera, dance)
_____ church events
_____ classes
_____ community organiza-
        tions
        (Junior League,
        Chamber of Com-
        merce, local boards,
        etc.)

_____ hobbies
        (photography,
        chess, gardening,
        etc.)
_____ card playing
_____ hiking and camping
_____ music groups
        (choirs, bands,
        orchestra, etc.)
_____ dancing
_____ bars/lounges
_____ informal get togethers
_____ parties

Isolation can be one of the most destructive aspects of human existence. With the mobility of our culture, families are often dispersed and with urbanization even greater isolation has resulted. Therefore, people even more imperatively need to learn the value of a community and skills in developing a community. People need each other. When pretenses are dropped, people are real with each other, and when conflicts are faced, love abounds (Peck, 1987).

Blocks to Relationships

Look at the kinds of issues which people use to impede the development of new relationships (Gambrill & Richey, 1985):

1. Fear of rejection: One of the most common blocks is that people won't like us. True, not everyone will like us. But, so what? Others will.

2. Fear of criticism: Many people are perfectionistic and fear looking foolish. But only by risking can we grow.

3. Feeling awkward: Initial encounters are awkward for many people. Even though many people appear confident and relaxed, most often people experience anxiety in some social situations. You're not unique in this. Learning certain skills (discussed later in this chapter) can help alleviate some of this anxiety and awkwardness.

4. Faulty beliefs: Beliefs such as the following can get in the way of forming relationships:

   I'm unlovable and not worth knowing.

   People will disappoint you.

   Relationships take too much work.

   People can't be trusted.

By identifying beliefs which may be blocking you from expanding your social support network and replacing these with more realistic beliefs, you can clear a path towards a happier existence.

INTERPERSONAL SKILLS

Communication: Verbal—Nonverbal

Communication has a significant effect on self esteem. The way an individual communicates with others (verbally and nonverbally) affects the way one feels about self, and affects the way others respond. Conversely, the way others respond directly affects one's self esteem. A number of primary communication skills are critical to maintain and enhance self esteem. A few simple skills can help take the edge off the anxiety of initial encounters.

Three important skills are necessary in initiating conversations: greetings or opening remarks, exchange of basic information, and small talk (Gambrill & Richey, 1985).

Greetings are remarks such as "Hi," "How are you," "Good to meet you," "Welcome." Such greetings are best delivered with a smile, full eye contact, and a clear, audible voice for good contact. When you know the person's name, adding that is helpful as well. Most people like to hear their names used.

Following the greeting is generally an **exchange of basic information** such as names, where you work or where you live, what you do for a living. Depending on the setting, other openers are also effective (Gambrill & Richey, 1985):

1. Requesting directions or help: "Can you show me how to work this machine?"

2. Asking simple questions: "How long have you worked here?" "Can I get you a drink?"

3. Complimenting the person: "That's a beautiful sweater."

4. Making a casual observation: "That salad looks delicious."

5. Asking to join the person: "May I sit here?"

6. Offering something: "Would you like to read this newspaper?" "Can I help you load that, it looks bulky."

7. Sharing an opinion or feeling: "This year's presidential race should be exciting." "This play is fantastic, isn't it?"

Small talk, while repugnant to many people, serves an important function with people who have not met before. It provides a chance for people to feel each other out for future topics of conversation. Having several small talk topics handy can help alleviate anxiety freeing up energy for responding.

In general, the more positive a person can be with any comments or questions the better. Focusing on assets, yours and theirs, is likely to increase comfort and receptivity. According to Gambrill and Richey (1985), a spark of humor is also useful if it is natural to you. As a general strategy, approach people as if they are treasure chests—your job is to identify the gifts they have to offer. Your curiosity and interest will pay off.

As relationships develop, other skills are required to deepen the interaction. People enjoy being listened to. Several skills can help with this: reflections of feelings, paraphrasing the content of a message, encouraging comments like, "That's great," "Yeah, I see what you mean," "Tell me more about it." Open-ended questions ("Tell me about your trip") are good to begin with followed by more specific questions.

A good balance must be achieved between receptivity towards and focus on the other and expressions of your own opinions and feelings. Dominating the conversation will alienate others as well as will too much passivity. The more genuine you are, that is, the closer your insides match your outsides (Satir, 1988), the closer you'll feel to others. Other skills such as self-disclosure, assertion, setting boundaries, filtering, meta-talk, and non-verbal activity also can enhance communication.

Self-disclosure. In order to make oneself known to others and closer to others, a person must use the skill of disclosure. Self disclosure involves sharing yourself. Examples of self-disclosure statements are

"I really like the feel of this room."

"I'm feeling anxious right now," and

"I really enjoyed being with you."

Self-disclosure involves skills such as speaking for self, making feeling statements, and speaking of one's intentions (Miller, Nunnally, & Wackwan, 1975). High disclosers are generally seen as friendlier though the context for disclosures must be appropriate and overly high disclosure too rapidly can put others off.

Although self-disclosure can improve contact, many people hide their true feelings and thoughts. People typically put up a front to gain acceptance, recognition, or simply to survive. For example, some images people adopt are good little girl, serious student, hood, and Don Juan. "Masks" or roles keep a person safe from the pain of rejection—but also "safe" from closeness, warmth, and love. What is intended as a means of protection ultimately deprives the individual of needed contact. Self-disclosure breaks down facades and allows for personal contact and enhancing of esteem.

When individuals play an exclusively nurturant role in order to please other people, they betray and despise themselves and resent others. Everyone, of course, plays certain roles at various times during the day, but roleplaying has reached a destructive level when one becomes alienated from self as well as others. Such individuals have lost touch with their feelings, wants, and needs. Roleplaying, defined here as facade, is different from legitimate role taking. When the self is hidden behind roleplaying, one is not harmed directly but neither does one receive nourishment to grow. The more one risks, the more nourishment is possible.

Through the skill of self-disclosure, people reveal feelings and open themselves to response (comfort, confrontation, encouragement). The self longs to express itself. Self-expression is a need of the organism, although the favored form of expression (dialogue, music, writing, and art, for example) varies from person to person.

Self-disclosure connects people to one another and enhances mental health (Jourard, 1971). Other skills which bond people are reflection of others' feelings, stating observations, and identifying mutually shared and uniquely experienced themes. Through self-disclosure, people discover how they are alike and different from others. These skills bond individuals together increasing the strength of their support thereby helping them to feel good.

Assertion. These *skills enable one to express needs as well as provide a way for those needs to be met. Individuals who lack this set of skills are unable effectively to meet their needs.* Assertion involves standing up for one's rights and expressing one's feelings, thoughts, and wants *in direct and appropriate ways* (Lange & Jakubowski, 1976). Examples of assertive skills for personal relationships are

> receiving compliments;
>
> refusing requests;
>
> returning an item to a store;
>
> telling someone you don't want advice;
>
> not allowing oneself to be interrupted without good reason;
>
> stating one's needs, wants, preferences;
>
> making positive statements about oneself;
>
> changing the topic of conversation;
>
> making a compliment;
>
> telling a person when he/she does something which bothers you;
>
> openly discussing someone's criticism of you;
>
> reporting good news about yourself; and
>
> expressing a divergent opinion.

Individuals who have such skills are able to meet more of their needs and improve their relationships. A belief system in which an individual values feelings, thoughts, and wants equally to those of others undergirds assertive behavior. As discussed earlier, assertive behavior is directly related to self esteem. When individuals are nonassertive as a characteristic style, they tend to violate their own rights and show a lack of respect for their own feelings, thoughts, and wants. Expressing oneself in a placating way often brings hostility and disparagement from others as well as self-hatred.

Nonassertive individuals are self-denying, allow others to choose, have difficulty in achieving goals, and often feel angry with themselves and others. Assertive individuals are generally self-enhancing; they feel good about themselves and are better able to achieve desired goals (Alberti & Emmons, 1974). Examples of assertive behavior are the following:

"Say, I wasn't finished with what I was saying."

"I'd like to go with you if I may."

"I'm not wanting to talk on the phone right now, may I call you tomorrow?"

"May I have a hug?"

Individuals who behave assertively reveal themselves through words and actions, have an active orientation to life; they go after what they want, respect themselves, hold reasonable beliefs about the world, and can communicate with people at all levels (Byrum-Gaw, 1981). According to Byrum-Gaw (1981), our self-image influences our assertive/nonassertive behavior which in turn elicits certain responses from others which further affect self esteem.

Along with assertiveness comes responsibility—the responsibility to respect others' rights in the process and to encourage others to assume responsibility for themselves. Mutuality is crucial—that is, respect self and others' rights equally (Lange & Jakubowski, 1976).

While some people habitually err on the side of nonassertion, others seem to lead their lives with almost continuous self-asserting. Fighting over every issue results in heavy energy depletion. Tubesing (1979) offered three questions in evaluating whether or not to fight: (1) Is the threat real? (2) Is the value or principle at stake important enough to one to expend the energy to fight? (3) If I choose to fight, will I be likely to be able to make an impact, or is the energy likely to be wasted? If the answer is "no" to any of these questions, Tubesing recommended letting the issue go. He warned against spending ten dollars worth of stress on a ten cent problem, or the reverse, spending ten cents worth of psychic energy on a ten dollar problem. Appropriate allocation of energy results in more efficient, positive functioning and, consequently, higher self esteem.

Once a decision to assert oneself has been made, the individual must develop those skills and attitudes (intrapersonal and interpersonal), and the tenacity to stand firm on the issue despite initial resistance. In so doing, one further defines the self and enhances one's self esteem.

Setting Boundaries. Related to self-assertion is the skill of setting boundaries. When parents are able to provide adequate caring and nurturance, the child internalizes the caring and the "me" becomes separate and distinct from the "not me." In other words, ego boundaries are developed which guard inner space. According to Fossum and Mason (1986), ego boundaries are the means by which one screens and interprets the world and regulates interaction with the world. Adequate ego boundaries are essential to the formation of identity. Fossum and Mason (1986) used the metaphor of a self with an internal or external zipper to explain the differences between people who have healthy ego boundaries (internal zipper) and people who have faulty ego boundaries (external zipper). These are illustrated in Figure 3.4.

For further description of healthy and unhealthy boundaries see Figure 3.5 which illustrates too permeable (unhealthy), healthy, and impermeable (unhealthy).

Internal Zipper	External Zipper
Can say "No"	Believe they are regulated by others and the outside world
Can walk away	
Can monitor closeness	Feel invaded and victimized
Express opinions assertively	Allow others to mind-read "You feel. . ." "You don't think that way"
Can wonder aloud	
Can ask questions freely	Have incomplete interpretingscreens
Can keep things private and secret without feeling guilt	Denial and repression prevent assessment of what is safe and what is harmful
Can stand up for his/her beliefs even when in minority	Display highly stereotypic sex role behavior—ex. helpless female
Can choose what feelings to express to others and has some control over feelings	Allow intellectual blurring. Created through criticizing, blaming, mind reading, prying, mind raping—attempting to turn her thoughts into his thoughts, comparing, belittling).
Able to maintain non-blaming stance	
Know that their failings are not dependent on other's actions or the cause of other's behaviors and feelings	
Can sit with another person in pain without taking feelings on	Allow physical blurring through incest, battering, rape, teasing about the body, bathing, enemas.
Respect others' distance boundaries	Allow *emotional blurring.* Created when parent shares with child secrets that should be for spouse only; when lonely, angry parents share intimate feelings with children; through emotional deprivation or psychological abandonment.
Have good esteem about physical self	
Able to touch and be touched with discrimination	
Able to nurture and receive	
Engage in regular exercise—balanced diet	
Able to be vulnerable when safe	
Know there is a dark side as well as light side to each of us	

Figure 3.4. Examples of healthy ego boundaries (internal zipper) and faulty ego boundaries (external zipper). Based on work by Fossum and Mason (1986).

(Too permeable) UNHEALTHY	HEALTHY	(Impermeable) UNHEALTHY
Telling all	I consider the other person's level of interest and caring before opening up to them. I also consider my own readiness to talk about particular subjects.	Not talking: not opening up at all.
Falling in love with anyone who shows interest.	When someone reaches out to me, I ask myself whether this person has the qualities I need. I selectively allow myself to love and be loved.	Not allowing anyone's love in and not allowing myself to love anyone.
Acting on first sexual impulse.	My feelings and my self-esteem decide whether I act on sexual impulses. "Will I feel good about myself?" is my first question.	Not allowing myself to be sexually excited or aroused even when I feel good about the person. Not allowing myself to act on these feelings even when I believe timing is right.
Letting anyone close who wants to get close.	I am wary of someone who wants to get too close to me too soon. I evaluate how close I want to be, with whom, and how soon.	Never letting anyone close to me.
Touching a person without asking.	I do not touch others without thinking about whether they have given me signals direct or indirect that it is okay. I ask for feedback about touching.	Not touching others ever.
Letting others describe my reality.	I assume that my perception of what is going on is just as accurate as another's perception. I refuse to allow others tell me, "You don't feel that way." I trust my own feelings and perceptions and filter feedback according to what fits for me.	Not being willing to listen as others describe their reality
Expecting others to anticipate my needs.	I do not expect others to read my mind about what is going on with me. I tell them what I want/need.	Not allowing others to take care of me or attend to my needs.

Figure 3.5. Boundaries—too permeable, healthy, and impermeable.

Adapted from handout acquired from Overeaters Anonymous.

Filtering. Another communication skill called filtering serves the function of sifting feedback which comes to one person from another. When people filter feedback, they accept that with which they can identify and refuse to accept that which does not fit. Good questions to ask are: What grain of truth can be identified with in this? What doesn't fit? Feedback is an important source of information about the self. Self-concept develops out of a relatively stable perception of oneself. In part, these impressions are formed from feedback one receives. Feedback has a direct effect on self esteem (Morran & Stockton, 1980). Individuals experience two common problems with filtering:

1. The personal boundary is almost impenetrable—little feedback is permitted to enter whether it is negative, positive, or neutral. As discussed in Chapter 1, feedback can help decrease the individual's blind area. The more aware people are, the more effective they can be. People may discover behaviors or attitudes which are not effective in meeting their needs, and they can change those behaviors or attitudes. Without awareness, change is inhibited. Feedback also may be positive, of course. Positive feedback helps to reinforce a person. Feedback can help people to become whole rather than to be filled with holes in their self-awareness.

2. The personal boundary is overly-penetrable—too much feedback enters without adequate discrimination. When people accept feedback indiscriminately they are likely to ingest others' "garbage" as well as their "gifts." For example, if Leon gives Jake feedback regarding Jake's behavior, the feedback may be truer for Leon than Jake. What is suggested is that there is always the possibility that the mechanism of projection is operating. In projection, an individual places onto others parts which the person considers unacceptable and, therefore, avoids recognizing in him/herself. The person one chooses to project onto usually displays at least a piece of the behavior/attitude which has been alienated. For this reason, Jake might ask himself, "What grain of truth can I identify with in this?" This kind of question facilitates the sorting which needs to be done so that

Jake does not take in that which more aptly belongs to Leon. Feedback also is laden with values. In sifting feedback, therefore, the individual might ask him/herself, "What value underlies this feedback? Do I agree with this value?" In so doing, the individual protects his/her esteem.

Either problem can inhibit the stability and enhancement of self esteem.

Meta-talk. The skill of meta-talk, or commenting on the process, allows the individual, at least temporarily, to avoid reacting and, instead, step out of the interchange to examine more objectively what is happening. A new direction may then emerge. For example, if person A, who normally is quite kind, suddenly becomes irritable and finds fault with everything person B does, person B can either respond with anger/hurt or say "I'm feeling upset that you seem to be picking at me. Is something going on with you?" In this way, person B responds by reacting to the process rather than to the content. In this example, the criticized individual emerges with his/her self esteem level preserved, rather than allowing his/her esteem to be diminished. The skill of meta-talk in allowing the individual to step out of the interaction permits the emotional distance necessary for greater objectivity of the process which may help protect self esteem. By stepping out, person B could observe that the partner was behaving in a peculiar way and could wonder what was going on with him/her rather than internalizing the criticisms or feeling hurt by the attack or defending or counterattacking.

Nonverbal Behavior. Flexibility in nonverbal behavior also is associated with higher self esteem and the individual's behavioral repertoire needs to include a balance of the following:

RECEPTIVE	ACTIVE
speaking softly	speaking loudly
respecting another's territory	intruding on another's territory
softening the eyes	hardening the eyes
pulling back	standing up
not touching	touching

Individuals who are capable of both a receptive mode (for example, silence, lips parted, small body movements) as well as an active mode (for example, more talking, larger body movements) can meet more of their needs. When nonverbal behavior is congruent with the verbal message, one's communication is most powerful (Mehrabian, 1972). The more needs one is able to meet, the higher the self esteem.

The more a person is able to tune in to the non-verbal aspects of communication, the deeper the exchange is likely to be. By noticing the non-verbal behaviors of others a person has more data to assess how best to proceed. For example:

> Joe confronted one of his employees, Larry, on his aggressive behavior with a customer. When he confronted Larry, he noticed Larry's mouth and jaw tighten as he responded in a bitey tone, "OK." Joe decided to report his observations to Larry and asked him what he was feeling. Larry replied, "I guess I'm angry. That customer is abusive to the sales personnel every time he comes to this store!" This was new information to Joe. Joe suggested that he and Larry discuss further more effective ways of handling difficult customers.

The above example illustrates how a person can use nonverbal observations to help draw a person out. Similar data can be used to gauge how a person responds. Words can hide feelings but nonverbal responses are not as easily masked. Nonverbal data holds a great deal of informational power. However, it should be noted that the same nonverbal cue can have different meanings so it is important to check out how the cue relates to the particular person. For example, a flushed face can mean the person is physically hot, angry, or embarrassed.

According to Gambrill and Richey (1985), to the extent people are receptive to nonverbal cues they will be more able to decode affect, interpersonal orientation (e.g., dominance, submissiveness, etc.), and intentions (e.g., when a person is ready to leave). Nonverbal skills also can assist people in differentiating literal versus metaphorical communication and in identifying sarcasm and joking. Attention to dress, mannerisms, and the like also can cue a person to role or social script (e.g., professional, priest, mechanic) which may help guide the interaction. An enormous amount of valuable information is available in physical appearance, touch, gestures, proximity, posture, gaze, and facial expression (Knapp, 1980).

Ingredients of an Interaction. Several common ingredients are involved in every interpersonal interaction and, are key concepts to understand in order to improve communication (Satir, Banmen, Gomori, & Gerber, 1987). When an individual delivers a message, he/she delivers the message both with words and affect (See Figure 3.6).

"Where's the newspaper!?"

The content of this message is a simple question requesting information about the whereabouts of a newspaper. However, in addition to the content (words), the person delivers the message with particular vocal qualities, a specific facial expression, gesture, gaze quality, and body posture all of which convey the attitude or feeling of the speaker. Perhaps this particular message was delivered with a slight bite in the voice, wrinkled forehead, and questioning intonation. Other nonverbal expressions may have been present as well, but we select what we attend to based on our feelings about ourself, our past experiences. What you see and hear represents Area 1 (Figure 3.6). This is our lens. For example, if self esteem is low, the person will attend to all that is negative. In essence, we tend to that which is familiar. In this example, perhaps the receiver had a father who regularly delivered his messages with a bite in his voice. Problems in communication develop when we react to behaviors and attitudes which we associate with important figures (parents, other authority figures, siblings) in early life. Sullivan (1968) referred to these inaccuracies in perception as *parataxic distortion.* Our selection of what we attend to is an inside job. What we select out of the totality of someone's communication, we run through past experience.

Based on what we attend to in the communication, we then put meaning onto it based on our past experiences (Area 2 in Figure 3.6). In this example, the person might assume that the sender in saying, "Where's the newspaper?!" is blaming the person for the newspaper not being on the table where it

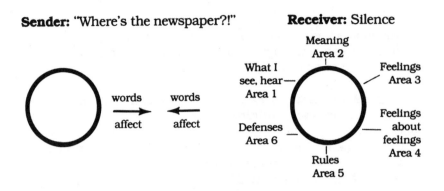

Sender: "Where's the newspaper?!"   **Receiver:** Silence

Figure 3.6. Ingredients of an interaction. [From Satir and Banmen (1984) and Satir et al. (1987)].

usually is kept. Sometimes the meaning we attach is based on projection where a person attributes to others rejected aspects of self. In this case, perhaps the receiver tends to blame others but is unable to own this attitude and, instead, attributes blaming to others. The receiver then reacts with feelings as a result of the meaning he/she attaches to the communication (Area 3, Figure 3.6). In this case, the receiver might react with fear and defensiveness. To complicate matters further, the receiver will then have feelings about his/her fear and defensiveness (Area 4, figure 3.6). Let's presume in this case, he/she feels ashamed about being afraid, unlovable. These feelings are usually connected with survival rules which are associated with that feeling. If I'm afraid and defensive does that mean I'm no good? Or that I shouldn't exist? Shouldn't live? These are survival fears.

How the receiver actually responds to the message, "Where's the newspaper?!" depends on the rules he/she has learned about commenting (Area 5, Figure 3.6). We all learn rules in our families talking about our thoughts, experiences, and feelings. In some families, commenting on our internal reactions is encouraged and safe. Rules such as the following inhibit commenting:

> "I shouldn't be afraid."
> "I should be perfect."
> "I should take care of my own problems."

Rules like this affect how we take care of ourselves.

When people experience survival fears, they typically utilize one of three characteristic defenses (Area 6, Figure 3.6), ignoring (I don't see it), denying (I say to myself, "It isn't so."), or projecting ("I believe you think I'm no good" rather than owning "I think I'm no good"). On the other hand, people with high self esteem can acknowledge their feelings, their survival fears and do not need to defend.

From this discussion, the reader can see how our past experiences, the rules we learn about commenting, and our survival fears, affect our perceptual filters, meaning attribution, and our ability to communicate effectively. All these elements Satir et al. (1987) called the ingredients of an interaction.

COMMUNICATION STANCES

A person's self esteem also affects the manner in which he/she communicates with others. Humans adopt communication stances which grow out of low self-worth (Satir, 1988). Satir (1988) outlined four communication stances which have been found in people all over the world. She outlined these four stances as placator, blamer, irrelevant, and super-reasonable.

Placator

This person apologizes for everything, tries to please everyone, promises anything, asks for nothing for self and hides his/her own needs. The person is in a one-down position. The feeling conveyed is "excuse me for my existence." According to Satir (1988), by evoking guilt, placators use this power to be spared. Nothing touches him/her. The placator position originates as a survival technique in a situation where an individual is completely dependent upon another for survival. Nonverbally, the person might display a caved-in posture with shoulders rounded, eyes averted, looking down, backing away, whiny voice. Underneath is the fear that comes with complete dependence.

Blamer

This person finds fault with everything, takes credit for everything, regardless of whether or not he/she had a part in it, and uses words and phrases as "never," "always," and "why don't you ever?" Satir (1988) explained that by evoking fear, the blamer gains power. The more fear and terror the person feels the more he/she needs to lay blame. As a result, the distance between that person and others grows, and painful loneliness develops. In relation to body posture, the individual puts his/her whole self on the line. Jaws, chest, and temples may tighten. The image the blamer conveys is that of an accusing pointed finger. This is his/her distorted way of saying, "Please love me," "Value me."

Irrelevant

This person is constantly moving both verbally and physically. These persons are very powerful in their irrelevance. One of their powers, explained Satir (1988) is to evoke fun. All survival needs are wrapped up in continual movement. Through distraction, needs, feelings, and relationships are ignored. These people avoid responding to the verbal point. They have a tremendous ability to distract and disrupt. These individuals go to extremes to get attention because underneath they feel unloveable. Physically, such persons are generally unbalanced.

Super-reasonable

These people are extremely erudite. They evoke envy, explained Satir (1988). They give long explanations and express little or no feeling. Their manner conveys the attitude that only ideas and things are important. They hide their feelings and needs. This person is likely to have a monotone voice and be very motionless. Underneath, the person feels alienated and withdrawn, hiding behind intelligence and a wide vocabulary.

According to Satir (1980), an individual becomes more congruent when able to allow feelings to come to the surface. Satir (1976, 1988) explained that through the use of each of these communication stances people try to prevent what is on the inside from showing. This creates great internal stress and hopelessness. Each represents a creative solution to allay fears and cover a lack of wholeness. Each stance needs something added to it for the person to become more whole:

Placator: Add "What do you want to do for yourself?"

Blamer: Add love.

Irrelevant: Add touches to make the words and movements more meaningful.

Super-reasonable: Add "How are you feeling?" Connect with touch, laughter, feelings; sidle up to the person, hold the person's hand; make the person laugh.

One goal, according to Satir (1988), is for people to learn how to apologize rather than placate, be reasonable without being a robot, change the subject without distracting, and state disagreements in a nonblaming way.

Satir (1980, 1988) believed that by adding these ingredients, people can become more congruent and improve chances of meeting their needs. This congruency would be reflected in the person's nonverbal demeanor in such behaviors as the following: upright, relaxed stance, a willingness to make relaxed eye contact, shoulders straight, knees slightly flexed, and breathing full.

The person with high self esteem is likely to display a balance in activity-reactivity, counterdependence-dependence, self-other responsibility, clear boundaries, and nonverbal behavior which is congruent with what is communicated verbally, what is going on inside one matches what is evident on the outside.

CRITICISM

In a variety of settings (both personal and work related) people are often faced with criticism which is directed towards them. If people learn to handle criticism well, they can avoid unfair blame while learning to accept responsibility for their behavior and while maintaining self-respect. Three frequent problem responses to criticism are defending, counterattacking, and distancing. With practice, people can learn more effective ways of handling criticism. Here are some guidelines:

1. **Relax and try to just hear the person.** Support yourself by breathing fully and keep your feet planted on the floor. (This doesn't mean you should allow yourself to be abused, however. If the person continues to yell at you, name call, etc., ask the person to change this behavior. If the person does not alter the behavior, you can end the exchange).

2. **Clarify the criticism.** Often criticisms are not specific or people use labels which could have various meanings. (Satir, 1988, Donahue Show).

   Example: "You're lazy!"

   Response: "Tell me more about that. What's your picture of how I'm lazy?"

3. **Agree with part of the criticism and give back the rest.** Parts of criticism often hold some truth. Avoid arguing over parts with which you disagree.(Satir, 1988, Donahue Show).

   Example: "You are so irresponsible! You're never on time, you don't pay the bills when you say you will, and I can Never depend on you."

   Response: "You're right, I was late. I'm sorry. I should have called." (McKay & Fanning, 1987; Satir, 1988).

4. **Own the criticism.** Agreement with a critic generally stops the criticism quickly. It should only be used when you actually can take responsibility for the criticism.

   Example: "I'm really having a problem with your controlling behavior in this group."

   Response: "Yeah, I have a problem with that part of me too. You're right and I'll pay attention to that."

5. **Tell the person how you're feeling.** For example, "I feel embarrassed about this mistake." or "I'm trying to listen but I have a hard time taking criticism."

6. **Consider asking for help in changing the behavior.** For example, "Let me know if I start to lecture you again. I'm not always aware."

At times you may be the recipient of criticism about a third party. This often happens since many people have as much trouble expressing their criticisms directly to others as they do hearing criticisms. If they do not know how and avoid expressing themselves, when tensions run high enough, they will look for another outlet. To stay out of the middle in such situations is best and to encourage the person to express the criticism to the appropriate person. Since people often find such exchanges risky, your support may be needed. Following are some guidelines for giving negative feedback to others (Clarke, 1983; Gambrill & Richey, 1985).

1. **Decide if it is an important issue.** Sometimes it's important to let some things go. Choose your "fights" carefully. Is it important to you? Will it be helpful to the other? Does the behavior happen frequently.

2. **Pick an appropriate context.** Timing is crucial to a successful exchange. Is there enough time and energy to thoroughly work through the problem? Is there privacy? Is the person in a receptive place?

3. **Be as specific as you can.** Providing specific examples is best.

4. **Own your criticism.** "I feel annoyed that you interrupted me when I was talking about my problem at work. This was hard for me to tell you."

5. **Avoid judgmental or emotionally laden words.** These are likely to close down communication.

6. **Offer recommendations for change.** Ask yourself what you'd like. This keeps things more positive and shows you're willing to share some responsibility for making things different.

7. **Keep your feedback to one issue and be brief.**

8. **Be alert and keep on the subject.** Many people will try to divert the conversation to other issues to relieve their discomfort.

9. **Assure the person that you care about them and the relationship and want to work through the problem.** Some people are so hypersensitive to criticism that they think it's the end of the relationship.

Most people are not very experienced in effective criticism—whether this be giving or receiving criticism. In a world where perfectionistic standards and people pleasing are rampant, many people are criticism avoidant. With practice, however, healthy criticism can lead to much more satisfying relationships.

STROKES

A stroke is any positive, affirming verbal or nonverbal message. Healthy rules around strokes are crucial to satisfying relationships and high self esteem. While complaints are common place, people are often very stingy about expressing positive feelings. Hogie Wycoff (1977) explained the stroke economy to which many people adhere:

> don't ask for strokes you want,
>
> don't take in strokes you get,
>
> don't reject strokes you don't want,
>
> don't give strokes to others, and
>
> don't give yourself strokes.

According to Wycoff (1977), such a "stroke economy" breeds a shortage of love. There's an old story about a town whose people started hoarding "warm fuzzies" for fear they would run out of them if they gave too many away. In the story the townspeople quickly started to wither and die. In a way, people in our culture seem to operate from a similar limitation mentality rather than from a premise of abundance.

Don't Ask for Strokes

Many people believe if they have to ask for a stroke it doesn't mean as much. The belief is that the stroke will not be genuine or meaningful if a person must ask for it. If this rule is to be broken, then people need to abide by a corollary rule that only genuine strokes will be given and that you only give what you want to give. Remember that asking for the strokes we want does increase our chances manifold of getting what we want. Wishing and hoping doesn't accomplish the same end since most people can't read minds.

Don't Take in Strokes

People often have difficulty in fully receiving the positive feedback they are given. People often deflect positives verbally ("Oh this was just something I threw together, yours is much better.") or nonverbally (for example, looking away). For those who are highly avoidant of strokes, it is easier to accept those based on fact versus judgment ("I appreciate your being on time" versus "You look beautiful today.") When receiving a stroke, breathe in deeply and allow at least 30 seconds to drink it in. Focus on absorbing the stroke. Some people feel so badly about themselves that they don't feel they deserve strokes. Others are afraid people will eventually find out they are frauds; that underneath they are incompetent or worthless. Still others fear they will never be able to make a mistake if they receive the stroke or eventually a price will have to be paid. Despite all of these obstacles, strokes are essential. Only continued repetition of strokes can make a dent in such automatic defenses against the very nurturance for which people are starving.

Don't Reject Strokes

When people do stroke us we often believe we can't reject the strokes. There are circumstances where we might better give ourselves that permission. For example, an extremely attractive female lawyer may need to learn how to reject strokes around her appearance in circumstances when strokes for her competence are more appropriate.

Don't Give Strokes

While there are innumerable times people could give strokes every day, many people withhold them. What would the world be like if we all went around looking for ways to compliment people? We're all hungry for strokes, the ideal praise—criticism ratio is 4 to 1. Stroke deficits can create all kinds of emotional and physical problems. Remember that people who are not used to getting strokes are likely not to reward you for your efforts at first. With persistence, however, change is possible. Don't despair.

Don't Stroke Yourself

All kinds of prohibitions are against stroking oneself. You wouldn't want to get too big an ego—a "big head" some call it. Bragging is not permitted. But putting yourself down or minimizing your accomplishments is acceptable. If you do give yourself a stroke, chances are someone (particular those with low self esteem) may try to tear you down. Instead of encouraging each other to build esteem, some people actively discourage such positive attempts. With permission and support, the "stroke economy" can be broken and a positive cycle can be generated. The pay off is great.

SUMMARY

A variety of forces, both internal and external to the individual, can serve to anchor, enhance, or diminish self esteem. Persons in one's support satellites help to ground self esteem and establish stability. When these systems support negative behaviors, attitudes which are nonproductive or even destructive, can negatively influence self esteem. By understanding the dynamics of self, individuals have the key to unlock doors to the self and make more healthy adaptations.

Individuals with low self esteem often have certain psychological/behavioral coping mechanisms which are self-defeating. For instance, the skill in self-criticism may be over-developed while the skill to stroke self and attack the environment may be underdeveloped. Another way of looking at it is that certain parts of the personality are not easily accessed or that certain coping skills have not been learned. The image of "unused muscles" might be a useful way to explain the phenomenon in that it

- assumes that the potential exists for strengthening these deficient areas,
- implies that with practice, attention, repetition, or use, this aspect of oneself can be developed,
- puts the person in charge of change.

Of course, exercising muscles requires considerable commitment and daily practice. Individuals most often are in search of an easier solution that requires less work and commitment. They want a magical cure, a pill that will make them "all better." The metaphor of exercising muscles heightens the awareness that the individual must make a real commitment to a moment-to-moment exercising of desired psychological/behavioral skills.

Opting to develop new skills and a new perspective thus raising self esteem involves venturing into new territory, facing fears, not running from the awkwardness of learning something new, and taking risks. The more stable and supportive the individual's external environment, the more prudent risks an individual is likely to take. Initially, goals must be focused on strengthening the individual's internal and external support systems. Once these are strengthened, the individual is in a better position to take risks, expand, and stretch self esteem to ever-higher levels.

With each goal individuals set and accomplish, they take another step to enhance self esteem. At the same time, individuals learn they are in charge of their life and can paint whatever picture they want. In order to accomplish this, it is important to identify what goals they would like to have happen in their lives and categorize them into long-term and short-term goals, and identify the smaller steps toward meeting these goals. Too often people with low esteem have

1. avoided the task of choosing major directions and goals;
2. neglected to outline, notice, and give themselves credit for the small, daily steps toward major goals.

The more an individual opts for safety (which low self esteem people generally do), the more he/she opts for security and status quo that can result in lowered self esteem especially as one moves through various life stages and takes stock of life. In extreme cases, this dependence on safety results in boredom, complacency, and, finally, death. Through self-chosen risk-taking a person stretches to achieve maximum potential. Without risk-taking, no new edges of the person are developed, the individual becomes stagnant and self esteem polarity is expressed. Self esteem also can suffer when the opposite occurs. Excessive, reckless risk-taking places too much stress on the organism. The individual is not allowed enough time to integrate changes before new ones are in process, or not enough attention is given to the consequences of a particular course of action. Thus, the individual is not functioning from a grounded, centered state. The healthy individual strikes a balance in this safety-risk dimension and is able to manage effectively. In Chapter 8 change and self esteem are presented in more detail.

Often, individuals "bite off too big a chunk" and cannot possibly accomplish a particular goal. The second half of this book includes activities which an individual can use in life-planning. Guidelines are included which can help an individual establish workable goals and avoid self-defeat. Each goal, then, becomes a step successfully completed, a victory for the person, a sign of hope.

Many people with low esteem have difficulty moving onward after pushing for what they want. They do not see themselves as able to transform, effect changes in their lives. Instead, they tend to collapse, or cave in, when resistance is encountered in the environment. Consequently, often the individual's needs go unmet. Seligman (1975) called this phenomenon "learned helplessness." The individual "gives up," feeling impotent to affect change. Each time the individual yields or presses without choice, the self esteem shrinks a bit more; each time the individual choicefully presses against the environment or yields, self esteem expands. Individuals can learn how to press again and they can learn to yield.

In addition to effectively managing one's "interface" with various systems, individuals with high self esteem must become aware of and learn to manage their own internal system, their intrapsychic dynamics. This is the theme of the next chapter.

ACTIVITY 3.1   TAKING THE LEAD

Introduction

This activity from the nurturance phase of intervention encourages participants to practice the skill of initiating so that they are better able to get what they want in life.

Time Required

Varied time length for homework part; 30 minutes discussion

Participants

Any number; adolescents and adults

Setting

Group or classroom after homework completed

Materials

None required

Procedure

Make a contract with a friend to take the lead in a particular situation. For example:

- plan an entire evening for you and your partner

- take the lead during a discussion with friends on a topic you'd like to discuss.

- Process in groups of 5 or 6. How did this feel to you? What did you learn? How did others react?

Outcomes

Increases your ability to get what you want and deserve.

ACTIVITY 3.2   NEW EXPERIENCE

Introduction

Participants are asked to venture into the unfamiliar in this activity, trying something they've always wanted to do, but never took the time to do nor had the courage or excuse to do. This activity expands one's world and is from the nurturance phase of intervention (See Chapter 6).

Time Required

Varied for homework parts; 30 minutes of discussion

Participants

Any number; adolescents and adults

Setting

Office or classroom

Materials

None

Procedure

Have three new experiences in the next week. *Examples:*

- *try skiing*

- *call someone for lunch whom you met recently who seems interesting to you*

- *buy a piece of clothing that is something different than you would normally wear*

- *contract for a massage*

- *get a reading from an astrologer.*

Choose something you've thought of doing at sometime but never took the initiative/risk to try.

Record your feelings/thoughts before, during, and after this activity.

Share in groups of 5 or 6.

Outcomes

Expands one's familiarity boundary and stretches one's ability to self-nurture.

ACTIVITY 3.3   NOURISHING

Introduction

This activity encourages people to share their ongoing appreciations with one another rather than to hoard them.

Time Required

20 minutes

Participants

Any number; all ages

Setting

Group or classroom

Materials

None

Procedure

Each person think of one or two people in class who has made you feel good. How did they make you feel good? What did they do? How did you feel? What did you like about what they did?

Go to the person you have these feelings toward and share your feelings and appreciations.

Outcomes

Frees up expression of positive feelings/appreciations.

———

ACTIVITY 3.4 WITH WHOM DO I HAVE THE PLEASURE

Introduction

This activity helps clear away blocks to fully experiencing a person for who they are, thereby heightening contact.

Time Required

40 minutes

Participants

Any number, adolescents and adults

Setting

Classroom or office

Materials

None

Procedure

1. Form pairs and sit directly across from your partner.

2. Conduct (leader does) a centering activity with partici-pants.

3. Direct partners to close their eyes and think of themselves as a camera and to think of their eyes as lenses.

4. Direct partners to open their eyes, take a picture of their partner, and then close their eyes.

5. With eyes closed, look at your picture of your partner. Is it clear? How do you feel about this picture? About the person in this picture? File that picture away for later.

6. Direct partners to open their eyes and look at their partner for any ways which he/she reminds them of anyone they have known/seen/heard about (e.g., eyes, coloring, hair cut, facial expression, shape of face, etc.).

7. Have partners close their eyes and if their partner did remind them of someone, they are asked to let themselves know how they feel about the person they remembered.

8. Ask partners to visualize this remembered person, bring back to memory the picture of their partner, and compare the two.

9. Instruct partners to open their eyes once again and let themselves pay attention to what they notice first about their partner.

10. Close eyes. What meaning do you put with what you noticed?

11. Open eyes. Make up a story about what you think your partner is seeing, hearing, and thinking in relation to you. Beware of what you told yourself and how you are feeling about what you told yourself.

12. Ask participants to close their eyes once again and to remember all information about your partner that came from a third party (person, newspaper, gossip). Be aware of what you feel and think as you gather this past information.

13. With their eyes still closed, ask partners to remember any previous contacts with their partner. Recall these contacts as well as how you feel about those contacts now.

14. Ask partners to share the information which came up with their partners and to be in touch with their feelings as they do so.

15. Check to see if you feel any different about your partner now. Take another picture. Check how you feel inside. Be aware of the differences.

Outcome

Helps one to recognize projections and other communication blocks and to increase contact with others.

Note: From Satir, V. (1984) Workshop at Tiyosopaye, Black Hills of South Dakota.

ACTIVITY 3.5   CHILDHOOD LABELS

Introduction

Through this activity you will identify and evaluate labels which were applied to you when you were growing up and recognize the effect of these labels on your self esteem.

Time Required

20 minutes

Participants

Any number; adolescent or adult

Setting

Classroom or office

Materials

Paper and pen

Procedure

1. *Think of four labels which were frequently used to describe you as a child. Pick two which you think are positive and two you find negative.*

2. *What memories do you associate with each label?*

3. *What other labels could describe you?*

4. *How did you get each label? (Describe the where, when, how, and with whom).*

5. *Which of your labels refer to physical aspect? Personality traits? Behavioral characteristics? Cultural background?*

6. *What do the labels say about the norms of the group, rules of behavior, or parental wishes and expectations?*

7. *Do you still apply these labels to yourself today? Do they need up-dating? How?*

Outcomes

Enables one to reevaluate old labels and update one's self-perception.

Adapted from: Duhl, Bunny (1983). *From the Inside Out and Other Metaphors.* Brunner/Mazel, New York.

——————

REFERENCES

Alberti, R. E., & Emmons, M. (1974). *Your perfect right.* San Luis Obispo, CA: Impact Publishers.

Banmen, J., Gerber, J., & Gomori, M. (1988). *The Virginia Satir growth model. A study guide on becoming more fully human.* N. Delta, B.C.: 11213 Canyon Crest, N. Delta, B.C., V4E 2R6.

Black, C. (1982). *It will never happen to me!* Denver, CO: MAC Printing and Publishing Division.

Byrum-Gaw, B. (1981). *Assertiveness training for Greene County Welfare Department.* Dayton, OH: Wright State University.

Carlock, C.J., & Hagerty, P.T. (1988). *Bridges to Intimacy: Couples Workbook.* Dayton, OH: Peoplemaking 1Midwest, 1105 Watervliet Avenue, 45420.

Clarke, J.I. (1983). *Ouch. That hurts!* Plymouth, MN: Daisy Press.

Clausen, J. A. (1976). The life course of individuals. In R. Atchley & M. Seltzer (Eds.), *The sociology of aging: Selected readings.* Belmont, CA: Wadsworth.

Curran, D. (1983). *Traits of a healthy family.* New York: Ballentine Books, Random House, Inc.

Duhl, B. (1983). *From the inside out and other metaphors.* New York: Brunner/Mazel.

Fossum, M.A., & Mason, M. (1986). *Facing shame.* New York: W.W. Norton.

Gambrill, E., & Richey, C. (1985). *Taking charge of your social life.* Belmont, CA: Wadsworth Publishing.

Gestalt Institute of Cleveland Post-Graduate Training Program. (1979). Cleveland, OH.

Gilles, J. (1976). *Friends.* New York: Coward, McCann, & Geoghegan.

Holmes, T. H., & Rahe, R. H. (1967, April). The social readjustment drafting scale. *Journal of Psychosomatic Research, 11*(2), 213-8.

Jourard, S. M. (1971). *The transparent self.* Princeton, NJ: Van Nostrand Insight.

Karpel, M. (1986). Testing, promoting and preserving family resources: beyond pathology and power. In M. Karpel & W.R. Beevers (Eds.), *Family Resources.* New York: The Gilford Press.

Knapp, M.L. (1980). *Essentials of non-verbal communication.* New York: Holt, Rinehart and Winston.

Lange, A., & Jakubowski, P. (1976). *Responsible assertive behavior.* Champaign, IL: Research Press.

Mehrabian, A. (1972). *Nonverbal communication.* Chicago, IL: Aldine-Atherton.

Miller, S., Nunnally, E., & Wackwan, D. (1975). *Alive and aware.* Minneapolis: Interpersonal Communication Programs.

Morran, K., & Stockton, R. (1980). Effect of self-concept on group member reception of positive and negative feedback. *Journal of Counseling Psychiatry, 27,* 260-267.

Peck, M.S. (1987). *The different drum.* New York: Simon and Schuster.

Satir, V. (1976). *Making contact.* Millbrae, CA: Celestial Arts.

Satir, V. (1980). Communications. A workshop sponsored by the Family Institute, South Bend, IN.

Satir, V. (1983). *Conjoint family therapy, 3rd ed.* Palo Alto, CA: Science and Behavior Books.

Satir, V. (1984). Tiyospaye. A workshop in the Black Hills, South Dakota.

Satir, V., & Banmen, J. (1984). *Virginia Satir verbatim.* N. Delta, B.C., Canada: Delta Psychological.

Satir V., Banmen, J., Gomori, M., & Gerber, J. (1987). *Satir model and ingredients of interaction.* Crested Butte, CO: Avanta Annual meeting.

Satir, V. (1988). Donahue Show. New York.

Satir, V. (1988). *Peoplemaking.* Palo Alto, CA: Science and Behavior Books.

Schur, E.M. (1971). *Labeling deviant behavior.* New York: Harper & Row.

Seligman, M. (1975). *Helplessness.* San Francisco, CA: W.H. Freeman.

Sullivan, H.S. (1968). *Interpersonal theory of psychiatry.* New York: Norton.

Tubesing, D. (1979). *Stress skills.* Oak Brook, IL: Whole Person Associates.

Wegscheider, S. (1981). *Another chance: Hope and health for the alcoholic family.* Deerfield Beach, FL: Health Communications.

Whitaker, C., & Napier, A. (1978). *The family crucible.* New York: Harper & Row.

Wycoff, H. (1977). *Solving women's problems.* New York: Grove Press.

CHAPTER 4

INTERNAL DYNAMICS
OF SELF

Individuals with high self esteem are protected from extreme fluctuations in self-concept. The effects of minor stresses are easily absorbed. Changes in self esteem across the life span are in the form of fine tuning rather than major changes. People with high self esteem are protected by a network of internal and interpersonal resources which shield the self from most traumas. Only in the case of multiple assaults to self esteem (for example sudden unexpected divorce, loss of job) will those with high self esteem be noticeably affected. The lower self esteem is, the more susceptible it is to disruptions from even the mildest life challenges and, conversely, the more highly resistant it is to positive growth and change.

But **stability** of the self also can be a problem if it develops into **rigidity.** Individuals with a rigidly fixed self image also can have low esteem if the flexibility is not present to adjust to different life demands or changes. Other problems occur when individuals hinge their self esteem on matters over which they have little control. An example of this might be a woman who lacks self-awareness, who never established a separate identity and, instead, adopted a definition of herself in the role of "mother" or "wife." Such a woman may rigidly hinge her self esteem on the actions of her children or husband over whom she has little control. If, for example, her children are not succeeding in her estimation, she may feel bad about herself.

Her self esteem could be characterized as stable but low. Calling attention to other assets this woman might display would not easily sway this person from her negative feelings about herself. The more rigid the self, the more singular the source of the person's self esteem, and to evoke positive change will be more difficult. The high self esteem individual strikes a balance between rigidity and flexibility, both internally and inter-personally. This chapter outlines the internal dynamics which affect self esteem.

BASIC CONCEPTS OF SELF

Organismic Self-regulation

The self-concept can be viewed as a steady state which attempts to maintain an orderly arrangement of elements. Actual personality dynamics of self can be viewed as attempts to satisfy needs, to reduce tension, or to maintain equilibrium.

Gestalt theory views the self as a process. The theory explains that the organism will seek to meet its needs (physiological, emotional, and intellectual). A person's sensory, body, emotional, and intellectual contact form the basis of his/her sense of self. To the extent that contact functions (visual, auditory, kinesthetic, olfactory, tactile) are limited or closed off, the person's ability to meet his/her needs is diminished. This leads to the development of a faulty sense of self.

CYCLE OF EXPERIENCE

Helpers can learn to assist people in bridging interruptions in the cycle of experience (see Figure 4.1). This cycle is a model of phases in need satisfaction, a way to describe human functioning. Chronic interruptions in the cycle erode self esteem, and in some instances, the inability to deliberately interrupt a cycle also can negatively affect self esteem. For example, some people chronically block expression of feelings, others need to learn to delay expression or learn to modulate that expression as in the case of those with impulse problems such as batterers.

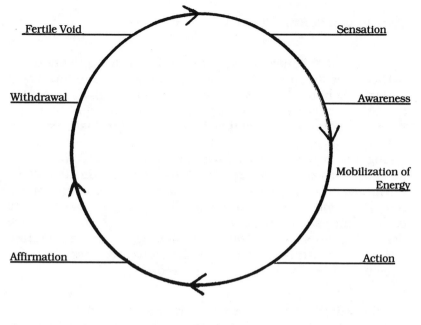

Figure 4.1. Fertile Void — Sensation — Withdrawal — Awareness — Mobilization of Energy — Affirmation — Action — Contact

Figure 4.1. Cycle of Experience. Gestalt Institute of Cleveland (1979).

The cycle of experience actually represents an excitation cycle. The level of an individual's self esteem rises as needs arise and are satisfied. Each completed cycle increases satisfaction. Breakdowns may occur at any point in the cycle of experience. Blocks in the cycle affecting self esteem can occur between any of the phases: sensation, awareness, action, contact, and withdrawal. The resistant forms of interaction common to these points are desensitization, projection, introjection, retroflection, deflection, and confluence. While interruptions that develop outside of awareness and become habitual can impair self esteem, interruptions choicefully employed can enhance personal functioning, positively affecting self esteem (Gestalt Institute of Cleveland, 1979). These resistances, employed with awareness, are necessary coping skills and are important mechanisms to maintain self esteem. A discussion of each of the common habitual and creative interruptions in the cycle follows (see Figure 4.1).

Interruption in Sensation-awareness

When individuals experience a block at the boundary between sensation (the raw data of experience) and awareness (organization of those data into meaning) they may identify certain internal feelings, thoughts, fantasies, or sensations, yet have not labeled these signals accurately. For instance, individuals with self esteem problems often have difficulty recognizing and expressing feelings and emotions as anger, fear, and longing. For example, a person's backache or arthritis may be attributed to repressed anger (see Chapter 9). Not recognizing repressed anger or resentments, the person is powerless to correct the situation and may tend to try to dull such disturbing sensations. Continued dulling or **desensitization** results in inadequate coping; the individual becomes incapable of being aware of and then meeting needs.

Sometimes people become desensitized to a part of themselves which they find hard to accept. In our culture the tendency is to identify with one force and to reject the contrasting element. Identifying with only one side of a duality creates imbalance. For example, a person may believe that giving and easy-going is acceptable but being firm or tough is not. Individuals may be viewed as a conglomeration of polar forces. For example, each person has not only the capacity for hardness, but also the capacity for softness; the capacity for passivity as well as activity; for kindness as well as uncaring; and so forth as represented in Figure 4.2. According to Zinker (1977), Satir (1976), and Satir and Bandler (1984) those individuals with high self esteem are aware of and able to accept polarities within themselves, including those characteristics which may be undervalued by society. These individuals' self-concepts are broad enough to incorporate even the most disparate traits, feelings, and ways of being, without causing undue anxiety. For instance, a woman might see herself as loving her son, yet sometimes when the child is whining and demanding, the mother may resent him and wish she were single again. When people wall off parts of self, they create emotional jails. These walls are composed of beliefs people adopt about how they "should" be in order to be loved (Satir, 1978). Parts that people have trouble accepting are often

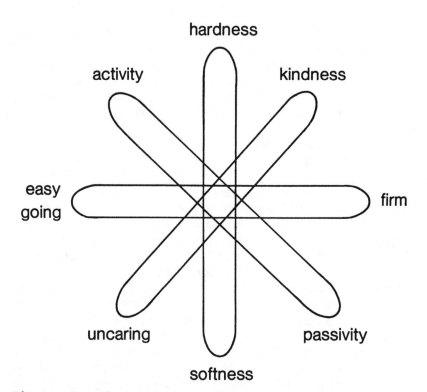

Figure 4.2. Mulitple polarities within an individual.

projected onto others. These can be parts which they consider exceptionally positive as well as negative.

Accepting all of one's parts does not necessarily imply approval of their use in all circumstances. Individuals can accept the shyness they display in certain situations and want to add to their behavioral repertoire other ways of being in different circumstances. The ability to accept even the most negatively valued parts of self and the ability to see inappropriate uses of positively valued parts demonstrates a depth of inner understanding/acceptance and movement toward wholeness.

While desensitization (numbing of sensation) that develops outside awareness can impair self esteem, choiceful desensitization can help preserve self esteem. For example, in a case where an individual in a situation is bombarded with feedback and other stimuli the ability to focus on one interaction and desensitize self to other stimuli can allow the person to manage the situation more effectively, thereby preserving self esteem. The individual might otherwise become overloaded and be unable to function (Gestalt Institute of Cleveland, 1979).

Interruption in Awareness— Mobilization of Energy

Individuals with low self esteem also may experience a block between **awareness** (organization of data into a meaning) and mobilization of energy. Individuals with this problem have accepted without question other people's values and beliefs. Introjection is useful at early stages of development when children do not possess the intellectual skills to judge and evaluate, or when expediency is demanded by a situation. The command, "Don't go into the street" protects children from harm at an age when they do not have the ability to judge when it is safe to go into the street. Likewise, in an emergency situation, if someone commands, "Don't move him, his neck looks broken," one would be wise to introject that message. Serious intrapsychic conflicts can occur when the person accepts two competing introjects. For example, a man may be taught "Be close" and "Don't touch." This may result in total immobilization. Individuals also may introject self attitudes (Mother hated me so I hate myself; Father abused Mother, therefore I see myself, a female child, as a bad person, worthy of abuse). People may introject self-destructive attitudes and rules such as: "Never argue with an authority figure," and "Always be good and obedient." ***Rigid rules are impossible to follow and result in diminished esteem*** (Gestalt Institute of Cleveland, 1979; Satir, 1980).

Interruption Between Energy and Action

Persons with low self esteem often experience a block between mobilization of energy (evidenced in movement, breathing, and skin color) and action (moving to meet a need). With this block, the person becomes aware and organizes all energies around that awareness, but is unable to act on impulses; unable to translate feelings/needs into action. Energy builds but the person does not move into action fearing failure, ridicule, or rejection and, instead, **retroflects,** directing the action on self. For example, a person experiences sensations in his/her chest and identifies this as a need for a hug. He/she begins to mobilize energy toward reaching out, but blocks this energy before taking action, resulting in an aching in his/her arms and shoulders (Gestalt Institute of Cleveland, 1979).

At the root of every well-developed retroflection, a tendency to do to oneself what one would like to do to others or would like others to do to oneself, is often a strong introject, a value adopted without conscious choice from a significant authority. In the previous example, the introject might be "Don't touch." Retroflection can be a creative response to a situation when it is done with awareness (Gestalt Institute of Cleveland, 1979). A person choicefully retroflects, for example, when he/she has an urge to express something to a superior but the context is not politically appropriate. A person might instead rub one's fingers together in that context, choosing not to express self until a private conference is arranged with the superior.

Individuals with self esteem problems tend to overuse self-evaluation, another form of retroflection. They are inclined to "step outside themselves" and critique their behavior, frequently emphasizing the negative. The act of stepping outside oneself splits the person's attention and prevents full contact with whatever or whomever he/she is involved (Gestalt Institute of Cleveland, 1979).

Interruption Between Action and Contact

Breakdowns also occur between action (moving out to meet a need) and contact (with self, someone, or something) through deflection and confluence. In this case, individuals work, eat, and interact, but are not nourished by the output of energy. In deflection, energy is split or diffused and, therefore, the person is not able to act pointedly or absorb the full impact of a message. For example, a person might become inattentive (averting glance, changing the subject, reporting excessive details, thinking about something else) when someone is giving him/her compliments. Contact is diluted and positive feedback, which might otherwise enhance self esteem, is blocked out.

Conscious deflection, however, can be used to block out unwanted feedback or as a distraction strategy to "take the heat off" a situation. When the interruption is habitual and the person exerts no choice in the matter, the person may be diluting the very nourishing contact for which he/she is starving. On the other hand, deflection in its creative form can be used by the individual to dilute a "hot" or negative interaction. Such inattention choicefully employed can help preserve esteem (Gestalt Institute of Cleveland, 1979).

In confluence, one behaves as if no boundaries exist between self and others; the point of contact is diminished and individual identity becomes blurred. Such persons typically have a difficult time sensing who they are and what they want. Early messages such as the following confuse boundaries:

"You're just like me."

"You're just like your father."

"You don't feel that way."

"Will you want anything more to eat tonight?" "No"— "O.K., then, I'll take out my false teeth."

"Are you hungry?"—"If you are . . ."

These individuals often also have problems saying "no" and being in touch with differences. Through this very process of saying clear "yeses" to some things and "noes" to others a person defines him/herself. Confluence with awareness, on the other hand, occurs at points of deepest intimacy between two people. The union can occur once the individual's personal boundaries are well-defined and the identity is well-formed (Gestalt Institute of Cleveland, 1979).

The ability to make and break contact is vital to adequate self esteem. Once chronic blocks are identified, then the work involves helping the person to choicefully bridge or interrupt the cycle so that the individual may experience greater satisfaction and, consequently, higher self esteem.

While chronic interruptions in the cycle negatively affect self esteem, paradoxically, so can a lack of a needed interruption negatively effect self esteem. In certain circumstances, interruptions are useful and increase self esteem. For example, if a man is extremely angry and wants to hit his wife, retroflection might slow him down and, hopefully, abort the action of striking her. It should be remembered, therefore, that each of the resistant forms of interaction (desensitization, confluence, introjection, and deflection) has an appropriate creative function in particular circumstances (Gestalt Institute of Cleveland, 1979).

Interruption Between Contact and Affirmation

Self esteem problems also can occur if individuals hang on to contact. Such people often have problems letting go of resentments and losses and avoid complete closure. Oftentimes this hanging on can be a signal that some aspect of the person has been projected and needs to be reowned. A very useful activity in the Alcoholics Anonymous "Big Book" directs people to list persons or institutions with whom you are angry. Next ask yourself why you are angry? (cause). Then, what were the injuries? (self esteem, security, ambitions, personal or sex relations.) Referring to the list again, now look for your own mistakes. Had you been dishonest territorial, frightened? Look for your own involvement. List your faults and make a decision to set them straight. (Alcoholics Anonymous, 1976). In this way projections may be reowned.

Interruption Between Affirmation and Withdrawal

Many people skip over the affirmation stage and do not fully take in or appreciate the satisfaction of the need. Closure is frequently incomplete as is *assimilation.* Ideally, in the assimilation process new material is utilized and irrelevant products are eliminated. It is a sorting through process. People who have problems in this part of the cycle do not savor their experiences. They have trouble with the stillness in life. They have trouble releasing the final bit of energy so that a small amount of residual energy is always there. Perfectionistic compulsive people (those who overwork, overeat or have other dosage problems) have problems here. They are not able to step back from an experience and fully appreciate it.

Interruption Between Withdrawal and Sensation

In the stage of withdrawal, the need commanding attention has receded into the background and the person moves into a "fertile void." In our Western culture, this void is resisted with people often mobilizing prematurely around a new need. Western culture is so production and action oriented that this receptive part of the cycle is undervalued and often avoided. Yet, in this part of the cycle equilibrium is re-established. Energy is turned inward and the self boundary is redefined. It is a pause, a zero point (Telfair-Richards, 1980). This time of **inner stillness,** when permitted, represents high contact with the self. It is an in-between place—neither leaning backwards towards a prior experience nor leaning forward toward a new figure/need. According to Telfair-Richards (1980), it is a time of alertness without arousal. Recent attention to various forms of meditation are attempts to help people experience this neglected phase more fully.

PARTS OF SELF

Awareness and ownership of everything about oneself leads to high self esteem (Satir, 1976; 1978). Satir (1978) stressed the importance of owning all of one's thoughts, images, feelings, words, body, voice, actions, gestures, fantasies, and triumphs. By owning all of one's parts a person develops a healthy productive relationship with self. According to Satir (1978), within everyone are all the resources to be effective and happy—all one needs to do is own and tap these parts.

Most people try to live by a set of rules, shoulds, and introjects which are impossible to follow. According to Satir (1978) when people are unable to meet these rules, they generally feel bad about themselves. Yet, people continue to try to cover over parts of themselves in order to try to please the outside world. If their rule is "Always be nice," then they have to sit on their angry feelings.

When one walls off parts of self, he/she creates an "emotional jail" (Satir, 1978). These walls are the beliefs one adopts about how he/she "should" be in order to be loved. Take a look at your beliefs. Do some of them need revision now? Take a look. What beliefs do you need to let go? Which rules are no longer applicable?

Many people reject various parts of themselves—anger, intelligence, jealousy, power, vulnerability (Satir, 1976). Yet, they reject these parts because they are inconsistent with the inhuman rules the person has adopted. Each of these self-estimates or parts is a potential resource given the appropriate context; each can help a person to survive.

Many times people have difficulty in getting along with their parts. In such cases often a part, anger or fear, needs to be listened to; perhaps the part is being neglected. The person has tried to cover the anger, but anger pervades the person's existence. Also, according to Satir (1981), people behave as if they are not in charge of their parts or self-estimates.

An important procedure is to determine whether an awareness of a part is missing. Is a part needed to balance another? In keeping with the Yin-Yang balance—do the parts represent one side exclusively? Perhaps sexuality is missing, or perhaps creativity is dormant, maybe rationality is overdeveloped and emotionality is underdeveloped. Perhaps nurturance is present but one only directs it toward others, never toward self (Satir, 1981).

When individuals move toward wholeness, toward owning all parts of self, they move toward greater personal effectiveness and higher self esteem. The greater the integration of and harmony of these parts, the higher the satisfaction level.

DIFFERENTIATION

Bowen (1985) coined a concept dealing with differentiation of self which is helpful in understanding behavior. It refers to the degree to which an individual has developed a "solid self" versus a "pseudo self". The concept is similar to emotional maturity. Differentiation is determined by the level of differentiation of one's parents, the type of relationship with parents, and the degree to which one has resolved his/her emotional relationship with parents (Bowen, 1985). Those with lower levels of differentiation are characterized by diffuse or rigid self boundaries while those with higher differentiation tend to have firm but permeable self boundaries. See Table 4.1 for the characteristics of each.

Certain common principles that Bowen (1985) identified are as follows:

1. Differentiation is best assessed during stress.

2. When one family member makes a microscopic step towards differentiation, others in the family will automatically take steps. However, family members will often disapprove of such steps and, therefore, need support. "You are wrong." "Change back." "If you do not . . . (consequences)."

3. One who is attempting to differentiate must stay on course without defending self, counter attacking, or seeking approval.

The togetherness or fusion amalgam is characterized by phrases such as "We think," "We feel," "It is wrong," "It is the thing to do." According to Bowen (1985), family members are defined as all alike in beliefs, feelings, principles, and values (confluence). In such families, a positive value is placed on thinking about others before self, sacrificing, and being responsible for others, even their happiness. Differentiation is treated as selfish and hostile (Bowen, 1985). On the other hand, with self differentiation, the "I" position defines principles and action. "This is what I think/believe/feel." Those with high differentiation do not force their own values on others (Bowen, 1985). Bowen continued and wrote that highly differentiated persons assume responsibility for their own happiness and avoid blaming and making demands on others ("I deserve," "This is my right/privilege"). They also do not yield to others' demands and continue to do what they need to do for themselves. Those with high differentiation are capable of concern for others without expecting something in return.

TABLE 4.1
DIFFERENTIATION OF SELF

Diffuse Personal Boundary

- fuses emotionally with others (emotionally dependent on others)

- floods intellect with emotionality

- bases decisions on feelings in order not to risk disapproval

- evaluates self based on interaction with others

- behaves dysfunctionally under stress

- creates pseudo self due to emotional pressure. Pseudo self is composed of a vast assortment of principles and beliefs which are random and inconsistent with one another.

- is often not aware of discrepancies

- becomes an actor and can be many selves

- responds to a variety of pressures (pseudo self unstable)

- orients self totally towards relationships. So much energy goes into seeking love that no energy is available for life goals.

- spends energy trying to keep relationships going and trying to achieve level of comfort and freedom from anxiety

- conforms or rebels

- fuses emotionally with increased closeness and then becomes distant and alienated

Table 4.1 (Continued)

Rigid Boundary

- resists change
- evaluates self unrealistically (far above or below reality) and as a result allows little input
- is impervious to feedback
- resists emotional fusion through exaggerated stance of rugged individualism
- finds it difficult to absorb stress

Firm but Permeable Boundary

- maintains autonomy
- separates feeling and thinking. Able to fully experience feelings and extricate self worth with logical reasoning when needed
- can engage in goal-directed activity or lose self in intimacy
- reacts less to praise and criticism
- evaluates self realistically
- recovers rapidly from stress
- defines beliefs, convictions, and life principles carefully. Incorporates into self after careful, logical reasoning (assimilation)
- states own beliefs without the need to attack beliefs of others or to defend own

With the lack of adequate emotional separation from parents/significant others, individuals fail to differentiate from their families. Such individuals often unconsciously live out their parents' message about who they are, their rules for living, carrying their parents' shame without awareness, or consciously trying to meet the parents' fantasy of the ideal child. The child's attitude toward self directly reflects attitudes of significant people in life. Children who grow up hearing messages such as "I don't know how you ever have any friends," "You're clumsy," and "You'll never be neat," are in danger of carrying these labels as life-long imprints if these messages are not re-evaluated. Even more harmful messages also can be carried such as "You don't have the right to exist." If a person was lucky enough to have been given positive, affirming messages, a good foundation is laid. Negative messages are often well entrenched before they are revised or discarded—if ever. Remember that for many, self esteem is based on distortions which have no basis in reality. These learnings are rarely intentional and frequently are drawn from incomplete, inaccurate, and outdated information (Satir, 1981). Our parents learned exactly the same way. Satir (1981) indicated that children see the world through the eyes of their parents and the interpretations they make.

The individual who acts out a self-image rooted in another is a prisoner of that person's construction of self-concept. The person who has not taken the opportunity to evaluate the validity of such judgments and make his/her own decisions about values, goals and aspirations is trapped in that image. A man living out his father's dream of success, who has not gone through the process of deciding whether this dream is his own, is not likely to experience much joy in his accomplishments. The dream either may be entirely unrealistic, or simply may not fit the person. Likewise, a man determined not to follow his father's dream, even though it might perfectly fit him, is equally controlled. (This concept was discussed in Chapter 2, psychological pathogens to the development of self esteem, involuntary identification.)

As children grow, they must begin to make a statement of protest and self-affirmation, to learn to say "noes" and clear "yeses." For some individuals this occurs spontaneously as in the case of the average two-year-old who stiffens all over, shakes his/her head, puts out his/her jaw, and says "No" to everything. In order to establish and maintain individuality, people must accept both pain and pleasure that they experience in taking risks and leaving their support (Keleman, 1975). Those who have a problem saying "No" have difficulty affirming themselves and exercising their ability to form and maintain personal boundaries. A state of pathological confluence (or blurring of identity) may result in which the individual cannot determine where he/she leaves off and others begin (Polster & Polster, 1973).

A crucial task in identity development is the ability to make clear "yeses" and clear "noes". When people say "yes" when they want to say no, self esteem erodes. Such behavior conveys the attitude, "Your feelings/rights are more important than mine." This creates an energy block inside which leads to a build up of resentment, anger, and hurt.

In confluence, discussed in greater detail later in this chapter, the person acts as if no difference exists between oneself and another. Many women, for instance, give up their personhood and fuse their identity with their spouse's or child's.

Others who succumb to pressure to think, behave, or feel a certain way do so for survival (emotional survival or literal physical survival in cases of emotional and physical abuse). **Emotional fusion** is a coping strategy in families where any attempts at individualization represent threats to the powers of authority.

As one's identity forms, values, beliefs, and guiding principles of behavior are revised to become uniquely individual. Throughout life, then, these value boundaries, belief boundaries, and behavior boundaries are challenged through life experiences and, in healthy people, are revised as necessary. These alterations are basic to growth and necessitate personal risk-takings in the expansion, contraction, or reshaping of these boundaries. For example, perhaps a person is reared in a family in which an explicit rule prohibits expression of disturbing personal problems to anyone outside the family and an implicit rule prohibits expression of disturbing personal problems inside the family—"Don't tell your mother that, she has a bad heart." Such a person might grow up stuffing feelings, becoming very introverted, perhaps manifesting psychosomatic symptoms. If those original family rules are identified, evaluated, and perhaps, revised, the individual then may take the risk of learning to express disturbing feelings to others, thereby expanding his/her expressive boundary.

Family rules cover a variety of areas, are conveyed either explicitly or implicitly, and govern conduct which maintain the family system and its power structure. Breaking family rules can result in guilt, admonishment, punishment, or even abandonment or banishment by family members (Carlock, Hagerty, & Verdon, 1985). Family rules cover such areas as play, space, privacy, touching, gender appropriate behaviors, religion, food, trust, and expressiveness. Refinements of such rules are made throughout the lives of individuals who are growth-oriented.

MAINTENANCE OF SELF ESTEEM
DEFENSE MECHANISMS

Freud (1936) outlined a number of defense mechanisms which people use to protect the self-concepts. These defense mechanisms which he called distortions are strategies by which individuals filter out unwanted information and, thus, temporarily cope with internal conflict. While defense mechanisms distort reality, they are to some degree adaptive measures. Without defenses one could not function. Defense mechanisms and their relationship to self esteem maintenance are shown in Table 4.2.

Experiences often have some aspects that run counter to people's standards. In order to protect their picture of themselves, people resort to various distortions (defense mechanisms) to protect the self-concept. People resort to defense mechanisms in order to adjust the demands of the external world to the demands of their consciences. The extra defenses which people employ, however, are only "stop-gap"

(Continued on page 125)

TABLE 4.2
Defense Mechanisms and Relationships to Self Esteem Maintenance

Definition	Example of How the Defense Maintains Self
Repression—know only that something which should be present has disappeared. Operates at an unconscious level.	If a young man feels intense jealousy toward older brother and wishes he would lose his family, etc., he may simply banish this intolerable thought from his conscious mind. (It operates outside of his awareness.) The hostility does not disappear but his self-concept as a loving brother is preserved.
Projection—symbolic objection by means of which something actually inside the ego is perceived and represented as though it were outside.	A woman who is unable to accept her own tension and anxiety as a speaker may complain that the audience seemed very anxious. In this way, she avoids dealing with her own anxiety.
Displacement—transfer of emotion. The object of emotion is switched.	A man whose self-concept does not allow him to feel or express hostility to his boss, may, after a day of having extra work piled on by the boss, come home and find some pretense to act out at his wife or children.
Reaction formation—involves repressing a feeling inconsistent with the self-concept and then professing the exact opposite of that feeling.	A woman unaccepting of her own sexual desires may join a campaign against "immorality." In this way, she avoids coming to terms with the sexual part of self which does not fit into her own image.
Intellectualization—hides unacceptable feelings behind a smokescreen of fancy intellectual analysis, avoiding the pain of directly facing these feelings. Another way of looking at it is that intellect is directed by the emotional process.	A man may talk about how difficult it is to make a relationship work, how many societal pressures put a strain on relationships. What he means is "I feel like a failure. My wife chose to leave me." Through social analysis, he blocks out his emotional response.

Table 4.2 (Continued)

Definition	Example of How the Defense Maintains Self
Denial—person simply denies whatever threatens self-concept. Awareness is narrowed. Secrets are kept from self.	A woman may refuse to believe that she has a drinking problem. Through denial, she presents herself as in control and adequately coping with life.
Sublimination—impulses are rechanneled from forbidden outlets to more creative outlets that are acceptable to the self.	A man channels some of his high sexual appetite into productive work activities rather than into extramarital affairs. Beating someone on the tennis court may be the person's way to release anger towards a boss. In this way he can avoid directly confronting his own sexual and aggressive urges.
Regression—an inability to go on functioning at fully mature levels (i.e., thinking, judgment become impaired). Preserves the integrity of the psychodynamic system at some level short of complete dissolution.	When a woman is faced with a crisis which she feels unable to handle, she dissolves into tears and retreats to bed, rather than dealing rationally with the situation. Enables the individual to avoid dealing with reality.
Dissociation—snapping of the associating link between visual and somatic elements of experience.	During a traumatic sexual experience a woman experiences herself viewing the event from a point above. She describes the event devoid of emotion or physical sensation.

adaptations. People can afford only a certain degree of distortions in perception before it negatively affects their functioning. If a person's self-image continually must be protected from one's actual feelings, the self-concept may be too rigid and unrealistic. For example, to the degree that persons believe they should always be nice, kind, and understanding, then they are likely to resort to a corresponding degree of repression, denial, projection or other defense mechanisms in order to maintain that image. In order to assess the adaptability of functioning one might ask: "To what degree am I functioning effectively in the world? To what degree is my behavior and thinking facilitating my movement towards my life goals? To what degree might my feelings be somaticized, that is, symptoms appearing in my body?" Defenses activated in the service of preservation of self image carried to an extreme can block out or distort awareness of important internal and external information.

Incoming stimuli is frequently distorted. When a person is desperate he/she will accept almost anything to satisfy that need. To a starving individual, a stale piece of bread satisfies the hunger as much as a steak. Likewise, a trace of a smile from an otherwise abusive, sadistic mother can be an oasis for a deprived child who yearns for some sign of acceptance and love. Needs can blind people to reality and can alter the standards which they normally expect. Fears, as well as any intense emotion, can blind individuals. Thus, such expressions as "blind with rage," "I was so angry I couldn't see straight," or "I was so afraid that I didn't hear anything you said after that." When the circuits become overloaded, the sensory and cognitive systems close down.

If people are unable or unwilling to face the reality of a situation they cannot evaluate effectively whether it is harmful or constructive. Individuals, in effect, block themselves from being able to take adequate care of themselves. These excessive needs and feelings result from the ineffective management of energy. After suppressing, denying, projecting, or using other additional forms of distorting the need or feeling for some time, the individual often suddenly becomes flooded with the need or the feeling and it finally breaks through the surface of its own accord, outside one's control, blinding a person at least temporarily.

Fooling oneself often helps keep people in situations which, though harmful, are nonetheless familiar. Many people adopt the positions, "What I don't see can't hurt me," yet in the long run, one cannot escape being hurt by self-deception. Self-deception is the primary tool used to preserve status quo.

Facing "what is" often necessitates change. Although change is a natural part of human existence, it is often dreaded and feared. Some people avoid giving up outdated self-images, for with change comes endings, and with endings comes chaos.

In order to face "what is" people must believe that they can handle any circumstance. Faith and trust in self must preside. Without facing "what is," individuals fall victim to fears and needs which results in a lowered capacity to cope, and consequently, lowered self esteem.

COGNITIVE CONSISTENCY

Another mechanism used to maintain the self-concept is what Festinger (1957) labeled cognitive consistency, discussed earlier in Chapter 2. According to Festinger, one of the most powerful motives of behavior is the drive for self-consistency, of having beliefs mesh with one another. When two beliefs do not mesh, a state of mental discomfort is created which Festinger called cognitive dissonance. The individual then resorts to distortion to relieve this tension. An attitude is changed or not changed in order to protect against inconsistency. This principle is considered central to the development of the self-concept. Even if a child's developing self is negative, he/she will use this standard to sort feedback concerning self. In a sense, the self functions as a magnet; it primarily attracts input of like valence.

Adults also tend to perceive reality in accordance with their self-concept. An interesting study by Fitch (1970) showed that individuals with high self esteem attributed their success to internal factors and their failures to external factors, while individuals with low self esteem tended to attribute success to external factors and failures to internal factors. In these examples, individuals attributed success or failure to factors which would preserve their original level of self esteem. This mechanism has a powerful effect, especially when it operates outside of conscious awareness.

COGNITIVE-PERCEPTUAL FRAMEWORK

Individuals with low self esteem exhibit a number of common distortions. Various authors emphasize the role cognition plays in the development and perpetuation of psychopathology (Beck, 1967; Ellis & Harper, 1976;

Meichenbaum, 1974). This view focuses on roles played by a person's cognitive processes, beliefs, and perceptions. Different individuals often view the same event through different perceptual filters which, in turn, affect and are affected by self esteem.

Figure 4.3 stresses the cyclic, reinforcing nature of thoughts, images, emotions, and behavior on self esteem. Each interacts with and influences the other. Evidence is that unrealistic and illogical thinking can seriously affect mental

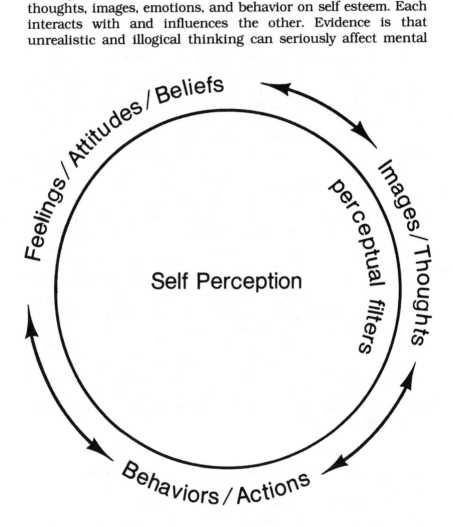

Figure 4.3. Bases of self-perception: Cycle of interaction and influence through perceptual filters.

health and serve to perpetuate a negative self-image. The following section further elaborates on the relationship of assumptions, shoulds, and self-blame on self esteem.

Beck (1967) and Beck, Rush, Shaw, and Emery (1979), and McKay and Fanning (1987) described a number of thought distortions related to self esteem. These distortions are represented in Table 4.3.

Assumptions—Shoulds

Beck et al. (1979) and McKay and Fanning (1987) described how assumptions can be related to self esteem. Assumptions are part of the foundation of self esteem and while some assumptions may be innocuous or even enhancing of self esteem, others may be harmful.

One's cognitions are based on untested assumptions learned early in life. These assumptions must be identified in order for high self esteem to be maintained. If I hold the assumption that "If I'm nice, bad things won't happen to me," then it's either my fault when bad things do happen (I wasn't nice enough) or life is unfair (because I'm nice and bad things still happen) (Beck et al., 1979). A number of automatic thoughts can stem from one primary assumption. The role that these assumptions play in the individual's feelings about self must then be explored and modified (Gardner, 1981).

Most negative emotions can be traced to self-defeating assumptions. Specific behavioral and cognitive techniques described by Beck et al. (1979) can be employed to modify assumptions. One subtype of assumptions are "shoulds" or rules for living. People often hold a partially conscious list of "shoulds" in their heads against which they measure their performance. These "shoulds" generally are adopted wholly from significant others and they cause people to judge themselves to be inadequate relative to this set of impossibly idealistic standards.

These standards, values, or rules for living are usually set in absolute terms (Beck et al., 1979). This arbitrary set of rules ultimately prevents individuals from identifying and/or enjoying

(Continued on page 131)

TABLE 4.3
Cognitive Distortions Related to Self Esteem

1. *Engaging in negative free associations unconnected to an immediate external stimulus.* For example, a high school student is given a surprise quiz by his/her teacher. The student begins to dwell on times in his/her childhood when a parent told the student he/she was inadequate, stupid, lazy.

2. *Little attempting to direct thoughts. The person feels thoughts arise automatically and involuntarily.* For example, clients tell counselors that negative self-thoughts (such as "I'm worthless") enter their minds all the time and that they can do nothing about it. It just happens.

3. *Magnifying failure or defect and minimizing or ignoring favorable characteristics.* For example, a counselor is faced with a female client who says she knows she will flunk a science course because she flunked the last test. Now the client believes that she is doomed for failure in science even though she has had some good grades on quizzes to date.

4. *Comparing oneself unfavorably with others.* For example, a young artist compares self with artists who have created famous masterpieces.

5. *Blaming self with no logical basis.* For example, a woman blames herself for all mistakes of her children. Typically the client takes responsibility for people and matters over which she has no control.

6. *Maintaining an enormous range of "shoulds" and "musts" with persistence even when it is infeasible for the person to carry out the "should."* For example, a person tells self that one should always be perfect on the job and never make a mistake.

7. *Having an overall systematic bias against self.* For example, a client almost always blames self for an unfavorable happening. Clients of this sort frequently apologize.

8. *Tending towards arbitrary inference where conclusions are drawn from insufficient evidence and when there is no evidence to the contrary.* For example, a client might be critical of self because of perceived inability to make friends when actually the client attends a school which is very "cliquish," and has attended only two months.

9. *Tending to focus on one detail of a situation, ignore other aspects, and conceptualize the situation based on this limited information.* For example, a male client might have low self esteem as a result of a recent argument with his parents. The client then blames self for an inability to get along satisfactorily with parents although, unbeknownst to him his parents might have been especially irritable that day due to an argument they were engaged in just before their son arrived.

Table 4.3 (Continued)

10. *Tending to magnify situations inappropriately.* For example, a person could develop low self esteem by telling oneself that because of lost job he/she is a totally worthless person.

11. *Perceiving a wide range of life experiences through the filter of low self esteem.* For example, individuals of low self esteem might develop a self-fulfilling prophecy that life just generally provides a "raw deal" because one deserves it.

12. *Polarized thinking.* In this case, the client sees everything as black or white with no gray areas. The client sees self as a raving success or a complete failure.

13. *Mind reading.* Here the client projects his negative self view onto others and assumes, for example, that others think he's boring, want to fire him, are being critical of his dancing.

Note. Table is original. Idea initiated from Beck (1967), Beck, Rush, Shaw, and Emery (1979), McKay and Fanning (1987).

their own successes and prevents individuals from determining their own priorities and deciding what they want. Trying to meet other's expectations consumes much energy and success is seldom attained. Shoulds create emotional jails (Satir, 1978).

As in Aesop's rhetoric: "You can't please everyone. If you try, you lose yourself." Competing shoulds complicate the picture and create additional conflicts as well as a "no win" situation. When these shoulds are examined thoroughly, individuals may want to retain some and discard others. The locus of control that comes from a clearer sense of "I" is generally more manageable, more easily incorporated into one's life, and more easily acted upon.

A person who tries to meet all the competing expectations/ shoulds from significant others is easily thrown into conflict. Such individuals often feel torn, used, and inadequate. Newman and Berkowitz (1977a & b) and Beattie (1987) pointed out several fears which arise when an individual contemplates giving up the need to please everyone: "Who will I be without others telling me what to do and how to be? Who will tell me what to do then? Will it mean that no one will love me? Who will I blame if things go wrong?"

Taking a stand means that individuals make their own decisions knowing and accepting the fact that some will work and others will not. When individuals define their own values, needs, and beliefs, they are no longer a patchwork quilt of the people in their environment—not some watered down version of themselves whose main goal is to avoid others' displeasure, but are, instead, distinct persons. In being honest, individuals risk rejection but at the same time, they reap the reward of knowing that when people like them they are liked for themselves.

In order to change, individuals need to value and honor themselves—honoring/valuing oneself involves knowing oneself. It means placing oneself in the central focus of one's life and identifying:

What you feel.

What you want.

What you need.

What you believe.

What you value.

Honoring the self involves formulating a point of view and valuing that point of view as equal to others. It involves making boundaries more distinct; determining the shape and direction of one's life. Honoring the self involves exercising the lost inner barometer that registers events and tells the person whether they bring happiness or satisfaction (Miller, 1976). Persons who live by others' "shoulds" have lost use of their inner barometer.

In examining cognition and its effect on self esteem, Ellis and Harper (1976) emphasized a slightly different point. According to them, events are filtered through one's personal beliefs, and feelings about self emerge at the other end. Ellis and Harper stressed the primacy of intervening in the belief system to affect change in self esteem. Because many beliefs are quite irrational and unrealistic, many painful emotional conclusions are made. In a sense, people are programmed with numerous mistaken beliefs and ideals which distort their perceptions. What they say to themselves, the internal talk in which they engage, may be highly correlated with their negative self-labels: "The world is big and dangerous and I'm small and weak." "Everyone must like me." "It's better not to try than to try and fail." By heightening awareness of self-talk helpers can assist individuals to affect change in feelings, performance, and ultimately self esteem.

Affirmations

Many books in the last ten years have stressed the positive effects of self affirmation and careful attention to thought forms which generate feelings of joy, peacefulness, and abundance (Gawain, 1978; Ray, 1980; Roman, 1986). Many believe that people have the power to create their own reality. Many people are limited by their thinking:

> I can't. . . .
> I don't deserve. . . .
> I have to. . . .
> I should. . . .

Such negative beliefs and thinking produce blocks to positive action and stress in one's body. Now, instead, notice what kind of feelings the following affirmative statements create:

> What I love to do is what I'm meant to do.
> I am bringing joy into my life.
> I am perfect just as I am.
> I am open to receive your love.

Affirmations state the desired outcome as already in the process of being realized. The belief espoused is that negative thoughts produce negative results, positive thoughts produce positive results.

Guidelines for Affirmations
(Acker-Stone, 1987; Canfield, 1986;
Gawain, 1978; Roman, 1986)

1. Begin with the words, "I am. . ."

2. Include your name in the affirmation.

3. Choose positive, expansive words.

4. Phrase in the present tense.

5. Keep statements short, simple, and specific.

6. Choose affirmations that especially fit you and express something you want to do.

7. Incorporate your strengths within your affirmations.

8. Choose action words.

9. Include positive, feeling words such as joy, serenity, peacefully, delightful, rejoicing, enthusiastic.

10. State affirmations which are in your control. (You cannot for example control whether someone else will marry you.)

11. Include a word ending in "ing" such as I am serenely accepting compliments.

12. Include a feeling word to motivate action (I am happy when I receive compliments).

13. Create as many scenes as possible when writing or thinking about the affirmation.

14. Once you have constructed an affirmation, close your eyes, repeat the affirmation several times (at least 3) and notice what inner images it evokes. If the images it evokes match your desired outcomes, your affirmation is a good one.

15. Use these images to deepen the effect of the affirmation. Draw a picture to represent each image or clip out pictures from magazines and elsewhere to represent your images.

16. Tell your friends your affirmations and share your pictures with them in order to prepare them for your changes.

Self-fulfilling Prophecy

Individuals tend to reinforce their self esteem by adjusting perceptions to conform with perceived self esteem. People with high self esteem tend to manifest success, while people with low self esteem tend to manifest failure—the picture of oneself becomes a self fulfilling prophecy which one often feels incapable of reversing.

By the individual's attitudes and beliefs, about self, others and/or the world, the person guarantees particular outcomes. For example, the attitude, "I'll never be able to stand up and give that speech. I'll be terrible," leads the individual to behave in ways that insure failure. Jourard and Landsman (1980) explained this clearly in writing

> Thus, when persons form self-concept, thereby defining them-
> selves, they are not so much describing that nature as they are making
> a pledge that they will continue to be the kinds of people they believe
> they now are and have been. One's self concept is not so much
> descriptive of experience and action as it is prescriptive. The self-
> concept is a commitment. (p. 187)

Of course, such prophecies can work to advantage when predicting success and/or growth. Merely changing the language people use to describe themselves can allow for the possibility of change (Satir, 1981). For example, one might change, "I'm terrible at giving speeches" to "Up until this time I've had a hard time giving speeches." Hope and hopelessness are revealed in the language of an individual.

Ray (1980) stressed the need for searching out buried negative thoughts which may be wreaking havoc in one's life. Negative thoughts once identified then may be replaced by positive thoughts, affirmations, which a person immerses into consciousness (Ray, 1980). According to Canfield and Self Esteem Associates (1986), the dissonance created by affir-mations produces motivation to achieve the outcome. By associating the desired outcome with a visual image, the affirmation can create even greater power.

Framing

Related to self-talk is the way a person frames a situation. How one frames a situation also can affect self esteem. The situation remains unchanged but the meaning (conceptual or emotional set) associated with the situation is altered (Bandler & Grinder, 1982; Borysenko, 1987; Watzlawick, Beavin, & Jackson, 1974). To illustrate this concept, Watzlawick et al. (1974) give the example of a man with a severe stammer who is forced by circumstances to become a salesman. This new position heightened his concern about his speech problem. His speech problem was reframed as an asset to him as a salesman as people generally dislike salesmen for their smooth barrage of words. Also pointed out to the man was that often people listen carefully and patiently to those with handicaps. His handicap was reframed into an asset. His handicap remained unchanged but his way of looking at it changed.

Reframing mistakes is necessary in order to increase self esteem (McKay & Fanning, 1987). No one is perfect; living necessitates making mistakes. In a way, mistakes are a sign that the individual is growing, taking risks, trying new things. McKay and Fanning (1987) also emphasize that mistakes are our teachers. An inventive professor at a University in Illinois gives students credit for giving wrong answers in class. He wants students to challenge themselves and stretch their thinking rather than playing safe. According to McKay and Fanning (1987), mistakes are our guideposts. Mistakes help keep us from going too far astray. McKay and Fanning (1987) emphasize that everyone deserves a quota for mistakes. They suggest as a rule of thumb, people be allowed an error quota of between one and three bad decisions out of every ten. McKay and Fanning (1987) also stress that mistakes are always easy to see after the fact. Can you love yourself, mistakes and all? Do you allow yourself an error quota?

Perspective

Satir explained that a direct relationship exists between what people notice, what their attention is called to, and how they interpret the world. Actions are taken based on those interpretations. She emphasized that in Western culture people tend to notice negatives. Most of the world has a highly developed attention to that which is wrong, bad, or destructive (Satir, 1981).

Satir (1981) further explained that what people notice and attend to also is determined greatly by their position. She used the analogy of a globe. "I will see what I am in a position to see. If I behave as though what I see is all there is to see and when you over there tell me what you see, I say, 'No, it's not true.' Then we can fight over who is right." According to Satir, this occurs all the time—fighting over who is right when people are in different positions. Satir stated that rigid people demand that you see the world through their filter and take the same actions they do.

Satir stressed the role of perception in self esteem. In summary, these perceptions are influenced by the following:

1. the position of the person, where he/she is located;

2. self-feelings the person has about him/herself; and

3. the interpretation one places on that data.

Satir (1981) contended that people's perceptions are often incomplete, inaccurate, and distorted.

Self-blame

Individuals who take more responsibility than necessary (most common for all the flaws, failures) experience a high level of guilt and self-blame which tends to erode the self-system. Such affective symptoms typically arise from extremely high standards of behavior.

Individuals who suffer severe guilt tend to level heavy blame on themselves. They often adhere to beliefs or values which are given them by important authorities with whom they interacted and upon whom their life depended during their growing up years. These authorities were typically harsh in their punishment and tended to project their own self hatred onto others.

Guilt is originally a response taught by parents in the service of oppression (Steiner, 1974). Steiner said that guilt prevents children from striving for the things that they want but which their parents don't want them to have. When individuals refuse or are unable to meet up to expectations leveled by significant figures, they experience intense guilt.

Guilt, then, is experienced when an individual's behavior, or even thoughts, transgress certain values, expectations, or shoulds as discussed earlier. To the extent that these values, expectations, or standards are freely chosen by the person, the guilt serves as a mechanism to alert the person to a violation of the integrity of the organism. Behavior then can be brought back in line with values, ultimately serving to enhance self esteem. To the extent that these values were adopted without critical appraisal, the guilt serves to notify the organism that these values deserve evaluation, reevaluation, and perhaps revision.

The origins of feelings/beliefs such as:

"I'm worthless."

"I'm defective."

"I'm bad."

"I'm flawed."

are from social determinants. Children are not born with these beliefs or low self esteem. They are trained into their negative self-image. Children are born precious and pure. An example of how this is socially determined is a woman named Joan who reported a network of negative self messages (see Figure 4.4).

Ingredients such as those in Figure 4.4 help form a distorted "bad self" belief. But this "bad self" belief is not an accurate reflection of self worth. Yet many swallow such beliefs about self indiscriminately. Having introjected such beliefs, many go on to act out that image through self or other destructive behaviors.

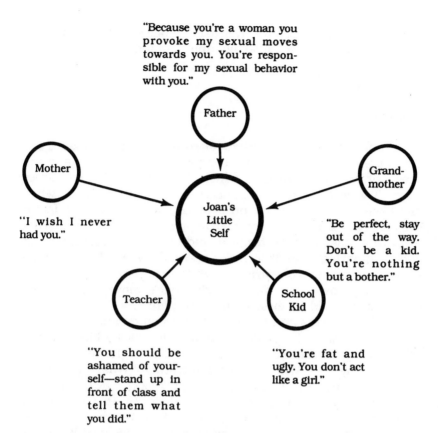

"Because you're a woman you provoke my sexual moves towards you. You're responsible for my sexual behavior with you."

Father

Mother

"I wish I never had you."

Grand-mother

Joan's Little Self

"Be perfect, stay out of the way. Don't be a kid. You're nothing but a bother."

Teacher

"You should be ashamed of your-self—stand up in front of class and tell them what you did."

School Kid

"You're fat and ugly. You don't act like a girl."

Figure 4.4. Formation of "Bad Self."

According to Whitfield (1987), family rules, family messages, and a lack of safety prevent the true self from emerging (see Figure 4.5). Compulsive behaviors, according to Whitfield

True Self

Defective "Bad" Self

False Self

higher self/pure precious child

vulnerabilities/shame/ negative messages/restrictive rules and beliefs

protections/facades/ defenses/compulsive behaviors

Figure 4.5. Layers of self.

(1987, are used to manage internal conflict between competing introjects (for example, "good me" and "bad me.")

Comparing Self to Others

Comparing oneself to others often results in diminished self esteem. Always when people compare themselves to another they will find some areas in which the other person surpasses them. These differences become even more pronounced when one bases the comparison on a person who is in a "different league." For example, a carpenter apprentice comparing his/her work to a master carpenter is bound to come out on the short end. Comparing oneself to other apprentices would be a more logical point of comparison, while comparing one's own performance over time or measuring one's movement towards one's goals would be even better. The person with healthy self esteem has dreams and believes in personal dreams. If I have a picture of how I'll be at 30, what my life will be like, but the reality of my life falls short of this image, it might be healthy to challenge myself—"What's keeping me stuck? What's happened to my dream? Am I taking enough risks?" If by making comparisons people feel bad about themselves, that method of comparison needs to be modified, for it is self-damaging rather than growth producing. Comparisons which are healthy result in individuals assessing their progress, highlighting the areas where they might need to add or transform or want to strengthen. If by making comparisons one more fully identifies uniqueness, or is encouraged to change, then the process of comparison, of simply identifying how the two are alike or different, has helped the individual to clarify and define without judgment. An internal reference base is helpful and healthy; however, an internal reference does not occur in a vacuum; it must some way relate to an external reference point.

Stilling the Mind

Many authors point to our lack of connection to our inner voice as a major source of emotional problems. One such author, Mariechild (1987) connected this loss of tie to ones inner voice to feelings of despair, alienation, and loneliness. She outlined a familiar sequence of events:

Our minds are often cluttered with thoughts. Stilling the mind requires practice. The mind can be trained through gradual disciplined cleaning. This cleaning then allows the inner voice to be heard. According to Vaughn (1979), fear (projection of anxiety) and desire (wishful thinking) are two of the main obstacles to this inner voice. Various mediatative practices guide the individual towards inner quiet (LeShan, 1974). A variety of meditative practices are available from which to choose: Yoga, Tai Chi, Transcendental Meditation, healing music, imagery, communion with nature.

In our culture we have become so attached to our minds that we have become separated from other aspects of ourselves. Once the internal chatter is quieted down, our inner voice, body feeling, vision, or dream can be experienced. According to Bennett (1987), our inner voice can help keep us on our paths and prevent us from straying into physical, emotional, or spiritual discord.

REPRESENTATIONAL SYSTEMS

In addition to defense mechanisms and cognitive-perceptual factors, individuals use different representational systems to reinforce self esteem. Representational systems are the methods (visual, kinesthetic, and auditory) that individuals utilize to gain access to their internal experiences. If people can come to understand how they maintain a negative self-image—by what processes, by what internal representational systems, they can more effectively short circuit the effects. Additionally, newer, more enhanced self-images may be developed through direct, purposeful use of these same systems. According to Bandler and Grinder (1975) and Grinder, Delozier, and Bandler (1977), individuals operate using three main representational systems—visual, kinesthetic, and auditory. Any one of these systems may function as the lead system, or the most highly valued and most often used system. Thus, any situation may be represented in at least three ways. Fire, for example, may be represented:

VISUAL—by sight of flickering flame,
KINESTHETICAL—by feeling of heat,
AUDITORY—by sounds of crackling flame.

By identifying an individual's lead system and patterns of representational systems employed, one can understand how self esteem may be reinforced or changed. A number of later books have addressed the application of NLP to a variety of problem areas (Cameron-Bandler, 1985; Cameron-Bandler, Gordon, & Lebeau, 1985). In Table 4.4 is presented an example of comparisons of the representational systems of students with high and low self esteem who are about to deliver a speech.

This work extends the idea of self-talk (Ellis & Harper, 1976) which involves the auditory representational system as the lead system. Prior to the work of Bandler and Grinder (1975), the role of negative thoughts in perpetuating low self esteem and the role that positive self-statements can exert in enhancing self esteem were considered as primarily auditory messages. Now what is known is that individuals tend to utilize different internal representational systems (visual, kinesthetic, and auditory) as their lead system or primary avenue of learning. Low self esteem may be maintained through automatic images, feelings, self-talk, while positive self esteem might be fostered by creating deliberate positive self-talk, kinesthetic responses, and images around particular experiences, and encouraging practice with these to raise self esteem and promote growth and change.

Other authors have emphasized the effectiveness of imagery—visualization in evoking positive change (Gawain, 1978; Lazarus, 1977; Singer, 1971). Visualization can help a person achieve goals on physical, emotional, mental, or spiritual levels. According to Gawain (1978), imagery is effective in dissolving internal conflicts into a harmony of being. Assagioli (1965) developed a theory of behavior change which utilizes

TABLE 4.4

**Representational Systems: Comparison of Students
of Low and High Esteem About to Deliver a Speech**

Representational Systems	Low Self Esteem	High Self Esteem
VISUAL	may picture self forgetting the speech and imagine the other children jeering.	may see self smoothly delivering the talk and may picture the other students as attentive and interested.
KINESTHETIC	may feel a sinking feeling in his/her chest.	may feel open, standing straight, breathing fully as he/she has experienced at other times when he/she felt success.
AUDITORY	may hear the other children laughing.	may imagine the other children silent in their attentiveness; imagine remarks of encouragement and support; may remember reassurance of his/her mother.

imagery as the primary approach in the revolution of internal conflict.

DEVELOPING INHERENT CAPABILITIES

Many people are like undeveloped land, just waiting to be tilled. Individuals are often unaware of the richness of the soil;

the buds just under the surface; the beautiful rocks hidden underneath. When individuals are aware of their resources and these treasures have not been brought to surface and been valued or encouraged, they become part of their burden and despair. A part of the self has been neglected—a part of its power source has gone unused, a part of the organism is deadened.

When these inherent capabilities are recognized and nurtured, the self becomes whole, grows, and expands. Self esteem rises as each personal "gift" is recognized and developed. The individual comes closer to utilizing total potential on behalf of self which leads to fuller functioning and greater satisfaction.

People cannot not change. Individuals are continually evolving. Even so, change is very threatening for some. The fear of letting go of old ways of viewing self, archaic behavior patterns, is the fear of death. A myriad of emotions arise through the process of self expansion and the shedding of outdated ways of being. By making room for this emotional journey and garnering support from others along the way, the disruptive aspects of change can be managed and the excitement of new beginnings may be experienced.

SUMMARY

Self esteem is a process. The ground work for the self-concept and self esteem is laid in early childhood, although the self-concept is gradually shaped throughout one's lifetime. The development of clear boundaries between parent and child is essential for normal psychological development and the development of one's identity. People's attitudes and beliefs about self influence how others view and treat them; one's pictures of self become self-fulfilling.

People have a repertoire of internal mechanisms to draw upon to protect their view of self. One group of internal mechanisms is "defense mechanisms." These "stop-gap" measures, when carried to extremes, inhibit growth of healthy self esteem and effective coping with reality. In a more positive light, however, these distortions can regulate incoming stimuli to protect the person from becoming flooded and unable to function. Cognitive consistency, another defense mechanism employed by adults, allows people to perceive reality in accordance with self-image. Such mechanisms help preserve the status quo. (Beck, Rush, Shaw, & Emery, 1979; McKay & Fanning, 1987).

A number of authors have outlined thought distortions which perpetuate negative self-images. Individuals can learn to challenge such distortions in order to improve self esteem. A number of related cognitive-perceptual factors also can influence self esteem. The ability to identify and meet one's needs is directly related to self esteem. The Gestalt cycle represents a model of the various phases of need satisfaction. Chronic interruptions in that cycle at any phase can erode self esteem.

The more one is able to face reality and deal with the world in a congruent way, the higher the self esteem. The increasing willingness to discover, own, and cherish all of one's parts (given the appropriate context) insures the building of higher esteem. Willingness to let go of those beliefs, attitudes, and defenses which no longer fit, are outdated, and no longer serve a positive function, insures a growing, healthy self esteem.

Self esteem seems much like a drop of water; it is affected by both social and internal sources. Just as a drop of water has a basic form, so does self esteem. Just as water can be influenced by the environment (i.e., wind might modify its shape, cold weather might change its form), so can self esteem (i.e., self-estimates change from time to time). Just as water is internally active, as can be seen by microscopic examination, self esteem also is internally active. Thus, self esteem is not a fixed, stable concept; it has fluidity based on social and internal factors. While self esteem has some basic form, it can primarily be seen as a process of development which occurs over a lifetime.

ACTIVITY 4.1   PARENT DIALOGUE

Introduction

In this activity from the nurturance phase of intervention, participants are invited to have a fantasy dialogue with one of their parents in order to come to terms with this parent.

Time Required

45 minutes

Participants

Any number; adolescents and adults

Setting

Carpeted office or classroom

Materials

None

Procedure

Sit comfortably and close your eyes . . . . Visualize one of your parents, sitting facing you. Take some time to really see your parent sitting facing you, and make contact with him or her. How is he/she sitting? . . . What is he/she wearing? . . . . What kind of facial expression does he/she have? . . . Notice all the details of your parent in front of you . . . . How do you feel as you look at your parent? . . . Now begin by being completely honest with your parent. Express all the things that you never told him/her and say these things directly as if you were actually talking to him/her now. Express everything that comes to your mind—resentments you held back, anger you were afraid to show, love that you didn't express, questions that you never asked, etc. Be aware of how you feel as you do this, and notice if you begin to tense your body somewhere, etc. Be sure you stay in contact with your parent as you do this. Take about five minutes to do this . . . .

Now become your parent, and respond to what you have just said. As your parent, how do you reply to what your child just said? . . . Be aware of how you feel as you do this . . . . How do you feel toward your child? . . . Now tell your child how you feel toward him/her, and tell him what you think of him/her . . . . What kind of relationship do you have with your child? . . .

Switch places again and become yourself. How do you respond to what your parent just said? . . . What do you say now, and how do you feel as you say it? . . . Tell your parent how you feel toward him/her now, and tell what you think of him or her . . . . How do you experience this relationship? . . . Now tell your parent what you need and want from him/her. Take some time to say exactly and specifically what you want your parent to do for you, and be aware of how you feel as you do this . . . .

Now, become your parent again. As parent, what do you reply to this expression of needs and wants from your child? . . . How do you feel as you do this? . . . What understanding do you have of what he/she is asking for? . . . Have you experienced anything similar in your life? . . . Now, tell your child what you need and want from him or her . . . .

Switch places and become yourself again. How do you respond to what your parent just said? . . . Do you have any better understanding of him/her now? Now tell your parent what it does for you to hang onto him or her in fantasy like this . . . . What do you gain by holding onto all these unfinished feelings toward your parent? . . .

Now, become your parent again and respond to this . . . . What do you say in reply? . . . What is your relationship like now? . . . Is any understanding developing, or is it still mostly fighting and conflict? . . .

Switch places and become yourself again. How do you respond to what your parent just said? . . . How do you experience your relationship, and what understanding do you have of your parent's situation? . . . Tell him/her whatever understanding you have now . . . .

Now, I want you to tell your parent what you appreciate in him or her. No matter how difficult your relationship is, there must be something about him or her that you appreciate. Tell your parent about these things now, and be specific and detailed . . . .

Now become your parent again. How do you respond to these appreciations? . . . Can you really accept them, or do you minimize or reject them? . . . Now, express your appreciations of your child. Tell him/her in detail what you appreciate in him or her . . . .

Now, become yourself again. How do you respond to the appreciations you just got from your parent? . . . How do you feel toward each other now? . . . Continue this dialogue on your own for some time, and switch back and forth between being yourself and your parent whenever you want to. Pay attention to what is going on in this interaction and make this explicit. For instance, if you realize that the parent is scolding and blaming, point this out and demand that he/she express self more directly. Notice when you are tense and holding back, and express yourself more fully. See how much you can express and clarify about this relationship . . . .

Time is required to clarify a relationship, and often you will arrive at a place where both sides are stuck in an unyielding deadlock. As you become more aware of the details of this deadlock, it will gradually become more flexible; when you become fully aware of the conflict, it will disappear. This may take many sessions of struggling, but each time some clarification and deepening of awareness is possible. Eventually, you can arrive at letting go of parents, giving up your demands that they be different, and forgiving them for their faults, and what they did or didn't do for or to you. You can recognize that they couldn't be other than they were, and that even "forgiving" is irrelevant. Perhaps hardest of all is to let go of a lost relationship. When an important person in your life has died or left you, he or she continues to exist in your fantasies as if he or she was still alive. In a kind of self-hypnosis, you continue to be involved with a dead relationship. When you can complete this dead relationship and say good-bye, you can wake up from your hypnosis and become involved with the living people around you. (Stevens, 1971, pp. 71-73)

Discuss in groups of 3 to 4.

Outcomes

A fuller appreciation of what a parent had to give and greater acceptance as the parent as a human being with strengths and faults.

Note: From *Awareness: Exploring, Experimenting, Experiencing* (pp. 71-3) by J. O. Stevens, 1971, New York: Bantam. Copyright 1971 by John O. Stevens. Reprinted by permission. Edited to some extent for this edition of *Enhancing Self Esteem.*

ACTIVITY 4.2   WEAKNESS-STRENGTH

Introduction

This activity from the strength-weakness phase of intervention helps participants to explore more fully what they perceive is their strong and weak side and what they gain/lose from each side.

Time Required

40 minutes

Participants

Any number; adolescents and adults

Setting

Carpeted classroom or office

Materials

None

Procedure

Close your eyes and turn your attention inward . . . . Get in touch with your physical existence . . . I want you to have a silent conversation between weakness and strength. I would like you to start by being weakness talking directly to strength. You might start out with something like "I'm so weak, and you're so strong, you can do so many things," etc. Be weakness and talk to strength for a little while, and be aware of how you feel, physically, as you do this . . . . Go into some specific details about how you are weak, and how he/she is strong.

Now switch roles and be strength replying to weakness . . . What do you say as strength, and how do you say it? . . . How do you feel in this role? . . . And how do you feel toward weakness? . . . Now tell weakness what it does for you to be strong . . . . What do you gain by being strong? . . .

Now switch roles and be weakness again . . . . What do you reply to strength, and how do you feel as you do this? . . . Now tell strength what it does for you to be weak . . . . What do you gain by being weak? . . . Tell him/her about the strength in your weakness. Tell all the advantages of being weak— how you can use your weakness to manipulate others and get them to help you, etc. . . . Go into specific details about the strength of your weakness . . . .

Now become strength again and reply to weakness . . . . What do you say as strength, and how do you feel now? . . . Now talk about the weakness in your strength. Tell about the disadvantages of being strong—how others lean on you and drain your energy, etc. Go into specific details about the weakness of your strength . . . .

Now become weakness again and reply to strength . . . . How do you feel now and what do you say? . . . Continue this dialogue for awhile on your own. Switch roles whenever you want to, but keep up this dialogue between weakness and strength for awhile and see what you can discover . . . .

(This kind of internal dialogue can be immensely useful for pointing out and clarifying the relationship that exists *within the individual,* between any pair of complementary people, roles, qualities, or aspects . . . . Some other productive sets of opposites are: husband-wife, parent-child, planner-spontaneous person, strange-familiar, helper-helpless, honest-dishonest, boss-employee, neat-sloppy, male-female, responsible-irresponsible, mind-body, stupid-smart, etc. Notice what you have difficulty with in your life, and then reduce this difficulty to a particular person, behavior, or quality. Then think of the *opposite* of this person, behavior, or quality and work with it in dialogue. If you really invest yourself in this dialogue, you will discover the symmetry and similarity that lies beneath the apparent opposition. In the example above, there is the strength of weakness and the weakness of strength, and also that both sides, are using different means to do the same thing—control each other.) (Stevens, 1971, pp. 169-171)

Discuss in group of 4 or 5.

Outcomes

1. *Increased awareness of how one expresses one's strength and weakness.*

2. *Helps one explore the relationship between one's strength and weakness.*

3. *Enables one to discover the similarities which underlie opposites.*

Note. From *Awareness: Exploring, Experimenting, Expressing* (pp. 169-71) by J. O. Stevens, 1971, New York: Bantam. Copyright 1971 by John O. Stevens. Reprinted by permission. Edited to some extent for this edition of *Enhancing Self Esteem.*

ACTIVITY 4.3 NAME WRITING

Introduction

This activity from the strength-weakness phase of intervention helps participants to discover parts of themselves and to tap the "child" inside.

Time Required

45 minutes

Participants

Any number; adolescents and adults

Setting

Carpeted room with no chairs

Materials

10 sheets of paper per participant
One box of oil pastels per 6 participants

Procedure

Go to the box of oil pastels and choose a color that pleases you and expresses something about you. Also take about ten sheets of paper from the stack, and sit where you won't be distracted by others near you . . . . In all of these experiments I want you to hold your pastel in the hand that you don't write with.

Now I want you to slowly write your name backwards, as if your name were reflected in a mirror. Use the top half of the sheet of paper to do this, and be aware of how you feel as you write your name backwards with your unaccustomed hand . . . . .

Now use the bottom half of the paper to do the same thing as before—writing your name backwards with your unaccustomed hand—but now do it with the **least possible effort.** Be aware of what you experience as you do this . . .

Take another sheet of paper and write your name forwards in such a way that you fill the whole sheet of paper . . . .

Now on the same piece of paper, write your name as small as you possibly can . . . .

Now put all these signatures where others can see them, and tell each other about your experience of doing these different kinds of name-writing . . . .

Take another piece of paper and write your name very slowly with your unaccustomed hand. Use this signature to draw a time-line map of your life up to the present time. The finished signature will somehow represent the different periods of your life and what you experienced at these times . . . .

Take another sheet of paper and on half of the sheet, use your name to draw a sketch of yourself as you really are . . . .

Now on the other half of the same sheet, use your name to draw a sketch of yourself as one of your parents sees you . . . .

Take another sheet of paper and on half of it use your name to draw a part of yourself that you like . . . .

On the other half of the same sheet, use your name to draw a part of yourself that you don't like . . . .

[Form groups of 5 or 6.] Now place your signatures where everyone [in your group] can see them and take turns telling about them and how you felt as you did them. Describe your time-line signature and your sketches of yourself in detail, and express your awareness of the process of doing them. After everyone has done this, take some time to discuss what you notice about each others' signatures and what they express . . . . (Stevens, 1971, pp. 286-288)

Outcomes

Helps one identify basic and early feelings and identify early self-images.

Note. From *Awareness: Exploring, Experimenting, Expressing* (pp. 286-88) by J. O. Stevens, 1971, New York: Bantam. Copyright 1971 by John O. Stevens. Reprinted by permission.

ACTIVITY 4.4   AN APPLE A DAY

Introduction

This activity helps participants to examine their tendencies toward introjection, their abilities to assimilate, and their resistances to both processes. It is an activity from the **strength-weakness phase of intervention.**

Time Required

40 minutes

Participants

No limit; adolescents and adults

Setting

Classroom or office

Materials

One apple per participant

Procedure

Ask each participant to bring in an apple. Participants are then directed to begin eating in their normal style. After a minute or two, **stop** and reflect on the style of your eating. How would you describe it? Share in groups of 3 or 4. Do you take your time in chewing? Do you swallow large chunks? Do you take small bites? How long do you chew each bite?

Now begin eating once again only this time, take a bite and chew on it until it is liquid before swallowing.

Reflect on what that was like. Did you notice any differences? Describe. How does this relate to how you assimilate ideas or how you move through life?

What relationship might this have to self esteem?

Meet in groups of 3 or 4 and discuss. Relate to Gestalt concept, introjection, which means "swallowing whole," values, advice, or ideas of authorities. What happens when you swallow such messages indiscriminately without fully assimilating them?

Outcomes

1. Increases awareness of the degree to which one filters external input resulting in greater selectivity.

2. Increases awareness of the roots of current behaviors/values/attitudes.

3. Helps one revaluate current behaviors/values/attitudes.

———

ACTIVITY 4.5   TIME OF YOUR LIFE

Introduction

This activity encourages you to take charge of your life by adding to your life more of what you find joyful and paring down those activities that you find unrewarding. It is an **identity phase activity** since it helps clarify values and set goals.

Time Required

20 minutes

Participants

Any number, adolescents, adults

Setting

Home, office, or classroom

Materials

Paper and pencil

Procedure

Think of a typical week. Section off the circle below like pieces of pie to indicate how you now fill your time (A) and how you'd like to fill your time (B).

(A) How I spend my life

Example: **Your Life:**

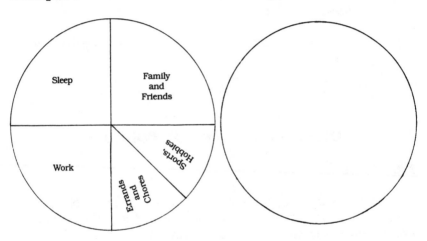

Evaluate how you are spending your time.

Is there a balance in your activities. For example:

—*work and play*

—*active and receptive*

—*body, mind, emotions, spiritual*

How much time do you spend in activities you consider joyful?

(B) How I'd like to fill my life

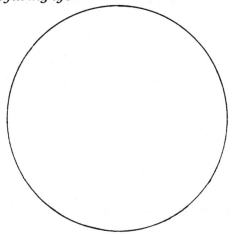

You have the power to change how you live your life. How could you make your life more joyful? What could you do now? You can practice inner freedom now. What is your inner being calling for you to do? What you love to do belongs in your life.

Write your reactions to this activity. Do big discrepancies exist between circle (A) and (B)?

What keeps you stuck?

—obligations, shoulds

—needs to be needed

—fear

—feeling undeserving

Discuss your thoughts and feelings in small groups.

Outcome

Heightens awareness of choices in how one spends time and sets goals to bring values in line with behavior.

———

ACTIVITY 4.6   INNER VOICE

Introduction

Hearing your inner voice requires time and practice in silent reflection. This activity directs you in that process. It is a **self nurturance activity** which redirects participants to attend to their inner life.

Time Required

20 minutes

Participants

Any number; adolescent, adults

Setting

Classroom or office

Materials

None

Procedure

Think of a question that's been on your mind. Meditate on that question for a few moments until it is planted firmly in your mind. Now imagine yourself in a beautiful magical garden. The colors are splendid here. Look around—at the sky, flowers, birds in the trees—take in everything. Listen to the sounds all around you. Take a deep breath and drink in the smells in the air. As you wander around, you come upon a small, clear pool of water. In the middle of the pool is a perfect lotus flower. Study this flower carefully. Notice the jewel in the heart of the flower. Allow yourself to be one with this jewel and listen for the deep voice inside. Allow yourself 5 to 15 minutes for this focused meditation.

Discuss the process with a partner. Of what did you become aware?

Outcome

Increases interoceptive awareness in order to strengthen trust of oneself.

REFERENCES

Acker-Stone, T. (1987). *What I say is what I am.* Hyannis, MA: Wonder Works Studio.

Alcoholics Anonymous. (1976). New York: Alcoholics Anonymous World Service.

Assagioli, R. (1965). *Psychosynthesis: A manual of principles and techniques.* New York: The Viking Press.

Bandler, R., & Grinder, J. (1975). *The structure of magic* (Vols. 1 & 2). Palo Alto, CA: Science and Behavior Books.

Bandler, R., & Grinder, Jr. (1982). *Reframing.* Moab, UT: Real People Press.

Beattie, M. (1987). *Co-dependent no more.* Center City, MN: Hazeldon Foundation.

Beck, A. (1967). *Clinical, experiential, and theoretical aspects.* New York: Harper and Row.

Beck, A., Rush, A. J., Shaw, B. F., & Emery, G. (1979). *Cognitive therapy of depression.* New York: The Guileford Press.

Bennett, H.Z. (1987). *The lens of perception.* Berkeley, CA: Celestial Arts.

Bernard, H., & Huckins, W. (1978). *Dynamics of personal adjustment* (3rd ed.). Boston: Holbrook Press.

Borysenko, J. (1987). *Minding the body, mending the mind.* New York: Bantam Books.

Bowen, M. (1985). *Family therapy in clinical practice.* New York: Jason Aronson.

Cameron-Bandler, L. (1985). *Solutions.* San Rafael, CA: Future Pace.

Cameron-Bandler, J., Gordon, D., & Lebeau, M. (1985). *Know how.* San Rafel, CA: Future Pace.

Canfield, J., and Self Esteem Seminars. (1986). *Self-esteem in the classroom,* Self-esteem Seminars, 17156 Palisades Circle, Pacific Palisades, CA 90272.

Carlock, C.J., Hagerty, P.T., & Verdon, T.R. (1985). *Satir family instruments.* Dayton, OH: Peoplemaking Midwest, 1105 Watervliet Avenue, Dayton, OH 45420.

Ellis, A., & Harper, R. (1976). *A new guide to rational living.* North Hollywood, CA: Wilshire.

Festinger, L. (1957). *A theory of cognitive dissonance.* Stanford: Stanford University Press.

Fitch, G. (1970). Effects of self esteem, perceived performance, and choice on causal attribution. *Journal of Personality and Social Psychology, 16,* 311-315.

Freud, S. (1936). *The problem of anxiety.* New York: Norton.

Gardner, P. (1981). Depression and self esteem: An investigation that used behavioral and cognitive approaches to the treatment of clinically depressed clients. *Journal of Clinical Psychology, 37,* 128-135.

Gawain, S. (1978). *Creative visualization.* Berkley, CA: Whatever Publishing.

Gestalt Institute of Cleveland Post Graduate Training Program. (1979). Lecture: Cycle of experience. Cleveland, OH.

Grinder, J., Delozier, J., & Bandler, R. (1977). *Patterns of hypnotic techniques of Milton H. Erickson, M.D.* (Vol. 2.) Cupertino, CA: Meta Publications.

Jourard, S., & Landsman, T. (1980). *Healthy personality* (4th ed.). New York: Macmillan.

Keleman, S. (1975). *The human ground.* Palo Alto, CA: Science and Behavior Books.

Lazarus, A. (1977). *In the mind's eye.* New York: Rawson Associates.

LeShan, L. (1974). *How to meditate.* New York: Bantam Books.

Mariechild, D. (1987). *The innerdance.* Freedom, CA: The Crossing Press.

McKay, M., & Fanning, P. (1987). *Self esteem.* Oakland, CA: New Heritage Publications.

Meichenbaum, D. (1974). *Cognitive behavior modification.* Morristown, NJ: General Learning Press.

Miller, J. (1976). *Toward a new psychology of women.* Boston: Beacon.

Newman, M., & Berkowitz, B. (1977a). *How to be your own best friend.* New York: Random House.

Newman, M., & Berkowitz, B. (1977b). *How to take charge of your life.* New York: Bantam.

Polster, E., & Polster, M. (1973). *Gestalt therapy integrated: Contours of theory and practice.* New York: Brunner/Mazel.

Ray, S. (1980). *Loving relationships.* Millbrae, CA: Celestial Arts.

Roman, S. (1986). *Living with joy.* Triburon, CA: H.J. Kramer.

Satir, V. (1976). *Making contact.* Millbrae, CA: Celestral Arts.

Satir, V. (1978). *Your many faces.* Millbrae, CA: Celestral Arts.

Satir, V. (1980). *Family communication.* Ann Arbor, MI: OASIS.

Satir, V. (1981, August). AVANTA Process Community. Park City, UT.

Satir, V., & Bandler, Jr. (1984). Virginia Satir Verbatim. N. Delta, B.C., Canada: Delta Psychological.

Singer, J. (1971, Spring). The vicissitudes of imagery in research and clinical use. *Contemporary Psychoanalyst, 7,* (2), 442.

Steiner, C. (1974). *Scripts people live.* New York: Grove Press.

Stevens, J. O. (1971). *Awareness: Exploring, experimenting, experiencing.* New York: Bantam.

Telfair-Richards, J. (1980). Energy: A Taoist/Gestalt perspective. Paper delivered at Gestalt Institute of Cleveland: Cleveland, OH.

Vaughn, F. (1979). *Awakening intuition.* New York: Anchor Books.

Watzlawick, P., Beavin, J. H., & Jackson, D. (1974). *Change.* New York: W.W. Norton.

Whitfield, C. (1987). *Healing the child within.* Pompano Beach, FL: Health Communications.

Zinker, J. (1977). *Creative process in Gestalt therapy.* New York: Brunner/Mazel.

CHAPTER 5

NEGATIVE
SELF-IMAGES

As discussed previously in the chapter on self-concept development, psychological pathogens often have pervasive effects on the evolving self-concept. What often occurs is that a person starts to develop a negative self-estimate based on the feedback received from one or several pathogens. For example, one might think he/she is not very adequate at interacting with peers. At the same time, the person might believe he/she is adequate at interacting with others who are older or younger than him/herself. The individual also might think that although he/she is not adequate in some other areas of self, there are also some areas of adequacy. Through continued exposure to psychological pathogens, this negative self-estimate develops into negative self esteem. The person begins to feel and think negatively about self in totality. Few, if any, areas of adequacy can then be seen by the individual.

These negative thoughts and feelings are manifested in various negative self-image types. Contrary to popular belief, low self esteem is not manifested in a singular manner such as saying, "I'm no good" or indicating nonverbally, "I'm no good" by slouched posture. Low self esteem can take on many different manifestations. Malmquist (1982) discussed the false facade which children of depression and low self esteem express. This is also the case for adults and individuals of varying types of low self esteem. These types are not necessarily mutually exclusive, and some individuals are a blend of types depending on their own life experiences and/or situations.

Nevertheless, it is helpful in studying low self esteem to become aware of its many faces and images. It aids in a more thorough and in-depth understanding. Regardless of the type of negative self-image, all these individuals experience high levels of psychological pain.

SCARED RABBIT

This person is hypersensitive and appears to be emotionally fragile. He/she sends out messages to others nonverbally and verbally which say, "Don't confront me, I might fall apart," and "Be careful with me, I'm fragile." Consequently, others back away and the person misses opportunities to grow because he/she does not receive constructive criticism. This person needs a change in focus to become more positive about self. This self-image type can benefit from becoming aware of internal conflicts and realizing that external feedback will not crush and defeat self. He/she needs to become familiar with inner strengths. This type could benefit from improved self-talk as discussed in Chapters 4 and 7. A good resource on self-talk for adults is *What to Say When You Talk to Yourself* (Helmstetter, 1986). *Vulture* (Simon, 1977) is a good resource for children on self-talk.

OSTRICH

This person denies both self and reality; his/her reaction to confrontation is usually, "What do you mean, it's not so bad." Often, these individuals, in an attempt to deny their negative self esteem, live vicariously through sports, television, movies, or their children. They will go to extremes not to admit negative self-feelings to others as well as to self. This person needs more self-awareness and self-vitality; he/she can develop this by facing people, problems, and events and learning more problem-solving skills.

Activity 6.5 , Who Am I?, is a helpful first start for this negative self-type. Activity 7.4, Robot, would also be a helpful technique for children of this type. These activities are discussed in Chapters 6 and 7.

CLOWN

This individual manifests low self esteem by excessive laughing and joking. This person is motivated by the idea "I'll make fun of me before you make fun of me." The person strives to make everything very superficial and funny to escape hurt or having to deal with negative self-thoughts.

This person needs to take self, others, and the environment more seriously. He/she needs both to learn to deal with others realistically and realize he/she will not be ridiculed. These individuals need to learn to get positive attention in other ways.

A helpful procedure for this negative self-image type is to learn to ask for what he/she is needing psychologically. Those of high self esteem are usually articulate about their needs. Individuals of low self esteem usually do not ask for what they need. Those low in self esteem often need to learn that "to G-E-T, one has to A-S-K." Sometimes one has to A-S-K and A-S-K and A-S-K. Usually others then begin to respond appropriately.

HOSTILE PERSON

This person is overly aggressive and tends to be particularly rebellious, especially against authority. He/she is often resentful, suspicious, and critical. These individuals relate very negatively with others in order to keep a safe distance between self and others and to vent negative self-feelings. Hostility is, thus, a form of projection.

These individuals need to become more aware and accepting of their fear and vulnerability. Often these individuals have a certain level of sadness underneath this behavior. Learning to deal with this directly becomes very important. Activity 7.10 Resentments and Appreciations, discussed in Chapter 7 can be helpful to this negative self-image type.

SCATTERED TYPE

This person utilizes so much energy in jumping from one event to the other that none is left for anything constructive.

This type of individual can become settled and efficient by becoming goal oriented. The scattered person needs to learn to distinguish self-goals from goals of others. Many of the techniques discussed in the maintenance phase of intervention in Chapter 6 are especially valuable to this type.

RATIONALIZER

Rationalizers refuse to face themselves and deny that circumstances are hurtful. These people need to become more aware of their feelings, especially those emotions of anger and sadness; they avoid feelings by "living" in the mind.

Activity 7.27, Journal Keeping, is an especially helpful technique for this type. This technique is discussed in Chapter 7. Through journal keeping this type becomes more aware. This is an important first step for this type.

PERFECTIONIST

This person operates by the maxim "A place for everything and everything in its place." If everything is not perfect about self, everything seems to come to an end. These individuals are hypercritical of self and others and are demanding and harsh. They feel that they must be in control.

A helpful procedure for perfectionists is to envision the absolute worst consequence possible to a given situation. Often it would not be as terrible as anticipated. Another procedure often helpful is to make a list of satisfactions derived from perfection (these two are not highly correlated although perfectionists illogically believe they are). By confronting fears about being imperfect, one often feels better about self. These people need to reverse their "all or nothing" thinking, such as "If I am not perfect, I am a worthless person." They also need to learn how to separate personhood from behavior and to learn that they are loveable regardless of imperfect behavior.

An interesting resource for this type is a book entitled, *Perfectionism—What's Bad About Being Too Good?* (Adderholdt-Elliott, 1987). Activity 1.1, I'm Not Perfect But. . .Parts of Me Are Excellent, in Chapter 1 is particularly helpful for this type.

BLAMER

This person says to self and others in various ways, "It's your fault I'm the way I am" (I don't like myself); "If it weren't for you . . . ." These people are very condemnatory, they put others down in an attempt to elevate self. Jealousy is a prevalent feeling with the Blamer. Blamers are usually unable to admit mistakes.

Blamers need to realize the consequences they suffer from excessive blaming—what blaming does to them and how it drives others away. The price paid for this type of behavior is high. Blamers also need to deal with the fear of looking at self.

Activity 1.2, What is Real? in Chapter 1, can be beneficial to this type as well as Activity 7.22, The Book of Me, Techniques discussed in Chapter 7.

TOUGH GUY

"Keep out," "Keep your distance," "I don't need you," are common attitudes with this negative type. These people put on such a tough exterior that few are inclined or able to interact on a personal level with them.

Tough guys need to accept the fact that they have needs, as it is their fear of having needs that frequently leads into this negative self-image type. Tough guys need to accept their soft feelings and allow for intimacy with others.

In Chapter 8, Activity 8.1 Risking, is described. This technique is especially helpful for this type.

THE WHINER

These people are fond of saying, "I can't do it" in a high, whiny voice. Over-dependency is the crucial dynamic of this type. The negative self esteem of such people is very evident by their attitude of helplessness.

This person needs to become more aware of inner resources and trust in self more. Often they are helped by learning to take more risks.

Two techniques often valuable to this type are Activity 8.1, Risking, and Activity 7.22, The Book of Me.

POLLYANNA

"Everything is just wonderful" and "Life is just a bowl of cherries" are statements reflecting this negative type. People avoid individuals with this attitude because such behavior is merely an attempt to mask negative self-feelings. Pollyannas seems to believe that if they express this attitude enough, it will be true. Pollyannas need to deal with the fear of looking at themselves. Self-acceptance and honesty are two important elements in overcoming this attitude. Learning to face conflicts rather than smoothing them over advances this person further toward positive self esteem.

Activity 6.2, Self-Sculpture, discussed in Chapter 6 can be a starting point for improvement in this type. Activity 7.1, Self-Portrait, (Chapter 7) is also a helpful technique.

PITY ME

"Feel sorry for me," and "Look at how I suffer" are statements this martyred individual makes to self and others. They spend so much energy feeling sorry for themselves and getting pity from others that little is left for constructive growth.

By facing conflicts and dealing with them such people can grow and become more complete. Pity me types need to develop an awareness of their own identity as they often bootleg their identity from others. They need to learn that they can receive approval for themselves.

Activity 6.8, Stroke Sheet, and Activity 7.14, Just Say "Yes," are useful focal points for this type.

MALLEABLE PERSON

These individuals are very self-effacing and approval seeking. Comments such as "Whatever you say" and "I don't care" are attitudes expressed by this type. They care so little for themselves that they can be molded in any direction; they are obsequious to others. Malleable persons need self-definition. They also need to learn to feel comfortable in the spotlight and accept attention.

In Chapter 6, the Activity 6.11, Group Affirmation, is described. This focuses on accepting attention and being in the spotlight.

THE GHOST

This person fades into the woodwork and makes comments expressing the attitude of "I'm not here," "I'm nothing." Because they do not regard themselves highly, they attempt to go very unnoticed to others. Their belief is that if they are not visible they cannot be a target for criticism. Thus, if they are invisible, they cannot be expected to give in any way to others. As a child, the Ghost type often behaved in this way as a defense mechanism. Ghost types need to learn that they are capable of giving and receiving both positive and negative feedback.

Activity 6.8, Stroke Sheet, would be a valuable intervention for the ghost type. Any techniques focusing on self identity are good starting points for this type.

OVERCOMPENSATOR

This person is excessively boastful. "I am the greatest" is often the attitude expressed. These individuals are often name droppers; they seek excessive amounts of recognition and are extremely verbal. They also need to learn to feel comfortable expressing their feelings and opinions even when they differ from others.

Overcompensators need to accept themselves as they are and realize that they do not have to be perfect to be accepted by themselves or others.

An excellent musical technique to use with this type is the song, "I Love Myself The Way I Am" in the cassette tape entitled Songs From the Heart (Alliance, 1987). The lyrics of this song provide insight and support, particularly for the overcompensator.

THE FRUMP

These individuals look very haggard and give one the impression that "I don't care about me." People with this self-image consider themselves to be a cypher, a zero.

They need to become aware of positive self-estimates as they are often phobic about good feelings. They need to develop assertiveness and learn how to acquire positive feedback from others. Frump types need to find people who feel good about them.

Activity 11.1, Personal Right, is a beneficial one for this type. Learning to ask for positive feedback is a valuable tool for this type also.

THE ACTOR

This person wears a different mask for each occasion, sometimes several layers of masks and facades at a time. These acts or roles become so pervasive that the person does not know who he/she really is. They have anesthetized themselves because of their negative self-feelings. Rosenberg (1965) found that these individuals are very likely to report psychosomatic symptoms.

Actors need to peel away the layers and masks and become more aware and accepting of their real selves. They need to become aware of what they need and have less of a focus on what others need and want from them. They need to become more aware of their feelings and thoughts and less aware of their behavior.

Activity 1.2, What is Real? is of value especially to this type. Activity 7.7, Three Boxes, also can aid this type.

PROCRASTINATORS

This person delays carrying out tasks because of negative self esteem. Frequently, he/she also may be indecisive. Such people seldom improve self esteem because they cannot make decisions. Consequently procrastination becomes an indirect decision with negative effects on self esteem. Procrastinators need to learn to ask questions and ask for help in order to learn how to proceed. Confronting the fear of success or failure is also helpful.

Of specific value to this type are the techniques of Activity 10.2, As If, and Activity 7.25, Imagining Alternative Endings, reviewed in Chapters 7 and 10.

FIERCELY COMPETITIVE

Individuals for whom recognition for their achievements, material possessions, and/or family is excessively important can be considered in this category. These people are desperate to dominate others. An excessive amount of energy is devoted to being "better than" others because of low self esteem. They need to redirect their energy to being aware of their own strengths and weaknesses. They need to turn their focus internally in order to balance their external focus.

In Chapter 7, Activity 7.13, Significant Others, is discussed. It has particular value to this type.

HIGH ENERGIZERS

This person is involved in everything. This excessive energy can be inner or outer directed. Such people can be constantly on the move and/or be compulsive drinkers, smokers, or eaters. In order to keep from looking at self, they are continually in motion. Often, such people appear to be very successful as in the case of a rock star who keeps an inordinately fast pace of numerous concert tours in a limited time. Sometimes, a professional helper is excessively involved in "straightening others out" as a means of directing attention away from self.

These individuals need to slow down and become aware of their feelings. They need to realize that accomplishments do not define personal worth.

Activity 7.16, Self Sabatoge (Chapter 7), is a helpful intervention for this type, as is any identity technique which causes the person to do some introspection.

SUMMARY

Rigid boundaries do not exist among these various negative self-image types, however some commonalities do exist among them. Almost all these types are hypersensitive to criticism. Most types overlap and some of these types can be situationally or person specific. For example, a person might behave like a Blamer while on the job, but feel adequate enough about self socially not to behave in ways which reflect negative self-image. Or, a person might be a Pity Me type around family members, but feel adequate enough with those external to the family to evidence positive self esteem. Of course, a person with an unstable self-concept, as discussed previously, might shift from one of these types to another depending upon the environment.

A life transition (i.e., marriage, divorce, or retirement) or a very devastating and traumatic event (i.e., death of a spouse, loss of a leg) could temporarily put one in a position of a negative self-image type.

Some people have behavior that is common to one or several of these types all their lives. To understand these negative self-image types, the helper must be aware of the psychological pain which is experienced by them. A valuable procedure is to look beyond the overt behavior of each type to the underlying feelings and thoughts discussed in this chapter. Such a thorough understanding of their needs helps in developing more positive self esteem. In Figure 5.1 is a summarization of these types. The following chapter on intervention is directed especially toward these negative self-image types and specific techniques to use in helping them.

ACTIVITY 5.1   NEGATIVE SELF-IMAGE

Introduction

This technique is to help you better understand how negative self-images have an impact upon one.

Time Required

15 to 30 minutes

Participants

Ages 10 and older

Setting

Office, classroom, or home

Materials

Self-image wheel with spinner. If not available, place the twenty items from Figure 5.1 on pieces of paper which are placed in a box.

Procedure

If using the self-image wheel, have a participant to spin a pointer in the middle of the figure (Figure 5.1). Identify the character on which the spinner stops.

If using the twenty items in a box, have a participant draw a character from the box.

Have the participant to assume the body post, voice, gestures, and attitude of this character and then interact with the group for a minute.

Process the Following:

How did that feel?

Of what were you aware?

Repeat the spinning or drawing and assuming as done the first time. Then repeat the processing.

Repeat the spinning, etc., until 4 or more characters have been assumed.

Process the following:

Do any of these characters seem more familiar than others?

In yourself?

In those around you?

Are you different in these characters with different people?

In different situations?

Underneath, what do these characters feel?

What might they be needing?

Outcomes

Develops increased awareness of negative self-images and their efforts upon self and others.

Figure 5.1. Negative self-image wheel

REFERENCES

Adderholdt-Elliott, M. (1987). *Perfectionism—What's bad about being too good?* Minneapolis, MN Free Spirit Publishing.

Alliance. (1987). "I love myself the way I am" in Songs From The Heart. Beverly Hills, CA: Go with The Flo.

Helmstetter, S. (1986). *What to say when you talk to yourself.* Scottsdale, AZ: Avalon Corporation.

Malmquist, C. (1982). The functioning of self esteem in childhood depression. *Seminar on Self Esteem Development and Sustenance.* Boston: Harvard Medical School.

Rosenberg, M. (1965). *Society and the adolescent self image.* Princeton, NJ: Princeton University Press.

Simon, S. (1977). *Vulture.* Niles, IL: Argus Communication.

CHAPTER 6

THE PROCESS
OF INTERVENTION

Every response to the environment is consonant with how one perceives self. Rogers (1951) stated,

> *As experiences occur in the life of the individual, they are either (a) symbolized, perceived, and organized in some relationship to the self, (b) ignored because there is no perceived relationship to the self structure, (c) denied symbolization or given a distorted symbolization because the experience is inconsistent with the structure of the self.* (p. 503)

These varying reactions result in many different behavioral manifestations, commonly called symptoms of low self esteem.

SYMPTOMS OF LOW SELF ESTEEM

These following 18 indications are common to most negative self-image types discussed in Chapter 5.

Negative Self-images

1. Verbal clues are often symptoms of low self esteem. A person may say such things as, "I'm stupid," "I'm ugly," "Don't ask me, I wouldn't know." Attitudes conveyed by such statements may be indicative of low self esteem.

2. A person who is very fearful of new experiences is often one with low self esteem. Such people do not trust themselves and, consequently, avoid anything new; little risk-taking is evident.

3. Exaggerated reactions to failure are common among those of low self esteem. Usually these individuals have a desire to be perfect; this makes facing failure very difficult.

4. Excessive boasting is another symptom. Those who continually boast and/or fabricate tales frequently do so as an overcompensation for feelings of inadequacy.

5. An extremely strong need for positive reinforcement and encouragement is symptomatic of low self esteem. Those who constantly need support and positive feedback do so out of a feeling of inadequacy.

6. Physical appearance also can be indicative of those lacking in self esteem. Those whose appearance reveals neglect or extreme perfectionism (ends of continuum) often reflect negative feelings about self. Physical appearance also includes gait, posture, eye contact, and other nonverbal indications. People who seldom maintain eye contact and who slouch in their chairs may lack self esteem.

7. An intense interest in the acquisition of material objects is often symptomatic of low self esteem. These individuals have the mistaken idea that material possessions will bring them enhanced self esteem.

8. Those reluctant to express their ideas often do not feel good about themselves. They do not express their ideas on any subject because they do not believe in themselves or have confidence in themselves. They really believe they have nothing to say. As children, their ideas were usually not valued.

9. Abdicating responsibility also is common among those with low self esteem. It is often related to feeling

powerless and defenseless. Refusal to take responsibility for self inhibits growth and experiential learning; "I don't know how that happened" is a commonly expressed thought.

10. Low energy level is another symptom; an insignificant task often looks monumental to those of low self esteem. "I can't, I'm too tired." Passivity also can be evident. These persons wait for something to happen. They are reactors, not actors.

11. Lack of self-awareness also is a symptom. A strain is involved in maintaining false images. The depletion of energy for this purpose leaves little for self-awareness. This individual usually can tell you little about "who" he/she is.

12. Excessive anxiety usually is prevalent in those with low self esteem. It seems that a circular-causal relationship exists between anxiety and self esteem: Anxiety leads to low self esteem and low self esteem seems to lead to increased anxiety.

13. An inordinate sensitivity to criticism is commonly evident. Usually those who feel worthless have difficulty accepting any feedback which might even border on being constructive criticism. These individuals usually feel that all others view self negatively.

14. Psychological isolation also is commonplace. Those who feel inadequate do not have support groups to aid them in times of increased stress, thus, all coping becomes the responsibility of one person. Feelings of loneliness are common.

15. Psychosomatic complaints also are common. Because they are deficient in self-awareness, low self esteem individuals commonly somaticize negative feelings about self.

16. Excessive criticism of others also is frequent. Often, those negative characteristics of others that are emphasized are the very qualities most disliked in self.

17. Dwelling in the past and catastrophizing are other symptoms of deficient self esteem. Both behaviors prevent growth. By continually analyzing and reliving the past, little is accomplished in the present. By overexaggerating what might happen in the future, self-growth is inhibited.

18. Excessive apologizing often can be observed in those deficient in self esteem. "I don't do this well," "Please excuse me," and "I'm so sorry" are all common statements expressed.

All of these symptoms need not be evident in one person for a person to be considered lacking in self esteem. These symptoms are common, however, across many negative self-image types as indicated previously. The person might be aware of symptoms or they might exist only at the unconscious level. If symptoms are only displayed in one or two areas of self, or are situational or personal specific, they probably are related to unstable self rather than to low self esteem. For example, a person who displays some symptoms **only** at work or **only** when with overbearing individuals is probably experiencing unstable self. Those symptoms which are more pervasive are associated with low self esteem. For example, the person who **consistently** uses excessive apologizing, withdrawal, and negative self-verbalization is probably lacking adequate self esteem. Most everyone may exhibit some of these symptoms occasionally.

According to Satir (1988) persons of high self esteem can feel low. Such individuals, however, do not condemn themselves, but see the low time as a natural, human condition with which one needs to cope. Only when symptoms are frequently evident, are displayed over long periods of time, develop into patterns, or are of great intensity is low self esteem present.

PHASES OF INTERVENTION

Too often, individuals who are interested in helping others improve their self-concept approach the task in a very haphazard manner. Frequently these helpers have only piecemeal background information about self-concept theory and treatment. Understanding the phases of intervention in self-concept problems aids the helper in understanding this process in totality, and, thus, prevents the helper from asking the low self esteem individual for a behavior, thought, or feeling he/she is developmentally unable to give. For example, asking low self esteem individuals to make a list of their positive qualities before they have an idea of their own identity is asking too much, too soon. Unfortunately, most helpers have focused only on part of Phase II—strength identification—rather than using a stepwise approach. This specific phase treatment approach has been found to be very successful in enhancing self esteem.

Phase I: Identity

Initially in intervention, an individual with low self esteem needs to discover his/her own identity. Because of distorted perceptions, such persons rarely have a clear understanding of who they really are. They often conceptualize themselves as having few or no strengths—physically, psychologically, or spiritually. Usually such persons do not see their whole self, but focus on small aspects of self. Such individuals might focus on their ideal self and how they have not attained that ideal, but they give little attention to their private self, as discussed in the Johari Window. They might be viewing themselves as they were in their past and not seeing their present selves. This is often exhibited in the life-scripting people do for themselves, such as when a 40-year-old man still tells himself he must compete with his sister for the attention of their parents. Activities such as those which follow and those discussed in the following chapter aid the helper in increasing the client's awareness of his/her own identity.

ACTIVITY 6.1   POLARITIES

Introduction

This identity activity helps put you in touch with the different sides of yourself.

Time Required

1 hour

Participants

Age 9 and older

Setting

Group setting, office or classroom

Materials

Paper
Pencil

Procedure

List five psychological qualities that would describe you.

Now, get in touch with the psychological opposites of each of these qualities.

How able are you to own both sides?

In groups of three or four, spend three minutes enacting one side and then three minutes enacting the other side.

The side with the psychological opposite probably represents your "dark side," the side you disown. Identify specific situations when each of these qualities was or could be a help to you. Now, identify specific situations when each of the qualities listed in the first procedural step might be a problem for you.

List your major learnings.

Outcomes

Helps one to list their major learnings.

Note. Written from memory of exercises conducted at Gestalt Institute of Cleveland Postgraduate Training Program (1979).

ACTIVITY 6.2   SELF-SCULPTURE

Introduction

Here participants are asked to create an image of themselves using clay. The activity encourages participants to allow the form to evolve and change through the process. This parallels the evolvement of the self through life. (It is an **identity phase activity.**)

Time Required

30 minutes

Participants

Age 8 and older

Setting

Office or classroom

Materials

For each person, have about 5 to 10 pounds of modeling clay and a piece of cardboard or plywood about two feet square for modeling on. You can use inexpensive painter's "drop cloths" to keep clay off a good floor or rug.

Procedure

Take a good double-handful of clay. Also get a board to put the clay on and find a comfortable place to sit, with some space around you . . . . Now take a few minutes to get acquainted with the clay . . . . Feel its texture and weight . . . . Feel the way it changes shape as you explore it with your fingers . . . . Try different ways of shaping it—squeezing, patting, rolling, pulling, pushing, stroking, punching, etc . . . . Discover what this clay is like and what it is capable of . . . .

Now that you have explored your clay, shape it all together into a fairly round ball and set it gently on your board in front of you. Close your eyes, sit in a comfortable position, and focus your awareness on your hands and fingers that have just been exploring this clay . . . . Notice how your fingers and hands feel . . . . Now turn inward even more and let your attention flow into the different areas of your body . . . . Become aware of what you feel in each different part of your body . . . .

Now visualize an image of your round ball of clay, and imagine that it will slowly change and shape itself into an image of yourself. This image might be a fairly realistic representation, or it might be quite abstract. Don't try to change this imaginary ball of clay; let it change itself slowly into some representation of yourself . . . . It might go through quite a few changes, or perhaps form two or more images of yourself . . . . Whatever it does, just watch it closely as it develops, without interference from you. (Stevens, 1971, p.288.)

Discuss what the person has learned or discovered about his/her identity.

Outcome

Helps one to review and possible gain a better self identity.

Note. From *Awareness: Exploring, Experimenting, Experiencing* (p. 288) by J. O. Stevens, 1971, New York: Bantam. Copyright 1971 J. O. Stevens. Reprinted by permission.

———

ACTIVITY 6.3   THE "ME" ALBUM

Introduction

This technique illustrates what was presented in Chapter 2. It is an **identity phase activity.**

Time Required

1 to 2 hours

Participants

Ages 6 and older

Setting

Office or classroom

Materials

Photographs
Family albums
Paper
Pen or pencil

Procedure

Look through your family albums and choose pictures which represent different developing phases of your life, which show important relationships in your life, and which convey your different moods.

Give your album a title and write a brief script which serves as a tourguide through your life.

Outcomes

Develop increased awareness of how self esteem evolves through human interaction.

––––

ACTIVITY 6.4   THREE DRAWINGS

Introduction

The individual is asked to make three separate pictures symbolically depicting three separate concepts of self. This is an identity activity.

Time Required

30 minutes

Participants

Children, ages 8 and older; adults

Setting

Office or classroom

Materials

None

Procedure

Close your eyes and relax as much as possible, taking time to release any tensions you may have in your body.

Quiet your mind and let go of any emotions you may be feeling at the moment; become receptive to your intuitive self.

Slowly open your eyes and answer these three questions:

1. How am I?
2. How do I want to be?
3. What is the solution?

Allow 5 to 8 minutes for each. Share in a group or process for oneself.

Outcomes

Enables one to become more aware of real self and ideal self and how to establish more congruency between the two.

———

ACTIVITY 6.5   WHO AM I?

Introduction

This activity teases out the Private area of the Johari Window as well as the Open area.

Time Required

45 minutes to 1 hour

Participants

Children or adults

Setting

Office, classroom, or home

Materials

Paper and pen or pencil

Procedure

Meditate on the question WHO AM I? and come up with at least 100 responses. Find a quiet place to do this where you won't be disturbed. Write words, phrases, images, colors, metaphors, similes . . . anything that comes to mind. Try not to censor.

After having done the preceding part of this activity, check for the following:

1. Are there any themes present in your responses?

2. Did you avoid or omit any of the following categories in describing yourself?

physical	social
spiritual	emotional
intellectual	self as process

3. After reviewing your list, what general statements could you make about how you view yourself?

Outcome

Causes one to reassess views held of self.

Phase II : Strengths and Weaknesses

Secondly, once self-awareness has been expanded, then a valuable procedure is to help the individual to see which areas of self are strengths and which are weaknesses. The assumption can be made that everyone possesses both positive and negative qualities which can be represented as in Figure 6.1.

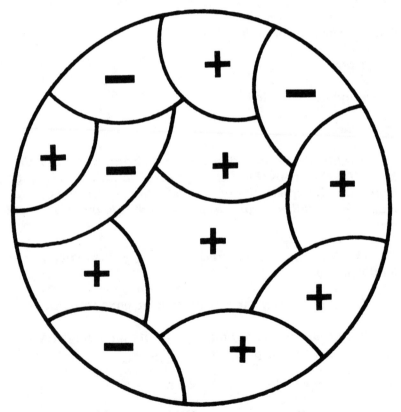

Figure 6.1. Self for positive self esteem.

In people with low self esteem, the self mostly is seen as in Figure 6.2 in which is emphasized mostly negative qualities.

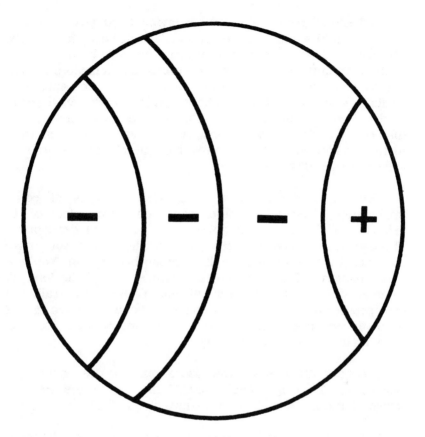

Figure 6.2. Self for low self esteem individuals.

The process of intervention helps the person to surface aspects of self for which he/she had little awareness and to reevaluate these aspects. The helpful procedure for a person to become more aware of a variegation of strengths. The more variegated one's strengths, the more stable one's self esteem.

Thus, a person is acquainted or reacquainted with self-strengths and weaknesses and learns a valid process for evaluating them.

Guidelines for Giving and Receiving Feedback. Feedback about strengths and weaknesses must be given with sincerity. Sincerity is determined by the receiver, not only by the content of the communication, but by the nonverbal behaviors as well (i.e., tone of voice, pitch of voice). These are affective elements of feedback which provide clues about how the sender really *feels.* If the feedback is insincere, the receiver will identify the insincerity and, thus, will discount the message and use it as further validation of his/her low-worth; the self-concept problem will be further aggravated.

Offering feedback in a concrete manner is of equal importance. Feedback should be made with reference to behavior of the person, not simply an adjectival description. Thus, feedback, such as "I really appreciate it when you arrive on time; it makes me feel good," is much better than "You're a great person." One's thoughts, feelings, and behaviors all compose different types of self esteem, of course. Generally the best procedure is to begin to focus on behavior when giving positive feedback. Then later in the intervention process focusing on thoughts and feelings.

Feedback about strengths also should be descriptive, not evaluative. The helper could say, "I like the colors you are wearing," rather than, "You are a sharp dresser."

Yamamoto (1972) indicated that a reward to punishment (R—P) ratio of five rewards for every one punishment is optimal in actualizing potential. When this ratio falls to two-to-one, neurotic symptoms begin to appear. He stated also that when the R—P ratio falls to one-to-one or below, feelings of despair develop. Consequently, a helper's ratio of five-to-one or at least three-to-one of praise to constructive criticism is helpful in this stage (the authors prefer the terms praise and constructive criticism to reward and punishment). Low self esteem individuals often experience a one-to-five ratio or worse, or experience an adequate ratio, but do not really integrate it into self.

These points for the helper are very important for a number of reasons. First, if sincere feedback is offered, the low self esteem individual is less likely to be able to rationalize away its motivation. Persons with low self esteem are frequently very adept at rationalizing away praise by saying that the person must "want something from me," "does not know me well enough to say that," "is not competent enough to make such a statement,"—to list only a few. When the praise is offered with sincerity, it is much more difficult to reject.

Also, second, if the feedback is concrete, specific, and nonjudgmental or evaluative, the person with low self esteem cannot reject it as easily. While a statement such as, "You are great!" is easy to reject, a statement such as "I like it when you bring in the groceries without being told to do so" is harder to deny. Either the person did the act or did not; to deny a behavior is difficult. When the helper does not place a value judgment on the behavior the person being helped has more difficulty in challenging the comment.

Keeping in mind the cognitive dissonance theory and the self-fulfilling prophecy theory, one can understand how individuals with low self esteem usually do not want to hear positive feedback about self. By understanding this ideation, the helper is more likely to penetrate the other person's negative cognition of self. Often the helper must be persevering and immune to criticism on the part of the other person when offering positive feedback, because many times low self esteem individuals will persist in negating positive feedback to the point of being verbally abusive to the helper.

Exploring Weaknesses. Looking at the individual's weaknesses also is helpful in this stage of intervention. According to Branden (1987), one of the most significant characteristics of positive self esteem is not being at war with oneself or others. If a person continues to avoid those negative aspects of self which keep him/her feeling poorly about self, then to change them becomes more difficult. Many negative aspects of self are either derived from messages sent by significant others or are ways of psychologically adapting to survive. Those warring subpersonalities, negative and positive self-estimates, are what prevent positive growth.

Satir (1978) believed people often view these negative aspects as being like hungry dogs which should be hidden and kept out of awareness. By caging them inside and feeding them only when absolutely necessary, people allow the dogs to become hungrier and hungrier. Consequently, they have to increase their guard to control the dogs. The continuation of this process is exhausting and leads to despair. The answer, according to Satir (1978), is not to get more guards, but to start paying attention to the dogs, caring and learning about them. Then energy can be used for discovery and change, not defending.

This increased awareness of weaknesses, their derivations and intentions, aids in effectively dealing with them, thus, enhancing self esteem.

Filtering Feedback. In this second phase, strengths and weaknesses, the helper teaches the low self esteem person how to receive feedback. Teaching people how to filter feedback and accept what is appropriate is necessary. Acceptance of feedback is related to the degree of self esteem (Morran & Stockton, 1980). Commonly, those with low self esteem accept feedback like a sponge, believing everything that is told to them. Through the process of intervention individuals are taught to accept what is true about themselves and to identify what is a projection of someone else. Feedback is then filtered through a screen, not totally absorbed as a sponge.

Van Buskirk (1983) discussed this filtering process using the metaphor of a semipermeable membrane. He stated that as an infant and toddler the self can be conceptualized as being surrounded by a very thin membrane which allows all feedback to enter. As the person ages this membrane becomes thicker and resembles a semipermeable membrane allowing in only some feedback. This decreases the hurt experienced when receiving feedback from unsolicited sources or which is incorrect. Those of low self esteem seem to have not developed this semipermeable membrane or have developed much too thick a membrane (denial or defensiveness) allowing little, if anything, to enter. Techniques for teaching this skill appear in the next chapter.

Three other valuable sources for dealing with criticism are *Ouch, That Hurts!—A Handbook for People Who Hate Criticism* (Clarke, 1983), *Negative Criticism and What You Can Do About It. . .* (Simon, 1978), and *The Mouse, The Monster, and Me* (Palmer, 1977). The latter book is a book for children. The others can be helpful for children or adults.

ACTIVITY 6.6   MANAGING YOUR PIG

Introduction

This activity helps people to identify areas of self-criticism and self-put-downs and teaches them a method for dealing with those negative messages. It is a strength-weakness phase activity.

Time Required

30 minutes

Participants

Any number; adolescents and adults

Setting

Homework assignment

Materials

Paper and pencil

Procedure

Things I get down on myself about. *Record things about which you nag at yourself.*

> *Physical*
> *Personal (psychological/intellectual)*
> *Social*
> *Spiritual*

Go through each of the previous points and record where you stand on each according to the following scale.

A. I'm not ready to change this yet.

B. I'm working on this one step at a time.

C. I'm wanting to work on this in the future.

D. I'm confused about what I want to do about this.

E. I'm working hard on this.

Check to see how many you noted "B" or "C." Are your plans realistic? Use goal-setting activity to set up a plan for change.

Outcomes

Sort through certain negative introjects, examine them, and decide one's position on each.

ACTIVITY 6.7   STICKS AND STONES

Introduction

This strength-weakness activity teaches filtering, an important skill in preserving self esteem.

Time Required

30 minutes

Participants

Any number; adolescents or adults

Setting

Classroom or group room

Materials

None

Procedure

Form small groups of 6 to 10 people. One person volunteers to be the pigger and throw words (sticks and stones) tailored to the groups' age, sex, and other special characteristics of the group aimed at pulling people down. After each pigging statement, the group responds in unison, "It doesn't matter what you say, I'm still a good person. I'm OK." The group is to respond louder and more convincingly each time. The volunteer continues to throw out insults, stereotypes, and put-downs with the rest of the group continuing to respond in unison.

Process feelings. What was it like to PIG? To talk back? How able were you to filter? What did you learn about yourself from this activity?

Outcomes

Increases one's skill in filtering. Helps individuals learn how to deal with put-downs. Helps one better recognize that he/she can possess negative qualities and still be a good person.

————

ACTIVITY 6.8 STROKE SHEET

Introduction

This group activity helps people identify their strengths. It is from the **strength-weakness intervention phase.**

Time Required

30 minutes

Participants

Any number; adolescents or adults

Setting

Classroom

Materials

One sheet of paper per member
Two pins for every member
One pen per person

Procedure

Pin sheets of paper to each other's backs.

Move around the room writing strokes or positive affir-mations you have for people on their sheets.

Take off sheets and fold—don't look at them.

When everyone is together, look at sheets and share the wording with each other.

Hang all sheets where they can be seen.

Outcomes

Through this activity, self esteem is enhanced by receiving feedback on strengths. The written stroke sheet can be used as a reminder to the person, as a reminder of his/her strengths at future low points when one might need a boost.

Note. Activity is original. Idea initiated by Wycoff (1971).

———

Phase III: Nurturance

In the nurturance phase, the individual is taught how to nurture this newly found identity with its strengths and weaknesses. The first two phases in themselves are not sufficient as newly acquired positive self esteem can be lost if it is not nurtured. Teaching nurturing helps the person to enhance strengths and use them to minimize weaknesses. As a person moves from one part of their environment to another, the praise/criticism ratio may change, especially when one is in more toxic environments.

Transferring Nurturing. The low self esteem individual needs to learn to utilize the high praise/criticism ratios from other environments to nurture self in less positive environments. For example, a person's home life may have a high praise/criticism ratio, but his/her work environment might be low in praise and high in criticism. Thus, the person needs to take strength from the positive environment to help nurture self in the other. The person also learns that a particular environment, behavior, or event does not define the self. If the person did poorly on an exam, this event does not make him/her totally inadequate. Viewing self as a complete picture is critical in intervention.

Identifying and Fulfilling Needs. Teaching low self esteem individuals to identify what their nurturing needs are and how to ask others to help fulfill these needs also is helpful at this stage. When the person of low self esteem also can validate others by telling them what he/she appreciates about their thoughts, feelings, and behaviors, he/she can be both nurtured and nurturing.

Self and Other Affirmation. The value of giving and receiving positive feedback cannot be underestimated. In the book *Games People Play*, Berne (1964) noted that positive feedback is as important and necessary to human life as physical needs such as for food, water, and shelter. Buber (1958) discussed the human need for affirmation. Studies in counselor effectiveness by Berenson, Mitchell, and Laney (1968) found that effective helpers use "confrontation of strength" more frequently than "confrontation of weakness." Focusing on the person's strengths rather than weaknesses is more effective. The nurturing phase of enhancing self esteem helps people learn how to affirm self and others.

More detailed explanation of affirmations appears in other chapters. An excellent resource for children on this topic is *Affirmation Ovals* (Clarke, & Gesme, 1988). Other discussions of affirmations appear in *Self-Esteem in The Classroom* (Canfield, 1986) and *What to Say When You Talk to Yourself* (Helmstetter, 1986).

Self-fulfilling Prophecy. In this nurturing phase, the helper can aid the disruption of the self-fulfilling prophecy of the low self esteem individual. Low self esteem truly is both the producer and product of ineffective behavior. Likewise, authentic, positive self esteem is both the producer and product of effective behavior. Low self esteem reinforces itself as self-fulfilling prophecies continue. In Phases II and III, this circular-causal relationship is broken and negative effects of the self-fulfilling prophecy of "I'm inadequate" is changed to a more positive self-fulfilling prophecy of "I'm adequate." This can be effected through the development of an effective praise/criticism ratio, an affirmation model for self and others, support groups for self, and/or through the disputation of faulty logic and reasoning. All of these are developed in the following activities and techniques. The format for this can be formal as in individual and/or group counseling, or informal as in the kind of growth which occurs from relating to effective friends and significant others.

Faulty Logic. In the nurturance phase of self esteem enhancement one learns to deal with the problems of overgeneralizing, selective abstraction, excessive responsibility, temporal causality, excessive self-referencing, dichotomous thinking, and catastrophizing, all of which can cause and maintain low self esteem.

The helper can teach one with low self esteem how to recognize faulty logic when **overgeneralizing.** For example, just because one felt negatively about self in one situation or at one time does not mean that he/she is a "terrible" person.

Learning to use logic to recognize when one is **selectively abstracting information** from the environment is helpful in disputing old ideas maintained by the subpersonalities. For example, when a woman tells herself that she is worthless because she is a bad cook, this abstraction needs to be recognized and characterized.

The helper aids the low self esteem individual in disattribution when the person takes **excessive responsibility.** Those low in self esteem need to learn that they are not responsible for everything and everyone in their environment; they are only responsible for themselves. **Temporal causality** is handled in the same manner. It is not true that because something was, it is. Those with low self esteem think that because their past was often negative, that the present or future will be the same. Helping these individuals involves assisting them to challenge the faulty logic of temporal causality. This can be done in numerous ways but one of the most effective is through reading biographies of others or by using **bibliotherapy** (learning about others' experiences through reading). Helping those with poor self esteem to challenge these ideas aids in enhancing self esteem.

Excessive **self-referencing** can be diminished by aiding the person with low self esteem to develop criteria to determine what the source of negative events is, as it is not always with the self. For example, when others give negative feedback, it is not necessarily true about the self or caused by the self. It could be offered by others out of jealousy or because the givers of feedback are not feeling well that day or were just given negative feedback themselves.

Helping those deficient in self esteem to calculate the real probability of an event and to recognize that the worst will not necessarily happen, greatly aids in lessening **catastrophizing.** For example, even though one might think he/she could never direct a meeting adequately and chaos would result, upon calculating the real probabilities objectively, it is unlikely that this result will happen. It could be the worst result of the meeting, but not the most likely. Helping the low self esteem person determine the best, most likely, and worst consequences of a behavior aids in disputing this illogical thinking.

Dichotomous thinking can be modified by placing negative events on a continuum. This helps eliminate the thinking of "I am either a good person or I am a bad person." These individuals need to be taught that all of one's behavior falls on a continuum—not all behaviors are negative.

Logical Self-talk. Just as individuals use illogical self-talk to prevent themselves from nurturing adequate self esteem, they also can be taught to use logical self-talk to nurture self and enhance self esteem. According to Satir (1988), since low self-worth has been learned, it can be unlearned, and new concepts can take its place.

A new dialogue then goes on in the mind. Self-talk can either inhibit or enhance self esteem depending on how logical and objective it is. Often the helper's role is to objectify self-talk for the helpee. For example, the helper might suggest to the person lacking adequate self esteem that he/she begin to tell self "I can do it," as contrasted to "I know I can't do it." A excellent recourse on this topic is *What To Say When You Talk to Yourself* (Helmstetter, 1986).

Support Groups. Developing effective support groups for self can be considered an aspect of the *nurturance phase.* A support group is generally considered to be a group of friends who are empathic, understanding, honest, straightforward, and encouraging of an individual. Support groups can be found in one's work, school, family, church, and/or social environment. If a support group is lacking in one of these areas, it can be compensated for in other areas. For example, if one does not have such a group at his/her work or school, he/she could form one through the family environment, social environment, and/or religious environment.

Ideally, one could have a support group in most of the different environments encountered. This support, however, frequently does not happen. For some, especially those with very low self esteem, no environment offers a support group. In these cases, the helper can teach the individual to develop self for support. If others fail them, low self esteem individuals always have themselves. For example, the helper can aid the low self esteem individual in learning how to be a friend to self by offering self-encouragement, empathy, and honesty. This reinforcement of self helps aids in enhancing self esteem. Too often, those with inadequate self esteem do not know how to make friends and develop support groups in those varying environments in which they interact. The nurturance phase aids those deficient in self esteem to identify their needs and develop a support group which will help meet needs. Various techniques are elaborated and listed as follows and in the following chapter.

ACTIVITY 6.9   KING/QUEEN FOR THE HOUR

Introduction

This activity gives practice in becoming aware of your needs, in being specific about what you want, and in receiving "good stuff" as deeply as you can. It is a **nurturance phase activity.**

Time Required

Two and one-half hours

Participants

Adolescents and adults; any number

Setting

Homework assignment for therapy or class

Materials

None

Procedure

Find a partner and contract with each other for an hour each to be King/Queen. During your hour you . . .

- *enjoy the privilege of identifying and asking for exactly what you want*

- *must not give, but must only receive.*

Pay close attention to your feelings in the role of King/Queen and in your role of server. This is a wonderful opportunity to get the nurturance all of us need.

Following the activity exchange your feelings/thoughts about the process.

Outcomes

Increases participant's ability to identify and express needs/wishes and to practice receiving.

ACTIVITY 6.10   POSITIVE MEMORIES

Introduction

By calling up positive memories from the past and conjuring positive fantasies for the future, individuals can create positive feelings in themselves. This is a **nurturance phase activity.**

Time Required

45 minutes

Participants

Any number; adolescents or adults

Setting

Office or carpeted group room

Materials

None

Procedure

Relax.

Imagine yourself in a beautiful place—your favorite place. Be in touch with the sights, smells, and sound of this place until you feel your body become fully relaxed . . . so very relaxed. Then, slowly, this scene will fade and you may imagine a movie screen—on it will flash scenes from your life—you feel excited to see this movie for it will be a happy, joyous film, full of warmth and life—positive scenes from your life will appear. You will remember your happy times, times when you felt really good about yourself—contented, peaceful, and oh, so alive.

I'd like you now to flash back over the catalogue of life events you have stored about your life and remember some times which were really important to you—times when you felt really good about yourself. Don't worry about whether the details are accurate or not—some may simply be fantasies about how you wanted things to be—others may be so true to life that you feel those same good feelings with great intensity once again—and, each time you remember one of these good feeling moments, you will feel a rush of brightness surge through you as you bring that scene into focus and step inside as you relive these precious moments in your history—these moments when you felt so good about yourself, about life— about who you are. So, go back now, back through your childhood, adolescent and adult years, and allow different scenes to flash upon your mental screen until you come upon the one which makes you feel oh so sunny inside—and when you have that scene—hold it there so still—while you take time to pay attention to all the details of that scene—while you let that scene play out, listening to and watching what's happening—and stepping into yourself and feeling those good feelings you felt then once again—notice how you feel inside as you feel this feeling-good-about-me feeling—notice your heart rate, your voice, the warmth of your skin, your eyes, how you hold your body—as you feel this feeling-good-about-me feeling once again.

Now, I want you to leave your past and move forward in time—to a time in the future—a time in the future when you will feel this feeling-good-about-me feeling once again— imagine times when you will feel those feelings once again— flash these scenes on your screen one by one until you come upon the one which makes you feel oh so good inside—so positive about yourself and when you have that scene, hold it there so still—while you take time to pay attention to all the details of that scene—while you let that scene play out, listening to and watching what's happening—and stepping into yourself and feeling those good feelings once again—notice how you feel inside as you feel this feeling-good-about-me feeling . . . notice your heart rate, your voice, your eyes, how you hold your body, as you feel this feeling-good-about-me feeling once again.

Discuss in groups of 3 to 4.

Outcomes

Participants will get in touch with their power to influence their moods positively.

ACTIVITY 6.11   GROUP AFIRMATION

Introduction

This activity helps participants to nourish themselves through their changes, to gain support for their steps. It is from the **nurturance phase** of intervention.

Time Required

30 to 45 minutes

Participants

Group of 6 to 12; adolescents and adults

Setting

Group room or classroom

Materials

None

Procedure

Members take turns being the focus person, going into the center of the group, and announcing one of the following:

- *a recent accomplishment,*

- *something of which you're proud,*

- *a goal you've set for yourself,*

- *a risk you took, or*

- *anything else you consider positive.*

The group then yells and cheers in affirmation and encouragement.

After everyone has experienced being in the center, the group then discusses the process, each member talking about his/her personal reactions and observations of others.

Outcomes

Enhances positive self-feelings; gathers encouragement and support.

Phase IV: Maintenance

The final phase of enhancing self esteem is **maintenance.** After one is aware of who self is, what his/her strengths and weaknesses are, and strategies for nurturing self, one needs to learn how to maintain adequate self esteem. Self esteem, as mentioned previously, is not a rigid, fixed concept. Self esteem is a process of evolution. At various times in one's life, this process of change is more rapid than at others. Various aspects within the self-concept change as one matures. One needs to learn how to maintain adequate self esteem just as it is necessary to maintain a car, house, or an interpersonal relationship if it is to grow and flourish.

During the maintenance phase, individuals are taught to turn experiences into learning situations, practice facilitative risk taking, set appropriate goals, forecast desired personal outcomes, and publicly affirm goals.

Learning From Experience. Many low self esteem individuals do not learn from experiences. They engage in what has been called the "neurotic paradox." They continue to engage in repetitive behavior without evaluating and assessing what was learned from the experiences. For example, a learning experience could be, "I can't study as well at night as I can in the morning." Studying could then be rearranged to occur on mornings when the individual does not have other commitments. By learning what made the experience undesirable or desirable, one can learn how to grow more fully in future situations.

Risk Taking. Low self esteem individuals generally risk too little or too much. In intervention, they are taught how to determine what risk level is appropriate. This can be facilitated by becoming aware of the risk/pay-off ratio. Risk taking is assessed in relationship to the "pay off" involved. Ideally, the ratio should be even—one to one. For example, telling off one's boss or teacher is a lot of risk for the pay off of being able to vent one's feelings. A more appropriate behavior might be to have a conversation as contrasted to an argument with an employer or teacher about what one dislikes or is upset about. This will help vent feelings, but at a time when they have not yet developed into extreme anger or rage. The helper might encourage low risk takers to assert themselves in order to facilitate the "pay off" of being able to return clothing which does not fit or food that is spoiled.

Goal Setting. Many individuals lack appropriate goal-setting skills. Sometimes goals for self are set too ambiguously and/or too high. For example, one might set as a goal self-actualization by the end of the year. This goal is too nebulous and too high an expectation to achieve in one year for most people. Sometimes goals are set which are not desirable for the person and/or not achievable. This can lead to self-defeating behavior and subsequently, to feelings of lowered self-worth. By dividing comprehensive goals into smaller steps, goals become more achievable and may be rewarded in intervals, thereby increasing motivation and self esteem, which results in a feeling of accomplishment. Activities are established in this phase of intervention to aid people in setting goals which are desirable, measurable, achievable, and realistic.

In addition to the techniques discussed here, another resource on goal setting can be found in *Self-Esteem in the Classroom* (Canfield, 1986).

Personal Forecasting. To have aspirations for the future aids one in becoming more fully actualized. The *maintenance phase* also helps individuals to learn to forecast for themselves what they would like to be doing five, ten, or fifteen years in the future. Brainstorming is helpful during these activities to aid in diminishing unnecessary false roadblocks to future goals.

Public Affirmation. Publicly affirming one's goals is helpful because once a commitment is made public, one is more likely to accomplish it. Once one publicly shares a goal, the dynamic of group interaction aids one in accomplishing the goal. Techniques to help one gain experience in public affirmation are included in the following chapter. The following is a sampling of maintenance techniques.

ACTIVITY 6.12   LETTER TO MYSELF

Introduction

*This technique can be done with children or adults, but needs to be done after a helper has been intervening for awhile. It is definitely a **Phase IV, Maintenance activity.***

Time Required

30 minutes

Participants

Ages 9 and older

Setting

Office or classroom

Materials

Paper
Pen or pencil

Procedure

After working with those of low self-regard for awhile, ask them to write themselves a letter. In the letter they are to write what they have learned about self, what they want to remember about self, and goals they have for themselves. Example:

> Dear Sue,
>
> I love you! You really made some important gains over the past few months, you've started to . . .
>
> You learned . . .
>
> I really liked how you . . . even though I didn't especially like your . . .
>
> I am concerned about your . . .
>
> I wonder if you . . .
>
> I appreciate you for your . . .
>
> By the way, what kind of progress are you making on your . . . I hope you . . .
>
> > Love,
> >
> > Me

The helper collects these letters and mails back to individuals a few months later.

Outcome

The letter serves as a follow-up device and aids in facilitating growth.

———

ACTIVITY 6.13   IDEALIZED SELF-IMAGE

Introduction

This activity helps one to narrow the gap between the ideal self and the real self. It is a maintenance phase activity.

Time Required

30 to 45 minutes

Participants

Age 9 and older

Setting

Office, classroom, or home

Materials

None

Procedure

Relax. Get as comfortable as you can. Close your eyes and visualize various pictures of yourself. In these pictures, see yourself demonstrating various qualities and skills that you want to find in yourself. Pick images that are within your ability. Keep the steps small and gradual—changes that can be made in a short time.

Compare and contrast your idealized self-image with your real self-image, note what you like and don't like, and set goals for yourself. Picture yourself doing something extremely well. Notice the feeling of accomplishment you have. How do you feel that in your body? Notice all the feelings and sensations. Imagine yourself feeling this way in your present life. Picture yourself feeling this way in the future. Settle on some clear images that represent this. Whenever you have a minute, bring these images of how you want to be into focus.

Picture yourself changing those factors. Begin to act and feel more like the idealized self-image.

Outcome

Help one act and feel more like the idealized self-image.

Note. Activity is original. Idea initiated by Susskind (Lazarus, 1977).

———

These four phases of intervention in enhancing self esteem are best viewed on a continuum, as in Figure 6.3. Although this intervention approach is a stepwise progression from Identity to Maintenance, there is obviously some overlap and vacillation between phases. Guidance along this logical progression by the helper, however, is much more effective than haphazard approaches which are currently in use.

| Identity Phase | Strengths/Weaknesses Awareness Phase | Nurturance Phase | Maintenance Phase |

Figure 6.3. Phases of intervention.

REASONS FOR RESISTANCE TO ENHANCED SELF ESTEEM

No approaches to intervention help others unless they want to improve their self esteem. Many individuals with low self esteem do not want to change. Some are afraid of success; they do not want to like themselves. Others have adapted to the habit of low self esteem and are afraid of the new experiences they might have to undergo to change. Still others might want to change but not enough; they have what is called an approach-avoidance conflict. Change is desired to a degree, but not to the point of being willing to do the work that change involves. The process of change is not always easy, it takes a certain level of anxiety and hurt to be motivated to change. The change process itself also involves some additional hurt. The benefits of change, however, are worth the hurt.

Festinger (1957) indicated that the level of resistance to change depends on

1. *the centralness of the idea to the person's total belief system;*

2. *the centralization of the new idea to the person's basic self-concept;*

3. *the value(s) the person attains from maintaining the originally held idea;*

4. *the threat level of the new idea; and*

5. *the pressure to change, too little minimizes motivation, too much results in resistance.*

The helping professional needs to assess all these areas to determine which area(s) is serving as a roadblock to further self esteem change.

Eisenberg (1979) discussed resistance to change. He concluded that individuals behave in such a way as to maintain their view of self regardless of whether it is positive, negative, neutral, or confused. In extreme cases, in order to avoid change, some clients make themselves physically ill with ulcers, migraines, headaches, colitis, and so forth.

Eisenberg offered several hypotheses to explain this resistant behavior. One is that changing self esteem develops an identity crisis for the person. Changing one's self-image can have a ripple effect which could threaten other parts of the person's life. A certain security exists in having an identity, even a negative one. Loss of this identity deprives the person of what little security he/she is likely to have; individuals might think that it is better to have a consistently negative view of self than to have no identity at all.

The second hypothesis Eisenberg (1979) offered is related to expectancy theory. In this theory is postulated that in maintaining a negative view of self has instrumental value. People with low self esteem are viewed by others as fragile and vulnerable. Often, these people are treated gently and in a nonthreatening way; therefore, little is expected of such fragile people. They do not have to perform much at all. Maintaining low self esteem sets up low expectations from significant others. Thus, low self esteem can become a shelter, encasing them in a cocoon that prevents much failure, stress, and risk taking.

The third hypothesis posited by Eisenberg comes from the psychoanalytic literature. Often, unresolved guilt from childhood events may exist at the subconscious level. This guilt prevents feelings of adequacy from developing by generating needs to punish self and by disallowing the person to like self.

None of these explanations are universal. Each helping professional will need to listen actively to his/her client to determine which hypothesis is operating in preventing self-concept change; at times, several may apply to the same person.

THEORETICAL ORIENTATIONS
AND INTERVENTIONS

The **intervention model** allows the practitioner to focus on change in self esteem in any number of ways depending upon his/her theoretical orientation to helping. From a **behaviorist's** point of view, the helper would focus on the overt behavior. Once the behavior changes from self-defeating to self-enhancing, the individual will begin to feel more positive about self in many aspects. This approach focuses on behavior first, with consequent changes in beliefs, attitudes, values, morals, perceptual field, environment (peers, friends), and core self.

On the other hand, the **insight approach** of helping attempts to change self esteem by focusing on the perceptual field, environment (peers, friends), beliefs, values, attitudes, and morals in order to enable the client to develop greater self-understanding, which would then lead to changes in behavior. Both behavioral and insight approaches can be incorporated into this intervention model.

COMMITMENT TO CHANGE

Usually, the commitment to change and work on continued improvement comes when one is in transition from the identity phase to the strengths/weaknesses phase. It can, of course, appear earlier, but is seldom seen later because individuals do not advance to the nurturance phase without a personal commitment.

A commitment to change the whole self at one time is not necessary. One can improve, for example, one's feeling about self at **home,** but not be ready to improve self at work or school. One could work on improving one's **intrapersonal** self and later improve one's **interpersonal** self. It is usually true that changes in self-estimate precede changes in self esteem. These changes in **self-estimate** often lead to an unstable self. This unstable self is often explained by the helper as resembling a puzzle in which the pieces do not quite interlock. The aspects of changed self do not interlock with the changed parts. Growth is gradual and can be incubating at times without the person's awareness of it. As total change occurs, the various aspects of self interlock and new self esteem is formed in totality. This can be seen in Figure 6.4. The nurturance and maintenance phases then follow to insure continued good feelings about self.

Characteristics of
Human Behavior Change

The change process, like much of human learning, is erratic. Improvement can be followed by a slight regression, which is in turn followed by improvement. This process repeats itself until some stabilization of changed behavior occurs. This change is graphically depicted as in Figure 6.5.

EFFECTIVE HELPING

Before any intervention can occur, an effective relationship must exist between the helper and the person deficient in self esteem. To be highly facilitative the helper needs to be empathic, congruent, genuine, and high in positive regard for the low self esteem person. If those with low self esteem feel that

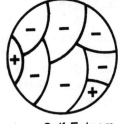
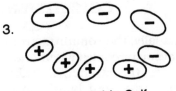
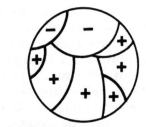

1.

Low Self Esteem

3.

Unstable Self

2.

Change(s) in Self Estimate

4.

Enhanced Self Esteem
(Self Estimates Interlocked Again)

Figure 6.4. Change process of self esteem.

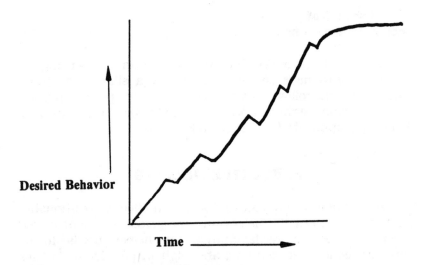

Desired Behavior

Time ⟶

Figure 6.5. Changes in self esteem.

214   Enhancing Self Esteem

the helper does not understand them, little can be changed. Rogers (1961) extensively elaborated on these conditions for the effective relationship. Other research on empathy and enhancing self esteem supports Rogers' findings (Williams, 1979).

INTERVENTION CONSIDERATIONS

After carefully developing a relationship with the individual, the helper can assess how severely deficient in self esteem the individual is and in what areas he/she seems to need the most help. This can be done in a variety of ways. Ablon (1982) suggested using the Rorschach and/or other format tests. Of course, one's professional judgment can serve as an informal assessment. The following method of using the Self-mandala also is helpful.

Self-Mandala

Satir (1981) developed a self-mandala, a circular design of concentric forms symbolizing wholeness, graphically depicted in Figure 6.6 (This mandala was also discussed more fully by Satir in 1988). In the center of the self-mandala is the "I" or that which one calls self. Around that self is the body or physical self. Around that self is the mind or intellectual self. Around this layer is the emotional self, the self which experiences pain, joy, satisfaction, anger, and varied other feelings. The next layer includes the sensual self—eyes, ears, nose, mouth, pores, and "holes" through which messages come into and out of the body. The interactional self is the next layer and includes the social aspects of self. Next is the nutritional self which includes how one nourishes the body. Around this layer is the contextual self which is composed of the environmental factors of time, space, light, air, water, sound, color, weather, and seasons. Extended to the fullest, this layer could include the Universe. Finally, the last layer is the life force which is similar to the soul. Satir (1981) stated that the basic chemical ingredients of the human being can be purchased at a drugstore, but to date, no one has been able to take those chemicals and create a human being. The soul, then, is the life source of each person.

All of these layers are interacting at any given time. Each part needs the others to function fully. For example, thoughts act on one's feelings, feelings can act on the body, and the body can act on one's thoughts or feelings. Discovering how these parts interact can aid the helper and the low self esteem individual in realizing how one is functioning relative to self and others.

Figure 6.6. Self-mandala.

Note: Idea initiated from Satir (1981).

ACTIVITY 6.14   SELF-MANDALA

Introduction

The following activity is intended for use in a group setting. It heightens awareness of all the various aspects of self. Before doing this activity review the Self-mandala by Virginia Satir (1981).

Time Required

30 minutes

Participants

One or more small groups

Setting

A large room

Materials

None (Review Self-mandala concept)

Procedure

Choose someone in the group to be each part of your mandala (i.e., physical self, intellectual self). Each person representing each part is free to move around you on a track in any way they choose. Acknowledge each part of yourself by saying "You are my . . . ." (Do not refer to the diagram in the chapter while doing this). Be aware of those parts you do not remember. Do you deny these parts? While the other parts of you continue their movements, tell the parts you do not remember to sit on the floor. They may give you little pinches to heighten your awareness. Ask the people representing the parts how they experience you. Take charge of your parts by bringing each person to you without talking. How do you use your parts to help you? Give a message to your parts to move in harmony around you. Allow your parts to pick you up and support you. After putting you down, the people representing *your parts encircle you and each one says to you, "I am your _____ (fill in blank) self; will you accept me? When you say "yes" the person puts his/her hand on your neck. This affirmation continues until all the parts participants have formed a necklace by putting their hands on your neck. Finally close your eyes and feel all the parts, recognizing that you have accepted all of them.*

Process this experience with your group. Discuss what you learned, relearned, or wonder about the various aspects of yourself.

Outcome

Enables one to explore various aspects of self.

Note. Activity is original. Idea initiated by Satir (1981).

———

By imagining that this self-mandala can be held up in front of others by the helper, one can experience what parts of the other person shine through dramatically and what parts are in the shadows or the dark. Viewing people through the mandala aids the helper to fully experience the person and not become overly focused on symptoms or labels. The question the helper can ask him/herself is, "How can I help tune in and turn on other parts of the mandala for this person to enable the individual to become a more fully functioning, positive person?"

For example, in the initial helping stages, the helper might notice that the person is very unaware of his/her sensual, nutritional, and emotional self. Perhaps, he/she is most aware of intellectual and interactional self. Possibly the person is living primarily in his/her thoughts with others and self to avoid feeling the pain of low self esteem. The helper could then aid this individual particularly in becoming more aware of these "shadow areas." While working through the four phases of intervention, techniques would be chosen which particularly related to enhancing the sensual, nutritional, and emotional self in addition to helping the person become more aware of how all these aspects of the self-mandala interact.

THEORIES OF HELPING

The effective process of enhancing self esteem involves both introspection and behavior change while working through the four phases of intervention. Both group and individual approaches to enhancing self esteem have been proven effective (Babensee, 1979; Zimmerman, 1980). These phases of intervention are adaptable to both group and individual approaches.

A variety of counseling and therapy theories are represented in the accumulation of techniques and activities discussed in the following chapter. Gestalt, Client-Centered, Rational Emotive, Behavioral, Transactional Analysis, Existential, and Ego Psychology approaches are evident in these intervention strategies. The techniques and activities are presented according to the phases of intervention previously elucidated and are specified according to their appropriateness for children or adults.

IDIOSYNCRATIC CONSIDERATIONS

Helpers must consider the type of low self esteem person with whom he/she is working, the various dynamics involved, the person's environment, and the helper's personality in determining which techniques will be utilized. For example, a young child might find it difficult to do techniques involving disattribution because of the level of cognitive functioning required. Or, perhaps the helper, after reviewing a technique, feels uncomfortable with it; it is not congruent with his/her style; a different technique should then be chosen. In certain instances, those of low self esteem might live in an environment not conducive to some techniques. For example, to encourage someone to develop an extensive support group would be difficult if he/she lived in a very remote area or worked and lived alone. Under such conditions a more appropriate procedure would be to choose other techniques.

Some individuals deficient in self esteem might learn better from auditory methods; others by more visual methods; and still others by kinesthetic methods (A comprehensive discussion of learning styles can be found in *The Creative Brain* by

Herrmann (1988). The large selection of techniques in each phase thus allows for the consideration of all these factors.

Lastly, helpers need to develop patience. People change at different speeds. Some individuals change more quickly than others, and much variability exists within individuals related to change. They might be slow to change at first, and then change quickly in another phase, then slower again at another phase. In the final analysis, however, the change is well worth the new feelings of positive self-worth and satisfaction acquired by all those involved, for, as Branden, (1987) stated, "I cannot think of a single psychological difficulty that is not traceable to poor self-esteem." A positive change in self esteem, therefore, has many benefits.

REFERENCES

Ablon, S. (1982, Dec.). Seminar in self esteem development and sustenance. Boston: Harvard Medical School.

Babensee, B. (1979). *Adjustment counseling with children of divorced parents.* Unpublished doctoral dissertation, College of William and Mary, Williamsburg, VA.

Berenson, B., Mitchell, E., & Laney, R. (1968). Level of therapist functioning, types of confrontation, and type of patient. *Journal of Clinical Psychology, 24* (1), 111-115.

Berne, E. (1964). *Games people play.* New York: Grove Press.

Branden, N. (1987). *How to Raise your Self-esteem.* New York: Bantam Books.

Buber, M. (1958). *I and thou* (R. G. Smith, Trans.). New York: Charles Scribner's Sons.

Canfield, J. (1986). *Self-esteem in the Classroom.* Pacific Palisades, CA: Self Esteem Seminars.

Clarke, J. (1983). *Ouch, that hurts!—A handbook for people who hate criticism.* Plymouth MN: Daisey Press.

Clarke, J. & Gesme, C. (1988). *Affirmation ovals.* Plymouth, MN: Daisey Press.

Eisenberg, S. (1979). Understanding and building self esteem. In S. Eisenberg & L. Patterson (Eds.), *Helping clients with special concerns.* Chicago: Rand McNally.

Festinger, L. A. (1957). *A theory of cognitive dissonance.* New York: Row, Peterson.

Gestalt Institute of Cleveland Post Graduate Training Program. (1979). Lecture: Cycle of Experience. Cleveland, OH.

Helmstetter, S. (1986). *What to say when you talk to your self.* New York: Pocket Books.

Herrmann, N. (1988). *The creative brain.* Lake Lure, NC: Brain Books.

Lazarus, A. (1977). *In the mind's eye: The power of imagry for personal enrichment.* New York: Rawson.

Morran, D. K., & Stockton, R. (1980, May). Effect of self-concept on group member reception of positive and negative feedback. *Journal of Counseling Psychology, 27* (3), 260-267.

Palmer, P. (1977). *The mouse, the monster, and me.* San Luis Obispo, CA: Impact Publishers.

Rogers, C. (1951). *Client-centered therapy.* Boston: Houghton-Mifflin.

Rogers, C. (1961). *On becoming a person.* Boston: Houghton-Mifflin.

Satir, V. (1978). *Your many faces.* Millbrae, CA: Celestial Arts.

Satir, V. (1981, August). Presentation at Avanta Process Community, Park City, UT.

Satir, V. (1988). *The new peoplemaking.* Moutain View, CA: Science and Behavior Books.

Simon, S. (1978). *Negative criticism and what you can do about it. . .* Leverett, MA: Author.

Stevens, J. O. (1971). *Awareness: Exploring, experimenting, experiencing.* New York: Bantam.

Van Buskirk, D. (1983). Clinical illustrations of a concept of the regulation of self esteem. In J. Mack and S. Ablon (Eds.), *The development and sustenance of self esteem in childhood.* New York: International Universities Press.

Williams, C. (1979). *Nurse therapist high empathy and nurse therapist low empathy during therapeutic—Group work as factors in changing the self-concept of the institutionalized aged.* Unpublished doctoral dissertation, Catholic University of America, Washington, DC.

Wycoff, H. (1977). *Solving women's problems.* New York: Grove .

Yamamoto, K. (1972). *The child and his image.* Boston: Houghton Mifflin.

Zimmerman, W. (1980). *Effects of short-term group counseling on gifted elementary students.* Unpublished doctoral dissertation, Brigham Young University, UT.

CHAPTER 7

TECHNIQUES FOR ENHANCING SELF ESTEEM OF CHILDREN AND ADULTS

Techniques and activities are organized according to the four phases of intervention previously discussed: Identity, Strengths and Weaknesses, Nurturance, and Maintenance. Most of these techniques can be used with both children and adults with some adaptation, and are, in most cases, appropriate for individual or group approaches. An introduction to each technique and/or activity reviews the highlights of the basic concept of each.

Techniques which may help one define identity are explored.

PHASE I: IDENTITY TECHNIQUES AND ACTIVITIES

Many people have only partial awareness of their many facets. The following activities help to broaden that awareness so that the individual can identify specific strong and weak areas.

ACTIVITY 7.1   SELF-PORTRAIT

Introduction

This activity focuses on Area I of the Johari Window—the Open area.

Time Required

45 minutes to 1 hour

Participants

Children and adults

Setting

Office or classroom

Materials

Clay
Pastels
Water colors
Crayons
Charcoal

Procedure

Allow the person to choose the type of art media in which he/she prefers to work: pastels, watercolors, clay, crayons, charcoal. The person then meditates for a few moments, getting in touch with self.

After meditating, the person tears off a sheet of paper (length individually determined) from a large roll of paper (unless person is working in clay, in which case he/she takes as much clay as wanted). It must be large enough to represent self adequately.

Individuals are then instructed to use the media they have selected to express how they see themselves. Do not be concerned with the **product** but rather attend to your **process** and concentrate on **expressing** how you see yourself. Express how you present yourself to the world and how you feel about your physical/image. Use colors, forms, line, contrast, and so forth to make your representation.

Process in first person present tense. "My outer layer is yellow—bright and cheery, lighting up all around me. But just beneath any surface, I am red and raw . . . and so forth."

Make note of the sequence of additions you made to your portrait.

Are any themes evident? How do you feel about your portrait? Do any similarities exist among the portraits? What did you learn or relearn about yourself?

Outcome

The person gains a better self-portrait.

ACTIVITY 7.2   THE MEETING

Introduction

This guided fantasy helps one to become more acquainted with symbolic representations of self-estimates.

Time Required

30 minutes

Participants

Children and adults

Setting

Office or classroom

Materials

None

Procedure

In this activity comfort is essential. Relax in the way that feels best to you. Slowly become aware of the various parts of your body, each one in its turn, relaxing one and then going on to the next . . . first your toes; then the foot with its arch, instep, ball, heel, ankle . . . let go of all effort. Rest the legs, hands, arms, shoulders, abdomen, chest, throat, facial muscles, and the eyes . . . let go . . .

Once your body is relaxed, your mind is ready to concentrate. Focus your mind on an object as simply and quietly as you would on a flower or a burning candle. Become absorbed in it. Don't pick it apart but see it in such a way that you can see all its detail even with your eyes closed.

Close your eyes now. I want you to go now to a place you remember having enjoyed and you would like to enjoy again. Go there now. It's twilight and the mist hides the landscape. As you start out with each step, count slowly from 10 to 0. With each step, the mist will lift. You will begin to take in the joy of your surroundings. With each breath, you take in the warmth and good feelings around you, which, like after a day of good exercise, gently lulls you into a deep dreamy sleep. And in this dream four animals will appear. You will spend time getting to know each of these four very different animals and you will watch how they interact together. Take 5 minutes to do this.

Make sure you take time to talk with **each.** Each animal may represent a different side of yourself.

Outcomes

The person is encouraged to share what they discovered and to process what meaning it might have for them. Various self-estimates are usually discovered through this imagery.

———

ACTIVITY 7.3   YOU, THE WRITER

Introduction

This activity is helpful in identifying themes through life and how varying sources of self esteem reappear.

Time Required

30 minutes

Participants

Children and adults

Setting

Classroom or office for individual or group setting

Materials

None

Procedure

You are asked to write a book on your life. Spend a few minutes meditating about your life. What might be the theme of your book? Now give your book a title.

Form small groups and share your theme and title and why you chose these and process this information by yourself.

Take some time to ask questions. What did you learn from this?

Outcome

The participant usually learns more about the various sources of self esteem and how they fit together to form an identity.

───

ACTIVITY 7.4 ROBOT

Introduction

This is an exciting technique for children as well as adults. The activity necessitates being done with a partner. The helper and the client could do this together or it could be done in dyads or groups.

Time Required

20 minutes

Participants

Children and adults

Setting

Office or classroom in dyadic grouping

Materials

None

Procedure

Pick a partner and decide who will be robot first. Robot maintains an unemotional, unresponsive nonexpression and pivots, turning away from and then turning back toward his/her partner. Whenever the Robot turns toward partner, he/she asks mechanically with his/her robot voice, "WHO ARE YOU?" and then waits for partner's simple response. The partner responds with a word or a phrase, a metaphor, an image . . . whatever first comes to his/her mind, without censoring, without evaluating, without trying to grasp the meaning—just let the image, the feeling, the thought, whatever voice you hear, speak its message through you. Do this now for five minutes.

Discuss your feelings. What did you learn about yourself? Were there any themes in your responses?

Outcome

Enables revelation of feelings.

_____

ACTIVITY 7.5
SELF ESTEEM DISCLOSURE WHEEL

Introduction

This activity helps participants to focus on what they know about themselves and encourages people to share with others.

Time Required

30 to 45 minutes

Participants

Age 9 or older

Setting

Office or classroom large enough for a group

Materials

None

Procedure

Group forms two concentric circles with the 8 chairs in the inner circle facing 8 chairs in the outer circle. Topics are given for discussion. After 2 minutes, the inner circle moves one seat to the left and works with a different partner and a new topic.

Possible Topics

1. Something I do very well
2. A way I'm creative
3. A person who totally accepts me
4. How I react to criticism
5. A place I feel very relaxed
6. An award I received
7. A goal I'm striving for

8. Something people appreciate about me
9. A time I felt very good about myself
10. A risk I recently took
11. A high point in my life
12. A favorite activity
13. Someone on whom I have a big impact
14. A time I felt bad about myself
15. A vacation I especially enjoyed

Outcome

Increases awareness about self.

ACTIVITY 7.6   EULOGY

Introduction

This activity helps participants to chart the current course of their lives and to determine if they want to make any changes.

Time Required

30 minutes

Participants

Ages 9 and older

Setting

Individual or group setting; classroom or office

Materials

None

Procedure

(Eulogy is the praise of someone, spoken or written)

If I were to continue my life on its present course, my eulogy might read:

If I were to actualize my dreams for myself, my eulogy might read:

Each person is invited to write two brief eulogies (each under 50 words) to be delivered at his/her funeral. Choose who you'd want to deliver each of the two versions and state why you chose this person.

Outcome

Increases insight about self-identity and future identity.

ACTIVITY 7.7   THREE BOXES

Introduction

The purpose of this activity is to provide insight about one's identity.

Time Required

20 to 40 minutes

Participants

Individual or group, children or adults

Procedure

Imagine three boxes in front of you. Each one will nest in the other such that you have in front of you a picture of the biggest box, the next largest, and the smallest.

In each box imagine an object. Any object will do. Think of the first thing which comes to your mind. You could draw a picture of each box and/or the object in each. Give each object a voice: "I feel ...", "I am ...."

The largest box is often representative of the way in which one relates to the environment the exterior facade. The middle size box frequently is representative of the types of defense mechanisms one uses. The smallest box often is symbolic of the inner self, the true self. Think of what each symbol means to you. Does it tell you things about your own identity? If you are in a group ask others about their views of your boxes. Think about your feelings as you process this activity. How could your inner self become less hidden? How many facades do you have? When is it appropriate to let this inner self out? With whom would it be appropriate to reveal this case self?

Outcome

Increases awareness of different aspect of self.

Note: This activity is adopted from *Psychotherapy Through Imagery* by Joseph Shorr, 1983.

ACTIVITY 7.8   OBJECT TALK

Introduction

Often individuals can learn about their identity through indirect ways. This activity reveals many different aspects of self.

Time Required

15 to 30 minutes

Participants

Individual or group, children or adults

Procedure

Discuss the idea of giving objects a voice. Suppose an object around you could talk; what would it say about you? Choose several of the following objects and tell what each would say about you:

toothbrush	school bus	coat
shoes	closet	comb or brush
pen or pencil	dresser	chair
bed	television	ring
car (bicycle)	radio	hair
soap	desk	lamp

Participants could share the object talk with others to receive increased feedback. If children are the participants, they could draw pictures of these objects talking, similar to cartoon pictures.

Outcome

Individuals will learn about different aspects of themselves (self estimates) in a nonthreatening manner.

———

PHASE II: STRENGTHS AND WEAKNESSES TECHNIQUES AND ACTIVITIES

Everybody has both strengths and weaknesses. People need to develop a full awareness of what strengths they possess so they can use them as a base from which to explore the side they label as weakness. These activities also try to help people determine how to transform weaknesses into strengths.

———

ACTIVITY 7.9   HOW NOT TO BE, HOW TO BE

Introduction

*This activity emphasizes that people often develop a highly detailed picture of how **not** to be. The emphasis in Western culture is on the negative—"don't do this," "don't be that way," and so on.*

Time Required

30 minutes

Participants

Adolescents and adults; any number

Setting

Classroom

Materials

Discussion questions, paper, writing instrument

Procedure

Participants are given two pieces of paper and ten minutes to write on one piece of paper everything they can remember they were told **not to be** and on the other piece of paper everything they can remember they were told by others **how to be**. After ten minutes participants are asked to compare their lists of "How Not to Be" and "How to Be." They are then asked to share some items from their lists in groups of 6 to 8 and discuss the following questions:

1. What are some of the ways you have been taught that you're not supposed to be?

   Don't be. . . .
   Never. . . .

2. Do you dwell on your negatives? What messages did your parents give you about your mistakes?

3. In what ways do you emphasize your successes and achievements? How were you rewarded for these as a child? As an adult?

4. *Do you spend as much energy on your successes as you do on your failures?*

5. *What have you learned from this activity?*

Outcomes

Increases awareness of negativity in our culture, our families, and ourselves and shifts to greater attention on more positive aspects.

ACTIVITY 7.10
RESENTMENTS AND APPRECIATIONS

Introduction

This activity allows participants to sort through their negative feelings about a person and also to identify what they are getting out of that resentment.

Time Required

45 minutes

Participants

Any number of adults or adolescents

Setting

Classroom or office

Materials

Paper and pens

Procedure

Think of someone you really resent—someone who annoys and disturbs you, or someone with whom you have some difficulty. Imagine that this person is in front of you, facing you, and looking at you. Visualize this person in detail. What is he/she wearing? . . . Now express your resentments directly to this person: "Bob, I resent—" Be very specific, and say exactly what you resent about this person. Try to get the feel of actually communicating with him/her. Take some time and express a long list of resentments to this person. . . .

Now go through this same list of resentments and cross out the word resent and substitute the word appreciate and say this to the person. Pause after you have said it, as if you were trying on a shirt for size. Notice how you feel as you say the sentence, and see if any realization comes (sic) to you. For instance, if my resentment is "I resent your weakness, because I have to do things for you," when I go back I might say, "I appreciate your weakness; it makes me feel strong and capable in comparison." [Be careful with this part. You're going to have to think about what you're getting out of that resentment. Do not just replace the word "resent" with "appreciate." Take it a step further.] Take a few minutes to do this and see if you can discover some appreciation of what you resent. Go ahead . . . . (Stevens, 1971, pp. 168-69)

Record your fantasy—appreciations and resentments.

What did you learn from this? Discuss at least three learnings in groups of 3 to 4.

Outcomes

Uncovers resentments and aids in discovery of what one can learn about oneself from those resentments.

Note. From *Awareness: Exploring, Experimenting, Experiencing* (pp. 168-169) by J. O. Stevens, 1971. New York: Bantam. Copyright 1971 by J. O. Stevens. Reprinted by permission.

ACTIVITY 7.11   STRENGTH EXPRESSION THROUGH ART

Introduction

This activity encourages people to focus on and exper-ience their good parts, parts of themselves they fully appreciate.

Time Required

60 minutes

Participants

Any number; adolescents and adults

Setting

Group room, office, or classroom

Materials

Paper and art media

Procedure

Place a big sheet of paper in front of you. Get in touch with the feelings you would have throughout your whole being if you felt **really good about yourself**—See an image of that feeling. (This is like the difference between watching a film of yourself on a roller coaster and feeling yourself actually on the roller coaster, flying down those slopes.)

Now express that feeling inside of you on this paper using any media and/or sounds and movements you wish. Be as abstract as you like. Use color, form, contrast, movement, and so on to capture the feeling.

Form groups of 3 or 4. Share and discuss.

Outcome

People will be able to get closer in touch with kinesthetic, auditory, and visual expressions of self-respect and self-love.

ACTIVITY 7.12 BOASTING CONTRACT

Introduction

Participants by doing this activity will be better able to make contract to announce their strengths and accomplishments to others. External and internal recognition of behavior strengthens their self esteem.

Time Required

15 to 20 minutes

Participants

Any number; adolescents and adults

Setting

Classroom or office

Materials

Paper and pen

Procedure

Make a contract to boast...

I agree to boast to _____ (number) people over the course of the next _____ (number) days about some of my current successes.

Signed
Date
Witness

Report to a friend/partner about what that experience was like—how you felt and other people's reactions.

Outcome

Increases the permission for self-boasting to expand the feeling of strength.

ACTIVITY 7.13   SIGNIFICANT OTHERS

Introduction

This activity helps one to understand the positive qualities and negative aspects of self.

Participants

Individual or group, children 8 and older or adults

Procedure

Ask the participant(s) to make a list of five individuals, past or present, living or deceased, real or imaginary whom they admire. After listing the five persons ask the participant(s) to describe the qualities each of these possess which causes the participant to admire them.

Do the same procedure for five people, past or present, living or deceased, real or imaginary, whom the participant greatly dislikes. Make a list of characteristics each of these people has which causes the participant to dislike him/her.

The positive qualities often represent the qualities one would like to have or already has (ideal self versus real self). The more one has these qualities, the more likely he/she is to feel good about self. The fewer of these qualities one has, the less positively one is to think of self.

If one has many of the negative qualities, likely he/she feels low self esteem. If one does not have these negative qualities, likely he/she would feel low self esteem if these characteristics emerged in the future.

If a group is doing this activity, each person could choose others in the group to represent or role play each significant other. Each person could then review their list and try to reorganize and/or own this quality in oneself.

Outcomes

Individuals begin to recognize both strengths and weaknesses of themselves based on their own value system. This activity also forecasts for oneself what one needs to do to continue to feel good about self and what one has to avoid in order to have positive self-esteem.

_____

ACTIVITY 7.14   JUST SAY, "YES"

Introduction

Often people have difficulty accepting positive feedback. This activity represents a stepwise progression to internalizing positive feedback.

Participants

Individual or group, children or adults

Procedure

Ask the participant to discuss his/her reaction to receiving positive feedback. Then suggest that the individual just say nothing after receiving such feedback instead of rejecting the feedback and/or rationalizing it away. A second step is to just say "thank you" after hearing the feedback. The third step involves accepting the feedback and then addressing the statement, "I couldn't agree with you more." Step four involves accepting the feedback, saying, "I couldn't agree with you more." and saying, "Tell me more." Step five asks the participant receiving the feedback to say, "Thank you. I couldn't agree   with you more and I also _____ (something additional which is positive about the person)."

If in a group, participants could practice doing rounds of these steps giving each other positive feedback and responding appropriately according to step.

Participants can practice these responses in their day to day environments until they become more comfortable with accepting compliments.

Outcome

Individuals will become more comfortable with themselves when receiving positive feedback.

ACTIVITY 7.15   CRITICISM CLUES

Introduction

In learning how to filter feedback often a helpful procedure is to understand the difference between constructive and destructive feedback. This is just one such activity which can help to achieve this goal.

Participants

Individual or group, children or adults

Procedure

Think about the times when you have sent or felt like sending destructive feedback. What were the circumstances? List as many as you can. The following are examples:

1. When I am tired.
2. When I am ill.
3. When you are not listening to me.
4. When I am scared.
5. When I think you won't agree with me.
6. When someone else just put me down.
7. When I'm upset about something else.

Often circumstances exist during which others give you destructive feedback. Think about what might be behind the criticism others give you. Try to become less impulsive in accepting it. Imagine a screen in front of you. Let in that feedback which is true of you. Do not accept feedback which might be given under the circumstances listed above.

Outcomes

Increases awareness of others' motivation for delivery of feedback and helps one to discuss what information is true about self.

ACTIVITY 7.16   SELF SABOTAGE

Introduction

By using sentence stems one can introspect to discover ways which one puts self down, resulting in self weaknesses.

Participants

Individual or group, Junior High School or older, adults

Procedure

Ask each person to orally respond or to respond in writing to the following sentence stems:

One of the ways I sometimes contribute to my own frustration is

_____

_____

One of the ways I sometimes make it difficult for people to give me what I want is

_____

_____

One of the ways I sometimes obstruct my own success is

_____

_____

If I were to take full responsibility for getting what I want

_____

_____

When I see myself making mistakes

_____

_____

Ask participants to give at least eight responses to each stem. By stretching for responses individuals access hidden messages about themselves.

Outcome

One gains a deeper understanding of self weaknesses through introspecting about these themes.

Note: These stems are from To See What I See and Know What I Know by Nathaniel Branden, 1986, Bantam Books.

PHASE III:
NURTURANCE TECHNIQUES AND ACTIVITIES

The nurturance phase involves two basic tasks: learning how to ask for and receive feedback from others and learning how to give feedback to others and to self. Nurturance can be given by both verbal and nonverbal means.

ACTIVITY 7.17   NURTURING RELATIONSHIPS

Introduction

Participants are encouraged to examine how they can positively influence a younger person. The activity puts people in touch with their personal power as a Nurturer.

Time Required

20 minutes

Participants

Any number; adolescents and adults

Setting

Office or classroom

Materials

None

Procedure

Form dyads.

Think of a person in your life who nurtured you, cared for you, gave you a lot of affection and esteem: neighbor, aunt, grandmother, teacher, someone other than a parent. Imagine a specific scene where you felt his/her positive influence on you.

Now, think of someone over whom you have the potential for such influence; someone who looks to you for guidance and love. Imagine a scene where you are a nurturing agent for this person.

Share with your partner your thoughts about the power people have to influence the lives of others, to help others feel better about themselves.

Make a contract to try to positively influence a younger person.

Discuss results with partner.

Outcomes

Enhances people's awareness of and use of their personal power.

Note. Activity is original. Idea initiated by Elkins (1977).

———

ACTIVITY 7.18
NURTURING PARTNER EXCHANGE

Introduction

This exchange creates the possibility for even greater closeness and nurturance between two people in an existing relationship.

Time Required

15 to 30 minutes for homework;
20 to 30 minutes for discussion

Participants

Any number; adolescents and adults

Setting

Group room or office

Materials

None

Procedure

Participants form dyads with a person they have known for some time and review the impact each has had upon the other.

Exchange feelings and thoughts on the following:

> what I give to you,
> what I mean to you,
> what I teach you,
> how I am special to you,
> perceptions of your most special moments together, and recount the positive changes your relationship has gone through.

In groups of 4 to 6 discuss the foregoing experience.

Outcome

Increases one's ability to nurture another

ACTIVITY 7.19 HOMEWORK: EXPECTATIONS AND APPRECIATIONS

Introduction

This activity provides an opportunity for participants to surface their expectations and appreciations with a significant other thereby providing an opportunity for greater closeness.

Time Required

30 minutes of homework;
30 minutes of discussion

Participants

Any number; adolescents or adults

Setting

Office or classroom

Materials

None

Procedure

Choose someone with whom you are involved in an ongoing relationship (ex-spouse, lover, friend, child, parent, and so forth). Use a tape recorder.

Sit face-to-face and exchange expectations for a few minutes. "I expect you to _____ (**Refer to specific behaviors**)." Spend approximately 10 minutes on this section. Include financial, social, personal, physical, and so forth areas. Include the ethics of your relationship. **Do not respond to each other's expectations.**

Quietly, reflect on your partner's expectations of you.

Tell your partner what you have heard those expectations to be. Do not discuss or argue about them. Just be sure you heard each other—you must have agreement on that before anything else is possible.

Take time to clear up any misunderstandings.

After expectations are clearly understood, take some time to respond to these expectations.

Ask the questions **am** I

willing to meet expectations?
reluctant to meet expectations?
unwilling to meet expectations?

Do not whine, blame, rationalize, deny, or judge.

After completing the procedure on expectations, prioritize those expectations you placed on your partner. Which are the most important?

What happened? How did you feel? How was this a different sort of interchange for you? Did you clarify your relationship any? In what ways did you try to evade your partner's expectations or impose your expectations?

Appreciations?

Continue sitting face-to-face and exchange appreciations—"I appreciate _____ ."
Use a tape recorder.

Refer to **specific** behaviors, attitudes, physical qualities, ways of being, ways of relating, and so forth.

Do this activity about **10 minutes.**

Tell your partner what you heard those appreciations to be. Be sure you **heard** all of them.

Quietly reflect on your partner's appreciations. How far did you let them in? How much impact did they have on you? Did you discount or deflect any? Let them in now. Share with your partner.

What did you learn from this activity? How do you plan to use these learnings?

In therapy or in class in groups of 5 or 6 discuss what you learned from this experience.

Outcomes

Causes surfacing of expectations, enhances communication, and may result in greater closeness.

ACTIVITY 7.20 SELF-LOVE

Introduction

This activity puts people in touch with the part of themselves that is capable of providing nurturance to themselves. The second one-half of the activity provides an opportunity for another to join in and play the role of nurturer, saying and doing all the behaviors the person desires.

Time Required

40 minutes

Participants

Any number; adults

Setting

Carpeted office, group room, or classroom

Materials

Crayons and paper

Procedure

First practice **relaxation.** *Fantasy—go in your mind's eye to a beautiful place. Nurturing parent visits—this forever-friend can be whomever you wish . . . What does your friend look like? How does your friend move? While in your fantasy say unconditional loving and supportive things. Say good-byes.*

Next take a crayon and on one side of a large sheet of paper, write words or phrases that describe what you would like **Nurturing Parent to be like:** *loves me, holds me, kind and gentle, always there, soft, warm, and so forth.*

Then on the other side of the paper write what you would like Nurturing Parent to say to you—"I love you, you're beautiful," and so forth.

Now locate a friend with whom you can practice. Then say messages to each other while the one holds the other on his/her lap or puts his/her arm around the other or cuddles him/her. Person being nurtured closes eyes. Let words soak in. Keep repeating.

After completing the practice, process experience with your partner.

Outcome

Increases the experience of self-love and deep love from another person.

Note. Activity is original. Idea initiated by Wycoff (1977).

ACTIVITY 7.21   WISHING WELL

Introduction

Many people cut off their wishes even before they reach total awareness. "I can't have that" is the familiar internal response which kills a wish before it is expressed. This activity supports people to formulate and express their wishes. These wishes are then immediately fulfilled.

Time Required

1 to 2 hours

Participants

Group of 6 to 12; all ages

Setting

Carpeted group room or classroom

Materials

None

Procedure

One person volunteers at a time.

He/she states three wishes that he/she wants fulfilled during a 15 minute span of time. Be as specific as you can so you get exactly what you want. Then:

1. Describe your process of determining your wishes.

2. How difficult was it for you to ask for and receive your wishes?

3. How can you apply this in your life?

Outcome

Increases one's willingness to wish and dream, hope, and go after what he/she wants.

ACTIVITY 7.22   THE BOOK OF ME

Introduction

This activity allows participants an opportunity to get in touch with their nurturing energies, to recognize their abilities, and to use their power to learn from every experience and to influence each day of their lives.

Time Required

45 minutes

Participants

Any number; adolescents and adults

Setting

Carpeted room

Materials

*Soft music (Example, Steven Halpern's **EVENTIDE**)*

Procedure

Get yourself ready by centering yourself on your chairs and feeling the support of your feet, your bottom, and your back. Maybe you could think of this as friendly contact between the back of your chair, the floor, the seat of your chair, and the rest of your body, as if you are one unit. Then, let your eyes gently close. Let yourself be aware of how easily and quickly your eyelids did your bidding. You just said the words and your eyelids followed. Maybe you could become aware that all the rest of your body could just as gently and easily follow your wishes in awareness. So, as your eyelids are closed, your eyelids act as shades helping you keep your attention within. And, now as your eyes are closed, let yourself come in touch with your breathing. You breathe all the time, but now you are conscious of the air coming into your body and filling all your body with its nurturing aspects. As you take in your breath and it fills in your body, perhaps you also can be in touch with any little tightness or tensions in your body and let them flow out on an outgoing breath until your body feels comfortably relaxed. Now, let yourself come in touch with the force of energy that comes from the heavens, coming down through your head and into your body, the energy of inspiration, intuition, imagination, your concentration with the cosmos. Feel this true energy moving, blending, and creating yet a third energy, positive, growth-producing, beneficial, and nurturing. Feel that ever moving. Feel it flowing through your body and out through your arms. If others were at the other end of your arms, your energy could flow with them and they with you. And, again, let yourself be in touch with your breathing, and perhaps this time, feeling even more the breath as it comes in to fill your body, your body which is alert, yet relaxing, supported, yet comfortable. Then, let yourself go to that place deep inside yourself where you keep the miracle called you, the treasure, the only one of its kind, **YOU**. Give yourself a message of appreciation for your ability to see, to hear, to move, to feel, to think, to touch, to smell and taste, to choose, to let go of that which no longer fits. Be in touch with the things that you use at the present that fit well for you, and take a moment to honor their usefulness to you at this time. Give yourself appreciation for your courage and your initiative to invent that which you need and to reach out for that which you now need. You can give yourself a message to appreciate your ability to do this sorting daily. And, again, be in touch with your breathing. Let yourself come in touch with a memory, of a time when you felt completely happy, full of feelings of well being, wherever that was, in a warm place, the seashore, the mountains, the plains, wherever that was. Let yourself go back in memory to that place now, to feel the feeling you felt then. As you move back to that place, let yourself notice anew, the colors, the people if there are any, the environment, the sands and the water, the wind and the sun. Just be in touch with those feelings and your feelings of well being. Let yourself relax into your deep feelings and give yourself a mental message that at any time you need comfort for yourself you can return to this place. It's only a journey in your mind, to refresh you, to remind you that you have many parts and many experiences.

Today, as you're here, you've probably been here many times before, but today somewhere about, maybe over on the left side, you notice something that you never saw before. It's a door, you look at it and it welcomes you to step toward it. As you approach it and put your hand on the knob, there's a warm feeling in that knob and another message of invitation to open it. You don't know what's on the other side, but it feels good to think of the possibilities. As you open that door, you see a room furnished in your favorite color, built with your favorite form, lighted in your favorite light, with all your favorite plants and pictures about. The floor is heavily carpeted, but as you step your foot on it, the carpet seems to sing with your presence. As you look around, you notice that there are many shelves filled with books. As you are in the wonder and the beauty of the light, the form, the color, there is a book on the shelf that seems to stand out from all the rest. You feel drawn to that book and as you move toward that book you notice that it's bound beautifully in your favorite leather and on the back of it your name is written in just the way you like it. The book seems to ask you to take it off of the shelf and open it, and as you do you look in the pages and you see that it starts with your birthday on this plane. There are many pages that are now full, full of the experiences of your life, of the joys, of the pleasures, the struggles as you have moved from that time long ago till now. This is a big book, it's light, however, and only about a quarter of it is filled with your experiences. You come to the page, the first page that is empty and on the top of it, it is written, "Today." You immediately know that on this page and all the following pages, there is time to write out your new experiences. The page is not entirely clear, for at the bottom in a footnote it is written, "Reading the foregoing pages is the essence of your learning. All of it can be used for your growing. As you read this, the pages in the book that are yesterday's writings seem to be filled with a curious light and through these pages you see the words 'whatever you do is your choice.'" You feel good and you decide this morning to write something on your new day. You take the book to a comfortable place to sit, a chair that's made exactly for you and fits you beautifully. You sit and write, comfortably, feeling good. Somehow, your hand writes without effort and as you write you feel a sense of completeness for this time, knowing that you can come back here any time and write more. You lay your pen down and gently and lovingly close this book for you know you will leave this place for now, very soon. You lovingly put the book back on the shelf. Somehow at this moment it is really clear to you that everything before this time in your life is something useful for you to learn, to love with, to have joy with for the coming days. You turn, leaving the room gently, perhaps walking a little more lightly, moving out toward the door, closing it, stepping out into this place you have known so well, where you have felt this great comfort and love for yourself, for other beings in the world. You move gently back, bringing those good feelings with you as come slowly to the here and now, going back to that miracle place inside yourself, the treasure that is you, feeling again your breathing, your body relax, reminding yourself of the sources of energy from the center of the earth and from the cosmos, and from your connections with each other, and you prepare yourself for the opportunity of a new day. As you come now fully here, aware of your opportunities, your choices, your awareness to taste whatever is there and swallow only that which fits, you feel ready. And, as you gently now open your eyes, if there are any sounds or movement that would like to come, let them. (Satir, 1981)

Share in groups of 3 or 4.

Outcomes

Increases one's awareness of choice of life and increases self-nurturance.

Note. From Presentation at Avanta Process Community by V. Satir, 1981, August, Park City, UT. Printed by permission.

ACTIVITY 7.23   SELF-FORGIVENESS

Introduction

Oftentimes it's hard for people to forgive themselves for real or imagined wrongs. This activity encourages you to examine events over which you feel guilt or shame and to try to move towards self-forgiveness. It is a **self-nurturance activity.**

Time Required

30 minutes

Participants

Any number: adolescents, adults

Setting

Classroom or office

Materials

Paper, pencil

Procedure

Think of an event in the past over which you feel bad about yourself.

Record the event

What was happening?
Where were you?
Who was there?
How did you feel? What feeling was underneath?
What were you needing?
What were you thinking?
What past pain might have influenced your behavior?

We all do the best we can with what resources we have at the moment. Can you accept yourself back then? Accepting yourself is different from condoning your behavior.

Imagine the nurturing part of you talking to the younger you. What would he/she say? RECORD THE MESSAGE.

What could you do to make amends and let go of your mistake? RECORD THE AMENDS.

Outcome

Achieves greater internal peace for individual through self-acceptance.

_____

ACTIVITY 7.24   THE WORTHY YOU

Introduction

At one time in everyone's life he/she was pure. At the very least, all of us were born innocent, devoid of low self esteem. This activity allows you to get in touch with that younger, worthy you and encourage you to nurture that part of yourself.

Time Required

30 minutes

Participants

Any number: children, adolescents, adults

Setting

Classroom or office

Materials

Paper, crayons, soft music

Procedure

Draw a picture of yourself at whatever age you consider yourself to have been most pure and worthy of love. Use crayons for this drawing. Place yourself in a safe, comfortable environment. Surround the entire area with a golden light of protection.

Send the child messages of his/her inherent goodness, spontaneity, and creativity. Tell the child anything he/she needs to hear. Be generous and anticipate any needs the child might have. Be sure to give the child such developmental affirmations as (Clarke, 1983) the following:

> "I'm glad you're here."
> "I'm glad you are a boy." or "I'm glad you are a girl."
> "You're needs are okay."
> "You don't have to hurry."

(Note: See Chapter 2 for other ideas)

256   Enhancing Self Esteem

Record on your drawing all the messages you give to the child.

Share your drawing and messages in a small group of four.

Pair up with someone in your foursome. Partner A identifies with the child in his/her drawing and partner B delivers the messages. Reverse roles. Discuss your feelings with your partner and then in foursome which messages were hardest to take in? Share in foursome.

Contract with your small group to repeat the messages you most need to hear over the months ahead. Think of other people in your environment whom you could also ask to remind you of these messages. Make a list of these people and contract to ask them. Choose people from various settings: family, school, church, work, and other organizations.

Outcome

Heightens self-love towards the inner child.

PHASE IV:
MAINTENANCE TECHNIQUES AND ACTIVITIES

The following techniques focus on how to maintain positive self esteem over time. The self-regulation effects of self esteem are clearly evident in the activities.

ACTIVITY 7.25
IMAGINING ALTERNATIVE ENDINGS

Introduction

This activity helps both children and adults to do more appropriate risk taking.

Time Required

20 minutes a day

Participants

Age 9 and older

Setting

Home, office, or classroom

Materials

None

Procedure

People tend to use their negative imagination to scare themselves out of acting assertively. They imagine the worst thing that could possibly happen thereby creating excessive anxiety. However our imagination also can be used to reduce our fears and help us to feel more confident about ourselves.

This technique involves expanding the types of assumptions a person makes about the possible outcomes of risky behaviors.

Think of a situation in which you'd like to act assertively.

Play out the same situation in your mind with the usual very negative ending.

Now play out the scene three more times.

Once with a very positive ending
Once with a somewhat negative ending
Once with a somewhat positive ending

Discuss.

What was the situation?
With what endings did you come up?
What did you learn about yourself?

*If you had trouble imagining **yourself** achieving a positive ending, picture someone else doing so.*

Practice this with at least one situation per day. To do so will take some retraining, however the potential may well be well worth the effort. Record changes in feelings/thoughts. What did you learn?

Outcome

Helps participants involve themselves in more risk taking.

ACTIVITY 7.26   SELF-TALK

Introduction

As discussed previously, self-talk (internal dialogue) can be either helpful or harmful to self esteem depending on how logical it is. The following activity increases awareness of self-talk.

Time Required

30 minutes

Participants

Age 12 and older

Setting

Anywhere

Materials

None

Procedure

Identify the debates or wars you frequently experience in yourself. Examine each issue at stake. List each issue. How are the sides drawn for each issue? What are the stances each takes? Describe the speaker for each side. What does each look like? How does each act, move, talk, walk? What attitude does each convey? How solid does each feel? What does each say? Feel? Create a dialogue between the characters and bring the conversation to some closure. Make sure each has its say.

What did you learn from this activity? Were any characters stronger than the others? Did you notice anything special or puzzling about any characters? What is the nature of your self talk?

Outcome

Enables one to gain a better perspective of self talk and its implications.

ACTIVITY 7.27   JOURNAL

Introduction

By keeping a journal and reviewing it, one can realize growth patterns and trends in self esteem. This technique is good for children and adults.

Time Required

10 to 30 minutes a day

Participants

Age 9 and older

Setting

Quiet place

Materials

Paper and pen

Procedure

Journals can be kept in a variety of ways, people generally develop their own style. Use whatever style suits you. Try experimenting with different methods.

You could use a Blank Book for your journal. Doing so seems to make writing more attractive. It's not just a pad you're writing on, you're **writing your book!**

You can include several different topics in your book:

dreams
fantasies
secret fears and desires
letters to yourself or other people
a quote which had a special impact on you
self-portrait
childhood memories
your passage through a current conflict
important decisions or commitments you made
images
metaphors of your life issues
cycles—positive and self-defeating

The possibilities are limitless and the rewards are endless.

Outcomes

Keeping a journal is an excellent tool for self-awareness and change. It can help you to

identify patterns in your behavior and feelings;

keep in touch with what is happening with your feelings, thoughts, and actions;

understand how you are changing and how you're remaining the same;

feel important—you're thoughts, experiences, and feelings are so special that you are writing a book about them;

record awarenesses which might otherwise slip from consciousness; and

expand your self-concept.

ACTIVITY 7.28
HEROES, HEROINES, VISIONS, AND DREAMS

Introduction

Hopes and aspirations for self are embedded in people's heroes, heroines, and dreams. Hope and future visions are essential for high self esteem.

Time Required

30 minutes

Participants

Adults

Setting

Office

Materials

None

Procedure

Think back to when you were a child and later as an adolescent. Get in touch with the following:

Who were your favorite television and movie heroes and heroines? What did you admire in them?

Who in real life did you admire (teachers, ministers, aunt, uncle, grandparent, neighbor, and so forth)? For what kinds of things did you admire them?

When you were little, what did you hope to become? What dreams did you have of yourself?

What did you fantasize about as a child?

Outcomes

Develops a focus on the future and how one would like to continue developing positive self esteem.

ACTIVITY 7.29   BOUNDARIES

Introduction

The ability to define our boundaries contributes to identity formation and the ability to function well in the world. The following activity represents a beginning exploration of this concept. For further exploration of this topic see Carlock and Hagerty (1988) and Mason and Fossum (1986).

Time Required

30 minutes

Participants

Any number; adolescents, adults

Setting

Classroom or office

Materials

Paper, pencil

Procedure

Record your answers to the following questions under each category of body, value, expressive, and space.

BODY

How free are you to move your body? Express yourself physically?

Are you restrained? Free?

Are your gestures small? Large?

How aware are you of different areas of your body?

How comfortable are you in being touched or in touching others?

VALUE

List 10 values you hold dearly

Next to each write the name of the person who taught you each value.

Have you been heavily influenced by someone?

Have you ever reviewed your values? Revised them?

Are the values of any other early significant others missing from your list.

EXPRESSIVE

How free are you to express yourself verbally?

Are you talkative? Friendly?

Do you censor much of what you think?

What rules existed in your family around expression?

Could you express feelings freely? Which ones?

Were there lots of family secrets?

Did people keep confidences?

SPACE

Do you have certain spaces that you can call your own and into which you control entry? What are they? What are your rules?

Do people regularly invade your space or use your belongings without your permission?

How do your answers to the above relate to how people operated in your family of origin?

Share your responses in small groups. What conclusions can you draw? How do your responses relate to how well you take care of yourself and how well you defined who you are?

Outcomes

Expands awareness of rules around boundaries and provides opportunities for revising these.

ACTIVITY 7.30
SELF ESTEEM MAINTENANCE KIT

Introduction

Virginia Satir in Satir and Banmen (1984) put together this self esteem maintenance tool kit which contains a wishing stick, a medallion with a clear "yes" and a clear "no" on either side, a detective's hat, and the golden key.

Time Required

30 minutes

Participants

Any number: children, adolescents, adults

Setting

Classroom or office

Materials

None

Procedure

The golden key allows you to go places or try things to satisfy your curiosity. The key gives you courage to take the risks to move into the unfamiliar—alone if necessary.

What have you always wanted the courage to do?

Without dreams—small and large— our spirits die. The magic wand gives you permission to put out your wishes and keep your dreams alive. Verbalizing your dreams is the first step towards actualizing them.

What do you wish in life?

What wishes do you have regarding a significant relationship?

What about your wishes in relation to work/career?

One sign of high esteem is the ability to make clear "yeses" and clear "noes" in relation to choices in your daily life. It allows you the permission and courage to say what fits at a moment in time. Are you able to say "yes" to what you want? Do you believe you deserve to have what you want?

Can you say "no" to those things which do not fit for you at the moment? Can you do this without excessive guilt. To whom do you have trouble saying "no?"

The detective's hat enables people to observe without judging, to see and hear and to comment on those observations. Are you able to state your observations and report data without attaching values? Without judging yourself or others?

Outcome

Provides some tools helpful for self-care.

———

ACTIVITY 7.31   AFFIRMATIONS

Introduction

This activity teaches you how to begin to create your own positive reality. Daily work with affirmations will help you maintain high self esteem.

Time Required

1 hour

Participants

Any number; adolescents, adults

Setting

Classroom or office

Materials

Paper, pencil, and 3 x 5 cards

Procedures

List three specific outcomes you desire—three wishes.

Write in detail why each is important to you.

Describe how you imagine your life would be if you achieved these outcomes.

Describe how you might accomplish each.

Share your response to items 1 through 4 with a friend.

Describe the resources you possess to achieve each outcome.

Describe everything you can think of which could get in your way.

Record in Figure 7.1 your negative thoughts in Column A. Then, in Column B transform each negative into an affirmation. In Column C record your reactions to the affirmation. Keep re-writing your affirmation (Column B) and reactions (Column C) until you have exhausted everything which stands in the way of you and your goal. An example is provided in Figure 7.1.

Work with one affirmation every day. Gradually try to temporarily suspend your doubts and negative reactions. Write the affirmation on a 3 x 5 card and carry it with you. Post it on your bathroom mirror, car dashboard, or other conspicuous place as a reminder.

Outcome

Increases ability to affirm self.

———

(A) Negative thought or outcome desired	(B) Affirmation	(C) Thoughts, beliefs, feelings in response to affirmation
I'll never be able to maintain a lower weight. I have no will power. I don't like to exercise	I, Carol, now freely allow myself to be comforted by God's love, the love of family and and friends, and the joy of body movement. I am growing lighter and lighter each day.	That's not enough. I'll never be able to do that. I wish! No one will be there for me.

Figure 7.1. Example of changing negative thoughts into an affirmation.

ACTIVITY 7.32 GRATEFULNESS

One way to practice receiving is to pay attention to even the simplest, smallest thing we appreciate—a sunny day, the sound of birds chirping, a kind word from a shopkeeper, a smile from a stranger. Spend an entire day making notes of all the little things for which you are grateful. High self esteem is maintained by paying attention to the gifts all around us.

Introduction

All too infrequently do we stop and count our blessings. Yet there is so much for which we can be thankful. By highlighting how we are blessed, we make ourselves all the richer.

Time Required

Moments throughout the day

Participants

Any number; all ages

Setting

Any setting

Materials

None

Procedure

Keep a lot of your reactions and report in your group the impact of this activity.

Outcome

Directs awareness at the small, daily aspects for which we can be thankful thereby increasing joy in life.

REFERENCES

Branden, N. (1986). *To see what I see & know what I know: A guide to self-discovery.* New York: Bantam.

Carlock, J., & Hagerty, P. (1988). *Bridges to intimacy couples workbook.* Dayton, OH 45420: Peoplemaking Midwest, 1105 Watervliet Avenue.

Clarke, J. (1983). *Ouch, that hurts!* Plymouth, MA: Daisy Press.

Elkins, D. (1977). *Teaching people to love themselves.* Rochester, NY: Growth Associates.

Mason, M., & Fossum, M. (1986). *Facing shame.* New York: W.W. Norton.

Satir, V. (1981, August). Presentation at Avanta Process Community, Park City, UT.

Satir, V., & Banmen, J. (1984). *Virginia Satir verbatim.* N. Delta, B.C. Canada: Delta Psychological.

Shorr, J.E. (1983). *Psychotherapy through imagery.* New York: Thieme Medical Pub.

Stevens, J. O. (1971). *Awareness: Exploring, experimenting, experiencing.* New York: Bantam.

Wycoff, H. (1977). *Solving women's problems through awareness, action and contact.* New York: Grove.

CHAPTER 8

TRANSITIONS AND SELF ESTEEM

Management of transitions is intricately related to attitudes about self. The more positive one's self esteem, the more able is the person to cope with imposed changes of all types. Also, the more positive the self esteem, the more likely is the person to initiate transitions which result in self-expansion/self-improvement. For example, "I feel competent and confident; I do quality work; I am offered a promotion; I accept it."

RELATIONSHIP OF SELF ESTEEM
TO TRANSITIONS

The higher one's self esteem, the more able is one to cope also with "negative" transitions; that is, change which results in diminished choice. One is more flexible and better able to shift sources of esteem; self esteem deepens and does not rest so heavily on external factors. If a person is confident, he/she will remain that way regardless of external changes—unless those external changes are multiple, occur in a limited time span, or the person attaches a great deal of meaning to the changes. Such conditions may result in a temporary blow to self esteem. The higher one's self esteem, therefore, the more resilient is the person to such blows.

Likewise, however the more negative self esteem, the more likely is the person to provoke negative changes and/or take responsibility inappropriately for some negative changes. For example, "I feel bad about myself; a co-worker makes fun of me in public; I lose control and hit him; I get fired." Unless intervention occurs, self esteem may continue to plummet. People with low and/or unstable self esteem lack a certainty about themselves and often lack support in their environment. They lack the resources, internal or external, necessary for negotiating transitions adequately.

The Inevitability of Change

Everything is always moving, always changing. The sun rises, the sun sets, the earth moves, continually, imperceptively, seasons change, tide flows in, tide flows out.

This is an age of **rapid** change. But change has always been a part of human existence. Human beings have evolved through the ages. This evolvement is expressed in one's person and is expressed in one's environment.

While certain qualities and aspects of life remain somewhat constant (love, art, friends, a good play), problems of living change considerably over time. Using Maslow's (1954) hierarchy of needs (discussed in the chapter on self-concept development) as a basis for comparison, one might observe that while the major focus of Early Americans was on securing physical necessities (food, warmth, staying alive), the 1960s, 70s, and most of the 80s were, for the most part, a time of prosperity when most Americans were well fed and were struggling instead with problems in choosing how they could better their lives. During times of economic recession and depression, on the other hand, basic survival needs are threatened. Throughout history, one can note such broad swings in the nation's economic and political climate which reverberated down to the level of every individual. Wherever the nation is on the arc of that swing poses a set of dilemmas with which people must cope. Some changes seem to occur in big swings or with breathtaking speed: high inflation, high unemployment, fast moving technological changes.

Many people do not expect change. They expect the world to remain the same; always run smoothly and provide plentifully. The natural ups and downs then become major catastrophies. The downs are not anticipated and accepted as a part of life (mistakes, losses, weaknesses, sicknesses). As a consequence, people tend to be less able to "roll with the punches," less able to cope. People with low self esteem also tend to take responsibility inappropriately for some losses and/or fail to take appropriate responsibility for other losses and certain gains. They also tend to turn everything into a life or death matter. For example, "I'll just die if we have to move."

People not only are affected by their own actions and attitudes, but also are affected by external circumstances. Like a domino effect, changes at higher levels reverberate to the lowest levels. Internally generated changes as shown in Figure 8.1, on

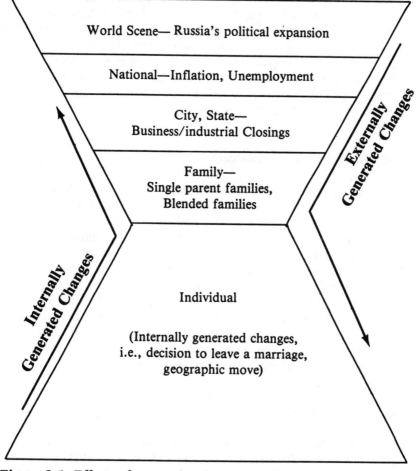

Figure 8.1. Effects of internal and external change.

the other hand, have far less dramatic effects, except at the immediately higher level. A few exceptional individuals, however, also can exert a great deal of change at higher levels.

People are continually forced to deal with situations over which they have little control. Combine the stress of change and the stress of the Puritan work ethic with a lowered capacity to cope and you will wonder why more people do not fold under the pressure. People *are* rather strong and resilient.

The fact is, however, some *are* caving in from the pressure. This is evidenced in a variety of ways: problems with depression, anxiety, psychosomatic complaints, drug abuse (particularly tranquilizers), and alcoholism to name a few. Such symptoms are signs of inadequate coping. Therefore, a crucial necessity is for people to learn better coping strategies so that they can preserve their esteem through the inevitable "ups and downs" in life. Each of these "ups and downs" are transitions with which people must cope.

Self-Estimates and Transitions

Self-estimates are important in transitions. Some individuals may, indeed, be able to identify qualities they possess or behaviors they display which generally are considered positive. However, the person possessing this quality/behavior may not value those. For example, a woman might see herself as open but only concentrate on the negative aspects of openness. Self-estimate refers to one's evaluation of thoughts, feelings, and behaviors that are all a part of self. By helping the individual to focus on the positive self-estimates and by helping the person to value more the positive manifestations of each of his/her behaviors, feelings, and thoughts, the person's strengths may then be used to aid the individual in transition.

Types of Transitions

Transitions are turning points in one's life which are either internally generated or externally induced. They involve passing from one condition, stage, or place to another and have within them dimensions of differentness. Transitions are inevitable. The process of life involves a series of transitions. These transitions mark points of growth for individuals and larger systems (i.e., families, organizations). Transitions make it necessary for people to reorganize their way of experiencing and perceiving the world (Parkes, 1971). These are times of incredible possibilities. Openings are created so that even in change which might be viewed as negative, very positive outcomes also can occur. Sometimes the road gets very bumpy and rocky and one needs to sit down and rest on one of these rocks along the way. Other times the road seems so very dark. One can easily scare self into believing that no light will ever be seen again. Painful as transitions may be at times, they are opportunities of growth.

Satir (1987) also made the point that internal transitions involve two types. The first, **automatic change** is a natural part of living. It is automatic, universal. Our hair and fingernails keep growing, our skin ages, wrinkles, and begins to sag. Then, **conscious change** involves an effort to develop a different outcome. Conscious change is always possible given the right attitude, willingness, hope, timing, circumstances, and so on.

Conscious change, according to Satir (1987) is fueled by a clear picture of **what you want,** not what you don't want. In order for a person to get in touch with what he/she wants, the impediments against realizing wants must be identified. "I can't have that," "This too much to ask for," "Girls can't do that." Many beliefs limit people and impede adaptation to change. Each turning point in one's life journey is a landmark of possibilities, a time of loss and a time of gain. If people view the next leg of their journey negatively ("Old age means I'm useless."), their spirits will wither as they relegate themselves to the back shelf of life. If they believe that they still have much to contribute, they will find creative ways to make that happen.

Some examples of those circumstances falling outside of a person's control, which necessitate change are loss of a significant other through death or divorce, loss of a job due to recession, hereditary medical problems, or forced retirement. Such transitions are hard on self esteem. They put people in touch with their powerlessness, their utter vulnerability. Even with the examples cited, however, individuals may cushion the jolt of such transitions by taking certain preventive measures when things are going well through adequate financial planning, maintaining an adequate support network, developing leisure time interests and activities, and adequate exercise and nutrition. Some control does exist. However, if a "no choice"/ unplanned-for transition occurs during an off-time, when other facets of a person's life are shaken as well, the repercussions will be magnified.

Phases of Transitions

Each passage of a transition involves three distinct phases: endings, the middle ground, and new formations (Keleman, 1979). These phases permeate the individual's life as *endings* (something ends or changes in one's life), *middle ground* (a time of disorganization), and beginning or *new formations* (time for trying out new behaviors). These phases appear in all transitions and provide a common base of experience.

Before the stage of endings, the individual is in a phase of status quo (Satir, 1987). According to Satir (1987), at this time, the individual holds a group of expectations and validations on which he/she can count. For example, "On Tuesdays, I drive 15 minutes to work in my Prelude, see several clients, and meet my women's group." These expectations and predictions are clear and repeatedly reinforced. As they are reinforced they gain power. Satir (1987), believed we then grow to believe that this is the right way for us to be and we then come to connect these expectations with our survival. According to Satir (1987), "changing is like a whole new birth; it is hard." If a young man is continually reinforced to believe "You're no good just like your father. You'll never amount to anything," re-writing this script is no easy task. Satir (1987) stated that most change is initiated in response to *threat* and only recently are people moving towards *comfort* as a motivator for change.

Endings. *Endings involve a cessation of imbeddedness in a particular way of doing things, a separating. It is an indication that some part of the person, some way of being, some circumstance has outlived its usefulness.* It usually involves the introduction of a foreign element or an intervention (Satir, 1987). Given the fact that people are continually dealing with endings, Bridges (1980), contended that most people do not handle endings very well, minimizing or catastrophizing those endings. It is a time of unbounding, withdrawing, and self-collecting where great conflict brews between staying and going. Sickness is a clue that ending is occurring—headaches, intestinal problems, heart attacks. The more energy one has invested in the pattern, the more excitation, the more an ending of that pattern poses a threat of loss of identity. According to Keleman (1979) in order to survive endings, one must confront situations in a state of emerging helplessness and resist falling back on automatic, counter--productive responses.

Bridges (1980) outlined four different aspects of endings: disengagement, disidentification, disenchantment, and disorientation. Bridges (1980) described these aspects as follows:

> **Disengagement** involves separating oneself from the context in which a person has known him/herself; one's identity is shaken (for example, a newly divorced middle aged woman might move from the home in which she and her husband resided for 30 years).

> **Disidentification** involves doing away with the outward signs of the former identity. Oftentimes people make changes yet continue to identify with their former self-image. In such cases, disidentification has not been completed. Self-perception has not caught up with changes in behavior (for example, the divorced woman described above may have a difficult time viewing herself as a free agent able now to make a wider range of choices now that she does not have to consider the impact on her spouse).

> **Disenchantment** involves the discovery that what one believed and expected is no longer real. The person discovers that a significant part of that reality was fantasy. Disenchantment also is a sign that one is entering a transition (for example, a growing feeling of dissatisfaction usually precedes a job change or career move).

Disorientation results when one's reality—one's way of orienting him/herself—has been shaken. Confusion, emptiness, and resulting fear abound. The person's sense of space and time are altered.

The person must pass through each of these four phases before the ending is complete. Incomplete endings may negatively affect self esteem.

Individual growth can become arrested between endings and the middle ground. People may refuse to go on when something ends. With such persons, giving up certain ritualized patterns feels equal to death. New interactions are inhibited, new learnings are avoided, and the growth process is slowed down, eventually leading to distress.

Middle Ground. *The middle ground, according to Keleman (1979), is a time of chaos; a period of being unformed, a no man's land, a time of feeling lost or overwhelmed.* One can easily see why this phase is often avoided. A flooding of emotion exists here, a swelling, and what evolves seems crazy, illogical, irrational. According to Bridges (1980), in old rituals, people learned to call on spirit guides to help light the way through this phase. Images and feelings are dominant, not rationality. This is the greatest time when people "hang hats on" (project onto) others. Strong, often unjustified, emotional reactions often appear. I really like (*person*) or I hate (*person*) (even though the people are really strangers). People project their familiarity from the past onto the present at such times (Satir, 1981).

Safety and trust are crucial in this stage. Therapists and other helping professionals can help provide this safety by taking charge of the process, by setting boundaries that prohibit harmful interactions, by responding honestly and congruently, and by having the ability to look ahead to anticipate needs (Satir, 1987). Satir emphasizes that this chaos period is the crack. She believed that no real change can happen until chaos appears. Superficial changes do not stick. Many therapists become frightened when clients begin to experience this chaos. Some will be tempted to medicate the client to relieve their own anxiety. This should be avoided if clinically possible. According to Satir (1987), the change agent holds total responsibility for the process in this phase. She emphasized that during the chaos stage the change agent must be

- in control of the process (creating safety and trust);

- devoid of judging;

- very creative;

- observant by the second; and

- straight talking, congruent, and loving.

The agent of change must be the clearest he/she has ever been so as not to get caught up in the chaos which would render the agent ineffective. The more flexible and unbiased the agent of change, the more he/she will be able to guide the person.

Satir (1987) warned that when the going gets tough in the chaos period, people often want to retreat to the familiar. Through the guide's centeredness experienced through eyes, touch, tone of voice, people can be helped to move forward instead of back to what is familiar. No lasting change can occur until the desire to "go back" is acknowledged and the chaos is passed.

For those going through the change, to relieve the anxiety of this period, they often want to start doing something right away. To relieve tensions, people often overeat, overwork, drink too much, become oversexed (Keleman, 1979). These types of behaviors can further diminish one's self esteem. The mature organism learns to pause, wait, inhibit impulsiveness. Many people find getting away and being alone for awhile is helpful in this phase so as to attend to their inner selves (Bridges, 1980). At other times, encouragement from friends to stay with the experience and not run may be needed. It is an in-between time—a time of discovering: how one wants to live life, the needs one wants to satisfy, how one wishes to satisfy those needs, and how one wishes to be in the world. It is a time of grasping certain truths about oneself. Bridges (1980) described this period as a time of gestation, when a new self is growing. People must learn to surrender to the emptiness. People cannot really move ahead with tasks involved in reconstruction until they acknowledge this chaos period (Satir, 1981). Satir (1981) called it a time of active patience (waiting, moving, but not always knowing what one is doing), a time when one must be able to say and think what one feels and be heard. This middle ground is a time of formlessness; a primal experience, a state of pure energy from which every new beginning develops (Bridges, 1980).

Satir (1987) asserted that people cannot move on until they have had enough experience with the new beginning. This involves forming a clear picture of the desired change and trying on that behavior so that the body has the experience of behaving differently, letting new words pass through one's mouth, and so on. Identifying the body cues which go along with both the old experience and the new behavior will help facilitate the process of change (Satir, 1987). All of this, explained Satir (1987) gives the person an experience in re-wiring. Heightened awareness facilitates the change process.

New Formations. *New formations is a period of trying out new behaviors and reinforcing the change.* Repetition and a symbol reminding oneself of the desired change can aid the person at this stage.

The period of new formations is a time of heightened experience of one's spurts of outgrowth; now a new birthing begins. During this period, commitments are made to truths learned about self. An internal alignment occurs which allows people to get in touch with their deep wants and become amazingly motivated, even overcoming difficult obstacles (Bridges, 1980). This period is a time of getting oneself ready to do something, gathering one's inner resources, and mobilizing one's images, information, and muscular patterns to form another shape (Keleman, 1979).

Often through adult transitions, people begin anew, making dramatic changes in their lives (Bridges, 1980). Gandhi, Lincoln, Roosevelt, and Walt Whitman are a few famous figures who truly turned their lives around through an adult transition.

In essence, through transitions many people begin to make their lives their own, beginning a path to their own dreams rather than rebelling against or living out someone else's. The fertile ground turned during a transition can provide a more nurturing environment for dormant seeds to grow. This growth can enhance self esteem if a person really acknowledges to him/herself and others the process of that growth. Artwork, movement, and other expressive forms are helpful in aiding people in fully taking in the experience of their growing.

Depending on how central or peripheral the change is, movement through this cycle can be either rapid or very gradual. For individuals to look at life and find out how they prevent complete endings is very important. Keleman (1979) stressed that in order to end something, people must have contact with how they are immersed in a particular pattern. Endings create separation. Many endings involve more a change of form rather than a total obliteration of connections. According to Keleman (1979), unbounding, unforming, and destructuring are part of the inescapable rhythms of life. He pointed out that to experience living as a process is to see the possibility for living and forming one's life—not as a slave or victim, but as a pioneer.

The psychological journey cannot be ignored as one moves from point "A" to point "B" (Satir, 1981). For example, with the addition of a new infant into a family, the family cannot proceed with business as usual—though people often try. The family must make room for the new person, physically and emotionally. Members must learn to deal with the inevitable losses and gains that result from such an addition and to let their feelings develop: their anger, their wish to be taken care of, whatever is there, without expecting anyone else to do something about those feelings (Satir, 1981).

Time is not the relevant factor in change, awareness is (Satir, 1981). According to Satir (1981), time only provides the opportunity.

Approaching desired change with joy and exhilaration requires completion of a number of cycles through the phases of changes until a high comfort level is reached and anxiety is minimized. Through more cycles, looking forward to change and peace with change can come.

DEVELOPMENTAL TRANSITIONS

Another group of transitions which involve changes both outside of one's control and within one's control are developmental changes. They are normal, predictable crises people experience or tasks people face in the course of their lives. Perhaps the first to explore these passages in a lively, descriptive way was Sheehy in her books, *Passages* (1976) and *Pathfinders* (1981), which very quickly became best sellers. These books as well as others (Levinson, et al, 1978), provided a map for people so that they could begin to see their current transitions in the context of a life journey. Development, according to Bridges (1980), means "unfolding" and it continues throughout life.

Bridges (1980) outlined three basic steps in life with a pivotal transition point between steps, thus two pivotal transition points:

1. dependency;

2. separateness and independence; walking on one's own two feet; and

3. suffering, deepened awareness, and disengagement.

According to Bridges (1980), a lifetime has these three natural steps, each with its characteristic style. The movement from one step to another often is not easily negotiated.

Dependency

The first step in human development is a stage, a sort of beginning, awakening of all the senses, emotions, intellectual capacities, physical capabilities. "I" and "Thou" are more one. "I'm someone else's legs, thoughts, values, and so on." The "I" is not clear. This stage is more completely discussed in Chapter 2.

Adolescence

The movement away from dependency during adolescence is characterized by such questions as "Who am I? How do I want to be? What do I want? Who should I be? How should I act? Whom should I respect? What is expected of me?" Clarke, Clemes, & Bean (1987) pointed out that the struggle with such issues dominate frequently this chaotic time in life. Adolescents are just beginning to separate from their parents, associate more with a peer group, and establish an individual identity. With the increasing freedom of this period individuals also must learn to take and handle responsibility.

Adolescence is a period with a myriad of changes: physical, emotional, social involving a movement towards more independence, identity formation, and values clarification. Numerous studies have looked at shifts in self esteem in this major transition and have reported mixed results. Longitudinal studies tend to show increases in self esteem during adolescence (Backman & O'Malley, 1983 for example) while cross sectional research tends to show either no relationship or a possible decline in esteem (Wallace & Cunningham, 1984). Wallace et al. (1984) performed a longitudinal study which showed slight increases in male self esteem in school behavior between 9 and 14 years old and gains in social esteem for girls. By age 14 girls and boys exhibit comparable levels of both social and school behavior as earlier differences level out. According to Wallace et al. (1984), 69% of the males and 68% of females scored higher on the total scale of self esteem at age 14. These authors provided convincing data which rule out possible methodological problems to explain these increases in self esteem. McCarthy and Hoge (1982) posited that increases in global esteem during adolescence may be accounted for by increased role taking, increased autonomy, and increased realism about ideal self.

Nottelmann (1987) and Cohen, Burt, and Bjorch (1987) reported early adolescence to be a relatively stable period with most young people able to effectively negotiate the transition into secondary school and adapt to higher demands. Overall, adolescents perceive their competency to increase and remain stable during this period (Nottleman, 1987; Cohen et al., 1987).

However Jaquish and Savin-Williams (1981) showed that adolescent girls (grades 7 through 9) consistently self-report lower esteem than adolescent boys although when behavioral measures are used, no differences appear. Those problems which do occur are usually the result of multiple concurrent changes (for example, significant physical development, early dating, physical advances from boys, change of schools).

Later adolescence poses more problems with the enormous pressure within self and from the peer group to be sexually active (Wolf, 1988). Adolescent girls often feel ambivalent and guilty about sexuality as they struggle with competing messages of old and new sexual morales from parents, peers, and the media. Those girls who do become sexually active often feel anxious, worthless, depressed, and guilty and as Malmquist (1985) pointed out, are more likely to display defenses of turning against self. This punishing of self is likely to appear through unwanted pregnancies, abortion, or promiscuity.

While adolescent girls are likely to begin to feel surges of aggression as well, they are taught to repress it resulting in a tendency for females to experience greater anxiety and guilt in regard to aggression (Malmquist, 1985). According to Malmquist, in girls, dependency is reinforced in boys aggression and projection are common acceptable defenses. Stake, DeVille, and Pennell (1983) demonstrated that assertiveness training is effective for girls in improving self esteem, particularly in those with very low self esteem. If the aggression is repressed, it typically appears in depression or acting out (alienation, drug and alcohol abuse, truancy, suicidal gesturing, weight loss or gain, or frequent illness). Adolescents need help in accepting, coping with, and constructively expressing emerging anger.

Negotiating peer relationships and coping with divorce and other increased pressures (academic, social), also can put a strain on some adolescents particularly when change and pressures come all at once. Elkind (1984) pointed out that the current variations in family form (remarried families and single parent families for example) and the loss of traditional markers which set off adolescence as a distinct phase (even infants are wearing designer clothers, and young teens are increasingly being adultified in films and magazines) have created even more pressures.

The independence step of adolescence involves several critical transitions: learning to stand on one's own two feet, determining one's values and directions, striving toward a dream. In this step, individuals come more and more to trust their own senses, judgments, intuitions, and feelings of rightness and wrongness. Self-support and reliance on others is in balance (Bridges, 1980).

Early Adulthood

Early adulthood is a phase which involves several tasks: differentiation from family of origin, the development of peer relationships, the establishment of a work identity, gradual establishment of economic independence, and the decision to form a committed relationship. Of course, many young adults now are still in school. Finkelstein and Gaier (1983) showed that prolonged student status has a negative effect on identity formation since it fosters emotional dependence. Prolonged student status also contributes to feelings of inadequacy, lowered self-worth, and delayed vocational identity formation. Their results suggest that non-traditional study programs spreading education over the entire life cycle might better serve developmental interests.

Marriage represents not only the joining of two individuals but the joining of two families. The place of marriage in the life cycle has changed in recent years since people are marrying later and living with one or more partners before marrying (Carter & McGoldrick, 1988). They pointed out that currently 10% of women are choosing to remain single. For the first time in history, women have a choice to complete a crucial step in adult development—differentiation from parents, establishment of life goals and career, and the movement into an autonomous life style instead of moving from one dependent relationship to another (father to husband). Carter and McGoldrick (1988) indicated that 12% of young women will never marry.

The family life cycle of the 1980s is very different from that of the 50s. An important procedure is to recognize these changes in family structure and life course and attempt to transform our thinking to view such changes as the following in a positive frame (Carter & McGoldrick, 1988):

1. decision not to marry (3% of all individuals),

2. women living alone,

3. decision not to have children or to have fewer children,

4. single-parent adoptions,

5. dual career marriages,

6. divorce,

7. single parent families,

8. remarried couples,

9. expanded life span, and/or

10. retirement years.

Many people choose their mate in an effort to enhance their self esteem. They seek to complete themselves by marrying someone who displays disowned qualities. Marital choice also may reflect unresolved issues in the family of origin (Carter & McGoldrick, 1988). For example, in an effort to separate from a fused family, a son of a Jewish couple might marry a Catholic Phillipino woman, a clearly unacceptable choice to his parents. Carter and McGoldrick (1988) explained that if partners have not completed the process of establishing emotional independence from their parents, they will not be able to appreciate differences in their partner.

For those who marry, the wedding marks the transition point into marriage. A helpful occurrence is when the couple realizes that the wedding is a family event, not an event just for the couple. The event, explain Carter and McGoldrick (1988) marks the joining of the two families and the shifting position of each partner within his/her family. As a nodal event, it can be an opportunity to reopen cut-off or estranged relationships or to diffuse emotional issues through the natural emphasis on recognizing generations of family ties (Carter & McGoldrick, 1988).

While family social support is important for young adults in sustaining positive self perception, relationship with spouses serves as a partial replacement Mortimer and Lorence (1981). Their study showed that interpersonal relationships are of greater importance than achievements in enhancing well-being. Their research also demonstrated stability of self concept over a 14 year period (upon entry into college, end of college, and 10 years later) spanning late adolescence and early adulthood. The study also showed the importance of experiences of autonomy in developing competency. Note should be made, however, that this study was based on a highly advantaged group (graduates from the University of Michigan, with 93% from intact families and where the majority of fathers were professional or managerial).

Adulthood

Typically, childbearing is increasingly being postponed until later in marriage and a growing number of couples are choosing not to have any children at all. (The prediction is that 20 to 30% of women in present generations will not have children). With the transition of parenthood comes a sudden confrontation with the problems of traditional sex roles and transgenerational patterns. Carter and McGoldrick (1988) explained that while women are moving on their careers and looking towards a more equal sharing of household and child care responsibility with their spouses, change is coming slowly.

As Carter and McGoldrick (1988) pointed out, no phase in the life cycle creates as much change and disruption as the addition of a child to a family. Prospective parents should consider:

1. Can I make emotional space for the child in my life? What am I willing to curtail or give up in order to have time to devote to a child. Who will help care for the child (especially when extended family are not close at hand)?

2. Is the child being used to fill a gap of loss of my own parents? Emotional distance from spouse? Replacement for unrealized personal goals?

3. Am I prepared to allow for the emotional journey which comes with the changes created by the introduction of a new child into a family? All kinds of feelings are likely to emerge and space is needed for voicing them all.

Due to the tremendous stresses of this transition, a majority of the divorces occur at this time. Many women become depressed as a result of changes the birth of a child imposes on their lives and some men may tend to become further estranged from the family. Other couples struggle over responsibilities (parenting, childcare, household chores, financial). According to Carter and McGoldrick (1988), successful adaptation of this period requires negotiation of these issues of gender and sex-role.

Middle Age

Carter and McGoldrick (1988) indicated that whereas child rearing used to absorb adult attention for their entire life span, it now involves less than one-half of adult life since old age has been extended. They point out that for women, this further forces the issue of their need to develop a personal identity beyond the role of mother and homemaker. For marriage partners, this change also puts partners face to face with each other after the last child has left—for another 20 years, the newest and longest phase of family life (Carter & McGoldrick, 1988). Partners now have the task of reviving the marital relationship which may have been neglected during the child rearing years or deepening the level of intimacy.

During the middle years, both sexes display peak levels of masculinity though levels of femininity do not change significantly for either sex according to Puglisi and Jackson (1987). Their study also substantiated prior claims that androgenous individuals report highest levels of self esteem followed by masculine sex-typed persons. Masculinity continues to be a better predictor of self esteem than does femininity.

Many people in the middle years also are faced with the prospect of caring for ailing parents or somehow providing for their care. When elders do have to be placed in an institution, adult children often struggle with guilt over abandonment and anxiety about their care. Carter and McGoldrick, (1988) stressed that dealing with an aging parent who is struggling with a lengthy terminal illness also can create considerable internal conflict particularly around decisions which must be made in regard to procedures to prolong life or facilitate death. Coping with feelings of helplessness and guilt are often difficult.

The middle years are a time when people often stop to evaluate their progress on their career goals and modify their success dreams according to the realities of what they've accomplished so far (Bianci, 1987). Some may choose new careers at this time in an attempt to infuse new life into their work.

Another theme of the mid-life transition is a renewed inner directedness with a more spiritual orientation and a clarification and owning of values (Brewi & Brennan, 1985). Not all opt in this direction, however. Many frantically seek out more superficial ways to rejuvenate their vitality through romantic episodes with younger women or men, others settle for resigned coping (Bianci, 1987).

Carter and McGoldrick (1988) indicated that the fastest growth in divorce rates is occurring among couples with adolescent children during the so-called mid-life crisis when many women resume or begin work or return to school and men also tend to re-evaluate their lives including marital and career satisfaction.

Divorce

Carter and McGoldrick (1988) emphasized the prevalence of divorce in current society—almost 50% of marriages end in divorce. Often a grueling transition requiring one to three years is necessary for a family to go through the divorce process, restablize, and continue to grow. Many divorced people become vulnerable to greater psychological risk (six times more likely to be hospitalized than married people according to Bloom, White, & Asher, 1978). Bloom et al. (1978) further presented evidence that divorced people are more vulnerable to suicide, car accidents, and physical illness as well. Divorce definitely tends to produce a major crisis which throws a family into the chaos period (described elsewhere in this chapter) and requires many adjustments before a new equilibrium can be reached. A number of factors can influence adjustment through the process of divorce (Carter & McGoldrick, 1988):

- Initiators of divorce report greater life satisfaction than non-initiator spouses.

- Women who have worked during marriage and make enough money to be self-supporting adjust more easily.

- Women who have marketable skills adjust better.

- Sudden and unexpected divorce results in more difficult adjustment.

- Bitter divorces create loyalty conflicts across generational lines and result in poor functioning.

- Older children and girls adjust better (children 6 to 8 years old have hardest time adjusting).

- Ongoing high parental conflict (regardless of marital status) impairs adjustment of children.

- Continued, high quality, frequent contact with both parents post-divorce facilitates adjustment of children.

- The fewer changes post-divorce, the easier children adjust.

- Least disruptive are those newly married and with no children.

- Women over 40 have a tougher time adjusting particularly if their primary role has been in the home and they have never worked.

According to Carter and McGoldrick (1988), between the no-fault divorce which has resulted in the near disappearance of alimony and father's defaulting on support payments (47%), women and children have become victims of divorce. A solution many people choose to try to resolve the financial and psychological disruption created by divorce is to remarry—65% of women and 70% of men according to Glick and Lin (1986) and Norton and Moorman (1987). When a thorough exploration of the divorce decision including the steps which led to that decision as well as an exploration of his/her share of responsibility in the disintegration of the marriage has not been made, then inevitably these situations will lead to problems in the new marriage (Carter & McGoldrick, 1988). If children are involved, this only further complicates the picture. Adopting the intact family structure as a model is likely to doom the remarried family to failure (Carter & McGoldrick, 1988). A new model based on current research on remarried families is essential for a healthy formation (Visher & Visher, 1988).

While divorce is becoming normative in this country, it still is not treated as such. Consequently the growth possibilities of this transition are not underscored. Unfortunately, for many women, while the post-divorce period may be their first experience with autonomy, allowing for the development of a greater sense of competency, it also often brings with it a crisis financially. Carter and McGoldrick (1988) quoted a figure of over 50% of mothers who head up single parent households live in poverty. Men frequently have great difficulty maintaining a close relationship with their children after divorce. As a result of increasing feelings of alienation, 50% of noncustodial parents have no contact with their children in a year. The departing father also must function with a much reduced economic base in order to contribute to two households, one from which he no longer receives any benefit (Carter & McGoldrick, 1988).

Later Years

Over the years, the time between the launching of the last child and death of one spouse has expanded to from two to twenty years according to Carter and McGoldrick (1988). They contended that this expansion is the result of smaller nuclear families and increased life expectancy. It has resulted in a whole new stage of marriage which involves new tasks of spouses learning how to relate to each other, to their adult children, and to aging parents.

Retirement also poses a challenge to couples who must adjust to reduction in income, increased time together in the home, and re-ordered roles. If relocation of residence is also necessary, a sense of connection with neighbors and community is also lost (Carter & McGoldrick, 1988).

Women, more than men, are also more likely to have to face widowhood sometime which is a transition creating much chaos and loneliness (Carter & McGoldrick, 1988). Widows must come to grips with a solo life-style, realign relationships, and are often forced to relocate or give up independent living if financial or medical problems persist (Caine, 1988). Males who become widows have more options to remarry even as elders due to the greater availability of women. Carter and McGoldrick (1988) pointed out that most elders fear physical and mental deterioration (86% have chronic health problems). Since most of these are not maintained in institutions, this poses a significant strain on adult children both emotionally and financially.

Many elders find this dependency eroding to self esteem. The losses often pile high at this time—death of loved ones, health problems, financial constraints, even diminution of one's mental capacities. And, of course, underneath it all lurks the inevitability of death (Bianci, 1987).

If elders can divest themselves of the self-limiting myths about aging, they can find ways to maintain their productivity either through continued involvement in work, volunteer service, grandparenting roles, deepened avocational interests, community service projects, work on national issues, or other such avenues (Erickson, Erickson, & Kivnick, 1986). New levels of spirituality also may be attained as elders reach for comfort and help with the inevitable losses of old age.

The potential is also available in the later years for greater intensity of experience. The limitation of time can help make every minute count, heightening our contact not only with a higher power but also with friends, family, nature, and even ordinary events. With a deeper appreciation for the little gifts which each day brings, even the ordinary can become extra special.

Death is, of course, the ultimate transition. Levine (1987) encouraged people to take advantage of one last opportunity to finish business from the past, to put one's affairs in order, to open up one's heart wider than ever before letting go with trust in the face of death.

Movement into this last stage of life involves readjusting one's dream to reality, dealing more and more with loss, and developing a deeper sense of what is meaningful in life.

Summary

Of course, what has been presented here is merely a skeleton of the myriad of changes one faces in a lifetime. Stagnating or lagging behind at any stage in the developmental cycle can negatively affect self esteem.

The wide popularity of Sheehy's (1976) book demonstrated the obvious hunger people feel for some guideposts against which they can view their own lives. With other guideposts changing as evidenced by Carter and McGoldrick's book (1988) which outlined changes in the current family life cycle, education is necessary in order to reframe certain transitions and increase awareness of new tasks brought about by these shifts. In a sense, this kind of information provides clues to what kinds of issues, tasks, behaviors, and feelings are common in a given life stage. Such guidance helps to normalize what might otherwise be a very anxiety-producing journey through uncharted territory. The individual's sense of disorientation is relieved as the landscape is made more familiar through the revelation of other people's passages. Individual self esteem is, thereby, supported in the difficult twists and turns of life.

Since many changes are self-initiated, they can be planned to minimize the degree of personal upheaval generated. Some examples of transitions which planning often can ease are birth of a child, job changes, and relocations. In order to minimize the effects and a transition, however, a person must become aware of

1. probable feelings, issues, and stresses one is likely to face;

2. available internal support to meet these demands; and

3. external resources upon which one might call.

In addition, one must develop confidence and forethought for planning along with the attitude that one can control, manage, and direct one's transitions.

Being quite naive about how to negotiate through life and so groping in ignorance, many people place themselves unwittingly in precariously stressful situations. Even when a person realizes a particular transition is likely to be difficult, the individual may feel nothing can be done about it—"I just have to grit my teeth and bear it." Often people are not able to see that they can take deliberate measures to alleviate the stress and modulate the change process.

NEGOTIATING TRANSITIONS

Identify Real Need

In order to negotiate transitions adequately, one must first learn to be aware of what really needs to be changed. Many people, for example, are prone when feeling discontent, to change more **external aspects** of their lives—jobs, geographic location, marital partners—when one's **internal life** might be a more fitting focus of change. People who repeatedly make external changes are thinking, "There must be a place where life will be better." Their focus is outside themselves rather than on their communication patterns (Satir, 1981). Satir (1981) believed that one's pattern of communicating effects one's health, productivity, intimacy, and ability to negotiate change effectively.

Identify Attitude Toward Change

Another important factor in effectively negotiating transitions is one's attitude toward change. Those who resist change experience physical and psychological symptoms. People are always changing, always going through stages. A person's attitude effects whether he/she will be able to get into the new flow or will try to keep the status quo (Satir, 1981). Trying to keep the status quo when a person is always changing is like trying to stay at the same level step on a moving stairway (Satir, 1981).

To try to create change is in some sense to stop it—to try to change oneself or somebody else, is to interrupt what is already happening. In a sense, it could be said that people don't change, but, rather, more of the person is made available—people discover more of themselves. In the process of uncovering oneself, the person creates change.

Responses to change—to disruption—fall between two polarities:

overbounded |___|___|___|___| underbounded

The **overbounded** individual is rigid and unyielding (Keleman, 1979). Change is resisted. Energy is constricted and the individual does not allow excitement to expand and grow. Such persons press life in and ward off the world, reaching out as little as possible. There are no springs to absorb shock of inevitable change (Keleman, 1979). The **underbounded** person is a victim, surrendering to every impulse. His/her shape is weak and toneless. Such persons let their process leak out; they erupt and expel life. Vacillation and caving in predominate. Individuals must come to find a place in the middle.

In Satir's (1981) view, transitions are never the problem, one's coping with the transitions is. People must learn to make room for the psychological journey.

Release Old Picture and Discover New One

As is depicted in Figure 8.2, the present situation consists of one's life as one presently knows it. One's present situation is familiar regardless of how comfortable or uncomfortable. When a person decides to make a change, or when a change is forced on a person, the system is disrupted and the person must prepare to make room for the feelings that go along with the inevitable endings that are to come (Satir, 1981). For even when something positive is added, the old picture is lost. Allowing space for the acknowledgement of feelings in the various phases of a transition improves one's ability to manage the shift. Other factors which affect how a person copes with change are

1. ability to accept that he/she is changing and moving;

2. willingness to meet strangers (people, places, and objects which are alien);

3. ability to look forward and picture the ultimate integration of the new parts—faith in the process of life; and

4. attitude toward risking, exploring, and discovering. (See activities at the end of this chapter).

When individuals move through transitions, they move through a state of disequilibrium. The system has been shaken up, and a state of confusion reverberates throughout. Satir (1979) used the analogy of driving through the fog to describe the feelings associated with movement through that state of disequilibrium. Driving through the fog can be rather scary

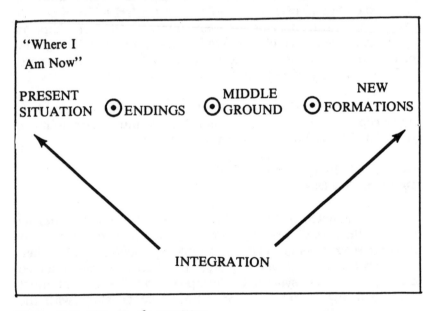

Figure 8.2. Phases of transition.

because people cannot see very far ahead; they must trust themselves and use whatever data they have available to negotiate that passage, waiting for the fog to lift. Yielding to the moment while moving through the fog is difficult, but, if mastered, makes that period of confusion more tolerable and serves to clear the mind for better judgment.

The ability to be flexible and to adapt to changes is certainly one of the most important skills a person can develop in him/herself. This is particularly true for the generations of the future, because things are changing so rapidly. With computerization, for example, the future is likely to present an even faster pace. What was true of the past may not be true for the future.

FACTORS INFLUENCING ADAPTATION TO CHANGE

Schlossberg and Kent (1979) summarized a number of factors which may influence an individual's adaptation to change. These factors include such aspects as whether the source is internally based or externally induced. Another factor which affects ability to adapt to change is whether the stress occurs on-time or off-time. This is an application of Neugarten's (1976) "social clock" principle which points out that there are social penalties for blooming early or blooming late. Applied to the area of transitions, it is less stressful to be widowed at 75 than to be widowed at 30; it is less stressful to move at the beginning of the ninth grade than at the beginning of the senior year in high school.

Whether the transition is perceived as essentially positive (job promotion) or essentially negative (death of spouse), whether the transition necessitates a permanent or a temporary change (permanent move vs. temporary handicap due to broken bone), all affect one's ability to adapt.

Characteristics of the Environment

People generally do not exist in isolation. People need people. They can enhance the quality of each other's life, help each other become more whole, and help steady each other through changes. Objects such as books and biofeedback equipment, for example, also can enhance one's existence as well as can the geographic location or time of day. Many aspects of one's environment can affect one's ability to cope with change. Analyze your environment by considering the following:

- What is the interpersonal support system like?

- Are intimate relationships available?

- How extensive is the network of friends?

- How cohesive and adaptable is the family?

Degree of Change Required

Goodman pointed out another factor which may influence change. In her book, Goodman (1979) proposed that to understand why one person changes and another one does not, one might look at the degree to which a particular change might threaten the meaning of the person's life. In defining the phrase "meaning of the person's life," Goodman explained this kind of threat would be related to that which might jeopardize an individual's experience of attachment, how the person comes to understand his/her life, where the person invests a commitment, what the person values, on what the person hangs his/her self esteem. For instance, a woman who is in the home, caring for her family while her husband works would likely be highly invested in her husband and children. Husband and children have been her sole sources of meaning, and, therefore, esteem. If the woman decides she wants to go to school, and the husband strongly disapproves, she would likely have difficulty continuing with the idea of school. On the other hand, adding a new piece of furniture to her home would likely be a much lower risk change because such a change would not threaten a central belief or source of meaning. (See Figure 8.3.)

Goodman (1979) stressed that people are more likely to make changes that "conserve" the meaning of their lives and avoid those that threaten to disrupt their lives. She also

LOW RISK CHANGE		HIGH RISK CHANGE
◄─── Growth ───►		
adding a new piece of furniture	graduation	crisis
	promotion	involves a significant loss
change in schedule to accommodate children	more mixed feelings start occuring at this point	quitting a job
		moving to another part of the country

Figure 8.3. Relationship of risk to change

distinguished between people's reactions to different degrees of change:

> change—becoming distinctly different;
> alter—partially changing; and
> modify—producing a minor change.

Modifications are clearly easier to yield to than are real **changes.** She also pointed out that changes which arise from expanded choices are easier to incorporate than are changes which involve a diminished number of choices—living on double one's salary rather than one half of one's salary would be an easier adjustment.

SUMMARY

Transitions are inevitable. Anyone or anything that is alive and growing goes through transitions. Even a general sketch of the territory can ease the journey through life's changes. Other factors which may ease the journey are one's attitude toward change, one's ability to be flexible and to operate more from an internal locus of control, and one's ability to let go of past images and form clear images of what one is moving toward. In all transitions, people must learn to leave room for the emotional journey, from the initial movement toward an ending through the reintegration of the new beginnings. They are times of great opportunity.

Self esteem is both affected by and affects transitions. Individuals may wish to learn additional skills to better negotiate transitions and, therefore, better preserve self esteem. Some of these tools involve active behaviors, others involve more passive attitudinal changes.

───

ACTIVITY 8.1   RISKING

Introduction

The following activity helps people to begin to identify and evaluate specific behaviors which they would consider risky.

Time Required

15 minutes

Participants

Any number; adults

Setting

Classroom or office

Materials

Pencil and paper

Procedure

Read the following statements and rate each on this five-point scale according to your subjective feelings of the degree of risk involved.

```
┌──────────┬──────────┬──────────┬──────────┐
1          2          3          4          5
Low                                        High
Risk                                       Risk
```

1. Start a new project at work.
2. Visit a city to which you've never been.
3. Express anger at someone.
4. Ask someone for a personal favor.
5. Admit you're wrong about something.
6. Ask directly for attention.
7. Touch someone other than your family.
8. Ask someone for feedback on how he/she sees you.
9. Go to dinner or a movie alone.
10. Make a career change.
11. Fill in a suggestion of your own.
12. Fill in another suggestion of your own.

Choose one of those listed which you rated 2 or 3 and carry it out. Make a record of your feelings/thoughts throughout the process as well as how you supported yourself.

Outcome

Expands self-concept through modulated risk taking.

Note. Activity is original. Idea initiated by Pfeiffer and Jones (1973).

ACTIVITY 8.2 VISUALIZATION ONE: WHAT DO YOU WANT?

Introduction

This activity encourages people to develop a picture of what they want.

Time Required

15 minutes

Participants

Any number; adults

Setting

Classroom or office

Materials

Paper and pen

Procedure

Visualize whatever it is that you want for yourself. See yourself having what you want, being the way that you want, doing what you want. Fill your picture with detail. Many people have a finely tuned picture of what they don't want, but a very vague and blurry picture of what they do want. This activity encourages you to spend some time focusing that picture of what you do want.

For someone unhappy in his/her job:

1. List **all** the things you want in a job.

2. List **all** the things you know how to do.

3. Imagine a job title that sums up both what you want and are capable of doing. Make a detailed picture of that.

4. Keep bringing the image into focus at various times during the day.

Outcome

Supports one's dreams and encourages an attitude of abundance.

Note. Activity is original. Idea initiated by Bry (1978).

ACTIVITY 8.3   VISUALIZATION TWO: COPING

Introduction

The following activity allows people the opportunity to create models of ways to cope with particular situations.

Time Required

15 minutes

Participants

Any number; adolescents or adults

Setting

Classroom or office

Materials

None

Procedure

Picture someone else coping easily with a situation that would normally be difficult for you. Now, imagine yourself imitating these actions.

1. What are the behavior traits you value and wish to have as your own?

2. Think of someone who possesses those traits.

3. Imagine this person reacting to situations you encounter. How would he/she deal with it? See it in your mind's eye. Now imitate him/her.

4. Practice this imagery regularly, before physically enacting the behavior.

Outcome

Expands one's behavioral repertory.

Note. Activity is original. Idea initiated by Lazarus (1977).

ACTIVITY 8.4 NEGOTIATING A TRANSITION

Introduction

This activity helps the participant assess external resources available to them in managing a change.

Time Required

20 minutes

Participants

Adolescents or adults

Setting

Classroom or office

Materials

Paper and pen

Procedure

Respond to the following questions. Use additional pages as needed.

1. What institutional supports are available that can help you make this change (e.g., libraries, churches, schools, community mental health agencies, women's centers)? (Schlossberg & Kent, 1979)

   _____

   _____

2. What particular people could be helpful to you. List names and resources they would bring.

   _____

   _____

3. What services do these supports offer that can help with this transition?

_____

_____

4. What environmental changes will occur as a result of this transition (e.g., sunny, clear, rural vs. cold, barren, polluted, big city, small school vs. large school)? (Schlossberg & Kent, 1979)

_____

_____

5. How much does the environment change pre- and post-transition?

_____

_____

6. What changes are in a positive or negative direction?

_____

_____

7. How much weight do you assign to each of those changes?

_____

_____

8. How can you cope with what you assign negative value?

_____

_____

Outcome

Facilitates smoother transitions and anticipates the degree of disruption in transition.

_____

ACTIVITY 8.5
ASSESSING YOUR ADAPTABILITY TO CHANGE

Time Required

30 minutes

Participants

Adolescents or adults

Setting

Classroom or office

Materials

Paper and Pen

Introduction and Procedure

To gauge your level of ease in making transitions, write your answers to the following questions:

1. *Sex-role identity (Schlossberg & Kent, 1979).*

   How whole are you? This is, how able are you to own your male or female parts?

2. *Psycho-social competence (Schlossberg & Kent, 1979).*

   What is your attitude toward yourself?
   How curious are you about yourself?
   How optimistic or pessimistic are you?
   How able are you to cope?
   > *to recognize your needs?*
   > *to show initiative?*
   > *to set realistic goals?*
   > *to express one's feelings?*
   > *to establish relationships?*
   > *to enjoy success, to fail?*
   > *and to learn from both? (Moos & Tsu, 1976).*
   Are you able to ask for help? Are you able to trust your senses?

3. Is your locus of control more internally or externally based? (Solvesson-Lane, 1980)

4. Have you had previous experiences with transitions? (Schlossberg & Kent, 1979)

5. How would you characterize your current level of functioning: overall mental health, level of life satisfaction, adequacy of role, and social functioning? (Schlossberg & Kent, 1979)

6. How willing are you to take responsibility for yourself? Answer to yourself the following:

I have to—
I choose to—
I can't—
I won't—

   How willing are you to take responsibility for your choices?

7. How flexible are you?

Outcome

One becomes better prepared for change by assessing personal resources.

REFERENCES

Backman, J.G., & O'Malley, P.M. (1983). Self-esteem in young men: A longitudinal analysis of the impact of educational and occupational attainment. *Journal of Personality and Social Psychology, 35* (6), 365-380.

Bianci, E. (1987). *Aging as a spiritual journal.* New York: Crossroad Publication.

Bloom, B.L., White, S.W., & Asher, S.J. (1978). Marital disruption as a stressor: A review and analysis. *Psychological Bulletin* (June).

Brewi, J. & Brennan, A. (1985). *Mid-life psychological and spiritual perspectives.* New York: Crossroad Publishing.

Bridges, W. (1980). *Transitions.* Reading, MA: Addison-Wesley.

Bry, A. (1978). *Visualization: Directing the movies of your mind.* New York: Barnes & Noble.

Caine, L. (1988). *Being a widow.* New York: Arbor.

Carter, B., & McGoldrick, M. (1988). *The changing family life cycle,* 2nd ed. New York: Gardner Press.

Clark, A., Clemes, H., & Bean, R. (1987). *How to raise teenager's self esteem.* Los Angeles: Price, Stern and Sloan.

Cohen, L.H., Burt, C.E., & Bjorck, J.P. (1987). Life stress and adjustment: Effects of life events experienced by young adolescents and their parents. *Developmental Psychology, 23*(4), 583-592.

Elkind, D. (1984). *All grown up with no place to go.* Reading, MA: Addison-Wesley.

Erickson, E., Erickson, J., & Kivnick, H. (1986). *Vital involvement in old age.* New York: W.W. Norton.

Finkelstein, M.J., & Gaier, E.L. (1983). The impact of prolonged student status on late adolescent development. *Adolescence, 18*(69), 115-129.

Glick, P.C., & Lin, S.L. (1986). Recent changes in divorce and remarriage. *Journal of Marriage and the Family. 48*(4), 737-747.

Goodman, E. (1979). *Turning points.* New York: Fawcett Columbine.

Jacquish, G.A., & Savin-Williams, R.C. (1981). Biological and ecological factors in the expression of adolescent self-esteem. *Journal of Youth and Adolescence, 10*(6), 473-485.

Keleman, S. (1979). *Somatic reality.* Berkely, CA: Center Press.

Lazarus, A. (1977). *In the mind's eye: The power of imagery for personal enrichment.* New York: Rawson Associates.

Levine, S. (1987). *Healing into life and death.* New York: Doubleday.

Levinson, D.J., Darrow, C.N., Klein, E.B., Levinson, M.H., & McKee, B. (1978). *The seasons of a man's life.* New York: Knopf.

McCarthy, J.D., & Hoge, D.R. (1982). Analysis of age effects in longitudinal studies of adolescent self esteem. *Developmental Psychology, 18*(3), 372-379.

Maslow, A. H. (1954). *Motivation and personality.* New York: Harper & Row.

Malmquist, C.P. (1985). *Handbook of Adolescence.* New York: Jason Aronson.

Moos, R.H., & Tsu, V.D. (1976). Human competence and coping: An overview. In R.H. Moos (Ed.), *Human adaptation: Coping with life crises* (pp. 3-16). Lexington, MA: Heath.

Mortimer, J.T., & Lorence, J. (1981). Self-concept stability and change from late adolescence to early adulthood. *Research in Community and Mental Health, 2,* 5-42.

Neugarten, B. L. (1976). Adaptation and the life cycle. *Counseling Psychologist, 6*(1), 16-20.

Norton, A.J., & Moorman, J.E. (1987). Current trends in marriage and divorce among American women. *Journal of Marriage and the Family, 49*(1), 3-14.

Nottelmann, E.D. (1987). Competence and self esteem during transition from childhood to adolescence. *Developmental Psychology, 23*(3), 441-450.

O'Malley, P.M., & Backman, J.G. (1983). Self-esteem: Change and stability between ages 13 and 23. *Developmental Psychology, 19*(2), 257-268.

Parkes, C.M. (1971). Psycho-social transitions: A field for study. *Social Science and Medicine* (Vol. 5). London, GB: Pergamon.

Pfeiffer, J.W., & Jones, J. (Eds.). (1973). *A handbook of structured experiences for human relations training* (Vol. 4). Iowa City, IA: University Associates.

Puglisi, J.T., & Jackson, D.W. (1987). Sex role identify and self esteem in adulthood. *International Journal of Aging and Human Development, 12*(2), 129-138.

Satir, V. (1979, August). Presentation at Avanta/Process community. Park City, UT.

Satir, V. (1981). *Communication in families.* South Bend, IN: Family Institute.

Satir, V. (1987). Process of change. Presentation at Avanta meeting. Crested Butte, CO.

Schlossberg, N., & Kent, L. (1979). Effective helping with women. In S. Eisenberg and L. Patterson (Eds.), *Helping clients with special concerns*. Chicago: Rand McNally.

Sheehy, G. (1976). *Passages: Predictable crises of adult life*. New York: Dutton.

Sheehy, G. (1981). *Pathfinders*. New York: William Morrow.

Solvesson-Lane, S.A. (1980). *Life transitions: Friend or foe? Self-concept, flexibility, and locus of control as moderator variables*. United States International University. H. Greenwald (Chair).

Stake, J.E., DeVille, C.J., & Pennell, C.L. (1983). *Journal of Youth and Adolescence, 12*(5), 435-442.

Visher, E.B., & Visher, E.B., Jr. (1988). *Old loyalties, new ties; Therapeutic strategies with step families*. New York: Brunner/Mazel.

Wallace, J.R., & Cunningham, T.F. (1984). Change and stability in self-esteem between late childhood and early adolescence. *Journal of Early Adolescence, 4*(3), 253-257.

Wolf, T. (1988). *I'll be home before midnight and I won't get pregnant*. New York: Vintage Books.

CHAPTER 9

BODY AND
SELF ESTEEM

Body esteem can have ramifications in various aspects of self-image. Body image is a person's picture or mental representation of his/her own body at rest or in motion at any moment. It is derived from internal sensations, postural changes, contact with outside objects and people, and emotional experiences and fantasies (Salkin, 1973). According to Hutchinson (1983; 1985), body image includes feelings, attitudes, and beliefs about one's body.

A sense of body image begins developing during the last one-half of the first year of life, although body image becomes more defined as a person develops a sense of self-identity. Some theorists such as Sears, Rau, and Alpert (1965) believe that early body image has a critical influence on developing self-concept. However, the development of body image occurs over a period of time and is subject to later modification.

DEVELOPMENT OF BODY IMAGE

Infancy and Childhood

Through the process of feeling, handling, and tasting, infants gradually distinguish between what is theirs and what is not, where they physically end and where the world begins. This process of identity exploration begins from birth (Sullivan, 1953). Babies make full use of their bodies and are completely absorbed by their bodies. Each newly found ability, to grasp with the hand, to kick, to crawl, to bounce on a bed, totally captures the child's attention (Nelson, 1975).

Infants' early attitudes towards their bodies are influenced not only by kinesthetic pleasures they derive from their bodies, but also by attitudes their primary caretakers hold about sex and bodily processes. These attitudes are first conveyed through touch and sound of voice and only later by words. (This is more thoroughly discussed in Chapter 2.)

The origins of guilt, shame, and unhealthy sexual attitudes are likely to begin during this initial period of bodily exploration. A blocking of the child's total body absorption begins at this point created by physical illnesses, inability of the parent to determine and respond to the child's actual needs, criticism of the child's early clumsy spills and falls, or disapproval of the child's natural exploration and enjoyment of body. According to Lebe (1986) body image among girls is more complex than for boys since their sexual organs are partially internal and, therefore, are not easy to see and touch.

In order for children to stop their fears or anger or protect their newly developing body, they learn to constrict muscles associated with such expressive functions. Steadily, the disconnecting from their body proceeds unless deliberate attempts are made to help children regain this connection through such methods as body awareness and movement games (Barlin & Greenberg, 1980; Nelson, 1975).

Another important element in the evolution of selfhood is the increasing control over one's body. The child's self picture grows as motor control increases and the child is able to do more and more. The way people respond to a child's growth also influences the child's attitude toward his/her body. Later, in the years of middle childhood, changes in the size and rate of growth and increasing ability to coordinate affect the child's success both in school and in his/her peer culture, ultimately affecting self esteem.

Children also seem to be influenced early by cultural stereotypes and incorporate other's opinions about their weights (Lerner & Gellert, 1969). Even young children are conscious of the weight of adults and children. They tend to favor normal weight children as compared with obese children. Children who are overweight have lower opinions of their bodies and appearance than normal weight children (Mendelson & White, 1982). Although in some studies, the overall self esteem of overweight children has been found to be lower, the findings are inconsistent. Mendelson and White (1982) in their study of 7 through 12 year olds, may have identified that period as a time when being overweight affects body esteem but often has not generalized to self esteem. If this is accurate, then early intervention becomes important.

Adolescence

According to Jersild (1952), the greatest concern with one's body seems to come after elementary school years. The body seems to take on intense meaning during adolescence. During adolescence many overt bodily changes take place along with inner hormonal fluctuations and dramatic morphological changes (Hoover, 1984; Peterson & Taylor, 1980). Even minor deviations are viewed with alarm (Huenemann, Shapiro, Hampton, & Mitchell, 1966). From ninth to twelfth grade an increasing number of girls described themselves as fat and as dissatisfied with their physical appearance, even though objective classification of the number of obese girls **did not** increase (Huenemann et al., 1966).

According to Lebe (1986), at puberty, girls often feel rejected by fathers who out of their own anxieties about their sexual feelings in response to their daughter's developing sexuality, withdraw from the relationship. Such abandonment at the time of these significant body changes may result in conflicted feelings about their developing bodies.

Female adolescents also tend to be more critical of their bodies than male adolescents (Clifford, 1971). For females, self-concept is tied more closely to their ratings of their body parts than to their ratings of self-effectiveness; for males, the reverse is true (Lerner, Orlos, & Knapp, 1976; Lerner, Iwawaki, Chihara, & Sorell, 1980). Worsley (1981) has shown that body image in adolescence may be of greater importance to girls than to boys. A study by Offer, Ostrov, and Howard (1981) also showed that normal adolescent girls are more negatively affected than boys by normal bodily changes. They report feeling ugly and ashamed of their bodies. Overweight teenage girls are often predisposed to feelings of anxiety and inferiority and inadequacy at this difficult time (Hoover, 1984). According to Huenemann et al. (1966), boys over the same age report increasing concern with becoming more muscular. The perception of self esteem during this developmental period is influenced by the body build, height, weight, physical appearance, physical adequacy, rate of maturity, and the appearance of secondary sex characteristics (Biller & Liebman, 1971; Jones & Mussen, 1958; Mussen & Jones, 1957; Strang, 1957; Yeatts, 1967).

By late adolescence, the body reestablishes an equilibrium. To the degree adolescents accept their physical uniqueness from others and the disparity between their real physical self and their ideal physical self, they will be satisfied with themselves.

Adulthood

One study by Calden, Lundy, and Schlafer (1959) provided information related to college students which showed that they are no more completely happy with their physical characteristics than with their psychological attributes:

1. Women were less satisfied than men with attractiveness of both their bodies and their faces.

2. About one-half of the women desired larger busts, about one-half of the males desired larger chests.

3. Both sexes felt their nose was the facial feature they would most like to change, usually to have it smaller. Men also wanted more prominent chins and less prominent ears, women wanted bigger eyes and more oval shaped faces.

4. All women who were dissatisfied with their weight wished to weigh less.

5. Women viewed "muscle men" as less attractive than men did.

In a more recent study (Bergner, Remer, & Whetsell, 1985), 80% of the female subjects, while within normal weight range, still held a negative body image. Women tend to have greater dissatisfaction with their bodies than do men. (Mintz & Betz, 1986). Women tend to perceive themselves as overweight while men tend to perceive themselves as underweight and wanted to gain rather than lose weight (Mintz & Betz, 1986). For both sexes less positive attitudes toward one's body were related to lower levels of self esteem (Mintz & Betz, 1986), although the relationship for women is stronger than for men.

Body image undergoes transition with each major life event. Once a person reaches adulthood, body image is more resistant to change. However, some researchers have reported evidence of changes in body image even in adulthood. For example, changes have been noted following significant weight loss (Leon, 1975; Leon, Bemis, Meland, & Nussbaum, 1978; Leon, Eckert, Teed, & Buchwald, 1979). Evidence of change in adult body image varies depending on the type of measurement instrument used to assess the change.

Generally by middle age people begin experiencing traumatic losses and various degrees of breakdown of their bodies. These losses tend to continue and accelerate through later life. Beginning in midlife, for example, visual and auditory acuity diminishes; a general slowing of the nervous system occurs after age 50; and chronic disorders such as arthritis, cancer, cardiovascular problems, and diabetes occur more frequently (Diekelmann, 1977; Finch & Hayflick, 1977). Some physical deterioration may, however, be related to people's beliefs about aging and the cumulative effects of abuse and neglect of one's body as much as to the inevitability of physical breakdown. Luce (1979) wrote an inspiring book which helped shatter self-limiting beliefs about aging, longevity, and sexuality in later life.

THE LONG BODY

Keleman (1979) presented a different perspective on body form and body image than have other authors. This difference is called the "long body." One of the qualities of biological process is that organisms continually evolve and change shape (Keleman, 1979). Human beings change from egg and sperm, to a multicelled organism, to a being with a primitive nervous system, to a fetus that begins to resemble human form. The human form evolves onward throughout life according to

Keleman (1979) who encouraged people to look at old family albums to understand the idea that people have many bodies in a lifetime. According to Keleman (1979), at least four different bodies exists in each person in a lifetime: young child, adolescent, adult, and older adult. Each has a totally different world view, attitude, and perception of its own realm of truth about the world. Keleman's contention was that these past images still exist within people, though they currently may be expressed in a different form or may be temporarily covered over, forgotten, and require revivification. (to experience this idea more fully, see Activity 9.1 The Long Body). Through this method one can recapture lost parts of self. All of one's past emotional experiences are expressed in the body.

The body speaks clearly, revealing the character of the life a person has lived. Body and mind are reflections of each other. Emotions and experiences which form personality directly affect the formation and structure of muscles and tissue. As such, the body offers the person trained in body awareness a wealth of data and an avenue for helping. As a result of the expansion of knowledge about the body, counseling has expanded from a purely verbal approach to approaches which directly comment on body processes (alterations in breathing, muscular tensions, postural changes, or eye movement, for example). As Keleman (1975), and Kurtz and Prestera (1970) emphasized, the body not only reveals the person, the body is the person. By examining a number of dimensions of the body, such as muscle tone, skin color, posture, proportions, tensions, and movements, one can develop a sense of life and history of the person within.

CULTURAL ASPECTS ON THE SELF ESTEEM AND BODY IMAGE

How people feel about their bodies is closely related to how they feel about themselves (Rosen & Ross, 1968; Secord & Jourard, 1953). In a culture which places so much stress on measuring up to rigid and idealized standards of beauty and acceptability, it is small wonder very few individuals escape self esteem problems related to body image. Increasingly, awareness of the effects of such rigid standards in weight, physical attractiveness, and even height (Gillis, 1982) has been emphasized.

Standards of Attractiveness

Not many people can measure up to the images the media establishes as the standard of attractiveness. Those images leave little room for differences. Such standards vary widely from society to society. Perception and evaluation of one's body is highly influenced by cultural and societal standards. Bruch (1973) and Chernin (1981) have both commented on the detrimental effects of American preoccupation with thinness.

Physical attractiveness is highly valued in this culture. People whose body images are not congruent with their physiological images often find themselves in emotional difficulty. As mentioned in Chapter 1, the more congruent the real and ideal self are (including physical selves) the higher the self esteem. While having been programmed to adopt these rigid standards, most people cannot meet them. As aging continues, even those few who manage to meet such standards inevitably suffer losses. Those who place primary emphasis on the body as the main source of self esteem, for example, body builders and models, run the risk of increasing damage to their self-worth over the course of their life span.

In a culture which places such a premium on measuring up to an unrealistic image, one can easily imagine the damage which can occur to self esteem when

a woman ages and her skin loses some of its elasticity,

a man starts balding,

physical endurance diminishes,

hair starts graying, or

a person looks in the mirror and notices deep wrinkle lines in his/her face or bags under eyes.

Rigid and perfectionistic body ideals leave no room for the appreciation of differences or respect for the natural transformation one's body undergoes through the life cycle (see Boston Women's Health Book Collective, 1984).

Obsession with Weight

Demand to conform to such an unrealistic image of a "good body" has had a distorting effect. Women's magazines, diet clubs, diet foods, and diet drinks all attest to the big issue on people's minds: fear of fat. As a result of socialization, women have equated physical attractiveness with self-worth (Greenspan, 1983). Our culture is obsessed with thinness (Chernin, 1981; McCoy, 1982). The "fat industry" is an eleven billion dollar industry (Mayer, 1978). Even slim people experience a nagging terror over every bite they eat for fear that they will become fat if they ever "let themselves go." Mayer (1978) indicated that people are divided into two groups: those who fear getting fat and those who are ashamed of being fat.

Women, particularly, are persecuted for their weight through fluctuating diet and fashion advertisements which convey the message that only slim women are worthy of love. People are placed in a double-bind situation. They are given the message: "LOSE WEIGHT," even though approximately 99% of all attempts to lose weight end in failure (Mayer, 1978). Fat people are in a double-bind. If they lose weight, and try to maintain a goal weight that is considered normal on weight charts, they must accept some degree of hunger and unsatisfied appetite as a way of life (Asher, 1974).

The belief is that certain body processes impede efforts at weight loss. Research by Keesey as discussed in Stunkard (1980) showed that a set point exists around which body weight is regulated which defends the body against weight loss despite efforts to lower it (Stunkard, 1980). This occurs partially through a decrease in basal metabolism. Natural body processes, therefore, impede our ability to shed excess weight. Another hypothesis regarding the difficulty in maintaining weight loss posits that while the fat cell number can increase at any age by weight gain, the number of fat cells cannot be reduced by weight loss. Given the previous information, then prevention of weight gain rather than weight loss might be a better goal. If overweight individuals repeatedly lose and gain weight, the evidence is that this fluctuation can lead to arteriosclerosis, leading to heart attacks and strokes (Stunkard, 1980). If they choose not to try to lose weight, they are likely to be subjected to ridicule, continued persecution, and resultant self hatred. Many people are on a dangerous rollercoaster of binging and starving (Rosen, 1982).

One of the few programs to help compulsive overeaters maintain long standing positive results is Overeaters Anonymous. This is a 12-step program modeled after Alcoholics Anonymous which addresses all dimensions of a person—physical, emotional, intellectual, and spiritual—in an effort to relieve the compulsion to overeat (literature on the organization may be obtained from Overeaters Anonymous, Inc., 4025 Spencer Street, #203, Torrance, CA 90503). Many people struggle again and again to control what they eat by dieting, joining weight reduction programs, exercising, reading popular literature with none of these producing lasting results. When nothing works, some are ready to admit their powerlessness over food and the unmanageability of their lives. The Overeaters Anonymous 12-step program, which encompasses a spiritual solution may then be embraced, albeit with initial skepticism. Some beginning materials which may be helpful are the book Overeaters Anonymous by Bill B. (1981), Listen to the Hunger (Anonymous, 1987), and Twelve Steps for Overeaters by Elizabeth L. (1988). Overeaters Anonymous provides a positive model for living in a world with ups and downs and numerous stresses without escaping into harmful dependencies. Overeaters Anonymous helps satisfy the spiritual hunger which gives rise to compulsive behavior.

A number of additional books can be helpful to a person who chooses to depart from the dieting solution and seek a more well-rounded approach which may increase chances of lifelong abstinence. Susie Orbach (1979, & 1982) perhaps offered the first divergence of perspective with regard to compulsive overeating. She emphasized that compulsive overeaters are out of touch with themselves and that preoccupation with food masks other problems. Orbach (1979, 1982) also stressed the relationship between compulsive eating and women's overgiving role in society and the complicated social meanings of food, femininity, and body size. She was one of the first to view compulsive eating/dieting as an addiction.

Roth (1982) continued to correlate the relationship between a person's physical self and emotional well-being. If people hate their bodies, they will experience problems with their self-esteem. Roth (1982) emphasized that eating was not the real issue and that the core of the problem was an "inside job." Compulsive eating serves a function and until those needs are addressed, the person will continue to regain weight.

Hollis (1986) expanded on this idea and introduced the role of family in the dysfunctional process. Hollis maintained that compulsive overeaters develop an "as if" personality as they try to please others. This is also directly related to the encultured female role in our society. According to Hollis (1986), food is used to drown out the true person inside and recovery involves a journey to the real self. Hollis (1986) stressed that family members help overeaters to live the lie and recovery depends on increasing awareness of their role as well. Hollis (1986) emphasized the issues of control and vulnerability in the recovery process.

In the last 20 years, according to Chernin (1981) and Neuman and Halvorson (1983), widespread incidence has developed of additional eating disorders: anorexia, a disorder where primarily women starve themselves in order to become very thin, and bulimia, a condition predominately of women who eat and then fast, eat and then purge (through vomiting, laxatives, diuretics). Bulimia is now epidemic on college campuses (Chernin, 1981, Boskind-White & White, 1983). As a result of this intense fear of being fat, significant distortion in body image has been found among anorexic subjects. Most anorectics overestimate their body size (Bell, Kirkpatrick, & Rinn, 1986). Obese subjects, on the other hand, tend to distort their body size (Bell, Kirkpatrick, & Rinn, 1986). The researchers also found that the further the subject placed from the weight norm, the greater they tended to over or underestimate their appearance. These results were replicated by Birtchell et al. (1987). Thompson and Thompson (1986) also have related self esteem to overestimation of body weight in normal weight subjects.

Much of the research on preoccupation with body weight has focused exclusively on females. While a few studies have compared overweight males and females, the effects of being underweight have been ignored (Harmatz, Gronendyke, & Thomas, 1985). Harmatz et al. (1985) found that underweight males have extremely negative self-images and evidence poor social adjustment that matches or exceeds that of overweight females. Tucker's (1982) research supported the idea that the muscular male body is the most socially desirable. Muscular males receive much more positive feedback and tend to feel better about themselves. According to Tucker (1982), to the degree male bodies deviate from the mesormorphic type, their self-concepts tend to decline rapidly.

Body Detachment

Women also have a greater need to camouflage their "deficiencies." They accomplish this through the application of cosmetics, "putting on a face" or, more radically, through plastic surgery. Men are increasingly seeking to change their appearance as well through hair transplants and other cosmetic corrections. While women have been pressured into a preoccupation with weight, up until recently they have been discouraged from pursuing physical activity unless it has been defined as sex role appropriate. Consequently, women have been conditioned to comply with external appearance standards in order to please others and conditioned to avoid physical activity which would develop physical strength, fitness, and tonality which might benefit their bodily attachment and sense of self-sufficiency and independence.

The average person has difficulty taking a good hard look at his/her body and really seeing it as it is. Many people avoid looking at themselves in mirrors and wear clothes meant to conceal or deceive. Strong emotions such as guilt and shame are often aroused when people do look at themselves. This, then, often produces an avoidance reaction. Looking at one's own image becomes unpleasant, causing the person to look away as a defense.

According to Fisher (1973), the average person "keeps a distance" when viewing self. People even have difficulty accurately visualizing the size of certain body parts. Individuals have a hard time recognizing what they look like even though they have more contact with their bodies than with anything else in the environment.

Hooker and Convisser (1983) claim that many women separate their bodies from their person. This perpetuates the problem of body distortion. Some body parts are simply difficult to examine visually: the anus, genitals, back of the body. Most people only have a vague notion of their internal organs and body's systems. While practical limitations restrict one's ability to examine some parts of one's body visually, one can use other sensations such as pain, temperature, and touch, for example, to become more aware of one's body.

Many people also learn to have a negative attitude towards their body from religious and moralistic sources. Montague (1971) suggested that many body taboos probably grew out of a fear closely related to the Christian traditions, the fear of bodily pleasure. Most people are body phobic. That is, they do not attend to their bodily sensations except when they become sick, or are consulting a physician. Body awareness soon becomes associated only with matters of health or illness.

According to Satir (1981) and Baker and Kepner (1981), people also detach from their bodies to avoid uncomfortable sensations. Uncomfortable feelings arise when a person's experience does not fit with the rules an individual thinks he/she must follow in order to be loved. For example:

> Experience: "I am angry."
> Rule: Anger is **not** OK.
> Result: I tighten my jaw. I squeeze in.

According to Kepner (1987), under normal conditions, emotion is expressed through movement out to the environment where needs can be completed. For example:

> longing—reaching out with arms and hands
> sadness—vocal sobs, facial expressions, contraction of
> the muscles involving breathing

Where family/cultural rules prohibit expression, physical tensions develop to block such expressions which would otherwise be punished or criticized. For example:

Rule	Prevents Expression of
Boys don't cry	crying
Be nice	anger
Be strong	fear

Parts which are denied as a result of such rules gradually become inaccessible and also are projected onto others. In fact, many relationships are based on projective identification where each partner reflects disowned parts of the other (Scarf, 1987).

Chronic tension eventually results in a lack of sensation. Muscular contractions were first employed as a creative method of survival when the person was powerless, unable to change the environment. Muscular contractions at that time were used to protect the person from a flood of "dangerous" sensations (Baker & Kepner, 1981; Satir, 1981). Unfortunately, these tensions often become chronic and habitual, gradually developing into structure (for example, caved in chest). More appropriate responses to a changed environment often are not developed.

An inner drive seems to exist in most people to regain the body sensitization which has been blocked. According to Baker and Kepner (1981), increased awareness of body sensation improves one's contact with reality, enhances self knowing, and increases self assurance. Baker and Kepner (1981) described two main sources of sensation: internal stimuli, which ground people in themselves, and external stimuli, which ground people in the world. Internal stimuli include kinesthetic stimuli, sense of movement; proprioception, one's sense of location of body parts; and visceral receptors, sensations of pressure, pain, internal images and thoughts (Baker & Kepner, 1981). Baker and Kepner described external stimuli as experienced through vision, hearing, smell, taste, and touch. In recovering sensation, Baker and Kepner suggested that the individual discipline his/herself to concentrate on sensations and stay with those sensations avoiding premature labeling. The senses require reawakening and re-education.

Smith's (1985) review of the meaning of a number of types of sensory experiences is shown in Table 9.1. He explained how each of these body phenomena reveals particular energy dynamics. Such a body scan can pinpoint precise areas in need of body work and can help to identify which are in need of exploration to determine the presence of toxic introjects (see Chapter 4) which may be interfering with awareness.

TABLE 9.1
Types of Sensation

Hot Spots—when energy charge exceeds discharge; charged and held energy.

Cold Spots—deadened or de-energized areas; areas where energy has been withdrawn to prevent aliveness.

Tension—the experience of chronic muscle contraction.

Pain—the result of strong, prolonged tension.

Numbness—the result of nerve pressure due to prolonged tension or pain. Sensation of coldness may coexist if tension interferes with blood flow.

Tingling, Prickly Feelings—these sensations appear when deadened areas (cold and/or numb) become enlivened.

Energy Streamings—deep vibrations which run up and down the body; free flowing excitement.

Most people do not live in their bodies—they live in their heads. This is understandable, given the negative messages people often receive about their bodies and prohibitions against bodily pleasure. The body is typically not viewed as a temple but rather often as a place of sin. If individuals could instead become better friends with their bodies, get to know their bodies, the body could become a finely tuned feedback instrument, invaluable to coping (Jencks, 1977).

Body awareness is inhibited not only by early experiences interacting with caretakers as described earlier, but also by the body depersonalization which is encouraged in Western culture (Fisher, 1973). In Western culture a dualism exists between mind and body. This split is evidenced linguistically when people say "I like my body," "My body is tired today." Inherent in the language people use is a split. People do not have a body, they are their bodies. In the process of civilization people have shown increasing disregard for their bodies.

Even the fashion industry encourages detachment from body sensations. People are forced to conform to current styles regardless of their comfort, or compatibility with their own feelings, or even with practical considerations. This is one way people ignore, do not tend to, do not respect their physical preferences.

However, in a number of ways, people resist body depersonalization. They attempt to regain a connection with their feelings and sensations in both constructive and in potentially self destructive ways (See Table 9.2).

Direct body manipulation through massage, Trager Psychophysical work, Reichian therapy or other body focused approaches may be used to enhance awareness of sensation (Jourard & Landsman, 1980). According to Lowen (1967), "The feeling of identity stems from a feeling of contact with the body. To know who one is, and individual must be aware of what (he/she) feels." The average person has much difficulty developing a clear, meaningful picture of his/her body. Such methods have been successful in increasing levels of self and body satisfaction.

TABLE 9.2
Examples of Attempts at Resensitization

Potentially Destructive	Constructive
Extremely spicy foods	Body awareness work (Trager, Massage, Aston patterning, etc.)
Fast Driving	Saunas
Smoking	Yoga
Drugs	Sports or other forms of movement (dance, martial arts, Tai Chi Chuan)
Thrill seeking, dangerous activities	Touch (light stroking, rubbing, vibrating, tapping, rocking)
Films packed with violence, suspense	Breathing work

Sensation

The opposite of body detachment is being sensorily aware. Sensation is the raw data of our experience (Baker & Kepner, 1981). Development of one's sensory apparatus is crucial to healthy functioning and high self esteem. Explore your senses by considering the following questions:

1. When you look, what do you see? Is there a difference between looking and seeing?

2. How much do you take in with your hearing? Can you close off your hearing?

3. How do different things feel? Texture, warmth, pressure, form? How much do you give/receive through touch?

4. Really taste your food today. What do you notice when you focus on savoring your food? What kinds of tastes appeal to you most? Least?

5. Can you identify different smells? How keen is your nose?

6. How tuned in are you to your internal world? Of what internal sensations are you aware (such as, cold spots, numbness, tensions, warm areas)?

7. How much do you take in through each sense? Which are your favored senses? How can you resensitize the underdeveloped ones?

Another aspect of resensitizing one's body involves revitalizing deadened areas (Baker & Kepner, 1981). To determine which areas of the body are deadened look for areas which

> lack arousal—feel numb—are hardened (muscular armor, for example, in man's overdeveloped chest)—are flaccid.

According to Baker and Kepner (1981), resensitization of these deadened areas involves rubbing, moving, touching, exercising that part of the body.

Mind-Body Connection

Fisher (1973) associated various physical problems with specific psychological issues as a way of reading one's body in order to become more closely attuned to one's emotional state and, therefore, to be able to cope more adequately. Feelings usually have a somatic base. By attending to sensation, people may be guided to reconnect with lost feelings. For example, awareness of your tensing your jaw may give you a clue to anger you are feeling. Increased body awareness can help people find their way back to feelings. If one considers the body a metaphor for what is happening emotionally with a person (as presented in Table 9.3), numerous relationships can be hypothesized.

TABLE 9.3
Body Metaphors

Body Condition	Emotional Condition
Sprained ankle	emotionally ungrounded
Hemorrhoids	holding onto feelings too tightly
Stomach problems	up-down issues; self esteem issues
Headache	perfectionism; anger and frustration
Astigmatism	feeling unbalanced
Pimples	irritation
Asthmatic	dependent on a person or situation, afraid to break away, wants to control or dominate; full of ideas to get ahead but fearful of pushing against opposition for fear they can't succeed; have not learned free expression; rage trapped in chest
Cold	combination of helplessness and suppressed anger; an inner "crying" over something they feel; they can't do anything about and are angry because they can't
Ulcers and stomach	great need to be loved and secure; great need to be successful in business to justify being loved; rooted in the feeling of guilt; great need to be loved but they may not feel worthy of love; introverted types have "inside" ailments
Mononucleosis	"victims" were pressured, consciously or not, by higher ups beyond what they could or wanted to do; young people out of school and on their own for the first time and finding a career or romance hard to handle are susceptible
Gallstones, Kidney stones	people hold in things which bother them and bury them deep in their system rather than letting them go

Table 9.3 (Continued)

Body Condition	Emotional Condition
High blood pressure	Suppression of inner hostility and rage for fear of hurting someone they love
Diabetes	The sweets of life have been taken away from them; may have been caused by a loss of a loved one
Lower back ache & other back pain	thrown out of balance; feelings about the injustice of balance of power; not feeling fully supported or feeling the burden of supporting another; not being able to ask for help in carrying the load; people who can give but have a hard time accepting; living with or being a perfectionist
Foot problems	relates to one's foundation; one's footing; feeling stepped on and feeling sorry for oneself
Heart	symbol of the love of one's life and the people in one's life; relates to loneliness, loss of love and connection to others
Sore throat	restrained anger

Borysenko (1987) cited that recent major studies show that 75% of visits to doctors are either for illnesses which would improve without care or are related to stress and anxiety. Even the most conservative sources, Pelletier (1977) explained, classify such illnesses as arthritis, migraine, bronchial asthma, hypertension, and certain types of colitis as psychosomatic. Other sources (Fisher, 1973; Steadman, 1979) stretched to hazard guesses about other possible relationships between body symptoms and emotional states. Steadman (1979) and Hay (1985) encouraged people to look at pain in the body as an indicator that they are "off the path." Kepner (1987) postulated that a correlation exists between body estrangement and illness.

Siegel (1986) stressed that the fundamental vulnerability to illness comes from people's inability to love themselves which he believes is the result of not having been loved in childhood. Siegel's (1986) work attempted to help people learn how to behave lovingly towards themselves and to develop a greater spiritual awareness. Meditation and visualization are two of the tools he recommends in the healing regimen to promote inner peace and harmony of mind, body, and spirit. Both Siegel (1986) and Borysenko (1987) also emphasized the importance of faith, hope, and prayer in unlocking healing energies. Anxiety, tension, and stress release increased adrenalin and cortisol which while providing quick energy also inhibit the immune system (Borysenko, 1987). Daily meditation along with a practiced flexible attitude toward adversities of daily life can yield physiological as well as psychological rewards, according to Borysenko (1987). Learning to let go, to stay open and patient, and to accept oneself, imperfections and all, can help reduce stress and improve physical health (Borysenko, 1987).

Body as Friend

Most people treat their bodies as their enemies rather than experiencing a unity of mind and body. For example, the typical person might say, "Oh, I have a headache. Wish it would go away. I'll take two aspirins. Can't get anything done like this." The pain is treated as an inconvenience/annoyance which needs anesthetizing. However, another way of viewing it is to see the headache pain as a signal. The body is trying to give the owner a message about something—overstress, the need to cry. One would use the pain as a signal to tune inside and identify the need expressed by the symptom. In this case, the owner's response was to try to silence the symptom without listening to its message. In reowning one's body for higher self esteem, individuals learn to listen to themselves, to use physical signals as resources for awareness of and fulfillment of needs.

The importance of developing a loving relationship with one's body cannot be stressed enough. Virginia Satir (1980) once told a story about a woman she met who hated her legs. Satir asked her, "Tell me, have your legs ever done you any good?" The woman thought a few moments and then replied, "Well, one time when someone tried to attack me, they helped me escape. I ran so fast he couldn't keep up." Satir replied, "Now your legs are receiving love, before they only got hate." Becoming healthy and whole requires learning to be in touch with and appreciate all parts of oneself, including one's body and to work in coordination with all parts. Hutchinson's (1985) book includes numerous helpful exercises combining visual and kinesthetic approaches aimed at restoring body awareness and a more positive body image.

In recent years a number of researchers have studied the effects of various forms of physical activity on body satisfaction and self esteem. Clance, Mitchell and Engleman (1980) demonstrated an improvement in childrens' satisfaction with their bodies and body processes through a group process consisting of awareness training and yoga exercises. Engleman, Clance and Imes (1982) also demonstrated significantly improved body and self-cathexis for adult yoga subjects as compared with controls.

Another study by Ben-Shlomo and Short (1986) suggested psychological benefits for use of aerobic conditioning with sedentary females. Brown, Morrow and Livingston (1982) suggested that a variety of conditioning programs may impact on selected aspects of self-concept in women if participants engage in a program long enough to effect change. Trujillo (1983) showed that women assigned to a weight training program evidenced significantly larger gains in self-esteem than those assigned to a mixed activity program or running group. Gains in strength, tonality, and success in a previously male dominated sport are suggested as a possible explanation of these results.

BREATHING AND GROUNDEDNESS

A person who has high self esteem, who feels good about him/herself, has a sense of having his/her feet firmly planted on the ground. One's personhood, one's feeling of solidarity are reflected in one's body. The more a person can feel contact with the ground, literally the earth underneath one's feet, and can maintain this position of contact, the more excitation the person can tolerate, the more feeling the person can handle, and the better the person will feel about him/herself.

An individual who is ungrounded, who exhibits a chronic lack of contact with the ground, is literally a pushover. The footing of one who is ungrounded is tenuous and their breathing lacks fullness. People such as this deal with high energy drives by containing them and live with a persistent terror of becoming completely disorganized. Fear immobilizes self-assertion; stress overwhelms, consequently, self esteem suffers. Individuals such as this are cut off from feeling and are unable to adequately support themselves.

Breathing, of course, is an essential element in the grounding process. According to Speads (1978), the quality of one's breathing is directly related to the quality of one's life. A person's bodily organs, emotional, and intellectual life depend on sufficient oxygen supplies. Despite this fact, the majority of Americans, as a product of our modern-day life, are almost breathless. By becoming aware of one's breathing, and by using its full support, one can increase the quality of life and heighten self esteem. According to Lowry (1980) one's breathing pattern influences one's outlook on life and one's feeling about self. He speculated that a relationship probably exists between chronic underbreathing, depression, low energy, and low self esteem.

More effective breathing results in clearer thinking and a positive change in mood. Speads (1978) emphasized that people are influenced by any variation in breathing, positively, when breathing supports them adequately; negatively, when breathing is blocked. Variations in breathing occur all the time. A person's breathing is affected by all life experiences. Instead of allowing breathing to fluctuate, people often cling to a disturbed pattern until it becomes habitual. Speads (1978) provided a series of well-sequenced exercises that aim at increasing awareness of breathing, feeling one's breathing and allowing it to change, and decreasing the time of recovery from poor breathing states.

Human beings tend to display a pattern of compressing excitement until it builds up to a certain point and then expressing it with focused satisfaction. This is true, for example, of verbal expression ("I couldn't hold it in any longer, I had to tell him") and in the orgasmic phenomenon, with its building to a climax. Blockage of this cycle, even at the bodily level, results in impairment of the individual's capacity to take in and discharge energy, thereby affecting self esteem. Interference with the rhythm of expansion and contraction of energy, according to Keleman (1975), is debilitating.

BODY AS COMMUNICATOR

Nonverbal communication conveys four times the information power as verbal communication (Knapp, 1972). Yet, even though this dimension holds such impact, people rarely are in touch with what their nonverbal behavior conveys or how they could express themselves more effectively.

The nonverbal dimension of human behavior involves several different categories: kinesics (physical characteristics, such as touching), paralinguistics, and proxemics.

Kinesics

Kinetic behavior includes gestures, movements of the body, limbs, hands, head, feet and legs, facial expressions, eye behavior, and posture. According to Knapp (1972), kinesics include furrow of brow, slump of shoulder, and tilt of head. Body shapes, height, weight, skin tone, general attractiveness, and body odors also are included in the study of kinesics.

Touching behavior encompasses such things as stroking, hitting, greeting, and holding. Even though the therapeutic use of the hands can be traced through ancient history, the American culture places strict limitations on tactile interaction. Yet, Krieger (1979) reported that therapeutic touch affects patients' blood components, brain waves, and elicits a generalized relaxation response. The importance of touch as a potent means of nurturing other human beings is generally underestimated (Wilson, 1982). Physical contact, in addition to tone of voice, is the earliest and most primitive means of communication (Frank, 1957). Stroking, verbal and nonverbal, is necessary for maintaining positive human functioning. Yet, most adults expect that touching be conducted in extremely personal and intimate relationships, which makes most touching "sensual" in nature and, thereby, a scarce commodity because the number of appropriate contexts are limited by that definition. Montague (1971) stated that early tactile experiences seem crucial to later mental and emotional adjustment. Likely ongoing tactile experiences are crucial to continued emotional adjustment. Touch serves a primary role in nurturing/consoling another person. Touch also has been shown to increase self-disclosure (Lomranz & Shapiro, 1974) and stimulate self-exploration (Pattison, 1973). Generally, people do not touch people they do not like except in fighting with them. The very act of touching says, "I accept you," "I care about you," "I want to give to you." Touch, therefore, is a critical skill in nurturing self and others and in helping people relate to the outside world.

Paralinguistics

Paralanguage concerns how something is said and includes voice qualities: pitch range, pitch control, rhythm control, tempo, articulation, and resonance (Knapp, 1972). This is a basic and early mode of preverbal communication.

Proxemics

Proxemics is considered to be the study of the individual's use and perception of social and personal space (Knapp, 1972). Individuals of low self esteem often spatially distance themselves from others to a greater degree than is average. Those individuals of high self esteem take charge of space around them and use it to enhance their life. They manage their space in such a way to encourage social interaction and development of their potential.

TOTAL BODY IMAGE

Certain nonverbal behaviors can be **clues** to self esteem problems. Feelings of insecurity might, for instance, be manifested in an individual's slouched shoulders, head tilted to the side, persistent self-touching, and a high pitched voice with many verbal segregates, for example, speech errors and latency.

People cannot refrain from communicating. Individuals communicate feelings through tone of voice, body posture, facial expressions, and gestures, as well as with words. People continually give clues regarding how much they value themselves (See Table 9.4). This statement, then, influences how others value one (Miller, Nunnally, & Wackman, 1975).

TABLE 9.4
Some Possible Physical Manifestations
of Low-high Self Esteem

Bodily Cues	High Self Esteem	Low Self Esteem
chest	soft but solid	sunken, constricted
eyes	bright	dull
skin tone	smooth	erupted
breathing	full	shallow
muscle tone	elastic	tight or flaccid
proportion of body	segments coordinated	top-bottom split, uncoordinated
gait	high, bouncy	burdened
neck	pliable	rigid
head	moves easily	does not move freely; immobile; movements jerky
pelvis	swings freely	frozen
alignment of body	aligned	off-center
hands	well cared for, smooth, nails clean and trimmed; expressive	rough, nails bitten or dirty; hidden out of sight
movements	coordinated	awkward
shoulders	relaxed	slumped/raised
actions	supported by total body, moving from the "center," flowing	incomplete, chaotic
posture	relaxed, spine straight	slumped or rigid
arms	animated	hang lifelessly
jaw	relaxed	juts out
total body energy	vibrant	dull

As Kurtz (1971) and Kurtz and Prestera (1970) pointed out, a person's walk can often give clues to his/her life style. With regard to self esteem, one might notice the following differences:

confidence—head erect, shoulders straight and loose, chest breathing fully and easily, gait light, movement generated from the person's "center," about two inches below the navel.

defeat—drooping head, slumped shoulders, caved-in chest, slow, burdened gait, unbalanced movement.

Discouragement of bodily contact produces intense longing for contact, feelings of helplessness, shame, self-hatred ("I hate myself for wanting"). According to Keleman (1975), this undermines the bodily self which is the basis of self esteem. A person having contact with his own body is in contact with feelings, desires, sensations, and pleasures. The principle avenues through which feelings are expressed are the voice, body, movement, and eyes.

CONCLUSION

A person's body is the oldest expression of him/herself. The body is a catalogue of one's life experiences. In a unified way, people physically express themselves to the world, making statements about themselves and their relationship to the world. Attention to one's physical sensations can provide a path to one's inner barometer. Through a close and friendly relationship with one's body, possibilities of higher functioning and enhanced self esteem are created. The body is a powerful avenue for human change and human nurturance.

———

ACTIVITY 9.1   THE LONG BODY

Introduction

Your body broadcasts what you have experienced. One's body is an image in the world that is meant to evoke responses. It is the result of the impact of the environment on self. Your body will tell you the story of all your experiences— how you survived.

Time Required

30 minutes

Participants

Any number; adolescents or adults

Setting

Office or classroom

Materials

Large sheets of paper and crayons

Procedure

Draw the current image that you have of yourself. What does your body say to you? Notice:

> *how your head sits on your neck (forward, back, balanced)*

> *hypertonics (forced rigidity) versus collapsed posture (self-worth not developed)*

> *attitude (defiant, defeated, etc.)*

> *the tensions? numbness? liveliness? rigidities? softness? where are they?*

From the previous statements, derive a few propositions:

> *What are you saying to yourself? about the world? about sexuality? What it means to be a woman? a man?*

> *What do you have to do to maintain yourself that way?*

> *What does your body say about who you want us to believe you are? Example, "I can handle things, I don't need you."*

How do you soften yourself? Walk that way.

What is it that your body inhibits you from doing?

What is it that you want to communicate?

The long body is the whole process of your body from neonate onward. The memory of the childhood body still exists now though you are mostly in contact with your surface body, your present form. Within each person are the following forms:

> child,
> adolescent,
> adult, and
> older adult.

What is it that you do to hide the previous body images? People oftentimes practice somebody's image of what they should be. . .good little girl, etc. What images are you practicing to be? What image is trying to be without all things which interfere with it?

Get in touch with images you had of yourself at different ages:

> *6 months—racing around in walker, energy, motion*

> *10 years—athletic, hand on hip, motion*

> Come up with at least five images from various life stages.

> What do those forms say about yourself?

> Was the world bigger or smaller than you?

> Were you angry, disappointed? What is the feeling conveyed?

Physically imitate each image from the inside out. Do this with each image. Go back and forth from 1 to 2 several times. Then 3, 2, 1, 2, 3, 4, 5, 2, 1, 3 . . . Feel all your body go up and down the track

> 1, 2, 3, 4, 5
> 5, 4, 3, 2, 1
> relax

Are 1,2,3,4 still alive in you now?

How did you know how to get from 1 to 4?

Run through each state—up and down. Stay with your own confusion, your own disorganization.

What did each image as you experienced each tell you about yourself in relation to sensation? Of what were you aware?

Outcome

Increases body awareness and awareness of the messages one's body image conveys to the world.

Note. Written from memory of exercise conducted at workshop (Keleman, 1976) and Keleman (1979).

ACTIVITY 9.2   BODY APPRECIATION

Introduction

This activity helps you to focus on what you appreciate about your body encouraging you to develop a friendlier relationship with it. The activity is a nurturance phase activity.

Time Required

30 minutes

Participants

Adolescents or adults, any number

Setting

Office or classroom

Materials

Paper and pen

Procedure

Look at yourself in a full-length mirror. Make a list of what you can appreciate about your body. Pay attention to your skin, hair, fingers, eyes, arms, everything about your physical self. Concentrate on what you like. Try to skip over areas you often criticize. Make affirming statements about what you appreciate.

Now, go back to those areas you tend to criticize. Is there anything you can find to appreciate about these parts.

Examples: "I don't like my hair because it's hard to manage since it's very fine. However, my hair is also very much like my deceased father's hair and so it reminds me of him. I like remembering him." Write whatever aspect you can find to appreciate.

For those areas you criticize and cannot find something to appreciate, go back and see if you can accept each. Write a statement of acceptance.

"I don't like the fact that my upper torso is large in comparison to my lower body but this is something God gave to me and I accept it."

Outcome

Focuses on the positive aspects of your physical self.

ACTIVITY 9.3   A LIFT

Introduction

Participation in this activity teaches a group how to physically nurture one person. It is an activity which fits in the maintenance phase of intervention. Being held, rocked, and hummed to by a group of loving individuals can provide warm comfort for a person.

Time Required

30 minutes

Participants

Adults; 8 to 20 participants

Setting

Carpeted group room or office

Materials

None

Procedure

One person lies in center of circle flat on his/her back. Group members hold hands in circle, close eyes, and move to deep, slow, peaceful breathing. Part your lips and breathe through your mouth slowly and deeply.

As you exhale, let some natural nurturing sounds come out. When you are ready, break contact with the circle and make some physical contact with the focus person and, as you breathe out, blow those nurturing feelings onto the focus person.

When the last person makes contact, members slowly place hands underneath the focus person and lift him/her slowly and ever so gently waist high into the air rocking and humming as they move.

After a few minutes, raise the person **slowly** higher and then **gently and slowly,** lower the participant, all the while making natural, nurturant sounds.

Again, make some kind of physical contact with the focus person to say goodbye. Resume holding hands with people in your circle and finish with a meditation on your positive, relaxing feelings. Discuss feelings if appropriate.

Outcomes

Provides a person with an intense feeling of nurturance and support.

ACTIVITY 9.4   RELAXATION IMAGERY: THE POWER OF THE MIND

Introduction

Performing this activity helps people learn how to relax. It teaches people a beginning step in how to work with themselves rather than against themselves. It is best used in the nurturance phase of intervention.

Time Required

45 minutes

Participants

Any number; adolescents and adults

Setting

Office, group room, or classroom

Materials

Paper and pencil

Procedure

Rate your degree of Tension-Relaxation.

> 100 = most tense you could ever be; tension is unbearable
> 75 = good deal of tension and anxiety
> 50 = moderate amount of tension
> 25 = calm, little tension
>   0 = calmest and most relaxed you could ever be

List some things that you do that are very relaxing to you.

List some things you do well.

Choose your favorite item from the relaxing list and your favorite of things you do well. I want you to then picture each, one at a time, fully in your mind with as much detail as possible, the more detail the better. Use those scenes which make you feel relaxed and happy. To design each scene effectively, follow the guidelines as listed:

> describe all the sights, sounds, and smells in the scene;
> describe exactly what you are doing; and
> describe how you look and how you feel.

Write each scene and read into a tape recorder at a slow, even pace.

Relax by the deep muscle relaxation method.

Picture the relaxation scene in your mind for 15 to 20 seconds. Picture the competency scene in your mind for 15 to 20 seconds. Picture the relaxation scene again, then repeat the competency scene, the relaxation scene, and so forth. Switch back and forth 5 to 10 times.

Rate your level of tension-relaxation once again.

Notice how one's images can affect one's mood and level of tension-relaxation.

Discuss in groups of 5 or 6.

Outcomes

One learns a method of self-relaxation as a skill to reduce/manage tension and anxiety.

ACTIVITY 9.5   BREATH OF LIFE

Introduction

Breath is really the Breath of Life. Breathing can have an important effect on one's feelings about self. The body literally has less energy to work with when an individual breathes very shallowly.

When people are young, they learn to hold their breath when they are afraid or tense, for in cutting off their breathing they cut off some of these painful feelings. This shallow breathing then becomes solidified into a pattern of holding in which describes an "up-tight" person. Lots of energy is invested in defending the person. People with low self esteem often feel low in energy and power, both emotionally and physically. This is a nurturance phase activity.

Time Required

30 minutes

Participants

Any number; adolescents and adults

Setting

Carpeted office or group room

Materials

None

Procedure

Find a comfortable place to lie down. Relax and take in a deep breath. Fill your chest, lungs, and stomach with air. Find your physical center and relax, with each breath you feel lighter and lighter. Stay focused on your breathing as you breathe out and blow all other thoughts away. Do this several times. Stay in the here and now. Notice how your body feels.

When you've had the time to thoroughly rest yourself, slowly come back to this room and open your eyes.

Questions:

How did that feel?
What were you aware of?
How hard was it to let go?
What did it do for your feelings about yourself?

Repeat frequently throughout the day

Outcome

Increases one's awareness of breathing and the supportive nature of breath.

————

ACTIVITY 9.6   LETTING GO

Introduction

Participants work with each other in a physical way to help each other get in touch with what it feels like to put oneself in another's hands and practice letting go. This is a nurturance phase activity.

Time Required

45 minutes

Participants

Adults and adolescents; any number

Setting

Carpeted room

Materials

None

Procedure

Go through relaxation and breathing procedures.

Sit Indian-style with partner in front of you lying on his/her back with head nearest your legs. Focus person is the partner lying down. Lift the focus person's head slowly and lovingly, being careful to support fully the neck. The focus person is **not to do any work.** Focus person is to let his/her neck go, leaving self totally in control of partner. Pay attention to your breathing and other experiences, feelings, images you have as you do this activity. Partner slowly moves focus person's head from one side to the other, pays attention to any rigidity or resistance and, then, slowly rests focus person's head on floor.

Very slowly, switch roles.

Process with partner. What did you feel throughout this experience? Was it difficult for you to let go? Was it difficult to put yourself in someone's else's hands? How did you avoid letting go? How did you let go? What did you learn from this experience? How did you feel about the love and caring? What effect did this have on how you feel about yourself? How does this apply to your life?

Analyze learnings.

Outcomes

Enables one to have an experience of letting go of oneself and to help allow another to let go through very gentle nurturance.

———

ACTIVITY 9.7   GROUNDING WITH YOUR BODY

Introduction

This activity helps one to become more aware of the body and how this awareness can help maintain self esteem. It is a maintenance phase activity.

Time Required

30 minutes

Participants

Children or adults; individual or group.

Setting

Office or classroom

Materials

None

Procedure

Place your feet 8 to 12 inches apart. Feel your feet against the ground. Tilt your body forward just a little while keeping your body in a straight line with your pelvis.

Keep your knees slightly bent and try not to collapse your chest. Be sure your heels remain on the floor and breathe through your mouth down deep into your stomach.

Allow your jaw to relax and imagine that you are breathing through every pore in your body. Soon you will feel some vibrations through your body. Allow these vibrations to come while you breathe slowly and deeply.

Make fists and place them in the small of your back while you pull your elbows gently towards each other.

Allow your body to bend back just a bit while your eyes still look forward.

Continue breathing through your mouth and be sure your knees remain bent.

Now relax, allowing your arms to gently move to your sides.

Breathe easily and rest for a moment.

Now, move your feet 18 inches apart. Turn your feet slightly towards each other.

Slowly bend forward at your waist. Relax your head and neck and just bob up and down a little.

Relax.

Allow the tips of your fingers to touch the floor without leaning on your fingers.

Your heels should be on the floor, your tailbone pointed up.

Keep your knees unlocked and your jaw relaxed.

Very slowly stand up straight once again and take a moment to rest.

This time spread your legs wide apart and place your feet outward while first bending your right leg. Most of your weight should be on your right leg while you stretch your left leg.

Be sure you keep breathing through this activity and keep your jaw relaxed.

Now reverse legs, bending your left leg while stretching your right leg.

Now, stand up once again, breathing, and keeping your knees flexed and jaw relaxed.

Slowly, come to a kneeling position.

Drop your chest to the floor, stretch your arms out.

Breathe easily and rest.

Outcomes

Helps one become more body aware through the use of breathing.

Note. Activity is original. Idea initiated by Lowen and Lowen (1977).

REFERENCES

Anonymous. (1987). *Listen to the hunger.* Minneapolis, MN: Hazelden.

Asher, W. L. (1974). Appetite suppressants as an aid in obesity control. In L. Lasagne (Ed.), *Obesity: Causes, consequences, and treatment.* New York: Kreiger.

B., Bill. (1981). *Overeaters anonymous. The basic text for compulsive overeaters.* Minneapolis, MN: CompCare Publications.

Baker, F., & Kepner, J. (1981, February). *Retroflection and desensitization.* Cleveland: Gestalt Institute of Cleveland.

Barlin, A. L., & Greenberg, R. (1980). *Move and be moved.* Van Nuys, CA: Learning Through Movement.

Bell C., Kirkpatrick, S., & Rinn, R. (1986, May). Body image of anorexic, obese, and normal females. *Journal of Clinical Psychology, 42*(3), 431-439.

Ben-Shlomo, L., & Short, M. (1986, Winter). The effects of physical conditioning on selected dimensions of self-concept in sedentary females. *Occupational Therapy in Mental Health, 5*(46), 27-46.

Bergner, M., Remer, P., & Whetsell, C. (1985). Transforming women's body image: A feminist counseling approach. *Women and Therapy, IV,* 25-38.

Biller, H., & Liebman, D. (1971). Body build and sex role preference and sex role adoption in junior high school boys. *Journal of Genetic Psychology, 118,* 81-86.

Birtchnell, S.A., Dolan, B.M., & Lacy, J.H. (1987). Body image distortion in non-eating disordered women. *International Journal of Eating Disorders, 6,* 385-391.

Borysenko, J. (1987). *Mending the body, mending the mind.* New York: Bantam Books.

Boskind-White, M., White, W.C. (1983). *Bulimarexia.* New York: Norton.

Boston Women's Health Book Collective (1984). *The new our bodies, ourselves.* New York: Simon and Schuster.

Brown, E., Morrow, J., & Livingston, S. (1982). Self-concept changes in women as a result of training. *Journal of Sport Psychology, 4,* 354-363.

Bruch, H. (1973). *Eating disorders: Obesity, anorexia nervosa and the person within.* New York: Basic Books.

Calden, G., Lundy, R. M., & Schlafer, R. J. (1959). Sex differences in body concepts. *Journal of Consulting Psychology, 23,* 276.

Chernin, K. (1981). *The obsession: Reflections on the tyranny of slenderness.* New York: Harper and Row.

Clance, P.R., Mitchell, M., & Engleman, S. (1980, Spring). Body cathexis in children as a function of awareness training and yoga. *Journal of Clinical Child Psychology,* 82-85.

Clifford, E. (1971). Body satisfaction in adolescence. *Perceptual and Motor Skills, 33,* 119-225.

Diekelmann, N. (1977). *Primary health care of the well adult.* New York: McGraw Hill.

Engelman, S., Clance, P.R., & Imes, S. (1982). Self and body—cathexis change in therapy and yoga groups. *Journal of American Society of Psychosomatic Dentistry & Medicine, 29,* 77-88.

Finch, C., & Hayflick, L. (1977). *Handbook of the biology of aging.* New York: Van Nostrand Reinhold.

Fisher, S. (1973). *Body consciousness: You are what you feel.* Englewood Cliffs, NJ: Prentice-Hall.

Frank, L. (1957). Tactile communication. *Genetic Psychology Monographs, 56,* 209-255.

Gillis, J. S. (1982). *Too tall too small.* Champaign, IL: Institute for Personality and Ability Testing.

Greenspan, M. (1983). *A new approach to women and therapy.* New York: McGraw-Hill.

Harmatz, M., Gronendyke, J., & Thomas, T. (1985). The underweight male: The unrecognized problem group of body image research. *The Journal of Obesity and Weight Regulation, 4,* 258-267.

Hay, L. (1985). *You can heal your life.* Farmingdale, NY: Coleman Pub.

Hollis, J. (1986). *Fat is a family affair.* San Francisco: Harper/Hazelden.

Hooker, D., & Convisser, E. (1983, December). Women's eating problems. An analysis of a coping mechanism. *Personal and Guidance Journal,* 236-239.

Hoover, M. (1984). The self-image of overweight adolescent females: a review of literature. *Maternal-child Nursing Journal, 13*(2), 125-137.

Huenemann, R. L., Shapiro, L. R., Hampton, M. C., & Mitchell, B. W. (1966). A longitudinal study of gross body composition and body conformation and their association with food and activity in teenage population. *American Journal of Clinical Nutrition. 18,* 325-338.

Hutchinson, M. (1985). *Transforming body image.* New York: The Crossing Press.

Jencks, B. (1977). *Your body: Biofeedback at its best.* Chicago: Nelson Hall.

Jersild, A. T. (1952). *In search of self: An exploration of the role of the school in promoting self-understanding.* New York: Columbia University, Teachers College.

Jones, M. D., & Mussen, P. H. (1958). Self-conceptions, motivations, and interpersonal attitudes of early and late maturing girls. *Child Development, 29,* 491-501.

Jourard, S., & Landsman, T. (1980). *Healthy personality.* New York: Macmillan.

Keleman, S. (1975). *The human ground.* Palo Alto, CA: Science and Behavior Books.

Keleman, S. (1976, December). Concepts and images of the body. A workshop with Joseph Campbell. Redwood, CA.

Keleman, S. (1979). *Somatic reality.* Berkeley, CA: Center.

Kepner, J. (1987). *Body process.* New York: Gestalt Institute of Cleveland Press.

Knapp, M. L. (1972). *Nonverbal communication in human interaction.* New York: Holt, Rinehart, and Winston.

Krieger, D. (1979). *The therapeutic touch.* Englewood Cliffs, NY: Harper & Row.

Kurtz, R. M. (1971). Body attitude and self esteem. *Proceedings of the 79th Annual Convention of APA, 6,* 467-468.

Kurtz, R., & Prestera, H. (1970). *The body reveals.* New York: Harper & Row.

L. Elizabeth. (1988). *Twelve steps for overeaters.* New York: Harper & Row.

Lebe, D. (1986). Female ego ideal conflicts in adulthood. *The American Journal of Psychoanalysis, 46,* 22-32.

Leon, G. R. (1975). Personality, body image, and eating pattern changes in overweight persons after weight loss. *Journal of Clinical Psychology, 31,* 618-623.

Leon, G. R., Bemis, K., Meland, M., & Nussbaum. D. (1978). Aspects of body image perception in obese and normal weight youngsters. *Journal of Abnormal Child Psychology, 6,* 361-371.

Leon, G. R., Eckert, E. D., Teed, D., & Buchwald, H. (1979). Changes in body image and other psychological factors after intestinal bypass surgery for massive obesity. *Journal of Behavioral Medicine, 2,* 39-59.

Lerner, R.M., Iwawaki, S., Chihara, T., & Sorell, G.T. (1980). Self-concept, self-esteem and body attitudes among Japanese male and female adolescents. *Child Development, 51,* 847-855.

Lerner, R.M., Orlos, J.B., & Knapp, J.R. (1976). Physical attractiveness, physical effectiveness, and self-concept in late adolescents. *Adolescence, 11,* 313-326.

Lerner, R.M., & Gellert, E. (1969). Body-build, identification, preference, and aversion in children. *Developmental Psychology, 1,* 456-462.

Lomranz, J., & Shapiro, A. (1974). Communication patterns of self-disclosure and touching behavior. *Journal of Psychology, 88*(2), 223-227.

Lowen, A. (1967). *Betrayal of the body.* New York: Collier Books.

Lowen, A., & Lowen, L. (1977). *The way to vibrant health: A manual of bioenergetic exercises.* New York: Harper & Row.

Lowry, T. (1980). Hyperventilation and hypoventilation. *The Journal of Biological Experience, 2,* 63-68.

Luce, G. (1979). *Your second life.* New York: Dell.

McCoy, K. (1982, July). Are you obsessed with your weight? *Seventeen, 41:* 80-81.

Mayer, V. (1978). *The fat illusion.* New Haven, CT: Fat Liberator Pub.

Mendelson, B., & White, D. (1982). Relation between body-esteem and self-esteem of obese and normal children. *Perceptual and Motor Skills, 54,* 899-905.

Miller, S., Nunnally, E., & Wackman, D. (1975). *Alive and aware.* Minneapolis: Interpersonal Communication Programs.

Mintz, L., & Betz, N. (1986). Sex differences in the nature, realism, and correlates of body image. *Sex roles,* Vol 15, No. 3 and 4, pp. 185-195.

Montague, M. F. A. (1971). *Touching: The human significance of the skin.* New York: Columbia University Press.

Mussen, P. H., & Jones, M. C. (1957). Self-conceptions, motivations, and interpersonal attitudes of late and early maturing boys. *Child Development, 28,* 243-256.

Nelson, E. (1975). *Movement games for children of all ages.* New York: Sterling.

Neuman, P., & Halvorson, P. (1983). *Anorexia nervosa and bulimia.* New York: Van Nostrand Rheinhold.

Offer, D., Ostrov, E., & Howard, K. (1981). *The adolescent: A psychological self-portrait*. New York: Basic Books.

Orbach, S. (1979). *Fat is a feminist issue*. New York: Berkley Books.

Orbach, S. (1982). *Fat is a feminist issue. Vol. II*. New York: Berkley Books.

Pattison, J. (1973). Effects of touch on self-exploration and the therapeutic relationships. *Journal of Consulting and Clinical Psychology, 40*, 170-175.

Pelletier, K. (1977). *Mind as healer, mind as slayer*. New York: Dell.

Peterson, A.C., & Taylor, B. (1980). The biological approach to adolescence: Biological change and psychological adaptation. In J. Adelson (Ed.), *Handbook of Adolescent Psychology*. New York: John Wiley.

Rosen, B. (1982, December). Love hate affair with my body: The story of a food addict. *Mademoiselle, 88*, 141-143.

Rosen, E. M., & Ross, A. O. (1968). Relationship of body-image to self-concept. *Journal of Consulting and Clinical Psychology, 32*, 100.

Roth, G. (1982). *Feeding the hungry heart*. New York: New American Library.

Salkin, J. (1973). *Body ego technique*. Springfield, IL: Charles C. Thomas.

Satir, V. (1980). Communication and the family. Workshop presented by Family Therapy Institute, South Bend, IN.

Satir, V. (1981, August). Presentation at Avanta process community. Park City, UT.

Scarf, M. (1987). *Intimate partners*. New York: Random House.

Sears, R., Rau, L., & Alpert, R. (1965). *Identification and child-rearing*. Stanford, CA: Stanford University Press.

Secord, R., & Jourard, S. (1953). The appraisal of body-cathexis and the self. *Journal of Consulting Psychology, 17*, 343-347.

Siegel, B. (1986). *Love, medicine and miracles*. New York: Harper & Row.

Smith, E. (1985). *The body in psychotherapy*. Jefferson, NC: McFarland.

Speads, C. (1978). Breathing: The ABC's. New York: Harper Colphon.

Steadman, A. (1979). *Who's the matter with me?* Marina del Rey, CA: DeVorss.

Strang, R. (1957). *The adolescent views himself*. New York: McGraw-Hill.

Stunkard, A. (1980). *Obesity*. Philadelphia: W.B. Saunders.

Sullivan, H. S. (1953). *The interpersonal theory of psychiatry*. New York: Norton.

Thompson, J.K., & Thompson, C.M. (1986). Body size distortion and self esteem in asymptomatic, normal weight males and females. *International Journal of Eating Disorders, 5,* 1061-1068.

Trujillo, C. (1983). The effects of weight training and running exercise. *International Journal of Sports Psychology, 14,* 162-173.

Tucker, L. (1982). Relationship between perceived somatotype and body cathexis of college males. *Psychological Reports, 50,* 983-989.

Wilson, J. M. (1982, January). The value of touch in psychotherapy. *American Journal Orthopsychiatry, 52*(1), 65-72.

Worsley, A. (1981). In the eye of the beholder: Social and personal characteristics of teenagers and their impressions of themselves as fat and slim people. *British Journal of Modern Medical Psychology, 54,* 231-242.

Yeatts, P. (1967). Developmental changes in the self-concept of children grades 3-12. *Florida Educational Research and Development Council Research Bulletin, 3*(2).

CHAPTER **10**

SELF ESTEEM AND CHILDREN OF SPECIAL NEEDS

As discussed in Chapter 2, the initial source of self esteem for children is their parents. Parents show an infant who he/she is in the manner in which they respond to the child. As children grow older, they have other mirrors which show them who they are. Teachers, friends, sitters, and significant others will perform this role. An apocryphal story told by Hartline (1982) emphasizes the importance of significant others to the development of self esteem in children:

> On the first day of school year an inner-city teacher picked up her materials and hurried to her classroom. Nearing the Christmas break, the principal dropped in on her class, since he knew it was a "difficult" one. He entered a room with happy busy children. He was amazed and whispered to the teacher, "My God, what's going on? Didn't you see their I.Q. scores?" The teacher responded that she thought those numbers were the children's locker numbers.

This story is illustrative of the positive effect a teacher can have on students if he/she believes in them. Unfortunately, many children are exposed to teachers and others who do not believe in them. Such individuals in a child's life often see others as they see themselves. If they do not have positive self esteem, very negative effects can happen with the children whose lives they touch.

If you happen to be a child with special needs, the understanding, acceptance, and assistance of others becomes especially important to the development of self esteem. While every type of special need child cannot be thoroughly discussed in this chapter, the available research about many of these children will be reviewed.

Research has demonstrated a high correlation between positive self esteem and academic achievement and low self esteem and nonachievement or under achievement (Hartline, 1982). Students who feel good about themselves and their ability to learn tend to learn more, like school better, and stay in school longer with regular attendance (Hartline, 1982). Students under the stress of failure perform at lower levels and have lower self esteem. Very often these children are special needs students, since they often have unique self esteem issues which are not addressed.

AFRO-AMERICAN CHILDREN

A vitally important procedure for those who study the self esteem of Afro-American children is to examine the developmental process within the child's social context and reference groups rather than from a perspective of the dominant culture (Spurlock, 1986). Spurlock listed five important considerations when studying Afro-American childrens' self esteem: skin color, impact of social change, positive role models, influence of family functioning, and influences from the broader environment.

Developmental Factors

Skin Color. The literature on skin color and its effect on self esteem of Afro-Americans is inconsistent. Some investigators have concluded that darker-skin children are more likely to have low self esteem while other studies have led to much different conclusions (Spurlock, 1986). Thus, the individual child's value and perceptions should be considered when studying self esteem since some children put less value on physical attractiveness while others place more value on this; and many times these children minimize the distinction between themselves and others, while some children maximize this distinction.

Impact of Social Change. The activities of the civil rights movement generated a resurgence of race consciousness and pride in Afro-Americans, thus reducing the influences of the negative attitude of the culture as a whole. In addition, a renewed interest has occurred in one's ancestral roots. These social changes have led to more positive influences on Afro-American children's self esteem. In a study of geographic regional differences in the development of self esteem, the discovery was that junior high school Afro-American students in a Southern city had significantly higher self esteem than did their white peers in the same city and their black counterparts in a Northern urban setting. Evidently, Afro-American students in the South benefited in self esteem from the cohesiveness and strength of their black community (Spurlock, 1986).

Positive Role Models. The presence of positive role models is a definite asset in the development of self esteem. These role models are often overlooked for Afro-American children because the role models for these children do not meet middle-class standards (Spurlock, 1986). Often a step-father who works two blue collar jobs, supports four children, and pays his taxes is not viewed by the culture as a whole outstanding role model. Actually social change has allowed for many more role models for Afro-Americans, but room for improvement still exists.

Influence of Family Functioning. Several studies negate the premise that separated or never-married families result in Afro-American children's low self esteem (Spurlock, 1986). Factors other than family structure alone need to be considered when discussing self esteem for these children. Health and security of the parents is a very important factor. Among the negative effects to healthy self esteem of these children is poverty, over crowded housing, and the high incidence of poisoning from inadequate storage of medication and cleaning supplies. Under stimulation of children is also a problem. The discontinuities in parenting which result from day care problems also can negatively affect self esteem. The strength of the extended family can be imperative, thus helping the children with self esteem issues. The family's relative position in the community is also a factor which influences self esteem.

Influences from the Broader Environment. As Afro-American children mature, they are exposed to social prejudice. Afro-Americans are overrepresented in exclusionary processes (Spurlock, 1986). For many, streets become the primary source of rewards. These children readily assimilate the interaction they view around them, resulting often in lowered self esteem.

All these factors have lead to the problem of dual identity for Afro-American children, in that the qualities attributed to Blackness are in opposition to the qualities rewarded in society (Mack, 1987). What are some interventions for enhancing Afro-American self esteem?

Interventions

Many of the interventions discussed thus far and in later chapters are, of course, very helpful to enhancing the self esteem of Afro-American children and adults. Some techniques, however, relate specifically to this population. Mack (1987) related four specific interventions for Afro-American children. One recommendation to enhance self esteem is to use members of the child's family or Black community as resources in teaching about the Black experience, thus providing excellent role models.

A second suggestion by Mack (1987) is for schools to use instructional materials which offer a multicultural perspective, thus providing a child with positive role models and an awareness of self-concept as it develops in the broader environment of the culture. Use of such materials aids in giving students a broader perspective. Education can use the student's culture and prior accomplishments as the context for discussing present accomplishments.

Third, Mack (1987) recommended that educators become more knowledgeable about Black/African heroes and major Black cultural issues. In this way teachers can help students to develop a sense of pride in their heritage and themselves.

Fourth, Mack recommended that when schools use a self esteem curriculum that direct attention be given to the evaluation of beliefs, feelings, and attitudes about students' own and different social/ethnic groups. This universal awareness aids in the development of self esteem. By implementing these interventions educators can provide an aware, nurturing, and supportive school environment which assures that Afro-American students will develop a positive view of their ethnicity and ethnic groups.

HANDICAPPED CHILDREN

Societal Factors

With current medical advances in more countries, the number of handicapped children is increasing. These children are often more vulnerable to a variety of psychosocial problems including lowered self esteem (Kashani, 1986). Handicapping conditions are often not such a problem to the children involved themselves as they are to others around them. Often the reaction of others to the handicap results in hurt feelings for a handicapped child. Although society has developed considerable intellectual tolerance of handicaps, beneath this surface most people harbor feelings of repugnance and abhorrence (Kashani, 1986). Realizing one is being avoided because of a handicap which cannot be changed is a painful discovery. When handicapped children discover the permanence of their handicap they often feel impotent, defective, and inferior, all factors which lead to low self esteem (Kashani, 1986). Negative attitudes towards the disabled have been shown to increase with the age of children, thus resulting in the reinforcement of low self esteem across the years of a child's development (Kashani, 1986).

Parental Factors

Parents of handicapped children play a special role in the development of self esteem. In a study of children with physical handicaps (Kashani, Venzke, & Millar, 1981) the discovery was that children of parents who had difficulty adjusting to their child's handicap exhibited more difficulty accepting their own condition. This was expressed by the children in self-reproach, suicidal ideation, and depression. Parent reaction often ranges from over-protectiveness to rejection. The effect of these reactions to the development of positive self esteem were discussed in Chapter 2—psychological pathogens. Lack of parental warmth may lead not only to low self esteem but also other serious childhood conditions including insecurity and feeling unwanted.

Severity of Handicap

Offer, Ostror, and Howard (1984) noted that severity and type of handicap also influences a child's self esteem. When the social stigma is easily noticed by others, self esteem is more impaired. If the handicap is not too prominent or incapacitating, however, the individual often can compensate for it in other ways. A handicap can even become a motivating factor to excel in other areas unrelated to the handicap (Offer et al., 1984). (Ray Charles, despite being blind, became an outstanding musician.) In this case, self esteem is less impaired.

Of special note when discussing handicapped individuals is the handicap of being hearing-impaired since this population represents the largest subgroup of the physically handicapped (Brooks & Ellis, 1982). The hearing-impaired seem to be more negatively labeled because of the pivotal role verbal language plays when interacting with others. Words such as "dumb" and "mute" are often used to describe the hearing-impaired. Many react to the hearing-impaired with pity rather than disparagement or derogation but the effect on self esteem for them is the same (Brooks & Ellis, 1982). This negative labeling continues to effect the self esteem of the hearing-impaired throughout their life.

While such labeling has negative effects on self esteem, these effects are often variable for the hearing-impaired (Brooks & Ellis, 1982). When the stigmatized person is surrounded by understanding others, the stigma of society is mediated, and low self esteem is ameliorated. Such significant others can be those who share the stigma or those who are not hearing-impaired but whose life experiences have led them to have intimate knowledge and understanding of the experience. The technique mentioned earlier about developing a social support system, filtering feedback, and managing self-talk are, thus, especially important techniques for this population.

Interventions

Parental guilt, insufficient knowledge, and feelings of inadequacy place handicapped children at risk for self esteem problems (Chess & Hassibi, 1978). Specific intervention strategies for these children, thus, involve frequent parental reassurances to assuage their guilt feelings, although some parents deny that they as parents have negative feelings (Kashani, 1986). When parents feel comfortable talking about a handicap, so do their children. This is an initial step in dealing with the self esteem issue which can accompany a handicap.

Second, Hastorf, Wildfogel, and Cassman (1979) found that disclosure and acknowledgment of a disability is a major deterrent to tension and social interaction difficulties. Mention of a handicap by the disabled person seems to reduce discomfort, anxiety, and uncertainty. Such disclosure also seems to minimize the chance of rejection by others. Parents and handicapped children should be encouraged to use this technique as a way of lessening the possible negative self esteem effect of a handicapping condition.

Third, a helpful procedure is for those significant others to a handicapped child to emphasize the child's abilities rather than disabilities. While to deny the handicap is not helpful, to dwell on it is not helpful. A positive, realistic orientation for the child aids in developing positive self esteem. Such children need to realize that many other aspects of their self can be emphasized other than that involving the handicap. As discussed in prior chapters, numerous self-estimates comprise the self concept of all individuals. Activity 1.1, "I'm Not Perfect but Parts of Me are Excellent," is a helpful one for everyone; it is especially helpful for these children. While other interventions discussed earlier in this book also are helpful for the handicapped, these specific suggestions can be beneficial in aiding these children to fully develop positive self esteem.

GIFTED CHILDREN

Global Versus Specific Self Esteem

As reviewed in the chapter on the measurement of self esteem, most assessments of self esteem are based on a global score although self esteem is generally agreed upon as being multifaceted. Consequently global measures of self esteem often result in insufficient information about various populations. This is especially true of the gifted. A review of the literature on the gifted and self esteem reveals many inconsistencies. To a large extent such inconsistencies exist because of varying global measures of self esteem. When self-estimates of the gifted are assessed in addition to global aspects of self esteem a more consistent picture emerges.

While the gifted generally show satisfactory, though not necessarily superior self esteem on global measures (Janos, Fung, & Robinson, 1985), they report more negative assessments about specific self-estimates. An exception to this are learning disabled gifted children, underachieving gifted children and gifted children not identified as having problems, who report lowered self esteem on global and specific measures (Janos, et al., 1985). Most, specifically the gifted, report low social self esteem but high academic self esteem. Being different from their agemate seems to have a negative effect on the self esteem of the gifted (Janos et al., 1985).

Perceptions of Being "Different"

In many ways the gifted are socialized to capitalize on their high ability, but if they mismanage this task alienation awaits them. When one conceptualizes oneself as different from others then more negative than positive effect occurs on self esteem. Some gifted children tend to overgeneralize the domains of superiority and focus on their differences from others rather than on their similarities (Janos et al, 1985).

In addition to and related to the differences these children feel from others is the exclusion they often experience by their peers. Although the gifted are frequently well trained in using their ability in cognitive areas, they are not well trained in how to use their intelligence to problem solve in the affective or emotional arenas of their lives.

Parental Influences

Another contributing factor to gifted self esteem is the perception the gifted student has of conflict in his/her family.

McGowan (1986) found the best prediction of gifted adolescents' self esteem was the perception of conflict in the family. McGowan found gifted adolescents had more negative perceptions of their families than did their parents. Differences between any pair of family members were negatively associated with self esteem. Thus, as discussed in Chapter 2, family conflict has a negative effect on the development of positive self esteem, especially among the gifted.

Sex Role Perceptions

Another important factor to consider relative to the gifted and self esteem is sex role. Robison-Awana, Kehle, & Jenson (1986) found levels of self esteem to rise commensurably with higher academic achievement for both sexes, but in general girls attribute significantly higher levels of self esteem to boys. Conversely, boys attributed significantly lower levels of self esteem to girls. Gifted girls, however, displayed an exception to this pattern. They rated boys significantly below themselves in self esteem.

These sex role differences in academically gifted girls were attributed to the fact that gifted girls often have more adrogynous characteristics than nongifted females. (Adrogynous characteristics are those which apply to both sexes.) The effect of sex role stereotyping on self esteem is greater for females than males (Lamke, 1982). Gifted girls seem to have rejected much of the sex role stereotyping.

Another explanation (Robison-Awana, 1986) for this difference in self esteem involves attribution theory. Low achieving girls often are victims of learned helplessness, whereas high achieving girls attribute their success to personal or internal causes not to external causes.

Interventions

A review of all these factors reveals that the gifted need to gain a balanced view of their self esteem in a social (discussed in prior chapters) as well as intellectual context. Such interventions as Weakness-Strength, (Activity 4.2), Self-Sculpture (Activity 6.2), The "Me" Album (Activity 6.3), and Who Am I (Activity 6.5) can be greatly beneficial in this area.

In addition, a social support network for these children is particularly valuable. Various possibilities for developing such a network were discussed in prior chapters. Earlier chapters also reviewed how to do such techniques as Nurturing Relationships (Activity 7.17), Nurturing Parents Exchange (Activity 7.18), and Expectations and Appreciation (Activity 7.19). These can all be of assistance in developing a sound network.

Problem solving skills are particularly necessary for the gifted, although this is also a valuable skill area for everyone. The technique, The Book of Me (Activity 7.22), discussed earlier, could be a helpful start in this area. Direct teaching of such skills in schools would greatly enhance the ability of the gifted to use their intelligence in this area. Parents of the gifted could share their skills in problem solving with their children such that the children become more adept at problem solving.

LEARNING DISABLED CHILDREN

Global Versus Specific Self Esteem

While global measures of self esteem have led to conflicting studies of self esteem of the gifted, so too has this problem existed with the learning disabled. Inconsistent results across studies have been difficult to integrate.

Recently more specific measures of self-estimates have revealed more detailed information about the self esteem of the learning disabled. In 1987, Kistner, Haskett, White, and Robbins found learning disabled students to have lower opinions of their cognitive abilities than normally achieving students. Also, compared to their peers, learning disabled children had lower self esteem about their physical abilities. Learning disabled and their peers did not differ in their social self esteem. In general self esteem measures, learning disabled students and normally achieving students had similar ratings.

Factors Related To Coping

Jacobs and Pries (1982) indicated that determining factors for whether a learning disabled child learns coping skills to deal with maturation lag or prolonged educational deficit are

1. number of compensatory skills available to the child;

2. encouragement for adopting compensatory skills; and

3. patience of family, school, and community.

Unfortunately, for many children, frustration ultimately leads to rejection or overprotection by parents of learning disabled students, thus decreasing sources for positive input to self-concept development. (Two activities are included which challenge negative self-talk—Standing Up to Myself (Activity 10.1)—and encourage thinking about ideal self—As If Technique (Activity 10.2).

ACTIVITY 10.1   STANDING UP TO MYSELF

Introduction

Negative self-talk can reduce self esteem rapidly. If the negative self-talk can be replaced with positive self-talk, the self esteem can be improved.

Time Required

5 to 15 minutes a day

Participants

Children and adults, any numbers

Setting

Any location if done alone
Office or classroom if done in groups

Materials

None

Procedure

Describe a situation in which you would like to be more assertive. Now let your negative self-talk speak. What this self-talk says can cause negative feelings in you. For example, imagine the situation of asking questions in class.

"Don't let them know you're dumb; you're a failure, you can't make them understand you. You'll never pass this test. Everyone understands this but you."

Now challenge each one of these statements. Ask yourself if this is 100% true at all times and in all situations, with all people? Pinpoint the flaw in the put-down. Also, reassure self . . . "So what if it were true, would that be the end of the world? Would I survive? Does one mistake make a person worthless? Can I forgive my imperfections?"

Try this at least once a day. Record all important points. How did you feel before and after each? What are you learning?

If done as a group, share in small groups of 2 to 4 persons how you challenged your negative self-talk, how you replaced the negative self-talk with positive self-talk, and how you felt before and after each.

Outcome

The individual will have better self concept, thus a better self esteem as a result of challenging the negative self-talk and then replacing it with positive self-talk.

ACTIVITY 10.2   AS IF TECHNIQUE

Introduction

Through the technique of imagination one can gain a feeling "as if" he/she had certain qualities, attitudes, or abilities.

Time Required

15 or 30 minutes

Participants

Children and adults, any number.

Setting

Any location if done alone
Office or classroom if done in groups

Materials

None

Procedure

Visualize yourself in various situations in real life acting "as if" you already possessed the quality, attitude, or ability you have chosen to develop. Practice in your imagination this new quality, attitude, or behavior. When you are visualizing yourself taking this next step, be aware of your eyes, expression, posture, gestures, voice, words. Feel what is occurring within you as you think and act this way. Refine your image.

If this activity is done as a group, share in small groups of 2 to 4 persons how you visualized yourself as being ("as if"). What quality, attitude, or ability did you choose to develop? How did you feel—inside? Did you notice changes in your posture, eyes, facial muscles, self talk rate or words, major muscle tension, or breathing rate?

Outcome

Though visualization one will be able to gain a feel "as if" he/she possessed already a quality, attitude, or ability the person wants to develop.

———

Social Perception

Disturbances in social perception are often the most debilitating of learning disorders because they interfere with the development of basic patterns of behavior. Many of these children fail to understand hazards and dangers in situations. Rules and sequences of games are difficult for them to understand. Disturbances in self-perception often lead to poor body image and body organization, body parts as they relate to the whole. The nonverbal world of experience is a deficit for such a child. Ability to make social judgments through observing nonverbal behavior such as facial expressions, actions, and gestures is difficult for the learning disabled child. Because emotions are typically communicated via nonverbal communication, many of these children lack affection and intimacy. They lack what Schutz (1972) has described as basic interpersonal needs: inclusion, control, and affection.

Nonverbal Communication

Good and Brophy (1972) reported that children who display positive, nonverbal behavior toward teachers are liked more and thought to be brighter than children who do not. Additionally, teachers communicate positive and negative judgments through the nonverbal modality of communication.

Children with learning disabilities are likely to misinterpret these messages because nonverbal communication is difficult for them. Consequently, the learning disabled child spends five or six hours a day struggling with a disability which causes much frustration as a response to both academic learning and emotional learning (expressed through nonverbal communication).

Interventions

To date, intervention with learning disabled children has been primarily focused on academic remediation with little or no emphasis on social and emotional development. Early identification and intervention with such children is necessary before low self esteem develops and augments.

Bibliotherapy and Counseling. One nonacademic intervention which has been tried with these children is bibliotherapy. Bibliotherapy is based on the concept that one is affected by what one reads and that guided reading can fulfill the psychosocial needs of low self esteem individuals. The following list contains suggestions for such stories.

THE LITTLE ENGINE THAT COULD

TEDDY ROOSEVELT

DEMONSTHENES: Overcame stammer and became a famous orator

HELEN KELLER

UGLY DUCKLING

THE MISSING PIECE

LIKING MYSELF

MYTH OF SISYPHUS: Condemned for all eternity to roll a large boulder up a hill only to have it slide down again

ALICE IN WONDERLAND: Conversation between Alice and the Mad Hatter

I AM LOVABLE AND CAPABLE

VELVETEEN RABBIT

Puppetry and music also have been tried as psychotherapeutic agents to enhance self esteem. Individual and group counseling have been tried with mixed results (Baty, 1969). Weinhold and Hilferty (1983) suggested a self esteem matrix of counseling approaches.

Parental Involvement. Parental involvement also has been tried as an intervention modality. Epps (1970) found that attempts to enhance self-concepts of students by changing parental attitudes resulted in only temporary results. Givelber and Schneider (1982) reported that all parents have difficulty with lowered self esteem during the vicissitudes of child rearing, but parents of learning disabled children are exceptionally vulnerable. Often parents feel they have produced a faulty product and experience diminished self esteem as a result. Such feedback by parents to the child also can produce deterrents to positive self esteem.

Teacher Intervention. Teacher involvement also has been tried as an intervention (Hamachek, 1971; Henderson & Long, 1968; Soares & Soares, 1970; Zirkel & Green, 1971). A correlation was found between children's perceptions of themselves and teachers' feelings toward the children. A teacher's high self esteem is a necessary prerequisite for developing children with high self esteem.

Mainstreaming. Mainstreaming of learning disabled students from their special classes into the regular classes in school is an intervention focusing on both the academic and emotional needs of children. Smith, Dokecki, and Davis (1977) indicated that one-half day mainstreaming of learning disabled students enhanced self esteem. The belief is that by having two reference groups to utilize for self-concept comparison, the special class and the regular class, the learning disabled students can make self-relevant comparisons based on whichever group they choose. Festinger (1954) posited that individuals at the lower end of an ability scale can remain influenced by one group situation if no other groups are relevant comparison groups for self-appraisal. Provided learning disabled students can maintain contact with similar others, one-half day mainstreaming can enhance self esteem.

Full day mainstreaming, according to Smith et al. (1977) can be seriously detrimental to the self esteem of learning disabled students because of the lack of choice of comparison groups. These students who are mainstreamed for the full school day suffer these same deterents to self esteem discussed earlier. Amount of time spent in special classes is an important variable in interpreting mainstreamed learning disabled childrens' self esteem (Kistner et al., 1987).

Decoding Interventions. Strategies to help learning disabled children learn to decode nonverbal communication are helpful in improving social perception and, consequently, enhancing self esteem. Techniques such as taking pictures of self and discussing the message communicated nonverbally helpful in changing this dysfunction and then enhancing self esteem. A form of charades used with the Negative Self Image Wheel (Activity 5.1), for example, is also a helpful experience. Many other techniques and activities discussed for each phase of intervention in the techniques chapter focus on nonverbal communication.

CONCLUSIONS

When students feel better about themselves in school, they are more likely to utilize the school environment as a source of developing self-concept and enhancing self esteem. School curriculum on self esteem needs to be planned and sequenced, not thought of as the hoped for by-product of more academic pursuits. When such affective components are included in school curricula materials, all special needs children benefit.

Eisenberg (1973) stated that children who have not mastered developmental tasks at the appropriate age can improve their self esteem if they are able to achieve some of their idealized self-image at a later time. For example, if a child had difficulty learning to read, and dropped behind his/her peers in achievement but later was able to strengthen his/her skills in mechanical abilities, a positive self esteem could be developed. Any interventions to strengthen existing positive self-estimates for special needs children can be very helpful in enhancing self esteem.

Changes in self-estimate are particularly important for these children. Improvement in one aspect of self esteem, even if it is peripheral and not the central core of self-concept, often is the catalyst for future changes. Changes in feelings about self as it relates to school are especially important to children, because school is one of the primary inputs to the development of self esteem at this developmental phase in life.

While just one chapter about special needs children cannot be all inclusive, it is a beginning to the understanding of these children. This chapter reflects what is currently known about different types of children. An omission of some special needs children indicates a need for research in that area. Special caution, of course, should be directed to responding individually to each child, not to a label or category. Each child has unique characteristics which deserve special attention. Our future rests on the self esteem of our children.

REFERENCES

Baty, C.H. (1969). *The influence of short-term intensive counseling of elementary school children with low self-esteem.* (Unpublished doctoral dissertation, University of Michigan, 1968). *Dissertation Abstracts, 29,* 2511A-2512A.

Brooks, H., & Ellis, G. (1982). Self-esteem of hearing-impaired adolescents: Effects of labeling. *Youth and Society, 14,* 1, 59-80.

Chess, S., & Hassibi, M. (1978). *Principals and Practice of Child Psychology.* New York: Plenum Press, 343-369.

Eisenberg, L. (1973). Psychiatric intervention. *Scientific American, 229*(3), 116-117.

Epps, E. (1970). Interpersonal relations and motivation: Implications for teachers of disadvantaged children. *Journal of Negro Education, 39,* 14-25.

Givelber, F., & Schneider, P. (1982). The parent-child relationship and the development of self esteem. *Seminar on Self Esteem Development and Sustenance.* Boston: Harvard Medical School.

Good, T., & Brophy, J. (1972). Behavioral expression of teacher attitudes. *Journal of Educational Psychology, 63,* 617-624.

Hamachek, D.E. (1971). *The self in growth, teaching and learning.* Englewood Cliffs, NJ: Prentice-Hall.

Hartline, J. (1982). *Me!? A curriculum for teaching self-esteem in the classroom.* Phoenix, AZ: Hartline Publications.

Hastorf, A., Wildfogel, J., & Cassman, T. (1979). Acknowledgment of handicap as a factor in social situations. *Journal of Personality and Social Psychology, 37,* 1790-1799.

Henderson, E.H., & Long, B.H. (1968). Self-social concepts of disadvantaged school beginners. *Journal of Genetic Psychology, 113,* 41-45.

Jacobs, D.H., & Pries, R. (1982). A court based program for servicing learning disabled delinquents. In G.L. Judy (Ed.), *Innovations from Family and Children's Service Agencies*. Springfield: Charles Thomas.

Janos, P., Fung, H., & Robinson, N. (1985). Self-concept, self-esteem, and peer relations among gifted children who feel "different". *Gifted Child Quarterly. 29,* 2, 78-82.

Kashani, J. (1986). Self-esteem of handicapped children and adolescents. *Developmental Medicine and Child Neurology, 28,* 77-83.

Kashani, J., Venzke, R., & Millar, E. (1981). Depression in children admitted to hospital for orthopaedic procedures. *British Journal of Psychiatry, 138,* 21-25.

Kistner, J., Haskett, M., White, K., & Robbins, F. (1987). Perceived competence and self-worth of LD and normally achieving students. *Learning Disability Quarterly, 10,* 37-44.

Lamke, L. (1982). The impact of sex-role orientation on self-esteem in early adolescence. *Child Development, 53,* 1530-1535.

Mack, F. (1987). Understanding and enhancing self-concept in black children. *Momentum, 18,* 22-25.

McGowan, L. (1986). Self-esteem and family environment of gifted adolescents. *Dissertation Abstract, 47,* 6, 2333-A.

Offer, D., Ostror, E., & Howard, K. (1984). Body image, self-perception, and chronic illness in adolescence. In Blum, R., (Ed.) *Chronic illness and disabilities in children and adolescence.* Orlando: Grune and Stratton.

Robison-Awana, P., Kehle, T., & Jenson, W. (1986). But what about smart girls? Adolescent self-esteem and sex role perceptions as a function of academic achievement. *Journal of Educational Psychology, 78,* 3 179-183.

Schutz, W.C. (1972). *Here comes everybody—Everyman's guide to encounter.* New York: Harper and Row.

Smith, M, Dokecki, P., & Davis, E. (1977, April). School-related factors influencing the self-concepts of children with learning problems. *Peabody Journal of Education,* pp. 85-195.

Soares, A.T., & Soares, L.M. (1970). Interpersonal and self perceptions of disadvantaged and advantaged high school students. *Proceedings of the 78th Annual Convention of the American Psychological Association, 5,* 457-458.

Spurlock, J. (1986). Development of self-concept in Afro-American children. *Hospital and Community Psychiatry, 37,* 1, 66-70.

Weinhold, B., & Hilferty, J. (1983, April). The Self-esteem Matrix: A tool for elementary counselors. *Elementary School Guidance and Counseling, 17,* 243-251.

Zirkel, P.A., & Green, J.F. (1971, February). The measurement of self-concept of disadvantaged students. *Paper presented at the Annual Meeting of the National Council on Measurement in Education,* New York.

CHAPTER 11

WOMEN AND
SELF ESTEEM

A person's gender identity is intimately tied up with his/her personal identity. People experience themselves first as human beings, and then as male or female. Sanford and Donovan (1985) claimed that by three years of age, gender identity has become the core of self-concept. In our culture, the contributions of women have been diminished. Many women have internalized these attitudes into their self-image.

Women often are not able to recognize and own their strengths. While many women are affected by the cultural devaluation of women and, therefore, experience problems with low self esteem/self-hatred, women differ in the degree of suffering they experience from the cultural training they receive and the attitudes towards women in this society. An important procedure is to view women's behavior (even seemingly self-destructive patterns) as attempts to cope with problems posed by society. As Miriam Greenspan (1983, p. 265) pointed out, "Within every symptom there is a seed of strength which lies dormant." Women hold many strengths. They need only discover the richness which lies within.

WOMEN'S ATTITUDES TOWARD SELF

Comments often made by women prior to experiences involving women only indicate a lack of trust and interest in women (Carlock, 1975; Schaef, 1981). Remarks such as the following were reported:

"What? A group with no men?"

"How boring."

"What will there be to talk about?"

Remarks like this are often heard from women entering an all-women's experience for the first time. According to Schaef (1981), when women say they do not like or trust other women they also are saying they do not like or trust themselves. She concluded that underneath that attitude lies the belief that "to be born female means to be born innately inferior, damaged, that there is something innately 'wrong' with us" (Schaef, 1981, p. 24). Schaef called this the original sin of being born female. She emphasized that no matter how competent a woman is, she will struggle with this "given." This given is actually a delusion which is developed through a woman's experience in life based on the picture she puts together as she observes the world around her and notices how she is treated.

In a culture where women's social roles, personal strengths, and work activities are devalued and women are not trained well in personal survival tactics, surviving life without enduring deep scars becomes almost impossible. Entitlement that comes with being born male is startling. Schaef (1981) pointed out that Freud, although misnaming his observation "penis envy," was one of the first to observe that women envied men their "innate superiority." Women envy the power to which men become heir simply by being born to the male gender. In this culture women are taught that they will be all right if they just find a man on whom they can attach themselves. This man will then protect and take care of them. In this system, Schaef (1981) explained women are placed in competition with other women for the resource necessary for survival, men.

Schaef (1981), contended that a woman's status is greatly enhanced when she bears a male child. The mother is then responsible for teaching her son the full meaning of this superior status, continued Schaef (1981). Mothers often give their male children special consideration, treating them with deference, catering to their needs. One woman stated:

I can remember watching how my brother and his wife treated my niece, their only girl child out of three. My brother gave her little attention or encouragement. He was always bragging about his sons and all the sports events they won or were involved in. He almost always attended their games and was very involved in their lives. And there sat his daughter, overweight and lonely, unsure of herself; not feeling special in any way. My sister-in-law passively allowed this. You don't ever question a man; you support him whether you think he's right or wrong. Not feeling good enough about herself, she could see little she could do to help her daughter. I thought to myself, "Heavens, that must have been what it was like for me in my family." I remember how I always hated my brother's special treatment. My mother always called him the "Apple Boy." Both my parents would cater to him and listen attentively to every word he said. My opinions were never valued. It's amazing how those attitudes and feelings keep getting passed down.

Many mothers, who are important role models, have incorporated the culture's rules about what it means to be a woman and have passed these on to their girl children (Dickstein, 1982). Many women have not adequately completed separation or individuation, according to Dickstein (1982) so that their behaviors/attitudes are not coming from a place of choice.

Society relies on physiology for direct cues to action. Roles are based first and foremost on age and sex differences: infant, boy, girl, adult male, adult female, old male, old female (Becker, 1971). Status and role are basic to understanding self esteem because they tell the individual what he/she is entitled to, obligated to do, and how he/she should feel about self when he/she does it. While the positive aspect of this is that this shared frame of reference makes joint action possible, identity becomes inseparable from the role one is assigned. The traditional role assigned to women by the culture is defined as inferior.

Assigned roles of women typically emphasize such traits as nurturance, dependence, and emotionality, while devaluing a cluster of traits labeled competence, which includes such traits as assertiveness, independence, rationality, and leadership ability (Broverman, Vogel, Broverman, & Rosenkrantz, 1972). In a culture which places high value on these competence traits, deficits in such qualities tend to erode self esteem and engender feelings of inadequacy with respect to these socially valued qualities. Understanding the impact the culture has on forming self esteem can relieve at least some of the responsibility women assume. Women are all too ready and eager to blame themselves for their perceived inadequacy, resulting in even higher levels of self-hatred. According to Schaef (1981), women tend to internalize their oppressors, blaming their unhappiness on some "flaw" inside themselves rather than being able to distinguish between psychological and social determinants. For example, when ignored, a woman is likely to hunt only for some flaw in her own character, "I must be too abrasive, not assertive enough," rather than to assume that just as likely her comments are ignored/devalued because they are coming from a woman.

Realizing the sources external to herself which have influenced her feelings about herself eases the burden. When a woman says, "I hate myself, I can't stand who I am. I hate my breasts, my legs, my face, my hair, my whole being. I'm horrible. I wish I'd die. I'm rotten and unworthy," one should not be surprised. This attitude is prevalent, though appalling.

CULTURAL ANTECEDENTS/MAINTAINERS OF LOW ESTEEM IN WOMEN

Importantly, each woman needs to uncover and analyze the influence of family scripting and societal scripting in maintaining her low self esteem. Analysis of one's psychological dynamics is essential, but analysis of broader social dynamics is imperative. A woman's self esteem cannot be understood in a vacuum; her esteem must be examined in the context of her family and of the culture in which she was reared. Women's problems, including the problem of low self esteem, are rooted in the social and political condition of their existence as people and as women. An analysis of self esteem in women must, therefore, take on personal and sociopolitical dimensions. Accordingly, creative solutions to women's esteem issues must be arrived at for both levels. Exploring the connection between the many difficulties a woman is experiencing and her socialization as a woman in American society can allow the woman to move beyond self-blame, feelings of personal failure, and being alone in her struggles (Kirk, 1976).

An examination of major societal institutions will quickly bring to focus woman's place in our culture, how she is **devalued** or at least undervalued. With women's contributions devalued, restricted almost universally, it is little wonder that women are plagued with low self-confidence and low self esteem.

Education

In an article by Hundley (1988), Dr. Kathy McMahon-Klosterman, an educational psychologist claims that children in classrooms are still being taught the ABCs of sexism. According to McMahon-Klosterman, girls' achievements tend to be ignored and they are not challenged as much in their performance. Boys are prompted, praised, and challenged more often.

With regard to the male-female balance in the teaching field, in elementary schools teachers are typically female (85.3%), whereas in higher levels of education (college and university) females represent 37.1% of the teacher population (*The World Almanac and Book of Facts,* 1989). Therefore, 62.9% of teachers at these levels are male. Overall, the higher the level of education, the more males predominate.

With regard to school textbooks, there still exists a bias towards male-oriented stories with male characters. If female characters do appear, they most often conform to stereotyped images according to Sanford and Donovan (1985). They are often portrayed as weak, dependent, fearful of risks, emotionally insecure, and obsessed with their appearance. A world history book currently used widely is entitled Men and Nations, according to McMahon-Klosserman (Hundley, 1988). This bias extends to the rest of the curriculum and simply reflects the broader cultural attitude.

Sanford and Donovan (1985) pointed out that even the generic term "man" used in school textbooks is often associated with male persons rather than a mixture of both sexes. Language patterns also, therefore, render women invisible.

Medical Establishment

There still exists a bias against women in both the practice of medicine and in whom the medical establishment allows into its ranks. Only modest progress has been made in increasing the number in the ranks of physicians. Statistics in 1989 show women in 1987 comprised 19.5% of the physician population (The World Almanac and Book of Facts, 1989); in 1970, 8% in the medical power structure were women (Bidese & Danais, 1981). In the medical profession, male doctors continue to reign King.

According to Mendelsohn (1982), male chauvinism is rampant in American medicine. Mendelsohn (1982) asserted, for example, that the number of operations in the U.S. is climbing steadily and those performed on women head the list. At the same time, continued Mendelsohn, no evidence exists to support that many of these surgeries enhance one's health. Increasingly, surgery is being performed for prophylactic purposes explains Mendelsohn. For example, at one time, hysterectomies were performed mainly when there existed a life-threatening situation. Today, only 20% are performed as a result of a life-threatening situation. In fact, Mendelsohn explained that Dr. Sammons, executive Vice President of the American Medical Association, asserted that hysterectomies could be considered clinically indicated for women with excessive anxiety. One out of every two women in the U.S. will undergo a hysterectomy by age 65 (Mendelsohn, 1982).

Sanford and Donovan (1985) also claim that the medical establishment has forced women to become dependent on physicians by their success in gaining control of birthing and gynecological care functions. Medical authorities have convinced women that they require physician care for safe pregnancy and birth and have positioned themselves as the only legal dispensary of birth control. Thus, women are tied to the physician (Sanford & Donovan, 1985). According to Sanford and Donovan (1985), the medical profession also has required that women entrust themselves in their physician's diagnostic skills and machinery and laboratory tests. This has eroded women's trust in their own body signals since if their symptoms are not corroborated by the physician and his/her tests, they doubt their own experience (Sanford & Donovan, 1985).

Sanford and Donovan (1985) also believed that the medical establishment has eroded women's belief in their own healing abilities and in their belief about the healing potential of other natural means such as nutrition, visualization, and spiritual avenues. They also pointed out that women with limited financial resources have even fewer choices in the medical care they receive. Since poverty among women is showing the most dramatic rise of all groups in the United States, women are highly affected by the pitfalls of this system.

One of the most useful resources for women desiring information about what they can do for themselves in regard to their physical health is a book, *The New Our Bodies, Ourselves, Boston Women's Health Book Collective* (1984). It contains very useful information on such topics as food, body image, alternative healing methods, alcohol and other addictive substances, sexuality, childbirth, and menopause as well as many other areas concerned with women's health. The beautiful aspect of this work is that it helps women to become more interested in and knowledgeable about their bodies. As the authors indicated, this increased learning prepares women to better evaluate services delivered by the traditional medical establishment as well as to give better care to themselves. Knowing more about their bodies gives women a stronger core to move within the world. Other resources which are helpful to women are the following:

1. *National Women's Health Network Newsletter* (National Women's Health Network, 1325 G Street, N.W., Washington, D.C.) which provides up-to-date input on such topics as osteoporosis, the hazards of cosmetics, questions about contraceptives, and mammograms.

2. *Ourselves, Growing Older* (Doress & Siegal, 1987) is an inspiring book which challenges older women to take charge of their health.

3. *Hot Flash,* a newsletter for midlife and older women produced by the National Action Forum for Midlife and Older Women, c/o Jane Porcino, Box 816, Stony Brook, New York 11790-0609. The newsletter discusses various issues related to menopause and the menopausal and after years. It is a very practical publication offering suggestions for small groups, keeping you abreast of legal issues of interest to aging women, and other pertinent health related suggestions for older women.

Religion

Males are still dominant and primary in the upper echelon of almost any religious denomination. Stone (1976) stated that our society, for centuries, has taught young children, both male and female, that a male deity created the world and all that is in the world was produced in his own image. As an afterthought, woman was created to serve the man. Stone (1976) indicated that the image of Eve, the woman who was supposed to have brought the downfall of humankind, has in many ways become the image of all women. According to Stone, as a result of this act, it was decreed by God that woman must submit to the dominance of man. Religions have played a key role in the initial and continual oppression and subjugation of women. Spretnak (1982) reiterated these points in her analysis of the partriachial ties which are perpetuated by the various religions of the world but goes on to define an emerging female spirituality.

Government

Women are still absent from the highest governmental posts. Women have made some progress in gaining offices at state and local levels, though the number of women holding public office is still incredibly low. Our government is still run primarily by white males (Sanford & Donovan, 1985).

Sanford and Donovan (1985) pointed out that women's issues are not taken seriously by the government. They remind us that it took more than 70 years for women to win the right to vote and the Equal Rights Amendment still hasn't passed after 50 years. While some progress has been made in winning equal rights, in many states marital rape is still not a crime, battering complaints are still not taken seriously, and increasing numbers of elderly widows and women who are heads of single parent families are living in poverty. Sanford and Donovan (1985) contended that the number of adult males has been reduced in recent years. The number of poor adult women has skyrocketed due to an increase in birth rates among young unmarried women and rising numbers of divorces.

Labor Market

Tokenism is still prevalent. More women are being allowed through the door but they are not privileged to the "Old-Boys Network," which increases one's chance for promotion. Occupational segregation still persists largely limiting women to lower-paying jobs (Bianchi & Spain, 1986; Fox & Hesse-Biber, 1984). According to Blau (1975), women earn between 57 and 60% the income of men. These statistics have only slightly improved. For example, 1981 figures by the U.S. Bureau of the Census (1981) showed that with five years of college, a man will earn around $1,301,000 in a typical 40-year career; a woman will gross about $699,000. With only four years of college, men will get $1,183,910; women can expect $461,340. With a high school education, women's earnings equalled 63% of men's. Another statistic by Thurow (1987) shows that while 22% of men earn $31,000 per year, only 3% of women earn this amount. He also found that women earn no more than 65% of what male counterparts earn, an increase of only 2% from 1980.

Sanford and Donovan (1985) summarize the findings of the 1982 United States Commission on Civil Rights which demonstrated that alarmingly high levels of sex and race discrimination still exist in the United States market. In a culture where money, power, and status are highly valued, those blocked from attaining such power symbols are likely to suffer esteem problems.

Literature

Women's literature—is it to be found to be in any high school or college course? Showalter (1974) indicated that the proportion of men to women authors on college course reading lists is typically 20:1. In the *Norton Anthology,* a standard two-volume anthology for example, Showalter (1974) revealed that 169 men compared to 6 women are represented. A review of the 1979 Norton Anthology, Vol. 2 (Gottesman et al., 1979) showed some improvement: 68 men to 22 women authors represented.

American fiction typically presents one-dimensional, stereotypic images of women. Beginning with fairy tales which launch the indoctrination into the fixed scenarios of men and women, and pornography with its carnal women and heroic men, literature has typically promulgated adherence to the deadly female sex role where to be anything but passive, innocent, and helpless is to be evil (Dworkin, 1974). To see the contrast, the reader is directed to current women's literature which presents very powerful female images. For example: *Cruiser Dreams* by Janet Morris, *Stone Angel* by Margaret Laurence, *Surfacing* by Margaret Atwood, *A Weave of Women* by E. M. Broner, *A Mother and Two Daughters* by Gail Godwin.

History

Glaringly absent from HIStory is HERstory. The roots of women in the U.S. have been largely ignored, or women appear in history texts as part of the domestic backdrop to the "real action" in history (Rosen, 1974). Textbooks typically exclude discussion of how women shaped life and culture in America, consequently, there are no strong female role models to draw upon. Sanford and Donovan (1985) pointed out that those few who do appear in history books are not ideal in what they validate. For example:

Joan of Arc—burned at stake

Betsy Ross—known for sewing

Carrie Nation—"moralistic battle-ax"

Florence Nightengale—"super-nurse"

Queen Elizabeth I—heir to throne by default since there were no males

While now, many excellent, though narrowly focused scholarly works exist, many people are still virtually unaware of the rich and diverse history of women in the U.S. (Hymowitz & Weissman, 1978; Sanford & Donovan, 1985). Looking at history increases women's awareness. Women are brought face to face with the fact that they have been systematically excluded from institutional and economic life. This is what makes Judy Chicago's (1979) artistic masterpiece, *The Dinner Party* such an important work. In addition to its artisitic significance, it has brought to light thousands of overlooked women in the world.

Media

Women are still being portrayed as whores, bitches, evil, Madonnas, dumb blondes, mentally ill, catty, woman behind the man, and victims. Sanford and Donovan (1985) pointed out that not only are women stereotyped by the media, they also are represented unequally. Sanford and Donovan (1985) quoted the *Boston Globe* and the *New York Times* regarding male-female representation in the media: male characters on prime time TV outnumber female characters by three to one; and, only 16% of the children's TV characters are female.

Laura Lederer (1980) cited a study by a group of researchers from Women Against Violence in Pornography and Media, which among other tasks, recorded themes and images in current table top pornography. They found a *Penthouse* magazine article entitled "The Joy of Pain;" an article in *Hustler* magazine, "About Face" where a man sticks his gun in a woman's mouth and forces her to suck it. Thousands upon thousands of men are being reared on these images of women. A recent cartoon in Penthouse (March, 1988) shows a nude woman in bed after sex with the caption "so . . . how was I?" gasoline is pictured streaming under and around her bed from a gas can in the door. A hand appears from the doorframe flickering a lighted match towards the spilled gasoline. The April, 1988 issue of *Hustler* contains two cartoons (pp. 40 and 83) which crudely disparage the natural odors of women's vaginas.

According to Lederer (1980) such examples of violence against and negative attitudes towards women are now filtering down through the larger mass media. She cited a December 1975 issue of *Vogue* which shows a male fashion model viciously slapping his female companion. Lederer also cited a record album called *Wild Angel* by Nelson Slater which presents an image of a plastic-looking woman, her head pulled back and a horse bit in her mouth.

In the film arena, Lederer (1980) claimed that women are portrayed as enjoying (or at least accepting as their fate) being raped, spanked, mutilated; or, turned on by anything men order them to do. Male power over women is celebrated in many films. In the last decade, Lederer continued, an increase has occurred in the appearance of films involving child prostitution.

In the mid-70s it seemed as if the movie industry were moving towards stronger images of women. Films such as *Julia*, portraying women trying to defeat Hitler and *An Unmarried Woman*, depicting women opting for independence over marriage, sprinkled an otherwise rather stereotypical collection of women's roles. TV also introduced stronger, more positive characters for women, for example, *Cagney and Lacey* and the female attorneys of *L.A. Law*. While some current roles for women portray them in the professions (e.g., Goldie Hawn as a lawyer), they are still largely playing the same stereotypical behaviors.

Family

Family is the ultimate source of patriarchal power. The sexual division grew originally out of rudimentary prehuman division between male defense and female child care. Early inequality was based on the need for prolonged child care and exigencies of primitive technology. Women's subordination increased with the rise of the state and of class society. Despite the fact that industrialization made equality between sexes possible, the family remained patriarchal in nature, though it was more democratic than ever before (Gillespie, 1975; Gough, 1975). Carter and McGoldrick (1988) indicated that most still view the one-up position of men in marriage as ideal. Both Laws (1975) and Bernard (1982) pointed out that current research shows that as marriage is structured now, statistically it is physically, psychologically, and socially a better investment for men than for women. Avis (1985) asserted that traditional family roles have a pernicious effect on women and all family members.

Summary

Women's oppression is reflected in all the major institutions of our culture. Dignity, respect, and adulation has typically been reserved for manhood.

In the major American institutions, women typically:

have been assigned lesser roles or weak roles,

are noticeably absent, and

are not celebrated for their accomplishments (nor are women encouraged or facilitated to expand beyond the limited image created for them).

While the limits of this chapter preclude a complete discussion of the impact of the myriad of institutions on women's self esteem, the previous brief discussion of a sample of those institutions makes the point. Women's place in other societal corners such as music, art, and law are but a few more places where women are not accorded recognition.

Without a woman's sense of her roots, her culture, her evolution and revolution, her grounding as a confident, competent woman is jeopardized. Without affirmation of women's common struggles, victories, and accomplishments, women cannot fully integrate these positive steps into their collective self-concepts. Without an understanding of their oppression, women needlessly hold themselves responsible for some perceived personal defectiveness.

IDENTITY DEVELOPMENT

Erikson (1968) proposed a formulation of female identity development which showed identical tasks for males and females until adolescence whereupon he believed the developmental tasks diverged. According to his model, males confront identity issues before intimacy issues whereas female adolescents confront identity and intimacy tasks simultaneously. In the 1960s a female's primary identity task was to locate a male partner to fill her inner void thereby completing herself. The female's identity was therefore closely tied with her selection of a partner. Erikson's theory was an accurate reflection of the times when the primary avenue to identity achievement (and self-worth) for women was determined largely by the assets of the particular man to whom she could attach herself. Changes in social norms have since introduced other acceptable options.

Marcia and Friedman (1970) challenged Erikson's formulation believing that women who achieve identity through intimacy, skipping the stage of identity moratorium, prematurely foreclose their development. During the identity moratorium, the task is to evaluate and define one's talents, skills, and values, experiment with and "try on" various lifestyles, life philosophies, career options, and other sources of identity before arriving at what fits (Marcia & Friedman, 1970; Prager, 1982). Premature intimacy aborts this process. Marcia and Friedman's (1970) ideas have been corroborated by later writers (Bardwick, 1979; Gilligan, 1982; Morgan & Farber, 1982).

Contemporary middle-class women are exposed to at least two variant value structures: A traditional one which places marriage and motherhood at the core of identity and a nontraditional one which places occupation and individual choice at its core (Morgan & Farber, 1982). Morgan and Farber (1982) believed that at some point in a woman's life she will face this conflict. Rubin (1979) found that many women describing disappointment in mid-life believe the origins date back to unquestioned internalization of the traditional female role. Employment status increases the psychological well-being of women in mid-life increasing self esteem and life satisfaction and reducing anxiety (Coleman & Antonucci, 1983). They did, however, find lower incomes related to better physical health since higher salaried positions often result in work overload and increased stress. Thus, whether employment status or salary is related to satisfaction is not clear. However, according to Coleman and Antonucci (1983), employment does attenuate the possible negative effects of mid-life. Baruch and Barnett (1986) stressed the importance of multiple roles.

Current thinking proposes that the crisis of identity is as important for women as it is for men. Kessler and McRae (1982; 1984) have pointed out that overall, women derive many positive benefits from employment particularly if they are satisfied with the work. Self esteem of employed women also has been found in some studies to be positively correlated with their salary (Morris & Markus, 1978). Many studies have stressed that psychological well-being is positively related to the number of roles a person occupies (Pietromonaco, Marris, & Frohardt-Lane, 1984; Thoits, 1983).

TRADITIONAL/NONTRADITIONAL FEMININITY AND SELF ESTEEM

Research shows that traditional femininity is negatively associated with self esteem (Connell & Johnson, 1971; Flammer, 1971) while high self esteem is positively related to a sense of competence (Baruch, 1973). Paradoxically, females who feel competent and communicate competence tend to be viewed as deviant in terms of the traditionally defined feminine sex role. They also are likely to feel anxious, conflicted, and vulnerable to rejection in addition to experiencing rewarding, ego-enhancing satisfactions (Horner, 1968/1969, 1972a, 1972b). The traditional female role also might be looked upon as socially sanctioned deviancy in that many of the traits which comprise the role of female are considered mentally unhealthy by a majority of clinicians (Broverman, Vogel, Broverman, & Rosenkrantz, 1972). Another interesting study by Miller (1972) showed that on some college campuses, conservative attitudes toward women's rights were correlated with low self esteem. Thus, seemingly either way a woman proceeds with her life, either pursuing a traditional or a nontraditional role pattern, her self esteem is likely to be challenged along the way.

Traditional Female Role

The traditional female role has typically not been valued (Broverman, Broverman, Clarkson, Rosenkrantz, & Vogel, 1970;

McKee & Sherriffs, 1959; Rosenkrantz, Vogel, Broverman, Broverman, & Clarkson, 1968). This role consists of traits such as nurturance, passivity, emotionality, and submissiveness. Partly, this lack of valuing may have come from the lack of balance in the personality—the lack of activity to balance times of passivity; the lack of dominance to balance the tendency toward submissiveness; the undeveloped logic to balance emotionality; and, therefore, the lack of wholeness in the individual. Kemlicka, Cross, and Tornai (1983) and O'Connor, Mann, and Bardwick (1978) showed high self esteem and high body and sexual satisfaction to be related to high scores on androgyny and masculinity among college women. In our highly competitive society, such traits are adaptive.

However, as Miller (1976) wrote, a bias exists against those "female traits" and in favor of more "masculine traits," logic, domination, activity. Men are equally unbalanced in the traits which comprise their personalities, yet the cultural response to them is different. Miller (1976) encouraged women to own and cherish their personality traits while at the same time remaining open to adding to them. The male-dominated culture is an imperfect one. Women can bring more wholeness to that culture if they are able to value, own, and affirm the traits they bring.

Self-Estimates

With this cultural overlay, not surprising, then, research shows that females of all ages typically devalue their own competence in comparison with their actual abilities and in comparison with male self-evaluations. This self-devaluation occurs in athletic performance (Cliffton & Smith, 1963), in academic ability (Baird, 1973; Wylie, 1963), and in the evaluation of other women's professional competence (Bernard, 1966; Goldberg, 1968). Later research has shown that while females generally show lower performance expectancies than males (Frieze, McHugh, Fisher, & Valle, 1975), women's expectancies for familiar tasks are comparable to or higher than men's (House & Perney, 1974). What this later research seems to suggest is that the traditional role assigned to women tends to construct their experience and women tend to be "protected" from a broad range of experiences.

Women who are reared to believe certain limitations in their capacities have difficulty accepting personal accomplishments which challenge those beliefs about themselves (Becker, 1987). Challenging this early formed internal self-image can generate considerable anxiety. The more basic the challenged images are, according to Becker (1987) the greater the anxiety. These findings suggest that parents would be wise to introduce their female children early to a broad range of experiences and liberal attitudes towards their capabilities as females.

Life experience is essential for mastery. Overprotection tends to inhibit a child's ability to master new situations. The degree to which a woman's range of movement is restricted affects her willingness to take risks. In order to grow, one must learn to take risks. By learning early how to move successfully into the unknown, women develop self-confidence and a positive self esteem; over-sheltering breeds insecurity.

Conflict Between Self and Others

Young men do not discuss sacrifice of friendship, marriage, or family for the sake of career but rather report loftier concerns—that "money grubbing makes you forget about being kind to others, and being a grind can be lonely" (Schnitzer, 1977). Among both males and females who fear success, however, an underlying tension seems to be common—that of satisfying oneself versus satisfying others. A high degree of anxiety may predispose a person to predict negative endings and to perceive him/herself as unable to tolerate and manage conflict.

When a woman's sense of herself is organized around being able to make and then maintain affiliations and relationships, threat of disruption of that relationship becomes closer to a loss of self (Miller, 1976). However, women's valuing of affiliation, in a way, is an advanced attitude. At a time when western man is bemoaning his feelings of alienation and lack of community, one can see the merit in placing a greater value on relationships (Miller, 1976). The mistake women have made, however, is to sacrifice willingly whole parts of themselves to meet their affiliation needs. When a woman comes to believe that everything she does is right only if she's doing it for someone else, not herself, she is in trouble—she has lost her inner barometer that registers how happy or sad a particular behavior makes her. The potentiality begins for her to harm herself—without even realizing it. Even the best of foods eaten in excess can make a person sick. Women must develop fuller relationships with others simultaneously with the fullest development of self. The female pull toward affiliation, then, is not personally destructive, but becomes a basic strength (Miller, 1976).

The Giving Myth

Woman as the all-giving figure, nurturing others selflessly is the image many people have been taught. "Be good to others and they will be good to you." "The more you give, the more you'll get." According to Becker (1987) women confuse being needed with being loved. Many women fear that if they reduce their caregiving behavior they may be abandoned. Of course, many women do not even give their compulsive caregiving a second thought. They have been trained so completely to put others' needs first that it never occurs to them to be concerned with their own interests.

Gilligan (1982) asserted that women's self-worth is intricately tied with how successful they are in maintaining relationships. This perpetuates over-giving in relationships. When women do differentiate themselves from these imposed expectations, they invariably experience anxiety (Lebe, 1986). This anxiety must be expected until the ego ideal expands to include aspects of caring for self and expression of anger. Following the limited belief that giving to others supersedes all other concerns has led many women down a lane of self-depletion, self-destruction, and consequently, low self esteem. Replenishment not forthcoming, internal resources gradually diminish. "I must be doing something wrong; I must be defective somehow; I'm not happy; What's wrong with me?" becomes the line of thinking which maintains low self esteem. Miller (1976) called this "doing good and feeling bad."

While the giving response is fully incorporated, a receiving posture is avoided. In fact, for many women the thought of "receiving" is a novel and often threatening idea (Collier, 1982).

Acting for oneself is made to seem like depriving others. In fact, acting for oneself, being able to articulate one's needs, is essential to ongoing nurturing of positive self esteem. This is discussed more thoroughly in a previous chapter. What can be readily seen, therefore, is how the internal conflict between being "all giving" yet needing to receive nurturance in return keeps many women in a low self esteem pattern.

Women often give to others instead of learning to give to themselves and to be compassionate to their own wants and needs—for exercise, affection, time off, time alone, a treat, or a new toy. Each time women give to themselves they add to their self esteem. Unfortunately, as Lebe (1986) pointed out, women's ego ideal includes being a good mother, a good wife, and successful career woman, but often does not extend to taking care of herself.

Women often do not feel deserving of or entitled to receive rewards from relationships or careers (Major, 1987). They have internalized the cultural devaluation of the contributions of women as well as the attitudes they carry in regard to their worth as females learned in their family of origin. This results in psychic costs. However, as Major (1987) contended, heightening women's awareness of their entitlement may breed discontent as women recognize the injustice. If this discontent is directed towards positive social change rather than self blame, Major (1987) suggested that women may be able to break this self-limiting cycle of expecting little and, therefore, receiving little. According to Major (1987), many women rationalize their meager rewards in order to preserve the myth that the world is fair.

Dependency

An important distinction can be made between various types of dependency. In self-imposed dependency, the woman plays out the role of victim, sees herself as helpless, sees others as responsible for her helplessness, and manipulates others to do for her what she could do for herself. In real dependency, on the other hand, actual shortages and inequalities exist.

The dependent woman exhibits the following characteristics:

1. Acts compliant. Does not see that she has power to choose. Internalizes expectations of others (Usher & Fels, 1985).

2. Sees herself as having limitations. Does not see options for developing internal resources for counteracting these limitations.

3. Manipulates her social system to get positive feedback.

4. Avoids thinking, taking action, and taking responsibility for herself.

5. Prefers the company of men—they are more okay and are, therefore, in a position to confer approval on her. Men give her a sense of self worth.

6. Assumes positively sanctioned roles—most of them under a male boss (wife, mother, nurse, secretary, mistress).

7. Believes that unless she has a man she is a loser.

8. Views normal needs for nurturance and intimacy as indicators of inadequate control and lack of independence.

The key mover out of dependency is the heightened awareness and expression of the pain which one feels in that dependent position. Increased awareness of how the consequences of that dependency must be fostered is described in Figure 11.1.

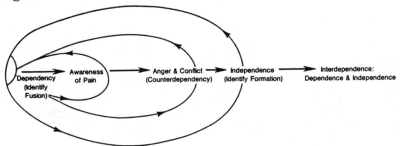

Figure 11.1. Phases of female self esteem development.

According to Greenspan (1983) dependency is a central issue for women and is related to women's reliance on men to provide a purpose for life. This reliance on men inhibits women from developing their own wholeness and often results in depression.

Counter-Dependency

Counter-dependency is an angry reaction to the dependent role. The expression of anger is vital to moving out of the role (Schaef, 1981). The woman must be willing to initiate conflict if she is to restructure an oppressive arrangement (Miller, 1976). The first step in this process involves encouraging women to take their needs seriously, to explore them, and to act on them. Many women have come to fuse their own needs with the needs of others. When women come to recognize and accept their needs as equal rather than secondary, they will initiate conflict (Miller, 1976)—or rather surface the conflict which exists.

Surfacing conflict is not easy for women since it requires facing fears of abandonment. Women often fear that relationships will not tolerate their assertion of differing wants, opinions, interests, and needs. While some women in intimate relationships may surface anger, they often do not challenge the basic rule that the man is the rulemaker and, therefore, the ultimate authority (Lerner, 1985). According to Lerner (1985) and Lemkau (1984), habitual giving in to pressure results in selflessness. Until women are able to initiate conflict, they are blocked from taking the next step.

During this phase of saying "NO" to the dependent style, women are typically hostile and blaming. They frequently withdraw from contact with males. In order to leave that role, the oppressor is often devalued (Schaef, 1981). Oftentimes, initially women revolt through passive aggressive means. However, at this point, the woman still does not feel good about herself. A critical skill for moving on to independence is the identification and expression of wants and the claiming of the right to make decisions without another's approval or permission.

The counter-dependent phase, as illustrated in Figure 11.1, is actually a false independence. On the outside, the woman tries to behave independently but she has not resolved her dependency issues, she has merely pushed them underground. Until she thoroughly deals with these needs she remains stuck. Many women never get past this phase for they are so judgmental and unaccepting of these unresolved feelings. The resulting internal tension created by this hidden conflict can diminish self esteem.

Independence

Focus shifts from the oppressor to the woman herself. During this phase, values and alternatives are explored and the woman begins to develop a sense of her own culture (woman's culture). Inner attentiveness increases as the woman begins to turn inward to get in touch with what she wants and needs. A celebration of her womanhood begins as she begins stroking herself and giving and accepting strokes from other people. She is more accepting of her dependency needs and begins resolving these needs in more self-enhancing ways.

Interdependence

Once the woman has more awareness of herself and is secure in knowing what she wants and does not want, she can then choose to relate with men and patriarchal systems from a stronger, more equal position. During this phase, the woman, while owning her own strength, reconnects with her more vulnerable, needy side. Movement through this phase rarely proceeds in a simple straight line progression, but rather more typically involves periodic returns to dependency issues (Collier, 1982), each time meeting that dependency from a stronger and stronger place (see Figure 11.1). However, one needs to realize that women could get "stuck" in one of the phases: dependency, counter-dependency (false independence), or the independent phase. Each phase is important and must be entered and worked through to maximize freedom of choice and opportunity for intimacy.

Nontraditional Female Role

The nontraditional female role ideally joins the positive elements of the traditional role with those elements which need to be added for balance. Sources of self esteem for the nontraditional woman are more diverse and, therefore, provide a more stable base. The expansion of the female role necessitates expansion of skills and, thereby, creates additional territories for developing one's expertise, applying creatively one's resources, and enhancing self esteem.

The locus of control of nontraditional female shifts from one heavily external to one which is more internal. She reclaims control of her life and her own personal power, discovers the inner strength required to surface conflict and take the risks necessary for growth.

Sources of Self Esteem

In the business world, a common method of ensuring viability of a venture is through diversification. For example, a person in the communications business might gradually expand his/her operation to include an answering service, mobile telephone operation, Western Union, and a federally assisted transportation project. The business has, thereby, protected itself so that if, for example, one of these ventures falters in a sluggish economy or is slower to develop, the other areas of the operation can keep the business afloat. A woman whose entire life revolves around a man places herself in a precarious situation. If her life is spent doing things for him, visiting with his friends, doing things he likes to do, living through his successes, and she is economically dependent on him, what happens when/if the man leaves? A woman whose identity is so fused with another's is treading in dangerous waters. She has put herself at the mercy of another person and has left herself utterly vulnerable. If he walks away, he walks away with a huge chunk of her. And even if he stays, she has little control over her own life and remains in an extremely powerless, submissive, subordinate position where she is not central in her own life. When "The Man" becomes more important than the woman herself, the woman's self esteem hangs by a thread and she has few resources for survival.

Women who have few resources for their self esteem become more dependent on these sources. A woman who has a greater number of sources for her self esteem and more of them internally based, has a better chance of feeling good about herself. She may want to be in a loving relationship with a man but she can function well without a man or without a man's constant reassurance.

Locus of Control

Women ask for approval in a number of ways. In many direct as well as subtle ways women beg, "Tell me I'm OK or that what I'm doing is OK or not OK." In this way, others are given powerful approval privileges. The seat of power subtly shifts from self to others, and the seat of self esteem becomes hazardously dispersed. Outside opinions in themselves are not detrimental. Through dependence on, idealization of, and overvaluing of these outside opinions a woman eventually erodes her own autonomy and emotional expressiveness in the service of placating the other. In addition, what frequently happens is that these outside sources, to whom she has given up her power, contradict each other, and furthermore, may not have her best interests at heart. The result is often massive confusion and intense anxiety, for never having learned to say "NO," to define herself, she fears rejection, and cannot find a way to please all these people who hold desperate views about what she should do.

This dependence on the judgment of others is understandable given the personal history of most women who are not encouraged early in life in an independent attitude. When the female self is billed as secondary, weak, and ineffectual, a view of oneself as capable of coping with the vicissitudes of life, making good decisions, and proceeding through life with confidence and optimism becomes rather difficult to form. Early on, women are "protected" from those life experiences which might have served as a primary training ground for positive self esteem. Unless one has had the opportunity to face and overcome obstacles in life, to master tasks of increasing difficulty and of increasing variety, one is severely handicapped in the development of adequate problem-solving skills and positive self esteem. In a sense, maturation in the female is forestalled when she is not encouraged to shift from environmental support to self-support and taught the skills to do so.

As women begin to listen to the inner voice which comes out of the still place within, they find an inner source of strength (Belenky, Clinchy, Goldberger, & Tarule, 1986). According to Belenky et al (1986), this shift from reliance on external sources of knowing to this more subjective form of knowing represents a significant developmental transition. By attending to their inner voice, women strengthen their self-concept, self esteem, self-protection, and self-definition. Many developmental theorists have recognized this shift to the authority within as a primary task of adolescence. Along with this shift comes the following awarenesses:

1. Personal experience is a valuable source of knowledge.

2. Truth is not absolute and often no one "right answer" exists.

3. Taking a stand different from that of others requires the willingness to stand alone, to be separate. For women, this process of separating and individuating can stir up feelings of fear and vulnerability.

Without this shift, women must become versatile and creative in securing environmental support and remain dependent on the opinions and judgment of others. Through very ingenious, though self-defeating maneuvers, women meet many of their needs using deceit, obsequiousness, syrupy sweetness, coquettish tactics, acting dumb, taking the back seat, pleasing, being perfect, sacrificing, and indulging—using an entire arsenal of self-defeating devices to avoid self-determined action and independent opinion. The price is high.

Some measure of pride is preserved when a woman maintains her viewpoint in silence, but doing so does not compensate for the erosion which occurs when a woman pretends to be unaware, to agree, or to be impressed when someone offers her some piece of elementary advice she has already considered, bowing and kowtowing and thanking him graciously for his "wisdom." To simply stop denying herself is not enough. Women also need to affirm themselves.

Power, acquired through manipulation, is a mixed victory for the woman cannot publicly acclaim and take credit for her victory. Her power is silent and its exchange in the stock market is far from equal.

Conflict and Risk

The goal which many women live out, "To avoid conflict at any cost," results in underdeveloped "muscles"—muscles which are essential for surviving, with self esteem intact, the ordinary everyday conflicts each of us faces. According to Keleman (1975), if people wish to establish and maintain their individuality, their personal integrity, they must accept the pain and pleasure that comes from risking and separating from support. For women, this represents an especially difficult task because their socialization often precludes aggressive strivings toward individuation. Early on, boys are encouraged towards separation and individuation; whereas, girl children are encouraged to take care of others and ignore their own needs (Caplan, 1981; Chodorow, 1971). Separation and individuation, therefore, remain key issues much longer in female development (Chodorow, 1978).

Risking conflict is to risk distance, separation, and loneliness. When a woman feels unable to say, "no," to disagree, to go up against someone, she never affirms herself, fails to exercise her ability to form and maintain her own boundaries— her own sense of selfhood. Becker (1987) asserted that through anger is how people establish the boundary between themselves and others. Through anger people establish their limits.

Chodorow (1978) postulated that this resistance to conflicts stems from the collusive binding in which mothers engage. This binding includes two elements: the mother's exaggerated tenderness which prevents the girl child's discharge of anger and the mother's coldness when the girl moves towards others. Combined, these elements prevent the normal loosening of the mother-daughter bond, thereby, forestalling the separation essential to healthy self esteem. As Levy (1982) emphasized, a female's movement towards individuation is culturally viewed as movement against nurturing others. Women are not socialized into "good enough mothering" according to Levy (1982) which involves a nurturing stance while also encouraging individuation.

Without adequate separation—individuation the girl child becomes easy prey to victimization or subtle exploitation which can take the form of prostitution, rape, psychological and/or physical battering, discrimination, or sexual harassment. The formative process requires a person to set boundaries to form the self and then soften boundaries and reform self. Females have trouble setting boundaries haunted by guilt; males tend to have trouble softening their boundaries.

In order to set firm boundaries, women must learn loving detachment, what Hollis (1986) described as being neutral in a healthy way. Detachment involves caring without hurting oneself. Detachment, according to Beattie (1987) involves several aspects:

1. Releasing a person or problem with love.

2. Separating one's responsibilities from other people's responsibilities.

3. Allowing other people to be responsible for themselves.

4. Living in the present.

5. Accepting reality; accepting "what is" and differentiating that from wishes, hopes, and fantasies. Women overlearn attachment and require much practice to achieve healthy detachment.

Nonverbal Power

At a very bodily level women tend to diminish themselves. For instance, Henley (1977) wrote that in general, females in our society exert less control over territory and their very bodily demeanor is more restrained and restricted spatially. Femininity, in fact, is gauged by how little space they take up (Henley, 1977). Marge Piercy (1973) described this pattern in a novel. She pointed out that women condense themselves, crossing their legs, keeping their elbows close to their sides, being sure not to take up too much space; not to touch, bump, or rub a man; and shrinking back if contact does occur. The psychological effect of this shrinking is to diminish one's sensations, and one's sense of pain and pleasure. The shrinking, originally a short-term defense for survival, becomes a negative pattern.

Women who reclaim their power and expand their self-concepts to include a diversity of roles and ways of being in the world reflect this attitude in their physical presence and nonverbal behavior. Nonverbally, they take up more space. Their gestures are more expansive; they allow themselves much more freedom of movement.

Macroview

Internal processes women have available to meet the demands of life directly affect self esteem. Without a complete set of working tools, any craftsperson is handicapped in producing a satisfactory product. As women's roles expand, their processes for coping with this expansion must keep pace if their self esteem is not to suffer.

Having traditionally been limited primarily to the home and family, women have developed an awareness of, and appreciation for, the finer details of their world. When one's territory is restricted, probability is high that the close-up lens will be more highly developed than a wide-angle view. Then the person cannot take in the panorama. What is interesting in such circumstances is the finer detail, the nuances, which close-up work can bring out. The relative smallness of a woman's world coupled with women's "place" in our society, has resulted in a high level of sophistication of her focusing ability. That is, women, in order to survive, have overdeveloped this focusing ability in order to protect themselves from the dominant structure. Henley (1977) explained that in order to survive, women, like Blacks and other minorities, have had to develop a finely tuned high level of nonverbal acuity, to always be on guard, to sense the reactions of those around. Nonverbal cues are vital in maintaining and changing the status quo. This outer-directedness, this highly focused stance is a necessary survival skill.

What has not been fully developed in women, however, is the wide-angle view—the ability to see the larger picture, the ability to unfocus. As women have stretched their boundaries and ventured out beyond home and family, they have, therefore, been handicapped because these additional skills have been largely undeveloped. Women typically lack the requisite skills to relate effectively to large social systems. The reader may be interested in experimenting with using his/her eyes as a camera lens—zooming in for close-up work, zooming out for a wider view. Zooming in or out requires refocusing. Notice what happens as you alter your lenses. What position feels most comfortable? Most awkward? What can you learn from each position and those points in between? Experiment with focusing and unfocusing your eyes. What do you notice? (Feelings, sensations, cognitions). What do you notice as you move from one position to the other?

Unfocusing may feel like a "letting go," similar to the relaxation response, characterized by a lack of vigilance, a lack of control. Focusing, on the other hand, involves directing awareness to a central point of interest, allowing for greater examination of, mastery of, or control over that particular point. Both the ability to focus and the ability to unfocus are processes vital to healthy functioning and positive self esteem. Typically, women with high drive to succeed, who have fought to establish themselves outside of the home environment, have had to develop sophisticated unfocusing processes. On the other hand, other women, typically those who do not venture out into unknown territory as frequently, those who opt for a safer, more limited existence for whatever reason, are quite adept at focusing and have a less highly developed unfocusing ability. Not faced continuously with new tasks to be mastered, their world being smaller, such individuals have little need to unfocus.

Anxiety in Change

Women in our culture are in transition, in an ongoing process of change. Women today, while striving for their rights, are still unconsciously tied to traditional thinking and values (De Rosis, 1979). Guilt, an emotion prevalent among women, indicates an underlying conflict, an inability to solve an old set of "shoulds." The pull towards the old set of shoulds, combined with a new competing set, exerts quite a pressure on the modern woman. The new set of shoulds is just as strong and unrealistic in its demand for formerly dependent "little girls" to become responsible women overnight. Failure to meet or even value these new standards can result in severe feelings of inadequacy. Those who attempt a career, independence, often still must carry 90% of the burden of the responsibility for childcare and housekeeping. Overburdened, these women typically experience much anxiety, guilt, and ultimately, fatigue. While the "opportunity" is more available for expansion, the external supports are lagging behind (i.e., structure of the marital dyad, split positions in the work world, adequate childcare). Expansion is possible, but not without struggle. Without a realistic assessment of those barriers, self esteem may plummet.

In the process of the transition to being progressive, women often are able to maintain their power, their personal ground (reflected, for example, in partaking equally in the leadership) in numerous contexts. They often exhibit, however, great difficulty holding their own in an intimate relationship with a man (and also, though less frequently encountered, with dominant women). Women tend to dissolve into a traditional dependent position. "Assuming one's place" feels like a safe alternative when faced with a dominant person. Another split, however, can emerge at this point with the woman: capitulating (acquiescing) on the surface while resisting inside.

The pressure for women to change, to rock the boat, to develop opinions, or to pursue a career is a heavy weight. This competing set of demands can become additionally oppressive if the woman fails to determine her own course of action. Adopting the current trend, whether it be in a traditional or revolutionary vein, can be equally binding. Women can choose and affirm the choices they make, fending off any implied derogation of those choices. People make innumerable choices in life, from the most mundane, what soap to buy, what to order for lunch, where to park the car, what blouse to wear; to choices which involve longer range implications such as whether or not to marry, have children, enter or change careers, go to school. People make the best choice they can, given their awareness of the options, and their own resources and limitations. Given the choice between path "A" and path "B," if I choose "A" now, this does not mean that path "B" is closed to me forever. People can make different choices at other times. No universally right or wrong path is available to follow. On the other hand, each choice further defines the character of one's life.

CONCLUSION:
THE ROAD BACK TO SELF

A number of approaches are useful to the enhancement and maintenance of self esteem in women. In working with women struggling with self esteem issues, a helper might experiment with a combination of the interventions listed:

1. Consciousness-Raising. Provide information substantiating the significant and negative association of traditional female behavior with self esteem. Help make women aware of various social explanations for low self esteem in women. Encourage role evaluation. Survey music, history, religion, education, science, and the arts to become more aware of the contributions of women to society.

2. Train in assertion, confrontation, conflict initiation, conflict management, and the politics of nonverbal behavior. Provide women with skills in dealing with double-binds, develop process skills; expand body awareness, encourage taking charge, develop verbal defense skills.

3. Teach cognitive restructuring, reframing, and dispassionate involvement; teach self-enhancing talk. Before being thrown in the ring and told "Now show your stuff!," women need to be trained in the tactics of survival in an environment where these behaviors are supported and women's other strengths are preserved rather than devalued.

4. One of the best survival tactics is to involve oneself in a support group. Women need skills in locating and forming support groups. They need the skills to recognize and ask for what they need. Women need to

become aware of what they have to offer, who can give them what they need, and how to make connections (Turner, 1983). Many cities have available groups peripherally connected with Al-Anon which address issues related to these presented in this chapter. They are often called *Co-dependency groups, Relationship Anonymous groups* or *Women Who Love Too Much groups.*

5. A rhythm needs to begin and a balance to be struck between identifying one's present state (feelings, ideas, needs, vacuums, wants, urges, hungers, longings), and expressing self, attempting to meet one's own needs, and *evaluating* how well the attempted solution has satisfied the need. Through this *self-oriented* feedback process, the seeds of an internally based self esteem are laid. Then, with every "I-me" oriented question, a woman waters and fertilizes that seed:

> What do I want?
> What is my next step?
> How can I do this?
> How does this feel to me?
> How good or bad does that make me feel?
> What do I think is important?
> I must do my own experiment.
> I must find what I can live with.
> I am my own person.
> What do I see?
> What are my choices?
> Do I agree with that?

With each affirmation of herself, the woman begins to shift her position—the "me"—from the background to the forefront of her life. A woman is best able to validate her own experience. She must literally pull herself into the driver's seat and increase the choices and control of her own life. A woman can honor herself and honor others.

6. Locating approximate models (especially in peers) and sharing mutually can increase self esteem.

7. Body awareness and body movement work is important for reconnecting women with their physical self as a source of experiencing, and a source of data to monitor what feels good and what does not, increasing their sense of integration, and facilitating and valuing an intuitive or inside-looking-out approach (Barlin & Greenberg, 1980; Jencks, 1977).

On an emotional, bodily, and cognitive level women have been trained to collapse, fold, withdraw. Women must now learn additional responses—to push back, to "come back at" in addition to giving in, to rise above, to watch from behind a screen, to bracket off their emotions and personhood when required, to respond as a computer filing data rather than allowing their insecurities to be hooked thus impairing their vision. Women need alternate ways to deal with their fears and anxieties. These additional ways of operating in the world also must be learned at the emotional, cognitive, and bodily level. The work is hard but joyous, for with each step she breathes in the air of life more deeply, giving herself new strength, energy, and robustness.

8. Analysis of one's family origin to identify what interpretations (conscious and unconscious) the woman took away with her and to determine what rules (implicitly or explicitly conveyed) about

what it means to be a woman,
how a woman should be treated, and
how a woman should treat herself.

While the challenges to women's self esteem are great now, opportunities for change are abundant. Now, more than ever before, awareness of the social-psychological dynamics which perpetuate low self esteem are heightened. Women's culture is slowly being brought to light. Women's music and literature, women's history, women's art, and other evidence of the female experience are gradually surfacing and receiving at least minimal recognition. This increased awareness opens the possibility of choice and the hope of freedom from oppression.

ACTIVITY 11.1   PERSONAL RIGHTS

Introduction

Asserting oneself helps one to grow. This activity helps one to enhance assertiveness and is appropriate for both children and adults. This activity is a **maintenance phase activity** as described in Chapter 6.

Time Required

45 minutes

Participants

Age 9 and older

Setting

Office or classroom

Materials

None

Procedure

Describe at least 3 situations where you felt you wanted to act assertively but held back. Now brainstorm your personal rights in each of these situations.

Imagine giving yourself this collective group of rights. Really take each one in deeply and hear these rights called out one at a time as you picture yourself growing stronger and stronger, as you feel yourself expand and glow.

Imagine how your life would be different. See yourself moving through a typical day while deeply feeling all your personal rights.

Did you have difficulty accepting any of the rights? Did you feel guilty when you assert your needs? How far did you let the rights in? How did you feel/act differently when you had all those rights?

Outcomes

This activity helps one bestow these rights upon self each day. When you find yourself in situations where you want to act assertively, take in all your rights and breathe deeply the strength they impart.

ACTIVITY 11.2 JOURNAL: HIDDEN SELF

Introduction

The goal of this activity is to increase awareness of your inner-hidden self.

Time Required

5 to 15 minutes a day

Participants

Any number; adolescents or adults

Setting

Classroom or office

Materials

Record log

Procedure

1. Record daily any positive feedback you receive. Are you able to absorb these positives? How do you block positives?

2. Record instances where you do things you do not want to do or say things you do not mean in order to gain approval. How do you feel about yourself when you do this?

3. Record times you stop yourself from taking risks. What goes on inside of you when you do this?

4. As you reflect on the above, do you find sources of fear, guilt, resentments, and shame? Many women are taught to devalue and be ashamed of their abilities, ambitions, and achievements.

Outcome

Increases positive self-evaluation.

ACTIVITY 11.3   RECEIVING

Introduction

This activity gives women an experience in receiving support and nurturance.

Time Required

30 to 45 minutes

Participants

Any number; adults

Setting

Therapy or workshop

Materials

None

Procedure

1. Find a partner.

2. Allow your partner to fully support one of your hands. Notice how you feel as you allow this support. Notice any resistance inside.

3. Allow your partner to explore and stroke your hand in various ways. Pay attention to fully receiving this stroking. Notice any ways you block this receiving. Give your partner specific feedback on how to touch you in a way that is more pleasing to you. Do this non-verbally. Ask for exactly what you want.

4. Process your feelings with your partner.

   a. How do you feel about receiving without giving in return?

   b. Were you able to fully receive?

   c. Were you able to be aware of and ask for the kind touching you wanted? How did you feel about doing this?

5. Reverse roles and repeat the procedure.

Outcome

Increases one's ability to receive.

ACTIVITY 11.4   MAKING REQUESTS

Introduction

This exercise helps participants to practice the skill of making simple requests to counterbalance the tendency to over-give.

Time Required

5 to 30 minutes a day

Participants

Any number; adults

Setting

Classroom or office

Materials

None

Procedure

Practice making small daily requests of those around you each day. Make the requests simple and able to be completed within 15 minutes time.

Some examples:

1. Would you give me a 15 minute back rub?

2. Will you make me a cup of coffee?

3. Will you listen to a problem I'm having for a few minutes?

Notice any resistances you have to completing this task. Make note of these.

How do you feel asking and allowing others to give to you?

How did people respond to you?

Note: If you get stuck trying to think of requests, notice small things you do for others. Often people do for others what they would like others to do for them.

Outcome

Increases the ability to ask for what one wants.

ACTIVITY 11.5   GIFT TO YOURSELF

Introduction

This is a self-nuturance phase activity designed to underline the importance of giving to oneself.

Time Required

5 to 15 minutes each day for one week

Participants

Any number; adolescents or adults

Setting

Classroom or office

Materials

Record log

Procedure

Think of some small way you can be good to yourself each day. Make it as important as eating and sleeping.

Record what you do for yourself each day for one week. At the end of each day write how giving to yourself in this way affected you. Describe any difficulties you encounter in completing this task.

Outcome

Increases self-nurturant behaviors.

ACTIVITY 11.6   INNER GUIDE

Introduction

This activity invites the participant to listen inwardly to the still small voice inside.

Time Required

5 to 30 minutes and repeated at other times

Participants

Any number; adolescents and adults

Setting

Classroom or office

Materials

Soft music

Procedure

Allow your eyes to close now. Pay attention to breathing. Breathe into that spot which you call the center of your body. For some, it is two inches below the navel. Allow yourself to breathe in and out of this center part of your being. With each exhalation, expel all of the air from your lungs. Allow your mouth to slightly drop open exhaling completely through your mouth and nose.

As you breathe in imagine filling your lungs and whole body with a cleansing, pure, white light. With each exhalation, expel any tensions you are holding anywhere. Continue this for a few moments.

Gradually, make your way to that safe, quiet spot deep inside of you. Perhaps you find a door to your secret room where you can relax in the comfort of your inner being. Find this place of comfort. Make yourself a place where you are *peaceful, undisturbed and open to yourself. Pay attention to your breathing as you make your way along the path to your inner quiet place. Notice everything about the place—colors, textures, smells—use all of your senses to experience your safe place.*

Find a comfortable position in the location where you are and ready yourself to receive any messages which might be forth coming from your wise one. Focus on a specific question on our mind or a problem in your life. When you have this in focus, ask your wise one for guidance. Do not search but merely wait to receive. Messages may come to you in many forms: colors, songs, images, memories, thought forms— perhaps you might find yourself moving in some way will be a symbol to you. Expect anything. Even the most seemingly insignificant experience you have in the next few moments may be a message to you. Open yourself to whatever comes and discover its meaning for you. Take a few moments now to rest in yourself as you open to your innerworld. Be aware of your breathing as you do this.

(Pause)

Take a moment to thank yourself for any messages which were delivered to you at this time. As you open more and more to your inner experience, many more gifts will be offered to you. If you had difficulty opening to yourself, repeat this activity intermittently over time. Be patient with yourself. Gradually, your breathing into relaxation will lead you to a deeper place inside yourself. Patiently practice and await what is to come.

Once again, breathe deeply into the center of your being. Then slowly, as you are ready, begin to leave this place carrying with you the messages you received.

Outcome

Increases inner-directedness.

ACTIVITY 11.7   ENSLAVING CARETAKER

Introduction

This activity heightens awareness of caretaking roles and the impact of self esteem.

Time Required

15 to 30 minutes to record plus 2 to 15 minutes to discuss later with a person selected.

Participants

Any number; adults

Setting

Classroom or office

Materials

Pen and paper

Procedure

In the middle of a piece of paper draw a circle and put your name in the center of it. From this circle draw lines outward. Allow space for many lines. At the end of each line draw another circle. In each outer circle write the role you fulfill daily or infrequently such as mother, wife, daughter, friend, sister-in-law, chef, church member—all the different roles you play.

For each role write a brief job description (one or two sentences). Ask yourself how often caretaking duties are part of each role. Is this helpful to your self esteem? Do you feel you must be nurturing, caring, supporting and caretaking to all persons all of the time? Have you confused caretaking with loving? How do you define yourself? How do you want others to define you?

For each role you indicated, write beside the circle ways in which you could ask the person involved for nurturing and support in return. Think of ways these relationships could be more reciprocal. Choose one role on which to work as a goal. Try to ask that person for what you are needing. If you want to G-E-T, you have to A-S-K.

Outcome

Creates more reciprocal relationships.

━━━━━━

REFERENCES

Atwood, M. (1972). *Surfacing.* New York: Fawcett Popular Library.

Avis, J. (1985). The politics of functional family therapy: A feminist critique. *Journal of Marital and Family Therapy, 11*(2): 127-138.

Baird, I. (1973). *The graduates.* Princeton, NJ: Educational Testing Service.

Bardwick, J. (1979). *In transition.* New York: Holt, Rinehart and Winston.

Barlin, A.L., & Greenberg, T.R. (1980). *Move and be moved.* Van Nuys, CA: Learning Through Movement.

Baruch, G. (1973). Feminine self-esteem, self-ratings of competence and maternal career commitment. *Journal of Counseling Psychology, 20,* 487-488.

Baruch, G.K., & Barnett, R. (1986). Role quality, multiple role involvement, and psychological well-being in midlife women. *Journal of Personality and Social Psychology, 51,* 578-585.

Beattie, M. (1987). *Codependent no more.* New York: Harper/Hazeldon.

Becker, C. (1987). *The invisible drama.* New York: Macmillan.

Becker, E. (1971). *The birth and death of meaning* (2nd ed.). New York: The Free Press.

Belenky, M.F., Clinchy, B.M., Goldberger, N.R., & Tarule, J.M. (1986). *Women's ways of knowing.* New York: Basic Books.

Bernard, J. (1966). *Academic women.* Cleveland: Meridian.

Bernard, J. (1982). *The future of marriage.* New York: Bantam.

Bianchi, S.M. & Spain, D. (1986). *American women in transition.* New York: Russell-Sage.

Bidese, C.M., & Danais, D. (1981). *Physician characteristics and distribution in the U.S. survey and data resources.* American Medical Association, Chicago.

Blau, F. (1975). Women in the labor force: An overview. In J. Freeman (Ed.), *Women: A feminist perspective* (pp. 211-226). Palo Alto, CA: Mayfield.

Boston Women's Health Book Collective (1984). New York: Simon & Schuster.

Broner, E.M. (1978). *A weave of women.* New York: Bantam.

Broverman, I.K., Broverman, D.M., Clarkson, F.E., Rosenkrantz, P.L., & Vogel, S.R. (1970). Sex-role stereotypes and clinical judgments of mental health. *Journal of Clinical and Consulting Psychology, 34,* 1-7.

Broverman, I.K., Vogel, S.R., Broverman, D.M., & Rosenkrantz, P.S. (1972). Sex-role stereotypes: A current appraisal. *Journal of Social Issues, 28,* 59-78.

Caplan, P. (1981). *Barriers between women.* Jamaica, NY: Spectrum.

Carlock, C.J. (1975). Development and analysis of a weekend workshop for the personal development of women. *Dissertation Abstracts, 36* (8), 5035A, 76-2628, 380.

Carter, B., & McGoldrick, M. (1988). *The changing family life cycle.* New York: Gardner Press.

Chicago, J. (1979). *The dinner party: A symbol of our heritage.* New York: Anchor/Doubleday.

Chodorow, N. (1971). Being and doing: A cross-cultural examination in the socialization of males and females. In V. Gornick & B. K. Moran (Eds.), *Women in sexist society: Studies in power and powerlessness* (pp. 259-291). New York: Basic Books.

Chodorow, N. (1978). *The reproduction of mothering: Psychoanalysis and the sociology of gender.* Berkeley: University of California Press.

Clifton, M.A., & Smith, H. (1963). Comparison of expressed self-concepts of highly skilled males and females concerning motor performance. *Perceptual and Motor Skills, 16,* 199-291.

Coleman, L., & Antonucci, T. (1983). Impact of work on women at midlife. *Developmental Psychology, 19,* 290-294.

Collier, H.V. (1982). *Counseling Women.* New York: The Free Press.

Connell, D.M., & Johnson, J.E. (1971). Relationships between sex-role identification and self-esteem in early adolescents. *Developmental Psychology, 3,* 208.

DeRosis, H. (1979). *Women and anxiety.* New York: Delacorte.

Dickstein, L. (1982). Women university students: Effects of inequality. *Women and Therapy, 1,* 83-88.

Doress, P.B., & Siegal, D.L. (1987). *Ourselves, growing older.* Simon & Schuster.

Dworkin, A. (1974). *Women hating.* New York: E. P. Dutton.

Erikson, E. (1968). *Identity: Youth and crisis.* New York: Norton.

Flammer, D.P. (1971). Self-esteem, parent identification, and sex-role development in pre-school age boys and girls. *Child Study Journal, 2,* 39-45.

Fox, M.F., & Hesse-Biber, S. (1984). *Women at work.* New York: Mayfield.

Frieze, I., McHugh, M., Fisher, J., & Valle, V. (1975, May-June). *Attributing the causes of success and failure: Internal and external barriers to achievement in women.* Paper presented at Conference on New Directions for Research on Women, Madison, WI.

Gillespie, D. (1975). Who has the power? In J. Freeman (Ed.), *Women: A feminist perspective* (pp. 64-87). Palo Alto, CA: Mayfield.

Gilligan, C. (1982). *In a different voice.* Cambridge, MA: Harvard University Press.

Godwin, G. (1982). *Mother and two daughters.* New York: Avon.

Goldberg, P. (1968). Are women prejudiced against women? *Transaction, 5,* 28-30.

Gottesman, R., Murphy, F., Holland, L., Parker, H., Kalstone, D., & Pritchard, W. (1979). *The Norton Anthology:* Vol. 2. New York: W. W. Norton.

Gough, K. (1975). The origin of the family. In J. Freeman (Ed.), *Women: A feminist perspective* (pp. 43-63). Palo Alto, CA: Mayfield.

Greenspan, M. (1983). *A new approach to women and therapy.* New York: McGraw-Hill.

Henley, N. (1977). *Body politics.* Englewood Cliffs, NJ: Prentice-Hall.

Hollis, J. (1986). *Fat is a family affair.* San Francisco: Harper/Hazelden.

Horner, M.S. (1969). Sex differences in achievement motivation and performance in competitive and non-competitive situations (Doctoral dissertation, University of Michigan, 1968). *Dissertation Abstracts International, 30,* 1078. (University Microfilms No. 69-12, 185).

Horner, M.S. (1972a) The motive to avoid success and changing aspirations of women. In J. M. Hardwick (Ed.), *Readings on the psychology of women.* New York: Harper & Row.

Horner, M.S. (1972b). Toward an understanding of achievement-related conflicts in women. *Journal of Social Issues, 28,* 157-175.

Hot Flash, Newsletter. National Action Forum for Midlife and Older Women.

House, W., & Perney, V. (1974). Valence of expected and unexpected outcomes as a function of focus of control and types of expectancy. *Journal of Personality and Social Psychology, 29,* 454-563.

Hundley, W.J. (1988, March 1). *The ABCs of sexism.* Dayton Daily News.

Hustler. (1988, April). Cartoons, pp. 40 & 83.

Hymowitz, C., & Weissman, M. (1978). *A history of women in America.* New York: Bantam.

Jencks, B. (1977). *Your body.* Chicago: Nelson Hall.

Keleman, S. (1975). *Your body speaks its mind.* New York: Simon and Schuster.

Kemlicka, T., Cross, H., & Tornai, J. (1983). A comparison of androgenous, feminine, masculine, and indifferentiated women on self-esteem, body satisfaction, and sexual satisfaction. *Psychology of Women Quarterly, 7,* 291-294.

Kessler, R. & McRae, J. (1982). The effect of wives employment on the mental health of married men and women. *American Sociological Review, 47,* 216-226.

Kessler, R.C., & McRae, J.A. (1984). A note on the relationships of sex and marital status with psychological distress. In J. Greenley (Ed.), *Community and mental health, Vol. III.* Greenwich, CT: JAI.

Kirk, S. (1976, March). Radical feminist counseling: Theory and practice. *CWSSS Feminist Bulletin, 6*(3). San Diego, CA: Center for Women's Studies, 908 "F" St.

Laurence, M. (1979). *Stone angel.* New York: Bantam.

Laws, J.L. (1975). A feminist view of marital adjustment. In A. Gurman & D. Rice (Eds.), *Couples in conflict.* New York: Aronson.

Lebe, D. (1986). Female ego ideal conflicts in adulthood. *The American Journal of Psychoanalysis, 46,* 22-32.

Lederer, L. (1980). *Take back the night.* New York: William Morrow.

Lemkau, J. (1984). Reflections on selflessness in the lives of women. Women & Therapy, 3, 3-36.

Lerner, H.G. (1985). *The dance of anger.* New York: Harper & Row.

Levy, S.B. (1982, Summer). Toward a consideration of intimacy in the female/female therapy relationship. *Women and Therapy, I*(1), 35-44.

Lynn, N. (1975). Women in American politics: An overview. In J. Freeman (Ed.), *Women: A feminist perspective* (pp. 364-385). Palo Alto, CA: Mayfield.

McKee, J.P., & Sheriffs, A.C. (1959). Men's and women's beliefs, ideals, and self-concepts. *American Journal of Sociology, 64,* 363-63.

Major, B. (1987). Women and entitlement. *Women and Therapy, 6,* 3-20.

Marcia, J.E., & Friedman, M.L. (1970). Ego identity status in college women. *Journal of Personality, 7,* 84-104.

Mendelsohn, R.S. (1982). *MAL(E) practice.* Chicago: Contemporary Books.

Miller, J.B. (1976). *Toward a new psychology of women.* New York: Beacon.

Miller, T.E. (1972, September). *Male attitudes towards women's rights as a function of their self-esteem.* Paper presented at meeting of APA, Honolulu.

Morgan, E., & Farber, B.A. (1982). Toward a reformulation of the Eriksonian model of female identity development. *Adolescence, 11,* 199-211.

Morris, J.D. & Markus, H. (1978, August). *Careers and career attitudes: Age, education, and timing effects.* Paper presented at the meeting of American Psychological Association, Toronto, Canada.

Morris, J. (1981). *Cruiser dreams.* New York: Berkley.

National Women's Health Network Newsletter. National Women's Health Network. Washington, DC.

O'Connor, K., Mann, D., & Bardwick, J. (1978). Androgynyard self esteem in the upper-middle class: a replication of Spence. *Journal of Consulting and Clinical Psychology, 5,* 1168-1169.

Penthouse. (1988, March). Cartoon, p. 65.

Piercy, M. (1973). *Small changes.* New York: Doubleday.

Pietromonaco, R., Marris, J., & Frohardt-Lane, K. (1984, August). *Psychological consequences of multiple social roles.* Paper presented at the meeting of the American Psychological Association, Toronto, Canada.

Prager, K. (1982). Identity development and self-esteem in young women. *The Journal of Genetic Psychology, 141,* 177-182.

Rosen, R. (1974). Sexism in history. In J. Stacey & B. J. Daniels (Eds.), *And Jill came tumbling after: Sexism in American education.* New York: Dell.

Rosenkrantz, P.S., Vogel, S.R., Broverman, I.K., Broverman, D.M., & Clarkson, F.E. (1968). Sex-role stereotypes and self-concepts in college students. *Journal of Clinical and Consulting Psychology, 32,* 287-295.

Rubin, L. (1979). *Women of a certain age: The mid-life search for self.* New York: Harper & Row.

Sanford, L., & Donovan, M.E. (1985). *Women and self-esteem.* New York: Penguin Books.

Schaef, A.W. (1981). *Women's reality.* Minneapolis: Winston.

Schnitzer, P.K. (1977). The motive to avoid success: Exploring the nature of the fear. *Psychology of Women, 1*(3).

Showalter, E. (1974). Women and the Literary Curriculum. In J. Stacey & B.J. Daniels (Eds.), *And Jill came tumbling after: Sexism in American education.* New York: Dell.

Spretnak, C. (Ed.). (1982). *The Politics of women's spirituality.* New York: Anchor Press Doubleday.

Stone, M. (1976). *When God was a woman.* New York: Harvest.

The World Almanac and Book of Facts. (1989). New York: Scripps Howard Company.

Thoits, P.A. (1983). Multiple identities and psychological well-being: A reformulation and best of the social isolation hypothesis. *American Sociological Review, 48,* 174-187.

Thurow, L. (1987). The surge of inequality. *Scientific American, 256*(5): 30-37.

Turner, R. (1983). Class and psychological vulnerability among women: The significance of social support and personal control. *Journal of Health and Social Behavior, 24,* 2-15.

U.S. Bureau of the Census. (1981). *Statistical abstract of the United States: 1981-81* (102d Ed). Washington, DC:

Usher, S., & Fels, M. (1985). The challenge of feminism and career for the middle-aged. *International Journal of Women's Studies, 8,* 47-57.

Wylie, R.C. (1963). Children's estimate of their school work ability as a function of sex, race, socio-economic level. *Journal of Personality, 31,* 203-224.

CHAPTER 12

MEASUREMENT OF SELF ESTEEM

As interest in self-concept and self esteem has increased so too has the measurement of these concepts increased. According to Demo (1985) research in these areas of self concept and self esteem has addressed itself to substantive problems of definition, measurement, and interpretation have been resolved. Paradoxically studies of the measurement problems of self esteem are infrequent and inconsequential.

SELF ESTEEM ASSESSMENT PROBLEMS

Validation

Bingham (1983) lists four difficulties in the measurement of self esteem. Validation of what comprises self esteem is the first problem area. Although a commonly accepted belief is that self esteem is multifaceted, many tests do not reflect this concept. Some tests measure global self esteem and some measure specific self esteem. Global self esteem refers to the over all evaluation of self esteem. Specific self-esteem refers to self evaluation in the more narrowly defined areas of self estimates, as discussed in Chapter 1. Global self esteem measurement can predict behavior across a wide array of situations, whereas specific self esteem measures may allow predictions in delineated areas of behavior.

Measurement of self esteem should be consistent with a conceptual model (O'Brien, 1985). For example, a test of specific self estimates should be consistent with a theory of self esteem which indicates that self esteem is composed of several self estimates. This consistency is not always the case when one reviews tests of self esteem. Frequently over reliance on traditional measures of global self esteem have resulted in self estimates being neglected (Demo, 1985).

Several theorists have criticized the global approach to the measurement of self-esteem (Gecas, 1982; Marsh & Shavelson, 1983). They argue that since self esteem is multifaceted and better prediction results from specific self esteem measurement, therefore, measurement of self esteem is enhanced when it focuses on specific factors. Although the number and type of factors of self esteem have varied across studies, most investigations have yielded at least one factor (self estimate) associated with the achievement area (i.e., feeling competent) and one association with the communal area (i.e., feeling likeable/ sociable (Stake, 1985). The use of specific self esteem measures have lead to greater success in predicting behavior and attitude. (The performance self-esteem scale and the social self esteem scale for adults are both examples of specific measures and will be described later in this chapter.)

Ceiling Effect

The second problem is with ceiling effect. Wylie (1974) concluded that *Rosenberg's Self-Esteem Scale* yielded impressive reliability and validity yet its ability to discriminate among adults have been less than adequate (Bingham, 1983). The report (Bingham, 1983) has been that usually two-thirds or more of adults score so close to the top of the scale on this test that differentiation is impossible. Thus the ceiling effect limits the usefulness of this instrument and some other instruments when studying adults.

Situation

The third problem with measurement of self esteem is often situationally specific. A person may be pleased with him/herself at work and not positive with his/her social self. An individual may have positive self esteem in a family context but not feel good about self in an academic setting. Measurement of self esteem asks the respondent to repeat only abstract or generalized ideas about self esteem. Self esteem has been measured almost exclusively in general terms (Bingham, 1983).

Sex Differences

The fourth problem is a conceptual difficulty in measuring self esteem which occurs in the inconsistency of results regarding sex differences. Sex differences in self esteem frequently have been discussed in the literature (Juhasz, 1985). Self approval of an act is called *intrinsic self esteem;* social approval—approval by others—is termed *extrinsic self esteem.* Boys more frequently manifest intrinsic self esteem and girls more frequently manifest extrinsic self esteem (Bingham, 1983). Kelley (1976) also found these sex related differences, and in addition found that these differences vary across time. Sex differences in self esteem therefore, need to be assessed along variables other than just level of self esteem.

Gecas (1982) reviewed the literature on self esteem measurement and confirmed that measurement is still a "serious problem" in self concept research. O'Brien (1985) concurred in stating that the over reliance on global self esteem measurement has lead to the neglect of other dimensions of self esteem and self concept. Consequently, well constructed measures for clinical use are difficult to acquire partly because few measures are subjected to close and systematic investigation (Hughes, 1984).

Children's Developmental Concerns

Hughes (1984) in an extensive review of the literature on measures of self concept and self esteem for children ages 3 through 12 years, stated that developmental concerns are also an issue in the measurement of self esteem of children. (This problem might be added to Bingham's 1983 list of methodological problems of self esteem assessment to bring the total to five problem areas.) Most tests of self esteem are experimenter or test designer determined for content, thus preventing children from specifying areas which comprise their self concept.

In addition a number of factors are unique to the measurement of children which must be considered when constructing a test. Children change in language skills and in their cognitive abilities which is reflected in their ability to understand certain concepts. These changes are crucial to item selection, method of administration, and test format. Also important when assessing children are intellectual levels. When designing tests for a particular age level that is a very important consideration. Attention span, memory capacity, and test-taking skills also are important to consider when testing children. All of these factors differ with age and developmental level.

Hughes (1984) in a review selected nineteen measures of self esteem. (Self concept and self esteem are often used interchangeably in test descriptions, however, as discussed earlier in this text there is agreement that the evaluative features of self concept are termed "self esteem". Since most tests in use require an evaluative response from subjects, the tests should more accurately be considered measures of self esteem, even if discussed as measures of self concept.) These measures were chosen only if they had some preliminary psychometric information available for review. Only self esteem tests which are "clinically relevant" were included in the review. Since Wylie (1974) argued strongly against the use of discrepancy scores due to difficulty in scoring and each of construct validity the *Sliding Person Test* (Karmos, 1979), the *Bledsoe Self Concept Scale* (Bledsoe, 1983), and the *Preschool Self-Concept Picture Test* (Woolner, 1966) were not recommended for use.

TEST REVIEWS

The measures selected as being the most "clinically relevant" were the *Coopersmith Self-Esteem Inventory*, the *Self-Perception Inventory—Self Concept Form*, the *Personal Attribute Inventory for Children* (and Revised form), the *Sears Self-Concept Inventory*, the *Piers-Harris Children's Self-Concept Scale*, the *McDaniel-Piers Young Children's Self-Concept Scale*, the *Primary Self-Concept Scale*, the *Pictorial Self-Concept Scale*, the *Brown IDS Self-Concept Referents Test*, the *Maryland Pre-School Self-Concept Scale* (and Revised form), the *Preschool and Primary Self-Concept Scale*, the *I Feel—Me Feel Scale*, the *Behavior Rating Form* (and Revised form), the

Behavioral Academic Self-Esteem Scale, the *Inferred Self Concept Scale,* and the *Barber Scales of Self-Regard for Preschool Children.* Each of these closed-end rating technique tests are briefly described in Tables 12.1 through 12.4.

The *Dimensions of Self-Concept (DOSC)* test is a measure of non-cognitive factors associated with self esteem or self-concept in a school setting—grades 4 to 6, grades 7 to 12, and college. Consists of five factor dimensions that help identify perceptions of low degree of self esteem or self-regard.

Summary and Recommendations

Self esteem measures for older children were developed earlier, therefore, more accumulated empirical support exists for these measures. To design tests for early elementary and preschool children is more difficult due to the developmental problems discussed earlier in this chapter. Consequently, recommendations for younger children are more difficult to make.

According to Hughes (1984) for the age range of 9 through 12 the measure of choice is the Piers-Harris Children's Self Concept Scale, due to the amount of empirical evidence for reliability and validity and percentile norms. The *Coopersmith Self-Esteem Inventory* and the *Sears Self-Concept Inventory* seem adequate for current use.

For the ages of 6 through 9 according to Hughes (1984) no one self-report instrument is best. Since the *McDaniels-Peirs Scales* have a large sample size, evidence for reliability, and a manual, it is the measurement of choice for this age group.

For the age range of 3 through 6, Hughes recommended the *Brown IDS Self-Concept Test* since it has more empirical evidence with larger numbers of children. The problem of self report instruments for this age range of children, however, is the egocentrism of young children and their drive to please adults. Adult reports of preschool children, therefore, may be the most adequate for measurement purposes. The *Behavioral Academic Self-Esteem* Scale is the measure of choice for children preschool age through sixth grade (Hughes, 1984)

(Continued on page 440)

TABLE 12.1
Self-Esteem Measures for Children Ages 9-12 Years*

Measure	Age	Description	Administration	Reliability	Validity
1.a. Self-Esteem Inventory (SEI) (Coopersmith, 1967)	9-15 years	Designed to measure evaluative attitudes toward the self in social, academic, family and personal areas of experience. 2 Forms: Form A: 50 items + 8-item Lie scale; subscales; General Self, Social Self-Peers, Home-Parents, School-Academic. Short Statements: 18 positive, 32 negative, 2 choices: "like me"—"unlike me."	self-report 25 minutes	Coopersmith (1967) N = 1700 Split-half Reliability r = .90 test-retest r = .88 5 weeks; test-retest r = .70 3 weeks	Kokenes (1974) Factor Analysis 8 Factors; 3 related to General, 2 related to Social. Moderate congruence with subscales.
		2 points per question: range 0-100. Form B: 25 items, no subscales, correlates r = .95 with Form A	10 minutes		r = .75 with Piers-Harris
1.b. Self-Esteem Inventory (SEI) (Coopersmith, 1981)	8-15 years	Same as 1.a. except for age change. Form A is now "School Form" with 58 items. Form B is now "School Short Form"	self-report		

Instrument	Age	Description	Administration	Reliability	Validity
2. Self-Perception Inventory (SPI) (Soares & Soares, 1980)	9-14 years	Designed to measure the component of self-perception which is how the individual sees the self at the moment. 20 pairs of bipolar statements or adjectives. 4-point rating scale: "very" positive + 2 "more" positive + 1 "more" negative - 1 "very" negative - 2 Algebraic sum yields index score ranging from - 40 to +40.	self-report 5-20 minutes depending on reading ability	Internal consistency r = .89	Correlates r = .68 with SEL Factor analysis— 7 factors identified
3.a. Personal Attribute Inventory for Children (PAIC) (Parish & Taylor, 1978)	9-13 years	Intended to measure the evaluative-affective component of self-concept. 48-item checklist: 24 positive, 24 negative. Check 15 words that best describe self. Score is number of positive words checked. Range 0-24	self-report 5 minutes	N = 390 test-retest r = .63—.98 4 weeks	N = 930 Correlate r = .32 with Piers-Harris total sample
3.b. Nonsexist Personal Attribute Inventory for Children (NPAIC) (Parish & Rankin, 1982)	10-14 years	Same as PAIC. 16 positive and 16 negative. Check 10 words best describe self. Score number of positive words checked. Range 0-10.	Self-report no time estimation	N = 300 test-retest 4 weeks r = .35-.66	N = 300 Correlate r = .49 with Piers-Harris

Table 12.1 (Continued)

Measure	Age	Description	Administration	Reliability	Validity
4. Sears Self-Concept Inventory (Sears, 1966; Sears & Sherman, 1964)	9-12 years	Assess child's expectations of solving problems and completing tasks. 48 items rate self compared with other children of the same age. 5 choices: (1) not so good to (5) excellent. Scores range 48-220. 9 subscales	self-report no time estimation	**N** = 488 Coefficient alpha = .94	N = 488 Correlates r = .58 with Piers-Harris Factors from factor analysis: (a) academic, (b) physical, (c) social, and (d) divergent mental abilities.
5. Piers-Harris Children's Self-Concept Scale (Piers, 1969)	9-16 years	Intended to measure general self-concept as it is reflected by concerns children have about themselves. 80 short statements: 44 negative, 36 positive. 2 choices "yes"—"no" 1 point per question answered in direction indicating high self-esteem. Range 0-80, scoring key provided. Cluster subscales.	self-report 15-20 minutes	test-retest 2-7 months r = .62-.75 3-9 weeks 4 = .80-.96	Correlates r = .10-.85 with other self-concept measures. N = 515 Factor analysis revealed 7 factors

*NOTE: Adapted from "Measures of Self-Concept and Self-Esteem for Children Ages 3-12 years: A Review and Recommendation" by Honore Hughes in *Clinical Psychology Review*, Vol. 4, pp. 654-692. 1984. Copyrighted 1985 by Pergamon Press, Inc. Reproduced by permission.

TABLE 12.2

Self-Esteem Measures for Children Ages 6-9 Years*

Measure	Age	Description	Administration	Reliability	Validity
1. McDaniel-Piers Young Children's Self-Concept Scale(E.D. McDaniel, cited in Johnson, 1976)	6-9 Years	Modification of Piers-Harris, extension downward in age. 40 short statements: 16 positive, 24 negative. 2 choices: "yes" "no." Scored like Piers-Harris. 3 subscales	Questions read to child individually or in small groups. 20 minutes. Special answer sheet with pictures rather than numbers.	N = 2000 KR_{20} = .73-86	N = 560 Factor analysis indicated 3 factors.
2. Primary Self-Concept Scale (Torshen, Krocker, and Petersen, 1977).	5-8 years	Designed to measure same construct as Sears Self-Concept Inventory. Scale I: 24 items [e.g., "if you learn things faster (same rate, slower) than most of your classmates"].	Questions read to a group. Child marks special answer sheet. 15 minutes per scale.	N = 77 Scale 1 test-retest 6 months r = .38-.73 sub-scales.	N = 240 Factor analysis yielded 7 factors congruent with 7 subscales.

Table 12.2 (Continued)

Measure	Age	Description	Administration	Reliability	Validity
3. Pictoral Self-Concept Scale (Bolea, Felker, and Barnes, 1971)	5-9 years	Constructed to measure self-concept based on Jersild's (1952) categories. 50 cartoon cards with central figure depicted. Child sorts cards into 3 piles: "like me," "sometimes like me," and "not like me." Male and female forms available. Scoring based on weighted values for each card.	Group or individual administration.	N = 1800 Split-half $r = .85$	N = 63 Correlate $r = .42$ with Piers-Harris 4th graders
4. Preschool and Primary Self-Concept (PPSC) Scale. (Stager and Young, 1982)	4-9 years	See Table 12.3 for description			

*NOTE: Adapted from "Measures of Self-Concept and Self-Esteem for Children Ages 3-12 years: A Review and Recommendation" by Honore Hughes in *Clinical Psychology Review*, Vol. 4, pp. 654-692, 1984. Copyrighted 1985 by Pergamon Press, Inc. Reproduced by permission.

TABLE 12.3

Self-Esteem Measures for Children Ages 3-6 Years*

Measure	Age	Description	Administra-tion	Reliability	Validity
1. Brown IDS Self-Concept Referents Test Brown, 1966 (cited in Walker, 1973)	3.5-6.5 years	Designed to measure "self-concept of young child." Polaroid picture taken of child. 21 bi-polar questions: either-or format. Adjectives or behavioral character-istics. Measures self-percep-tions, also how mothers, teachers and peers perceive them. 3 versions of instru-ment.	Administered individually. 10-15 minutes.	N = 38 Test-retest r = .71 3 weeks	N = 531 Correlate PPVT r = .30.
2.a. Maryland Pre-School Self-Concept Scale (Smith, 1978)	4-6 years	Developed to measure the evaluative feelings one has regarding one's capabilities and qualities. 30 pairs of descriptive statements. 10 pairs repeated for "con-sistency" score. 2 choices: choose one stick figure as most similar to self.	Individual administration. 15 minutes.	Spearman-Brown = .81	N = 100 Correlates r = .42 with Bolea Pictorial Self-Concept Scale

Table 12.3 (Continued)

Measure	Age	Description	Administration	Reliability	Validity
2.b. Maryland Pre-School Self-Concept Scale-Revised (Hughes, 1981)	4-6 years	Constructed to measure the evaluative feels one has regarding one's capabilities and qualities. 20 pairs of descriptive statements.	Administered individually. 10 minutes.	N = 54 Coefficient alpha = .77	N = 54 No correlation with PPVT-R.
3. Preschool and Primary Self Concept (PPSC) Scale (Stager and Young, 1982)	4-9 years	Developed to measure the child's thoughts and feelings in reference to him or herself or an object. Uses semantic differential format for concept "ME"; 7 adjective bipolar scales: happy-sad; strong-weak; good-bad; big-small; liked by other people-not liked by other people; fast-slow; busy doing something-not busy doing something. Measure has verbal and pictorial stimuli for each scale and 4 response options: "very good," a "little bit good," and "little bit bad," "very "bad."	Individually administered. 10 minutes.	N = 236 composite across scales. omega = .72	N = 46 Correlate r = .29 with Inferred Self Concept Scale.

| 4. I Feel— Me Feel (White and Human, 1976) | 3-6 years | Developed to measure "self/ social construct" of self- concept. 18 items with each item consisting of a black and white silhouetted picture depicting an event related to a young child's life. At the bottom of each item is a row of 5 faces which graphically represent very sad, a little sad, not sad-not happy, a little happy, very happy. | Individually administered. | N = 46 alpha = .73 | N not reported 1 factor "self/con- struct" |

NOTE: Adapted from "Measures of Self-Concept and Self-Esteem for Children Ages 3-12 years: A Review and Recommendation" by Honore Hughes in *Clinical Psychology Review,* Vol. 4. pp. 654-692, 1984. Copyrighted 1985 by Pergamon Press, Inc. Reproduced by permission.

TABLE 12.4
Self-Esteem Measures Completed by Parent or Teacher for Ages 4-12 Years*

Measure	Age	Description	Administration	Reliability	Validity
1.a. Behavior Rating Form (BRF) (Coopersmith, 1967)	9-16 years	Designed to measure general self-esteem based on Coopersmith's theory. 13 questions total. 10 measuring behavior reflecting self-esteem. 3 measuring defensive behavior. 5 point rating scale.	Adult rating (teachers, parents, clinicians)	N = 70 Interrater reliability r = .71.	N= 175 Did not correlate significantly with Piers-Harris or SEI
1.b. Behavior Rating Form-Revised (BRF-R) (Hughes & Pugh, 1984)	4-6 years	Designed to measure general self-esteem based on Coopersmith's theory. 14 questions measuring behavior reflecting self-esteem. No lie scale. 5 point rating scale.	Parent rating	N = 38 alpha = .81	N = 38, 44 No correlation with social desirability scores.
2. Behavior Academic Self-Esteem (BASE) (Coopersmith & Gilberts, 1982)	4-12 years	"Measures children's academic self-esteem by using direct observation of their classroom behaviors," then making ratings. 16 short statements focused on academic behaviors.	Teacher report	N = 4000 Item analyses: item/total mean correlation z = .61	(N not reported) 3 factor analyses supported 5 factors with more evidence for 1st three.

3. Inferred Self-Concept Scale (E.L. McDaniel, 1973)	6-12 years	Developed to measure the student's self-concept as the teachers infer it from the child's verbal and non-verbal behavior. 30 short statements covering mainly social relations. 5 point rating scale	Ratings by teacher or counselor. 10 minutes	N = 180 Test-retest r = .49-.87	N = 180 Correlates .16-.32 with intellectual variables.
4. Barber Scales of Self-Regard for Preschool Children (Barber and Peatling, 1977)	2-5 years	Designed to access developmental maturity. 7 rating scales	Completed by teacher or parent.	N = 35 Interjudge r = .49 between mother and father. Interjudge 4 = .97 between mother	N = 35 No correlation with Self-Concept and Motivation inventory.

*NOTE: Adapted from "Measures of Self-Concept and Self-Esteem for Children Ages 3-12 years: A Review and Recommendation" by Honore Hughes in *Clinical Psychology Review*, Vol. 4, pp. 654-692, 1984. Copyrighted 1985 by Pergamon Press, inc. Reproduced by permission.

ADDITIONAL ASSESSMENT STRATEGIES

Formal Techniques

Demo (1985) discussed the use of the *Q-sort technique* completed by observers and peer ratings. These formats were recommended for self esteem assessment since formal or informal observations of an individual over a period of time is likely to be more objective and generalized than self reporting by the individual being assessed. In the Q-sort method the individual or, as recommended by Demo (1985), the observer is asked to sort a large number cards into piles which range from most like to least like self. On each card are single words, phrases, or sentences equally representing positive and negative descriptions of self, with a smaller number of cards with neutral statements. The individual or observer is then asked to repeat the process representing how he/she feels about self ideal.

Brownfain's Self-Rating Inventory (Brownfain, 1952) yields four measures: (1) the private self, (2) the positive self, (3) the negative self, and (4) the social self. The subject is instructed to take the inventory four different times, each time yielding a different type of self-concept measure.

The semantic differential model polarizes attributes. The individual chooses where he/she falls on a continuum from negative to positive poles. The technique can be used with children and adults. The *Hodgkin Self-Concept Scale for Children* (HSCSC) uses a pictorial form of the semantic differential techniques. It is applicable at the nursery school, kindergarten, and first and second grade levels. The *Preschool Self-Concept and Picture Test* (PSCPT) also uses the semantic differential format in pictorial representation. Preschool children are shown pictures and asked "Which boy (girl) would you like to be?" These questions are designed to surface differences between self-ideal and self-real. Fiedler's semantic self-concept scale (Fiedler, Hutchins, & Dodge, 1959) is an often used technique for the type for adults.

Sociometric techniques which reveal how a person is viewed by others can be helpful in assessing self-concept also. However, the person doing the measurement must recognize that one can be well liked by a group and still have negative feelings about self. If a person is socially rejected by others, however, he/she is very likely to have low self esteem. A kit entitled *Classroom Sociometric Analysis* can be obtained from the Research Council of America.

Inferred self-concept measures, those based on the perception and judgment of observers, aid in assessing self-concept. Such observers rate the person being tested on a scale of items such as "sociability with peers, need for encouragement, child's reactions to failures." The *Coopersmith Behavioral Rating Form* (Coopersmith, 1967) is such an instrument for assessing self esteem of children. Observers also supply descriptions of others in the *Inferred Self-Concept Scale* of Combs & Soper (1963) and Parker (1966). To use these measures the researcher should establish that the observer has reliable information about the individual.

In contrast to closed-end rating technique discussed previously the *Twenty Statements Test* (Sptizer, Couch, & Stratton, 1971) simply asks the subject to identify self by supplying his/her own adjectives. Spitzer's *"Who Are You?"* technique also is popular for measuring self-concept. The *Adjective Generation Technique* (Potkay & Allen, 1973) also is an **open-ended technique.** Scoring codes for the *Twenty Statements Test* is difficult to obtain however, because such coding systems are usually published in unpublished theses and dissertations.

Projective techniques such as the *Draw-a-Person Test,* the *Rorschach,* the *Thematic Apperception Test,* and incomplete sentence tests also have been used to measure self-concept and self esteem. Such techniques require more time than the other techniques mentioned thus far and also more skill in scoring, administering, and interpreting.

Informal Techniques

Unstructured interviews for assessing self-concept are discussed by Silber and Tippett (1965) and Tippett and Silber (1965). These authors use a ninety minute face-to-face interview, which is audio tape recorded and typescripted for later coding. A psychiatrist does the interviewing and rating in a five category hierarchy:

1. nondefensive, high self esteem;
2. defensive, high self esteem;
3. inconsistent self esteem;
4. ineffective defensive self esteem; and
5. low self esteem.

Flexibility and qualitative depth are the major advantages of this approach.

A ramification of this technique is informal assessment through *conversation*. This technique is especially helpful for children by asking them such questions as:

"Name an animal you would like to be and tell why."

"If you could be changed from what you are, how would you want to change?"

"When you daydream, what do you daydream about?"

By listening to comments made by others, a researcher can often detect a person's perception of him/herself by such statements as, "I can't do that," or "Jeff's better than me."

For children, *puppetry* can often help express feelings about self that are not otherwise expressed. To achieve the best results, the puppets should represent persons important to the child such as parents, teachers, and peers. Asking the child to enact a story may reveal varying feelings about self.

Autobiographies also can aid in self esteem assessment. The qualitative comments in such a biography often indicate how the author feels about self and development.

Dreams often reinforce actual feelings about self-concept that are sometimes denied at the conscious level. Listening to dream content over a period of time can suggest patterns of feelings about self.

Observation of nonverbal behavior can aid individuals interested in self-concept assessment. By helping each individual become more aware of his/her nonverbal behavior and the meaning it holds, self-concept feelings are reinforced. An isolated behavior might not be significant but as it relates to the whole pattern of the person it becomes more meaningful.

Those involved with young children can observe muscle coordination as an indication of self-esteem of children. Some evidence is available to indicate that children who have difficulty in managing their body often have low self esteem.

A technique not often discussed in the literature either under the area of formal or informal techniques is the *interview.* This technique is reported by Demo (1985) to be very valuable in assessing self esteem. Demo interviewed adolescents using a standardized interview form of twenty questions. Each question was scored high (5) and low (1) yielding scale scores. Questions such as, "Would you say your friends like you? How much?; If you could change something(s) about yourself, what would it/they be? ; and Do you think you can meet the challenges ahead of you?" are examples of this interview format. Again, however, the same measurement difficulties are inherent in this approach to assessment as in other techniques: a reliance is on self report, a certain skill level is required of the interviewer to ascertain high or low scores, this interview technique is fairly global, and validity and reliability are not established, just to mention the most salient problems. Further use of this method is certainly warranted though if some of these issues can be addressed.

GENERAL MEASUREMENT CONCERNS

A number of general measurement issues are apparent after reviewing self esteem assessment. Social desirability, method variance, and construct validity seem to be most evident.

Social Desirability

The belief is that social desirability and approval motivation effect the manner in which individuals respond to test items.

Arlin (1976) argued that gain scores in self esteem that are not also controlled for by social desirability measures should be interpreted cautiously. The question in many studies of self esteem is whether true gains in self esteem have occurred or are the respondents reporting improvement to present themselves well and/or gain approval. In children this factor can be dealt with by using the *Children's Social Desirability Scale* (Crandall, Crandall, Katkovsky, 1965) developed for children in the third through the sixth grade or by using the *Young Children's Social Desirability Scale* (Ford & Rubin, 1970) constructed for children in preschool and early elementary school. Another approach would be to include items which indicate the need for social approval within the self esteem scale itself.

Method Variance

Method variance is also an element to consider in the use of self esteem subscales. This should be done with a great deal of caution. Test developers would do well to establish subscales through factor analysis, with norms for different subscales by grade and by gender.

Related to the issue of method variance is the issue of source variance, i.e., reports obtained from someone other than the person whose self esteem is being measured. Frequently various sources of reporting do not agree. Various reports should be treated as independent observations, each with essential information to contribute.

Construct Validity

Much of the current work in the field of self esteem assessment is focused on construct validity, that is, clarifying the definition of self-concept and self esteem. Damon and Hart (1982) contended that age related shifts occur related to self-concepts and self esteem with physical, active, social, and the psychological aspects of the self being most salient to the child as he/she moves through adolescence. Additional studies need to be conducted to investigate the developmental nature of self esteem. Also valuable would be to investigate the behavioral correlates of self esteem. This would greatly enhance the observational measures of self esteem. Researchers seem to need to move away from unidimensional conceptualizations of the self to explore self-estimates such as social confidence or self-efficacy and to assess the developmental change and stability of various dimensions. Various "cut-off scores" need also to be established to enable the identification of those with unusually low self esteem.

Each of the techniques discussed in this chapter has its advantages and disadvantages. Due to the problematic factors reviewed earlier, the test administrator is advised to consider the purpose of the assessment and the type of client being tested. Then multiple measures seem to yield meaningful results.

ACTIVITY 12.1   SELF ESTEEM INVENTORY

Introduction

The following activity is intended for individual or group use as an informal method of assessing self esteem. While this technique has inherent in it some of the measurement problems discussed in this chapter, it still is a starting place for informally assessing one's self esteem.

Time Required

30 to 45 minutes

Participants

Individual or groups, children or adults provided the concepts are explained in terminology which children can understand.

Setting

Office or classroom

Materials

Paper and writing material

Procedure

Review Satir's Self Mandala (Activity 6.14 and related content in Chapter 6) and the various self-estimates she discussed: physical, intellectual, emotional, sensual, interactional, nutritional, contextual, and Life Force. Beginning with the physical self, write as many words or phrases as you can to describe yourself. Try not to censor any thoughts which come to your mind. Include descriptions of your height, weight, facial appearance, quality of skin, hair, and descriptions of body areas such as your neck, chest, waist, legs.

Move on to the intellectual self. Do the same thing here. Include here an assessment of how well you reason and solve problems, your capacity to learn and create, your general amount of knowledge, your specific areas of knowledge, wisdom you have acquired, and insights you have.

Write as many words or phrases as you can to describe your emotional self. Include here ideas about typical feelings you have, feelings you seldom have, feelings you try to avoid, feelings you especially enjoy, feelings from your past and present, and feelings which are associated with each other.

In the area of sensual self, write as many words or phrases about how you feel about yourself as a sexual person. Also include how you feel about the different ways you take in information—through the eyes, ears, nose, mouth, pores, skin. In what ways do you let information in and out of your body.

Move on to the interactional self. Include descriptions of your strengths and weaknesses in intimate relationships and relationships to friends, family, co-workers, and strangers in social settings. Describe the strengths and weaknesses which your friends and family have noticed.

List the words and phrases which come to mind about your nutritional self. How do you nourish yourself? What do you like and dislike about this?

Next is the contextual self. Descriptors could be in the areas of maintenance of your living environment; reactions to light, temperature, space, weather, colors, sound, and seasons; and your impact on the environment.

Last is the spiritual self or Life force. Write words or phrases which tell about how you feel about yourself in this area. This could include your feelings about yourself and organized religion, reactions about your spiritual connections to others, feelings about your spiritual development and history, and thoughts about your metaphysical self.

When you have completed this inventory, put a plus by words or phrases which represent aspects about yourself which you like. Put a minus by items which you consider to be weaknesses or areas for improvement. Do not mark words which are neutral or factual, such as "5 feet 4 inches tall, 120 pounds." Take time to examine how many plus items and minus items you have in each category. Do some categories have more minus than plus areas? The larger proportion of minus to plus areas you have, the more effort will be needed to achieve positive self esteem. If the vast majority of your minus responses are in one or two areas, your self esteem is likely to be good but has a few self estimates which need to be improved.

Think of ways in which you could improve these minus areas. Review the chapter and/or activity which could help you most. If you are in a group, ask others for some feedback about how they have managed such dynamics.

Perhaps someone with mostly positives in the area you have mostly negatives could help you in personal growth.

Outcome

Provides one with a means of assessing self esteem.

REFERENCES

Arlin, M. (1976). Casual priority of social desirability over self-concept: A cross-legged correlational analysis. *Journal of Personality and Social Psychology, 33,* 267-272.

Barber, L.W., & Peatling, J.H. (1977). *A manual for the Barber Scale of Self-Regard—Preschool Form.* Schenectady, NY: Character Research Press.

Bills, R. (1954). Acceptance of self or measured by interview and the index of adjustment and value. *Journal of Consulting Psychology, 18,* (22).

Bingham, W.C. (1983). Problems in the assessment of self esteem. *International Journal of Advanced Counseling, 6,* 17-22.

Bledsoe, J.C. (1983). Self-concepts of children and their intelligence, interests, and anxiety. *Psychological Reports, 32,* 1253-1254.

Bolea, A.S., Felker, D.W., & Barnes, M.D. (1971). A Pictorial Self-Concept Scale for chidlren in K-4. *Journal of Educational Measurement, 8,* 223-224.

Brownfain, J. (1952). Stability of the self-concept as a dimension of personality. *Journal of Abnormal and Social Psychology, 47,* 596-606.

Coopersmith, S. (1967). *The antecedents of self esteem.* San Francisco: W. H. Freeman.

Coopersmith, S. (1981). *Manual for the Self-Esteem Inventories.* Palo Alto, CA: Consulting Psychologists Press.

Coopersmith, S., & Gilberts, R. (1982). *Behavioral Academic Self-Esteem (BASE) Professional Manual.* Palo Alto, CA: Consulting Psychologists Press.

Combs, A. W., & Soper, D. W. (1963). The relationship of child perceptions to achievement and behavior in the early school years. Cooperative Research Project #814. Washington, DC: Cooperative Research Program of the Office of Education, US Department of Health, Education, and Welfare.

Crandall, V.D., Crandall, V.J., & Katkovsky, W. (1965). A childrens social desirability questionaire. *Journal of Counseling Psychology, 29,* 27-36

Damon, W., & Hart, D. (1982). The development of self understanding from infancy through adolescence. *Child Development, 53,* 841-864.

Demo, D.H. (1985). The measurement of self esteem: Refining our methods. *Journal of Personality and Social Psychology, 8,* 6, 1490-1502.

Fiedler, F., Hutchins, E., & Dodge, J. (1959). Quasi-therapeutic relations in small college and military groups. *Psychological Monographs, 73*, 1-25.

Ford, L.H., & Rubin, B.M. (1970). A social desirability questionnaire for young children. *Journal of Consulting and Clinical Psychology, 365*, 195-204.

Gecas, V. (1982) . The self-concept. *Annual review of sociology, 8*, 1-33.

Hughes, H.M. (1981). *Revision of the Maryland Preschool Self-Concept Scale.* Unpublished manuscript.

Hughes, H.M. (1984). Measures of self-concept and self-esteem for children ages 3-12 years: A review and recommendations. *Clinical Psychology Review.*

Hughes, H.M., & Pugh, R. (1984). The Behavioral Rating From—Revised: A parent-report measure of children's self-estem. *Journal of Clinical Psychology, 40*, 1001-1005.

Johnson, O.G. (1976). *Tests and measurements in child development: Handbook II.* (Vol. 2, pp. 676-733). San Francisco: Jossey-Bass.

Juhasz, A. (1985). Measuring self-esteem in early adolescents. *Adolescence, 20*, 80, 877-887.

Karmos, A.H. (1979). The development and validation of a nonverbal measure of self-esteem: The Sliding Person Test. *Educational and Psychological Measurement, 39*, 479-483.

Kelley, G. K. (1976). A comparison of male and female levels and components of self-esteem. Unpublished doctoral dissertation, Rutgers University, New Brunswick, NJ.

Marsh, H.W., & Shavelson, R. (1983). Self-concept: It's multifaceted, hierarchial structure. Unpublished manuscript.

McDaniel, E.L. (1973). *Inferred Self-Concept Scale Manual.* Los Angeles: Western Psychological Services.

O'Brien, E.J. (1985). Global self-esteem scales: Undimensional or multidimensional? *Psychological Reports, 57*, 383-389.

Parish, T.S., & Rankin, C.I. (1982). The Nonsexist Personal Attribute Inventory for Children: A report on its validity and reliability as a self-concept scale. *Educational and Psychological Measurement, 42,* 339-343.

Parish, T.S., & Taylor, J.C. (1978). The Personal Attribute Inventory for Children: A report on its validity and reliability as a self-concept scale. *Educational and Psychological Measurement, 38,* 565-569.

Parker, J. (1966). The relationship of self-report to inferred self-concept. *Educational and Psychological Measurement, 26,* 691-700.

Piers, E.V. (1969). *The Piers-Harris Children's Self-Concept Scale.* Nashville, TN: Counselor Recordings and Tests. (Now available from Western Psychological Services).

Potkay, C., & Allen, B. (1973). The adjective generation technique: An alternative to adjective check lists. *Psychological Reports, 32,* 457-458.

Sears, P.S. (1966). *Memorandum with respect to the use of the Sears Self-Concept Inventory.* Dr. Pauline S. Sears, 1770 Bay Laurel Drive, Menlo Park, CA 94025.

Sears, P.S., & Sherman, V. (1964). *In pursuit of self-esteem.* Belmont, CA: Wadsworth.

Silber, E., & Tippett, J. S. (1965). Self esteem: Clinical assessment and measurement validation. *Psychological Reports, 16,* 1017-1071.

Smith, M.D. (1978). The development and validation of the Maryland Preschool Self-Concept Scale. (Doctoral dissertation, University of Maryland, 1977). *Dissertation Abstracts International, 38,* 416. (University Microfilms, No. 77-28, 755).

Soares, A.T., & Soares, L.M. (1980). *The Self-Perception Test Manual—Student Forms.* Soares Associates, 111 Teeter Rock Road, Trumbull, CT 06611.

Spitzer, S., Couch, C., & Stratton, J. (1971). *The assessment of the self.* Iowa City: Escort, Sernoll.

Stager, S., & Young, R.D. (1982). A self-concept measure for preschool and early primary grade children. *Journal of Personality Assessment, 46,* 536-543.

Stake, J.E. (1985). Predicting reactions to everyday events from measures of self-esteem. *Journal of Personality, 53,* 531-542.

Tippett, J.S., & Silber, E. (1965). Self-image stability: The problem of validation. *Psychological Reports, 17,* 323-329.

Torshen, K.P., Kroeker, L.P., & Peterson, R.A. (1977). Self-concept assessment for young children: Development of a self-report peer comparison measure. *Contemporary Educational Psychology, 2,* 325-331.

Walker, D.K. (1973). *Socioemotional measures for preschool and kindergarten children.* New York: Jossey-Bass.

White, W.F., & Human, S. (1976). Relationship of self-concepts of three-, four-, and five-year-old children with mother father, and teacher perception. *The Journal of Psychology, 92,* 191-194.

Woolner, R.B. (1966). *Preschool Self-Concept Picture Test.* Memphis, TN: RKA Publishing.

Wylie, R. (1974). *The self-concept.* Vol. 1. (Rev. Ed.) Lincoln, NE: University of Nebraska Press.

CHAPTER 13

ANALYSIS OF YOUR SELF ESTEEM

A plethora of ideas about self esteem have been presented in this book. The following information serves as a method of reviewing and summarizing major concepts about your self esteem. Rather than focusing on case study approaches of others, these approaches focus on interventions. A sequential approach for both understanding and intervening in your self esteem problems is presented. Guidelines serve as a synthesis of what has been discussed and, although applied to you the reader, they also can be used as a prototype for intervening with others.

ASSESSMENT

What Is Your Level of Self Esteem?

The first step in intervening is analyzing self esteem. The first area to assess is what is the current level of self esteem.

1. In reviewing the Johari Window in Chapter 1, decide how much of yourself is open.

   How well do you know yourself? Do you have many blind areas? Is this related to your willingness to accept feedback?

2. Remembering the definition of self esteem, do you have unstable self esteem?

Are you aware of your self estimates?

If not, review Activity 1.1, I'm Not Perfect, But. . . Parts of Me Are Excellent.

Do you believe that you must have achieved your self-ideal to feel good about yourself? If so, review the section on Fantasy Self in Chapter 1.

How Did Your Self Esteem Develop?

1. What were the social interactions which influenced your self esteem? Review Activity 2.1, Roots of Self Esteem, in Chapter 2.

2. What hereditary factors have influenced your self esteem? For example, your sex has had an effect on how your self esteem developed. (Review development of body image in Chapter 9).

3. How did your rate of maturation affect your self esteem? Were you an early maturer or a later maturer? Were you "on time" in maturing?

4. How did your belief system and values fit with that of your parents and significant others?

5. Review the list of psychological pathogens (Chapter 2). Which one(s) could have contributed to your self esteem?

What Are the Internal Dynamics of Your Self Esteem?

A third area in which you can assess yourself is in your internal dynamics. Internal processes contribute to high or low esteem.

1. How distinct a picture do you have of yourself? What are your values? How do your values and objectives for yourself differ from your parenting figures? How able are you to say "No?" To disagree with authorities? To determine your own priorities? How much are you influenced by the expectations of others?

2. Be sure your picture of yourself is accurate and up to date. Make a list of some statements about yourself and then ask yourself, "Is this still true of me?" Correct those self-statements which require modification.

3. Review Table 4.1 in Chapter 4, Internal Dynamics of Self. Which are your favorite defense mechanisms? How do each of these help preserve your esteem? How do each of these get in your way? Give two examples for each.

4. List five recent successes and five recent failures. Next to each write a brief analysis of the factors responsible for each of those successes and failures. Do you tend to attribute your successes to external factors and your failures to internal factors? If you do, try reversing that reasoning. Write what internal factors led to each of your successes and what external factors led to your "failures." What did you learn from each "failure?"

5. Review Table 4.2 from Chapter 4, Internal Dynamics of Self. Which cognitive distortions do you favor? Give a personal example of each of these. Now, practice correcting each distortion.

6. Make a list of all of your shoulds, attitudes, beliefs. Next to each write the source(s). (Dad, Mom, Grandma, Church, a Teacher). Examine each by asking the following:

> Were you influenced by one particular person?
> Is the should, attitude, or belief valuable to me as it is?
> Does it need revision to be valuable?
> Do I want to throw this away?

7. Pay attention to your internal self-talk and internal images in a number of different situations. Does this self-talk and/or do these internal images tend to be positive or negative? Choose another situation and deliberately try altering your self-talk and/or images to make them more positive.

8. Examine Figure 4.2 from Chapter 4, Internal Dynamics of Self. In the cycle of experience, where are your favorite points? Where are the points you tend to minimize? Give an example for each.

9. Complete Activity 6.1, Polarities, in Chapter 6. Work on owning all parts of yourself. Which parts of yourself do you find hard to accept? What parts of yourself are missing that you need in order to be a balanced person? What parts of yourself have you recently owned that previously you had difficulty accepting in yourself?

10. Make a list of your talents, fully realized or hidden. Maybe you used to doodle as a child and had fantasies of one day being an artist, but never made the investment to find out. Be generous with yourself, list them all. Which one of these might you wish to make a commitment to nurture more, to see what can happen?

How Does Your Social System Affect Your Self Esteem?

One's social system, the fourth area in which you can assess yourself, also can affect your self esteem. Through examining your social system, you can determine elements which contribute to low self esteem, remedy these, and strengthen the supportive elements.

1. Broadly, the culture sets the context in which your self esteem grows. Examine values which your culture supports. How do current economic, geographic, or political conditions affect self esteem?

Of what subcultures are you a member? Examples:

> Catholic
> Right to Lifer
> Women's Liberationist
> Gay Community
> Yoga Community
> Jewish
> Singles

How does each affect your self esteem?

How would you characterize your family? Draw a picture of your family defining them as persons and their relationship to each other. Who is close to whom? Farthest from whom? Who is leaning? Who is supporting? What is your role in the family? Choose five adjectives to define each person. Do not make a person either completely positive or completely negative. What did you learn about how to be in your family? What was valued? List implicit and explicit family rules. How would your family describe you?

2. Examine your support network by applying Figure 3.2 in Chapter 3, The Social System and Self Esteem, to your life. Complete the questions based on that support satellite figure. What is the praise/criticism ratio of each of the people is in your inner circle of friends, colleagues?

3. Examine your personal stance:

   a. Are you active as well as reactive? Which is your less well developed stance?

   b. Where are you on the continuum:

   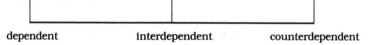

   dependent   interdependent   counterdependent

   c. How much responsibility do you take for your life? Your body? Your decisions? Your health? Situations over which you have no control?

   d. How aware are you of your verbal and nonverbal communication? Generally are you congruent? What statement do you make nonverbally: by the way you look, by the way you stand, by the way you move? Do you display both active and receptive nonverbal behaviors?

How self-disclosing are you? Do you tend to initiate conversations about yourself, tell personal stories about your life, talk about your beliefs and values? How long do you generally "hold the floor?" Is it easy for you to be in the spotlight, to reveal yourself or your awareness about others or the world? How able are you to identify, defend, and express these needs? How willing are you to defend the rights of others?

How able are you to filter feedback from others, taking in only that which fits?

How able are you to withdraw emotionally from an interaction and examine the situation from a step-back position to provide a slightly different view?

Which of Satir's communication stances identified in Chapter 3 as Blamer, Irrelevant, Super-Reasonable, or Placator fit you best? What does this stance cost you?

What Negative Self-images Are Present?

The fifth area of assessment is negative self-image(s).

1. In reviewing Chapter 5, Negative Self-images, do any of these seem to fit for you? Have the symptoms you discovered jelled into a negative self-image type(s)?

2. In reviewing the image(s) you have of yourself, what ideas do you have about intervention strategies? Use the Self-Mandala, Figure 6.6.

What Symptoms Are Evident For You?

The sixth area of assessment of self esteem is symptom-ology.

1. Review the section in Chapter 6 on Phases of Intervention. What symptom or cluster of symptoms seem to be true for you?

2. Are some of these symptoms true of you at some times or in some situations more than others?

3. Do symptoms overlap?

4. Use the Self-Mandala, Figure 6.6, to become more aware of self esteem deficiencies.

INTERVENTION

Some interventions have already been suggested in the foregoing assessments. In a way, heightening awareness, which as an inevitable part of the assessment process, is an important intervention in itself. What follows now, however, are specific interventions useful in each stage of helping, as discussed in Chapter 6, The Process of Intervention.

Identity

1. Complete and process Activity 7.4, The Robot, and Activity 2.4, Name/Symbol Inventory. In doing these techniques you will gain a better understanding about who you are, what your self-estimates are like.

2. Activity 6.5, Who Am I?, helps you to identify how you perceive yourself. Complete this activity and identify themes and categories you have used in describing yourself. What changes would you like to make?

3. To heighten your awareness of your emotional, cognitive, and behavioral self, think of several different situations in your life. What were you feeling, thinking, and doing at that time? How did you express these feelings, thoughts, and behaviors? If you do not have an awareness of all three of these areas, what is the most difficult one for you to remember? Perhaps this is a part of self which has been neglected.

Strengths and Weaknesses

1. Activity 4.2, Weakness-Strength, will enable you to explore the weaknesses and strengths of yourself and what you gain or loose from each.

2. Make a success chart:

- Break your life apart into four or five segments.

- List eight successes for each period.

3. Complete Activity 9.2, Body Map. Discover your strong areas and your undeveloped or weak areas. Which areas are tense? Which are relaxed?

4. Complete Activity 1.1, I'm Not Perfect But. . .Parts of Me Are Excellent. Can you identify and accept your weaknesses?

5. Ask six people you know for feedback. Ask them, "What do you see as my strengths in my work? As a partner? As a friend? And so forth? What areas would you like to see me develop?"

6. Record anything positive anybody says to you in the next three days.

Nurturance

1. Complete Activity 9.5, Breath of Life. Notice your breathing several times a day. Pay particular attention to how well your breathing is supporting you when you are under stress.

2. Complete the fantasy in Activity 7.14, Self-Love. Be a nurturing parent with yourself whenever you want or need it. Teach someone how to give you the exact kind of nurturing experience you like. Regularly, ask for it to be given to you. Each time, really let it soak in.

3. Enjoy the privilege of identifying and asking for exactly what you want by doing Activity 6.9, King/Queen for the Hour. You express your wishes and if your partner can, your wishes will be filled one after another. Through this, you will get more in touch with your needs and wants and also be able to practice receiving.

4. Activity 7.11, Nurturing Relationships, allows you to remember a nurturing person from the past. . .this will be a person who always brings back fond memories. Fully appreciate all that this person gave you. Do this with as many people who nourished you as you like.

After you have focused on those persons in your life who have the power to influence you, then recognize your ability and capacity to nurture. Think of someone whom you might nurture. In so doing you will become aware of how much you have to give. The power people have to influence positively another's life is awe-inspiring.

Maintenance

1. Take time to write about or think about what you **were** like and what you **are** like now. You could entitle this "I was. . .I am." Try to focus on thoughts, feelings, and behaviors which have changed.

2. Complete Activity 7.17, Imagining Alternative Endings. Practice this activity at least once a day. Record changes in your thoughts, feelings, and behaviors. What did you learn?

3. Whenever possible, make a public statement about your goals. When one publicly affirms goals, it helps to continue the motivation toward achieving them. It is a way acquiring some support from others also, because others will often inquire about how close you are to achieving your goals.

4. Activity 10.1, Standing Up to Myself, is a helpful maintenance strategy. Complete it and practice it once a day, record your learnings.

5. Review the guidelines for goal setting in Chapter 6.

   a. What am I doing? Is it getting me what I want? If not, what is it getting me?

b. If you are not getting what you want, it is your responsibility to change your behavior to try to bring about different results.

c. What other choices are open to you? What are the possible consequences of trying on a certain behavior? What's the best thing that could happen? What's the worst thing?

d. What are the general things on which you really **want** to work? What qualities do you **want** to manifest in your life? What specific behaviors do you want to try out for the next week, month, and so forth. Decide on a behavior and try it out.

e. Using the power of fantasy and belief, imagine yourself manifesting this new behavior in a variety of situations. Post affirmative statements to yourself . . . . meditate on a thought which reinforces this new attitude of behavior. Example: "I won't be cheated."

f. Map out steps you want to take.

g. Evaluate the results of your risk. How have you grown?

6. Five Years Ahead: Resume. Fantasize what kind of person you will be and what you will be doing five years from now if you are fully developed and use all the strengths you identified in yourself. Write a description of the person and what his/her life is like. Be specific and provide many examples. . .really bring the person to life. . .express this in whatever way seems right for you.

7. Write a letter to yourself as described in Activity 6.12, Letter to Myself. Ask a friend to send it to you in one month. Review your progress. Consider doing this several times.

METAPHORIC CONCLUSIONS

Only a few possible interventions have been suggested for each phase. Many more may be needed to produce change. Like a gardener who plants seeds, each activity, each new look at oneself is a seed. The gardener must sow many seeds to produce a few plants. Keep at it. Changing self esteem requires perseverance. The gardener patiently waits for the first seeds to sprout, providing moisture, light, and rich soil for the seeds to grow. . .and much love. People can provide all the elements for growth to occur. Then, at nature's right moment, growth may occur. The gardener does not despair—the gardener knows some seeds are bound to grow and in time, one by one, the sprouts come—each in its own time, some blooming early, some blooming late, but each a perfect form, a masterpiece of creation. The gardener takes care to weed the garden of that which might strangle the new growth, ridding the garden of any insects, animals, or fungus that might injure the young sprouts. What is newly developed tends not to be very strong and requires protection until it gains the strength to deal with adversity. Leaves sprout, buds develop, buds fall off, buds bloom, but the gardener prefers to keep his/her eye only on the growing, the blooming, the budding, welcoming and appreciating each new sprout into the world.

Effective gardeners learn from endings and deaths while choosing to direct most of their energy toward the growing, the living. Fixating on what dies or fails to grow may result in one's missing all the wonderful blooms and fruits of the magical garden of life.

In conclusion, enhancing self esteem can be thought of as being much like the metaphor from *The Wizard of Oz*, (Baum, 1900). The scarecrow who was in search of a brain, the tin woodsman who was in search of a heart, the lion who was in search of courage, and Dorothy who was in search of her home, all discovered through their various endeavors that they already had what they wanted. In order to gain this insight, they needed others to offer them increased awareness and guidance.

Enhancing self esteem is much like this tale. Most often, the positive qualities lie within the individual. It often takes others to activate these qualities and to begin the process of nurturing and maintaining positive self esteem. It is then that individuals discover the "wizard" inside themselves.

REFERENCES

Baum, F. (1900). *The Wizard of Oz*. New York: Grosset and Dunlap.

APPENDICES

APPENDIX 1
Children's Books Which Focus
on Self Esteem

APPENDIX 2
AV Material

APPENDIX 1

CHILDREN'S BOOKS WHICH
FOCUS ON SELF ESTEEM

NOTE: Any book that helps children see what they can do builds self esteem. Books that help children take pride in themselves, their family, their cultural history, etc., helps them focus on what is special about *them*. Books that help children sort out their multitude of feelings guide them in discovering "who they are" . . . and what they may choose to become. Carefully chosen books can help children to cherish the world and their place in it.

Aliki. (1982). *We are best friends.* New York: Greenwillow Books.

Ancona, George. (1985). *Helping out.* New York: Clarion Books.

Alexander, Martha G. (1971). *Nobody asked me if I wanted a baby sister.* New York: Dial Press.

Alexander, Martha G. & Blackboard Bear. (1972). *And my mean old mother will be sorry.* New York: Dial Press.

Alexander, Martha G. (1981). *Move over.* New York: Dial Press.

Blaine, Marge (1986). *The terrible thing that happened at our house.* New York: Four Winds Press.

Blegvad, Lenore. (1985). *Anna Banana and me.* New York: Atheneum.

Boon, Emillie. (1985). *Peterkin meets a star.* New York: Random House.

Brett, Jan. (1981). *Fritz and the beautiful horses.* Boston: Houghton Mifflin.

Buckley, Richard. (1985). *The greedy python.* Natick, MA: Picture Book Studio USA.

Caple, Kathy. (1985). *The biggest nose.* Boston: Houghton Mifflin.

Caray, Elizabeth. (1983). *My name is not Dummy.* Seattle, WA: Parenting Press.

Carle, Eric. (1977). *The grouchy ladybug.* New York: Harper & Row.

Caudill, Rebecca. (1964). *A pocketful of cricket.* New York: Holt, Rinehart and Winston.

Cohen, Miriam. (1967). *Will I have a friend?* New York: Macmillan.

Cooney, Nancy Evans. (1984). *The blanket that had to go.* New York: Putnam.

Craig, M. Jean. (1967). *The new boy on the sidewalk.* New York: Norton.

Crowe, Robert L. (1976). *Clyde Monster.* New York: Dutton.

Davis, Bruce. (1977). *Hugs and kisses.* New York: Workman Pub.

Delton, Judy. (1977). *My mom hates me in January.* Chicago: Whitman.

Delton, Judy. (1980). *Lee Henry's best friend.* Chicago: Whitman.

Edelman, Elaine. (1985). *I love my baby sister.* New York, NY: Puffin Books.

Fassler, Joan. (1975). *Howie helps himself.* Chicago: Whitman.

Freeman, Don. (1977). *Dandelion.* Harmondsworth: Puffin Books.

Freschet, Berniece. (1986). *Furlie Cat.* New York: Lothrop, Lee & Shepard Books.

Galler, Helga. (1982). *Little Nerino.* London: Neugebauer Press.

Goldsborough, June. (1981). *I can do it by myself.* New York: Golden Press.

Greenbery, Barbara. (1986). *The bravest babysitter.* New York: Dial Books for Young Readers.

Hamilton, Morse. (1979). *My name is Emily.* New York: Greenwillow Books.

Hazen, Barbara Shook. (1979). *If it weren't for Benjamin.* New York: Human Sciences Press.

Hazen, Barbara Shook. (1983). *Two homes to live in.* New York: Human Sciences Press.

Hazen, Barbara Shook. (1984). *Even if I did something awful.* New York: Atheneum.

Hines, Anna Grossnickle. (1985). *All by myself.* New York: Clarion Books.

Hitte, Kathryn. (1969). *Boy, was I mad!* New York: Parents' Magazine Press.

Isadora, Rache. (1987). *Max.* New York: Aladdin Books.

Keats, Ezra Jack. (1964). *Whistle for Willie.* New York: Viking Press.

Keats, Ezra Jack. (1967). *Peter's chair.* New York: Viking Press.

Krasilovsky, Phyllis. (1969). *The very tall little girl.* Garden City, NY: Doubleday.

Krasilovsky, Phyllis. (1970). *The shy little girl.* Boston, MA: Houghton Mifflin.

Kraus, Robert. (1987). *Leo the late bloomer.* New York: Simon & Schuster Books for Young Readers.

Krauss, Ruth. (1974). *The carrot seed.* New York: Scholastic Book Services.

Krauss, Ruth. (1988). *I'll be you and you be me.* New York: Scholastic.

Lakin, Pat. (1985). *Don't touch my room.* Boston: Little, Brown.

Lasker, Joe. (1972). *Mothers can do anything.* Chicago: Whitman.

Lasker, Joe. (1980). *Nick joins in.* Chicago: Whitman.

Laster, Helen. (1985). *It wasn't my fault.* Boston: Houghton Mifflin.

Leaf, Munro. (1938). *The story of Ferdinand.* New York: The Viking Press.

Levinson, Riki. (1985). *Watch the stars come out.* New York: Dutton.

Lionni, Leo. (1960). *Inch by inch.* New York: Obolensky.

Lionni, Leo. (1970). *Fish is fish.* New York: Knopf.

Lionni, Leo. (1973). *Swimmy.* New York: Random House.

Lionni, Leo. (1974). *Alexander and the wind-up mouse.* New York: Knopf/ Pantheon.

Litchfield, Ada Bassett. (1977). *A cane in her hand.* Chicago: Whitman.

MacLachlan, Patricia. (1979). *The sick day.* New York: Pantheon Books.

Mayer, Mercer. (1968). *There's a nightmare in my closet.* New York: Dial Press.

Mayer, Mercer. (1983). *I was so mad.* New York: Golden Press.

McConnell, Nancy P. (1988). *Different & alike.* Colorado Springs, CO: Current.

Morgan, Allen. (1987). *Sadie and the snowman.* New York: Scholastic.

Paris, Lena. (1980). *Mom is single.* Chicago: Childrens Press.

Piper, Watty. (1954). *The little engine that could.* New York: Platt & Munk.

Rosenberg, Maxine B. (1983). *My friend Leslie.* New York: Lothrop, Lee.

Ross, Dave. (1980). *A book of hugs.* New York: Crowell.

Ross, Dave. (1982). *A book of kisses*. New York: Random House.

Sabin, Francene. (1981). *The magic string*. Mahwah, NJ: Troll Associates.

Sage, James. (1978). *The boy and the dove*. New York: Workman Pub.

Scott, Ann Herber. (1967). *Sam*. New York: McGraw-Hill.

Sendak, Maurice. (1963). *Where the wild things are*. New York: Harper & Row.

Sharmat, Marjorie Weinman. (1980). *Sometimes Mama and Papa fight*. New York: Harper & Row.

Simon, Norma. (1970). *How do I feel?* Chicago: Whitman.

Simon, Norma. (1976). *Why am I different?* Chicago: Whitman.

Sinberg, Janet. (1978). *Divorce is a grown up problem*. New York: Avon.

Sinberg, Janet. (1979). *Now I have a stepparent. And it's kind of confusing*. New York: Avon.

Stein, Sara Bonnett. (1984). *The adopted one*. New York: Walker.

Stein, William. (1988). *Brave Irene*. New York: Farrar, Straus & Giroux.

Sugita, Yutaka. (1975). *Casper and the rainbow bird*. London: Evans Bros.

Udry, Janice. (1966). *What Mary Jo shared*. Chicago: Whitman.

Vigna, Judith. (1982). *Daddy's new baby*. Niles, IL: Whitman.

Viorst, Judith. (1987). *Alexander and the terrible, horrible, no good, very bad day*. New York: Aladdin Books.

Waber, Bernard. (1972). *Ira sleeps over*. Boston: Houghton Mifflin.

Wandro, Mark. (1981). *My daddy is a nurse*. New York: Lippincott.

Wilhelm, Hans. (1985). *I'll always love you*. New York: Crown.

Wildsmith, Brian. (1964). *The north wind and the sun*. Oxford: Oxford University Press.

Wildsmith, Brian. (1963). *The lazy bear*. Oxford: Oxford University Press.

Wildsmith, Brian. (1979). *Hunter and his dog*. Oxford: Oxford University Press.

Yarbrough, Camille. (1979). *Cornrows*. New York: Coward, McCann & Geoghegan.

Zolotow, Charlotte. (1966). *Big sister and little sister.* New York: Harper & Row.

Zolotow, Charlotte. (1969). *The hating book.* New York: Harper & Row.

Zolotow, Charlotte. (1972). *William's doll.* New York: Harper & Row.

Zolotow, Charlotte. (1985). *William's doll.* New York: Harper & Row.

APPENDIX 2

AV MATERIALS
(Audio Cassettes)

Branden, Nathaniel. (1984). *Raising Your Self-Esteem.* Biocentric Institute.

Branden, Nathaniel. (1985). *The Art of Self-Acceptance.* Biocentric Institute.

Branden, Nathaniel. (1986). *The Psychology of High Self-Esteem.* Nightingale-Conant Corporation; Distributed by the Biocentric Institute.

Burns, David D. (1983). *Feeling Good About Yourself.* Psychology Today.

Ellis, Albert. (197-). *25 Ways to Stop Downing Yourself.* American Academy of Psychotherapists.

Parker, Jonathan. (1985). *Building a Positive Self-Image.* Gateways Research Institute: Institute of Human Development.

INDEX

INDEX

A

Ablon, S. 215, 221
Abnormalities 35
Acker-Stone, T. 133, 159
Activities
  a lift 342-4
  activity inventory 48-9
  affirmations 267-8
  an apple a day 154-5
  as if technique 171, 368-9
  assessing your adaptability to change 308-9
  boasting contract 238
  body appreciation 341-2
  body map 460
  boundaries 263-5
  breath of life 346-7, 460
  childhood labels 102-3
  criticism clues 241
  cutting loose from parents 47-8
  enhancing self esteem developmentally 54-5
  enslaving caretaker 418-9
  eulogy 230-1
  expectations and appreciations 366
  gift to yourself 415
  gratefulness 270
  grounding with your body 348-50
  group affirmation 204-5
  heroes, heroines, visions, and dreams 262-3
  homework: expectations and appreciations 246-8
  how not to be, how to be 233-5
  I'm not perfect but . . . 9-10, 167, 454, 460,
  idealized self-image 209-10
  imagining alternative endings 171, 257-9, 461
  inner guide 416-7
  inner voice 158
  journal 260-2
  journal keeping 166
  journal: hidden self 411-2

just say "yes" 169, 240
king/queen for the hour 201-2, 460
letter to myself 207-8, 462
letting go 347-8
making requests 413-5
managing your pig 193-4
"me" album 365
name writing 152-3
name/symbol inventory 49-50, 459
negative self-image 173-4
negative self image wheel 373
negotiating a transition 306-7
new experience 98-9
nourishing 99-100
nurturing parents exchange 366
nurturing partner exchange 245
nurturing relationships 243-4, 366, 461
object talk 232-3
parent dialogue 146-9
personal right 170, 410-1
polarities 182-3, 456
positive memories 202-4
receiving 412-3
relaxation imagery: the power of the mind 344-5
resentments and appreciations 165, 235-6
risking 167, 302-3
roots of self esteem 454
roots of self-concept 44-6
self esteem disclosure wheel 229-30
self esteem inventory 445-7
self esteem maintenance kit 265-7
self sabotage 172, 242-3
self-forgiveness 254-5
self-love 248-9, 460
self-mandala 217-8
self-portrait 168, 224-5
self-sculpture 168, 183-4, 365
self-talk 259-60
significant others 172, 239
standing up to myself 367-8, 461

B

Bridges, W. 279, 280, 281, 282, 284, 287, 310
Brinthaupt, T. 40, 56
Broner, E.M. 386, 420
Brooks, H. 362, 374
Brophy, J. 370, 374
Broverman, D.M. 391, 392, 424
Broverman, I. K. 391, 392, 420, 424
Brown, E. 333, 351
Brown IDS Self-Concept Referents Test 428, 429, *Figure* 435
Brownfain, J. 440, 448
Bruch, H. 319, 351
Bry, A. 304, 310
Buber, M. 197, 221
Buchwald, H. 317, 354
Burt, C.E. 285, 310
Byrum-Gaw, B. 78, 104

C

Caine, L. 294, 310
Calden, G. 316, 351
Cameron-Bandler, J. 142, 159
Cameron-Bandler, L. 142, 159
Campbell, R. 3, 18
Canfield, J. 53, 56, 133, 135, 159, 198, 207, 221
Capabilities
    developing inherent 143-4
Caplan, P. 402, 420
Carlock, C. 66, 104, 123, 159, 263, 271, 377, 420
Carter, B. 287, 288, 289, 290, 291, 292, 293, 294, 295, 310, 388, 420
Cassman, T. 363, 374
Catastrophizing 199
Causality
    temporal 199
Ceiling effect
    of measurement 426
Change
    anxiety in 405-7
    automatic 277
    characteristics 213
    commitment to 213
    conscious 277
    cultural 35
    degree of 300-1

effects of, *Figure* 275
factors influencing adaptation 299-301
identify attitude toward 296-7
impact of social 359
inevitability 274-6
rapid 274
relationship of risk, *Figure* 301
self esteem, *Figure* 214
Characteristics
    environment 299-300
    fully functioning individuals 40-3
Chernin, K. 319, 320, 322, 352
Chess, S. 363, 374
Chicago, J. 387, 420
Chihara, T. 315, 354
Childhood 313-5
Children
    Afro-American 358-61
    gifted 363-6
    handicapped 361-3
    learning disabled 366-73
    special needs 357-74
Children's Social Desirabilty Scale 444
Chodorow, N. 402, 420
Chrzanowski, G. 22, 56
Clance, P.R. 333, 352
Clark, A. 285, 310
Clarke, J. 40, 54, 55, 56, 193, 198, 221, 256, 271
Clarke, J.I. 91, 104
Clarkson, F.E. 391, 392, 420, 424
Classroom Sociometric Analysis 441
Clausen, J.A. 61, 104
Clemes, H. 285, 310
Clewes, J. 21, 57
Clifford, E. 315, 352
Clifton, M.A. 392, 420
Clinchy, B.M. 401, 419
Clown 165
Co-dependency groups 408
Cohen, L.H. 285, 310
Coleman, L. 390,4 20
Collier, H.V. 394, 398, 421
Combs, A. W. 2, 18, 31, 42, 56, 441, 448
Communication
    nonverbal 74-87, 370

Harlow, H.F. 22, 57
Harmatz, M. 323, 352
Harper, R. 127, 132, 142, 160
Hart, D. 444, 448
Hartline, J. 357, 358, 374
Haskett, M. 366, 372, 375
Hassibi, M. 363, 374
Hastorf, A. 363, 374
Havighurst, R. 28, 40, 57
Hay, L. 331, 352
Hayflick, L. 317, 352
Helmstetter, S. 164, 176, 198, 200, 221
Help
    effective 213-5
Helping
    theories 219
Henley, N. 403, 404, 421
Heredity
    influence on self-concept 27
Herrmann, N. 27, 57, 220, 221
Hesse-Biber, S. 385, 421
Hierarchy of needs 29
Hightower, D. 26, 59
Hilferty, J. 371, 375
Hinsie, L.E. 3, 18
Hodgkin Self-Concept Scale for Children (HSCSC) 440
Hoge, D.R. 285, 311
Holland,L. 386, 421
Hollis, J. 323, 352, 403, 421
Holmes, O.W. 14
Holmes, T.H. 61, 104
Hooker, D. 324, 352
Hoover, M. 315, 316, 352
Horner, M.S. 391, 421, 422
Hostile person 165
Hot Flash, 384, 422
House, W. 392, 422
Howard, K. 315, 355, 362, 375
Huckins, W. 141, 159
Huenemann, R.L. 315, 316, 352
Hughes, H.M. 427, 429, 432, 434, 437, 449
Human
    interaction 21
Hundley, W.J. 381, 422
Hustler, 387, 422
Hutchins, E. 440, 449
Hutchinson, M. 313, 353
Hymowitz, C. 387, 422

I

I Feel—Me Feel
    Figure 437
    scale 429
Iames, S. 333, 352
Identification 34
    involuntary 37
Identity
    development 389-91
    intervention 459
    phase 181-8
Image
    body 336-8
Independence
    women 398
Individuals
    characteristics 40-3
    fully functioning 40-3
Infancy 313-5
Inferred Self Concept Scale 429, *Figure* 439
Influence
    culture-subculture, *Figure* 62
    environment 360
    family functioning 359
    parental 364-5
Informal Techniques 441-3
Information
    abstracting 199
    exchange of 74
Ingredients
    interactions 85-7, *Figure* 86
Insight
    approach 212
Integration 297-9
    Figure 298
Interactions
    ingredients 85-8, *Figure* 86
Interdependence
    women 398
Interruption
    affirmation and withdrawal 115
    Afro-American children 360-1
    awareness 112
    between action and contact 113-5
    between energy and action 112-3
    contact and affirmation 115

ABOUT

THE

AUTHORS

DIANE E. FREY

Dr. Frey earned her Ph.D. in counseling from the University of Illinois and is currently Professor of Counseling at Wright State University, Dayton, Ohio.

In addition to her teaching and writing, she maintains a private practice as a licensed clinical psychologist in Dayton, Ohio. Dr. Frey conducts seminars on self esteem, stress management, conflict management, the emotional needs of the gifted, and other personal growth topics for educational, business, and industrial clients. She has been guest lecturer at Indiana University and Purdue University. Dr. Frey has served as visiting professor of clinical psychology at the Hawaii School of Professional Psychology and the Forest Institute of Professional Psychology.

An internationally known speaker, Dr. Frey has appeared as a guest on talk shows in Hawaii, California, Ohio, and Indiana, as well as serving as keynote speaker and/or major presenter for the World Conference on the Gifted and Talented, The International Conference for Play Therapy, the National Conference on Supporting the Emotional Needs of the Gifted, the American Association for Counseling and Development, the American Psychological Association (A.P.A.), MENSA, and numerous state and regional conferences.

Dr. Frey has recently authored the book, *Intimate Relationships.* She is on the editorial boards of the *Elementary School Guidance and Counseling Journal* and the *Journal of Counseling Psychology.* In addition, she is on the Board of Directors of the Association for Play Therapy and the Board of Directors of the National Council for Self Esteem. Dr. Frey is also a member of the National Accreditation Board of A.P.A. and a board member of the Neuro Linguistic   Programming Foundation.

C. JESSE CARLOCK

Dr. C. Jesse Carlock earned her Ph.D. at the Florida State University in Tallahassee, Florida. Working with individuals, groups, couples, and families, she has been a psychologist in private practice for the past 12 years. Dr. Carlock specializes in work with those recovering from addictions, eating disorders, adult children of dysfunctional famlies, and survivors of childhood trauma. Currently, she is a Clinical Associate Professor with the School of Professional Psychology at Wright State University. She is also a trainer with the Gestalt Institute of Southern Ohio and Virginia Satir's Avanta Network.

Dr. Carlock is also co-director of Peoplemaking Midwest, an organization which offers workshops, training, consultation, and publications in Virginia Satir's model of self-esteem enhancement. She has written numerous articles in the areas of group work, couples therapy, alcoholism, and adult children of alcoholics.